Sunday Miscellany

Sunday Miscellany

A SELECTION 2018–2023

Edited by Sarah Binchy

NEW ISLAND

SUNDAY MISCELLANY
First published in 2023 by
New Island Books
Glenshesk House
10 Richview Office Park
Clonskeagh
Dublin D14 V8C4
Republic of Ireland

www.newisland.ie

Print ISBN: 978-1-84840-904-0
eBook ISBN: 978-1-84840-905-7

British Library Cataloguing in Publication Data. A CIP catalogue record for
this book is available from the British Library.

Typeset by JVR Creative India
Copy-edited by Susan McKeever
Cover design by Niall McCormack
Printed by ScandBook, Sweden, scandbook.com

New Island Books is a member of Publishing Ireland.
10 9 8 7 6 5 4 3 2 1

CONTENTS

SEPTEMBER

OCTOBER

NOVEMBER

DECEMBER

INTRODUCTION

It's a great pleasure to share this selection of broadcast scripts from *Sunday Miscellany* with you, to capture something of this programme's fleeting essence over the past few years, and to celebrate the sheer breadth of writing and storytelling talent we're lucky enough to be able to feature on it.

Although we commission some scripts, the vast majority of what you hear on air – and, therefore, of what you'll find in this book – has come in by open submission. This makes *Miscellany* a programme very much in dialogue with its listeners, and gives it a kind of power and intensity, fuelled as it is by stories that insist on being told, that don't wait politely for an invitation. Memories, reflections, tributes, historical or cultural scripts, comic pieces – we seek to keep the bandwidth as wide as possible, the voices various, the perspectives multiple, not settling on a single way of seeing things.

The book is arranged around the months of the year, with the scripts ebbing and flowing between 2018 and 2023. The Covid experience, in all its strangeness, features directly or comes through often, like a watermark; the war in Ukraine is there too, and various anniversaries and momentous events. But much of what you'll find here is drawn from the small moments of everyday life, captured in rich and precise detail. Our writers don't shy away from the darkness and complexity of human existence, but they are also interested in lightness, laughter, tenderness, friendship and family, and the beauty of the world around us, which demands that we slow down and pay attention.

For fifty-five years, *Miscellany* has maintained its immense popularity and has provided companionship, solace and joy on a Sunday morning – heralded by those glorious trumpets, which transport so many listeners into their own memory zone before a word has been spoken. Long may it continue to do so.

Sarah Binchy
September 2023

JANUARY

MOMENTS OF BEING
Lani O'Hanlon

It started when I was eight years old, then every Christmas or for my birthday in January, one of my relatives would give me a small, hard-backed diary – pink or blue – with a kitten or a puppy on the cover, a gold lock and two tiny keys.

'I thought you might like to write down your secrets the way I used to,' a favourite auntie whispered.

'Anne Frank,' another announced.

Intimidated, I'd put the diary in a drawer and forget about it until that lonely moment when I'd find it again, take the small key, insert it in the lock and pick up a pen. But what was I supposed to say? My name is ... I live in ... Today Jean and I slid on the ice.

I'd write dutifully for a few days and then lose the key, or else I'd find my little sister giggling at all the stupid things I'd written down. I didn't understand that the feverish scribbling on the backs of old copybooks or on bits of paper, the doodled hearts with boys' names in them, the notes I passed to Jean at the back of the class, the spat-out scrawls on my *Latin for Today: I don't give a toss about Caesar going into Gaul but I am interested in the Sabine Women* – this was my secret self, and as Anne Frank once said, 'People can tell you to keep your mouth shut but that doesn't stop you from having your own opinion.'

Then, as an adult, I discovered other people's diaries: Virginia Woolf, Henry David Thoreau, Anaïs Nin. I called into an antique bookshop looking for more of Nin's.

The owner lowered his voice. 'I have some in the back room.'

When he returned, he swiped the dust off an old hardback and then carefully wrapped it in brown paper, slipping it to me when other customers weren't looking. *Little Birds* was the innocent title, and I discovered that Nin had been writing erotica to support herself and the writers around her; she said she suspected that Pandora's box contained the mysteries of a woman's sensuality.

I read *Little Birds* then put it in the back of a cupboard. But what if I were to die suddenly? My family would think I was into some weird stuff and then what about my own Pandora's box? Notebooks piled up beside and under the bed or stacked up higgledy-piggledy against walls in the study. But surely no one would be able to read those dense scrawls in blue, black, red, green, and – I am sorry to report – purple ink. Secret thoughts set down beside lists: send out those invoices, submit poems, buy milk and cat food. Badly worked out income and expenditure for the month, then quotes that interest me, for example W.H. Auden describing his journal as a discipline for his laziness and lack of observation. Arrows then, linking a sentence at the end of the page with one on the top, doodles, spirals, the intimacy of page and pen more truthful and powerful than any analysis. As Freud is reported to have said, everywhere he went in the psyche he found that a poet had been there before him.

The writer Melanie Rae calls her diary *The Gospel of Grief and Grace and Gratitude*, and in her memoir *Are You Somebody?*, Nuala O'Faolain writes that there had been no steady accumulation in her life, it was all lived in moments. In her essay 'A Sketch of the Past', Virginia Woolf writes that life cannot be written about by saying where a person came from nor what happened to them, but rather, that the truth of a person is revealed by the moments of being in that person's life. Her novel *The Waves* is inspired by one of these moments of being: '… hearing this splash and seeing this light, and feeling, it is almost impossible that I should be here; of feeling the purest ecstasy I can conceive'.

Ecstasy, then. Is that the reward for this compulsion to scribble? Sometimes, but mostly these are also records of loneliness, rage, pettiness, grief, gratefulness: all the unlocked moments of being in a life. Though when I read back through the years, I realise that everything changes, including ourselves, and that all of this scribbling bestows an undercurrent of steadiness that allows me to be present enough to notice, just now, the slant of gold light on coppered ferns, and the joy of opening a new notebook with the date and my name written inside the cover.

A BIT OF MATTER
Niamh Campbell

I travelled to France in summer with my boyfriend. We took a train into airless, verdant Limousin. The walls of our room were bare, no light fixtures, a deal table, a bed; all around us airless, verdant countryside. We ate pastries, had one public argument, and spent a lot of time in the bed.

Passing through Paris on the return, I visited the Gallery of Geology and Mineralogy, and there, met with the real-life version of an image I've seen many times: the *Petit Fantôme*, a slice of mineral matter that looks as though a smiling spectre is trapped in it. The pattern is incidental, but its cuteness seems to address you consciously. It was kept as part of a collection of 'pictorial stones' by the surrealist Roger Callois, and when I was a student I had a photograph of it on my desk. Encountering it in Paris felt like finding a forgotten friend.

I also caught Covid in France. This meant that, a mere week after the deal table, the shutters open on a creamy bank of the Vézère, I lay alone in bed in Dublin, hallucinating from fever. Its pitch was unprecedented. I tried talking to it – the fever I mean.

'What are you doing?' I asked.

'Burning off the bug,' it replied, or so I fancied. In a hiss.

'Okay, I can accept this,' I told it, practising serenity. I closed my eyes, and in that moment – I do not exaggerate – I felt my temperature surge into the danger zone, then break immediately, and begin, right there, to heal.

One month later, I discovered I'd also gotten pregnant in Limousin: right there, somewhere between the table and the bed and the Vézère. The body in its fever, then, was hunting viruses and incubating the first spreading cells of life at the same time.

*

Every morning at four the baby begins kicking, inside me, in emphatic tattoo, like a tiny, reliable poltergeist. These slow thuds turn into bubbles. I think about the spasming glass of water on the dashboard in *Jurassic Park* because this is what it feels like – like a surface rippling.

I have become a universe.

At work, I spool and unspool nineties microfilm as the baby thumps around like a lottery drum. Scanned at a random angle is a note young Samuel Beckett seems to have left for someone. *Sorry to miss you last night, and again today, no chance of further meeting, 'bye.* This is funny to me, perhaps because it's the only thing I can read: everything else on the microfilm is written in Beckett's feathery cursive, mostly illegible. Beckett doodled ghouls and witches in his margins a lot.

I doodle cubes and cakes. The baby kicks.

Sorry to miss you
No chance of meeting
Goodbye!

*

Under the wand of the ultrasound machine, the baby shrinks away and hides her face, but suddenly her spine emerges, tensile as a quill, more like a fossil or a sigil than a person yet. One angry eye socket surges into view and makes me gasp.

Yes, they can be skeletal at this stage, says the nurse. Except she pronounces it *skeleetal,* with an extra e.

Beckett claimed to remember his time in the womb, to have what he called intrauterine memory, a sensation of entrapment and loneliness. In the archive I am chasing impressions, and most of these are repetitions or compulsions or habits of thought. An image of green larches recurs in his work, a rocking chair, familiar streets and rooms and orientations and *idées fixes* and calcifications: the 'sucking stones' of his novel *Molloy*, images of compression and blockage. Of things which will not dissolve.

I get bigger and I can't lie on my back anymore. In the book I am reading, a woman has mastitis; her breast is hard and bulbous like a ball, her baby cannot latch, it's as if she is ossifying.

*

Winter closes in. Rain flashes on the country roads that wind around the town. At night the baby wakes and so do I, and together we walk through the house. At four in the morning I am sitting in the cold darkness on a balance ball.

My pelvis, which I picture as a trencher of bone, is something I like to imagine gleaming underneath the archaeologist's brush on a rainy excavation site a thousand years from now.

I pull up a months-old Instagram picture of the *Petit Fantôme*, smiling wanly in its little cell of compressed matter, winking whitely from the blackness like a foetal scan. I go back to bed and wait. The baby is due in spring: there are long weeks of velvet darkness to get through.

INTO THE LIGHT

John MacKenna

It rises, even at this still murky time of year, out of the mist and fog and gloom. It rises on the other side of the river, miles and fields away. It rises into the clear sky and the darkened sky. It is there when I sit at my desk in the morning; it is there when I leave the work of the day behind. The mountain is a constant on the landscape, its sides catching the sweep of the wind, the shadows of the passing clouds running over its back, the sun glinting on its coats of snow and stone and heather.

Just after the Christmas of 2020, as the New Year was about to shoulder its way into the world, my constant companion and I climbed the mountain, as we've done every summer and every winter since we moved to south Carlow, ten years ago. We brought a picnic and we sat on a windswept rock and talked about the hopes and wishes and aspirations we had for the year ahead.

What the year brought was – as years are wont to do – a mixture of the good, the not so good and the bearable. But what it brought, too, at the height of last summer, was a Friday afternoon phone call telling me the clock was ticking, but not very steadily. Within a week, I was in hospital, preparing for open-heart surgery.

In those ironically dark midsummer days, I thought about a lot of things – mortality, the past, the present, the mistakes, the things I wished I had and hadn't said to people over the years, the cul-de-sacs I'd gone down and the open roads I'd never taken. Most of my thoughts were negative and a dark stranger seemed to loiter on every stairs I climbed.

But I survived the surgery and, as the days darkened and autumn blew into winter, my spirits rose, and Christmas and the New Year became beacons of light and optimism and anticipation. I realised I'm one of the lucky ones, and I realised, too, that I've been blessed in my life with two GPs whose care has spanned almost fifty years of living.

The first is a man called John MacDougald. He became my go-to for the minor ailments of my twenties; he was the man who stood in the kitchen at three o'clock in the morning getting the children through croup; the man who sat with me when silence was needed, and talked when words were required; the man who walked with me through the dark days before and after my brother's death. He was the true family doctor – his approach was holistic and his care and friendship and support were – and are, though he has now retired from practice – above and beyond what might rightly be expected of one man.

The second is a woman called Helen Delaney and, without her astute observation, I might not be here to write these words. The warmth of her personality, coupled with her medical skill, ensured that something that might otherwise have gone unnoticed was spotted and dealt with. At different times and in different ways these two medics have saved my life and kept me afloat.

So, this spring, as we climb the mountain and try to find a sheltered spot in which to hunker down and share our coffee, we will raise a cup to those two people and think of them with gratitude and a deep appreciation. And I will look to the brighter days ahead.

My hope for the year is that they, that we, that all of us find peace, good health and joy, after the bleak, hard times we've all been through.

The mountain is there to climb. It casts its shadow, it shelters the valley, it hides the sun and then reveals it. It lifts its head to the light of the stars and towers above the jigsaw of fields below.

The mountain offers darkness and light; challenge and recompense; indecision and optimism. But who would not want to go on climbing? Who would not want to stand on the summit and watch the sun set and the moon rise? Who would not want to remember the friends who save our lives in a multitude of ways?

THE SMELL OF SNOW

Tim Carey

I can smell snow. In fact, the smell of snow is one of my first memories. I'm three years old and our family is living in the tree avenue suburb of Shorewood in Milwaukee, Wisconsin, USA. I wake to see the world blanketed in snow. In the back yard a huge drift covers one half. As my mother puts me into a one-piece snow suit, zips me up and helps me put on my snow boots, I cannot wait to get out into this landscape.

My father and brother are in the backyard. My brother brings me over to what appears to my three-year-old eyes to be a mountain of snow. At the top there is an entrance. My brother sits on the edge of the hole and puts his feet into it. Then he pushes himself off and disappears. A few seconds later, he appears at the bottom of the drift. Then I'm on the edge and, without fear, push myself off and slide on my back down a steep incline into a snow cave. The walls of snow crystals emit a blue light. The only sounds are of my suit's synthetic material scratching the iced floor and my breathing. The only smell is the smell of snow.

I'm sure I am not the only person who can smell snow. I've met many who do not think snow has a smell. But I trust my nose as much as the weather forecasters when it comes to one of the most difficult of weather conditions to predict. If a chance of snow is mentioned by Met Éireann, I will go outside and sniff the air and make my own decision on the matter.

My greatest proof that I can smell snow came on a college night out. As we rolled out of the Lincoln Inn, I detected the unmistakable scent of snow in the air. I stopped and shouted, 'I smell snow!' – only to be largely ignored. But then, before we even reached the next pub, flakes began to fall from the night sky.

Growing up in the Midwest, deep snow was a fact of winter life, much in the same way that thunderstorms were in the summer. When I moved to Ireland at the age of twelve, among the many things I left behind was snow. I would have to become used to the Irish climate's lack of extreme cold or heat.

Snow did make an appearance sometimes, brief and tantalising. The occasional flurry, even if it brought the city's traffic to a standstill, didn't really meet my snow longing. But the big snow of 1982 brought me back to my old element, like the return of an old friend from my past.

And then snow became a distinct rarity. The years passed, and it began to feel as if it would never happen again. As climate change became an acknowledged fact, I began to believe that our two children would grow up in a world without snow.

Then came the big snow of 2010. To be followed by the big freeze of 2011. I don't know of any adult that got as much enjoyment out of playing in the snow with their children as I did. I was at least as much a child as Jen and Aaron were. We played American football with spectacular catches and dives, we built the biggest snowmen in the estate, we built an igloo. And we went to Killiney Hill with sacks, tea trays and anything else we could use to slalom the 300 metres down the hill's main avenue. We would stay until we were just too tired to walk back up the hill to race down again. They were some of the most memorable times I have had with my children and they've been immortalised in our YouTube video, 'Tea Tray Slide Killiney Hill'.

Snow returned briefly a few years later. But it wasn't the same. The children were no longer the eight- and ten-year-olds who'd play with me for hours. They had become teenagers and playing with their father in the snow didn't have the same allure it once had. And while we did go to Killiney Hill it wasn't as magical. Part of me knew Jen and Aaron would probably prefer to be with their friends. And I was selfish, because part of me just wanted them to always look at me in the way they had done. It was one of the saddest days. I figured that the next time it snowed, I probably wouldn't be out with them at all.

But still, throughout each winter, I get excited if I see the forecast predicting a cold front to move in from the east, to bring Arctic air and moisture from the Irish Sea. And each time I will go out, turn upwind and sniff the air, to try and get an early scent of ice crystals joining together to form snow, somewhere high up in the atmosphere.

NEVER TOO LATE

Gerry Stembridge

It was early March 1979, and I left the UCD campus mid-afternoon and went to my bedsit, a little back room over a shop in Windy Arbour, £5 a week.

Now, normally I haunted Belfield morning, noon and night. The Arts block was my stately pleasure-dome, my wonderful everyday and my Sunday best. My bedsit was for sleeping in and writing last-minute essays in. Being there in the afternoon was just weird.

Even stranger, I fell asleep. When I woke it was dark and, not having turned on the two-bar electric fire, very, very cold. Through the grogginess something dawned on me, and I checked the time. Oh God! It was … well, it was sometime after 8 p.m. And you see, I was acting in a play in Dramsoc that had started at eight.

But let's rewind a bit. Two years before, in Freshers Week, Dramsoc was one of the ten or so college societies I'd joined, once I got over the shock that the University Drama Society did not operate from an ancient ornate hall with a raised stage, my seventeen-year-old's notion of theatre.

Dramsoc HQ was a cold, black box space in the basement of the Arts building, called, with little regard for the romance of it all, LG1. Folding doors gave access to the equally glamorous LG2. Nonetheless, production photos on display of the previous year's triumph, Shakespeare's *Richard II*, suggested that some kind of magic could be created. I parted with my precious 50p and joined.

Some of my new college friends were convinced I was wasting my money. Dramsoc was a clique, full of weird types, a nest of homosexuals – an appalling stereotype which I am very glad to say I discovered to be largely

12

true. But the notion that this coven was unfriendly was not. The very first time I summoned up the courage to audition for a play, *The Bedsitting Room* by my comic hero Spike Milligan, I was welcomed and cast in a leading role. So here I was, starting my college life, acting in a play called *The Bedsitting Room* and renting my own bedsitting room. I was free as a bird.

I became, I admit, an inordinately selfish member of Dramsoc. Not for me the tiresome business of hunting down props, sticking up posters or manning the box office. I acted. I soaked up applause and laughter. Even learning lines was a tedious necessity, though I usually got there by opening night, while testing the nervous systems of my more studious fellow performers.

But I had never, ever missed a performance. So waking up in my bedsit when the show I was in had already started was a new and scary experience.

The play, by the way, was *Brand* by Ibsen, directed by Dr Joseph Long, a lecturer in the French Department. Remember the *Richard II* production photographs that had impressed me in Freshers Week two years before? He directed that. Something of a Dramsoc legend, everyone wanted to be in a Joe Long production, including myself although – dark secret – I'd read Ibsen's *Brand* and thought it was spectacularly boring.

When Joe offered me the minor role of the Provost, I found myself experiencing a very peculiar form of envy. I really disliked the play, but was furious not to have been offered the lead role. Perhaps waking after curtain time was some unconsciously psychotic howl of rage against Ibsen, *Brand*, Dr Joseph Long and the whole wretched production?

Well, I had no time to consider this fascinating psychological question, because I was grabbing a coat in the dark and cantering from my bedsit, out under the shadow of Dundrum Mental Hospital, along Bird Avenue, spinning left and then right at the Clonskeagh entrance to Belfield, and sprinting down the ridiculously long avenue past dark playing fields and the looming water tower, to the Science block and the lake, into the maw of the Arts building and down, down to the basement and LG1.

It was almost nine o'clock. Through the buzzing interval crowd, I spotted three faces huddled together in tense conversation: the auditor of Dramsoc, the stage manager, and Dr Joseph Long.

And now a reveal. An anti-climax perhaps. I had reluctantly accepted a smaller role in *Brand*. I did not mention that the character of the Provost did

13

not appear until the second half – when, as it happens, he had quite a big scene, but that's by the way. So, though I had been AWOL for the entire first half, and created serious trauma for the production team, I had not actually missed my bit.

Joe Long glared at my sweating, panting self and was brief: 'Get changed, please.' In the gloom of LG2, he who had been about to read in my part clambered out of the soutane and amusing hat that was my costume. And, without a whiff of warm-up, on I went. My scene … well, I remember nothing about it. It was fine, I think. Everything had worked out fine, really.

Afterwards, as I was getting out of my costume, I saw Joe coming towards me. I sighed and thought, here we go. Remember, this director was not a fellow student, he was Dr Joseph Long of the French department. I was resigned to a terrible tirade, a monumental dressing-down.

Joe spoke in a cold but very even voice.

'You may have no respect for your own work, Gerry, but please have some respect for mine.'

And he walked away.

That I can remember his words precisely, forty-two years later, indicates the intensity of their effect. No lengthy harangue could have humbled me more than that crisp sentence. Not only did I appreciate and regret the stress I had caused my fellow students, I realised something else for the first time: 'You may have no respect for your own work,' he had said, and my pain at this judgement told me that my involvement in Dramsoc was no passing college fling, but a serious affair. I had never given it a second's thought, but now felt at least a flicker of understanding that this theatre thing involved giving as much respect and applause as I received. If, that is, I wanted to do it right at all.

It is generally understood that going to college may change someone's life. What is not always appreciated is that the life-changing bit can happen, not in moments of achievement, but of shame. However, in a story about new insights, I should emphasise that one important detail remains unchanged since that time. Trust me, Ibsen's *Brand* really *is* boring.

IT WAS ALL IN THE STARS

Bibi Baskin

I didn't know anything much about astrology before I went to India. At that stage, like most people, I might browse through the star signs in a doctor's waiting room, select my star and then, while not really believing any of it, idly pick out the information that rang true to me, discarding the rest.

My first trip to India was for a holiday. And I did all the touristy things. I took a boat down the serene waterways of Kerala in south India, I saw traditional dance, called *Kathakali*, and I ate lots and lots of tasty curries. But I also included in my itinerary a visit to a Vedic astrologer. Now, the Vedas are the holy books of Hinduism, and Hindus take astrology very seriously indeed. It is used as a reliable decision-making tool for significant aspects of life such as picking a life partner, choosing a career, moving house and so on. In fact, today, you can study astrology in Indian universities, an idea which would probably bring out the raging sceptic in most of us in the Western world.

At that time, I was at a juncture in my life professionally. I had quit my television career in both Dublin and London. So what was going to be next? I was, at the very least, open to ideas. And so, when I heard that we, as tourists, could have a session with a genuine Vedic astrologer, I thought, why not?

Though I must admit that, as I entered his rooms, I was prepared to take it no more seriously than I did the star signs in the doctor's waiting room in Ireland.

He asked my name, and the time and date of my birth. The time was a bit of a guess. I was born in May so I figured around an early dawn might be reasonable, but I did caution him that I was uncertain.

He proceeded to look at various astrological maps, and over the next half hour or so, he a told me a few minor but accurate things about my life. So minor and incidental, I don't remember them now, but I do remember thinking, well, so far he hasn't been wrong.

He then asked me about my job, and I could feel a sense of something significant brewing. Well, I didn't think it would help my cause much if I told him I was between jobs. More than that, possibly between careers, and definitely between countries. Even continents.

So I told him a half-truth. I said I was a writer. Well, I'd had several articles published when I was a journalist, and at the back of my mind I had already decided that I would stay a bit longer in India and that I would use the time to write a book, in that vainglorious way that half the population say we'll write a book and we never do.

But his reaction was noticeable.

'No, Madam,' he said. 'In two years' time, you will have a different career entirely.' I protested. I said, 'That's out of the question.' He was having none of it. But he didn't indicate what that career would be.

It was only a couple of years later, when I came across the scribbles I'd made in his rooms, that it dawned on me. Two years had indeed passed, and during that time I had bought an old landmark residence with outhouses in Kerala, which I gradually converted into a heritage hotel. I had become, in effect, a hotelier. 'A different career entirely,' the astrologer had said. Well, from television presenter to hotel owner and manager. He had a point.

I also found, among my scribbles of his prophecy, something else intriguing. He had told me that I must do something substantial about Ayurveda, the Indian system of wellness, which I had been unofficially studying for decades.

'Madam, if you don't,' he had warned, 'the gods will be very angry with you when you die.' Well, I'd quite forgotten that caution, but as it happened, I had installed an Ayurvedic centre in my Indian hotel and since then have done quite a bit of Ayurveda work in Ireland. I hope I have paid my death duties.

Finally, though, and perhaps most significantly of all, he had said, 'Madam, you will never have much money but you'll always have enough money to do.'

Of all his pronouncements, that seemed the most likely. It's nearly twenty years later now, and my bank account proves that gentleman right. I have never been attracted by money, I don't know much about how to make it, and for sure I do not find it to be a hugely helpful factor in the pursuit of happiness, which is, after all, what everyone's life's goal should be, in my opinion.

Mr Astrologer, you were spot on, Sir. *Namaste.*

THE YOUNGER BROTHER
Dermot Bolger

It's hard being a kid brother. I speak from experience. Old neighbours often call me by the name of my big brother, whose footballing exploits I never matched.

But I've had it easier than Jack Butler Yeats. My big brother didn't win the Nobel Prize for Literature, wasn't considered the greatest poet of his era and didn't possess a self-important public aura.

Not that the Yeatses were rivals. W.B. was a supportive older brother, unthreatened by his sibling's talent. But when a big brother spends his life weaving a personalised mythology, and a kid brother declines to mythologise himself, it's hard to escape that big brother's shadow.

Nothing better sums up their difference than their epitaphs. W.B.'s epitaph was austere: 'Cast a cold eye on life, on death. Horseman, pass by.' As noted by Hilary Pyle in her monumental biography of the painter, Jack's epitaph was whimsical when told to a friend before his death: 'I have travelled all my life without a ticket: and, therefore, I was never to be seen when inspectors came around because then I was under the seat ...' [but] '... in the end, we who travel without tickets, we can say with that vanity which takes the place of self-confidence, even though we went without tickets, we were never commuters.'

They chose their wives differently too. When W.B. finally married, his bride was half his age and, humiliatingly, knew that she was his third choice, his other two other proposals having been recently rejected.

Jack was twenty when he became engaged to a fellow art school student, affectionately nicknamed Cottie. He spent three years working in a fireless room, producing comic magazine sketches until he earned enough to give his bride a home. Jack and Cottie were childless but shared a compatible happiness for fifty-three years until she died in 1947.

Jack never lost his childlike sense of wonder. While his elder brother dabbled in the occult and astrology, Jack enjoyed creating puppet shows for children and making model boats with the poet John Masefield. His early illustrations were simple depictions of West of Ireland life, but also captured the circuses he enjoyed with boyish enthusiasm.

These early drawings don't only convey sweetness: he illustrated the dreadful poverty that J.M. Synge chronicled in newspaper articles when they travelled through Connacht. But while capturing that poverty, he also caught the people's defiant spark.

What he witnessed never left him. But what makes him remarkable is that he described everything twice. He did so straightforwardly as a young man. But, working in oils when older, he revisited those memories in a way that made him a great artist.

His starting points in the later paintings didn't change: Irish landscapes, ponies, travelling shows. What changed was his depiction. He painted the layers of emotion within his memories, so that his canvases became not external landscapes but internal ones, infused with grief and passion.

He ceased being a factual illustrator, but rather, chronicled the human heart, even if this initially baffled his small audience. His monumental works were painted in a state he described as 'half memory': the original landscapes distorted with vibrant, emotional colour, flowing so quickly that brushstrokes weren't enough: daubs of paint were squeezed onto the canvas and moulded by his fingers.

In conservative Dublin, he was mocked, but a new generation of writers were mesmerised by the audacious, free-floating freedom of these paintings, by extraneous forces crowding onto canvases to give the logic of dreams. Young Samuel Beckett was in awe of him; James Joyce treasured a Yeats painting.

It took Ireland a long time to realise how the young sibling was as great an artistic force as his famous brother. But Jack B. Yeats was too engaged with life to worry about fame. Not that he was reclusive. Callers at his city-centre studio were served Madeira with twists of lemon peel. If persuaded to stroll along Fitzwilliam Street, he bought his visitors flowers from street sellers, regaling them with stories of beggars he had befriended.

After his wife's death he entered an old folk's home at Portobello Bridge. The modernist poet Thomas McGreevy visited every night, no matter how late the hour. Overhearing McGreevy's chatter, residents complained that Yeats 'has the BBC radio on every night after midnight'.

Jack Yeats chose to travel without a ticket and to hide from inspectors. But the kid brother has emerged from his big brother's shadow to become recognised as Ireland's greatest twentieth-century painter, his textured masterpieces displayed in the National Gallery.

I think of him whenever I walk the canal bank near Portobello Bridge, knowing how he loved to leave his nursing home and walk there, immersed in life. Two days before he died, aged eighty-six, he made his final drawing: two swirling ponies on a funfair roundabout. That captures him: joyous to the last, wrapped in wonder and unpreoccupied by any thoughts of genius.

THE BETRAYAL OF ANNE FRANK

Judith Mok

I first heard the name Anne Frank when I was five or six years old, in my parents' house in the dunes of Bergen aan Zee, a small, isolated village on Holland's windswept North Sea coast. We were sitting in the living room on a quiet afternoon, and for some reason I remember that my mother was talking about varnishing the floorboards in a deep purple colour, when the doorbell rang. My father answered the door and brought in a tall and somewhat sombre-looking stranger. I had no idea who he was, but later I was told that it was a man called Otto Frank, who had come all the way from Switzerland to visit us. He went with my father to his study.

Some time later they emerged, and my father was crying. I had never seen him cry before, so it made a strong and confusing impression on me. Mr Frank had come to visit my father to give him some letters and papers. They related to my father's sister, my aunt Saar. I knew that she had been murdered in a German concentration camp, but my parents rarely talked about these matters, or her, as they thought my sister and I were too young to fully understand the tragedies that had taken place in our family. From the adults' conversation I learned that my aunt Saar had known Mr Frank's daughter Anne in the concentration camp of Bergen-Belsen, where they had both died within days of each other.

That's how Anne Frank came into my life. It was years later that I read her diary, written in my native language, Dutch. But I knew she had been born in Germany, and had come to Holland with her family, fleeing the Nazi regime. Like many of the Dutch writers and intellectuals of his generation, my father, the poet Maurits Mok, spoke fluent and correct German. Whenever I ventured a sloppy sentence or made a grammatical mistake in the language he worshipped, a tortured frown would appear on his large brow.

How painful it must have been that the clipped language of his family's murderers was the same as the one he had learned to admire and love as an innocent Dutch teenager. We never spoke about it. I read the beautiful leather-bound German books by Heine, Goethe, Schiller and many others in our little black-and-gold painted library. I loved those books with their Gothic script, and I loved the smile on my father's face when he discovered our shared joy in the German language.

When I came to read Anne Frank's diary, I already understood why she had decided to write in Dutch, the language of the country where she was given refuge and grew up, and where eventually, as the world knows, she would go into hiding in an annexe with seven others, behind a house on the Prinsengracht. Then they were betrayed and taken off to the transit camp of Westerbork, like my aunts and uncles, my grandparents, my cousins – all the members of my family, ranging from toddlers to pensioners. After spending a short period there, they were loaded onto the trains heading east to the extermination camps. None of them ever came back.

After the war, everyone, including my parents, struggled to get back to life as normal, as if that was possible. Only in his very old age did my father open up about those closest to him, who had been betrayed by their fellow citizens and then murdered in the camps – just like the people who betrayed Anne Frank's place of hiding. A new book has appeared recently which seems to shed new light, after all this time, on the identity of her betrayer. But in Amsterdam there are few secrets. There was so much unspoken, but everyone knew what had happened. Everyone knew who had betrayed whom. Already as children, we understood that there were shops you didn't set foot in, restaurants you didn't eat in, families you avoided, people you didn't speak to. It was rarely talked about directly, but somehow we knew.

Only once, as a child, did I see my father's anger. We were driving past a busy restaurant, one of the best known in Amsterdam, with the owner's name in fat gold letters on the window. And time stood still. I knew that these were the people who had told the police about my aunt Saar's hiding place. These people were, it seemed, still doing well.

In Amsterdam the traffic is dense, and we sit in the car looking at that restaurant. We see eager people in front of their big plates of food. We're all quiet, waiting for the traffic lights to change, the rain to stop, the car to move on, when my father's rage comes out of nowhere. He shakes a white-knuckled fist at the over-lit restaurant and shouts through the opened car window: 'Informers!'

A YOUNG IRISHMAN AT CHURCHILL'S FUNERAL

Charles Lysaght

Unlike many Irish children of my generation I was brought up to admire Winston Churchill, Britain's wartime leader. My father, although nationalist enough, always uttered his name with reverence, believing he had saved us as well as the British from the evil Hitler. Churchill's defiant orations, received at home in those perilous years on our crackling Telefunken wireless, had made a deep impression.

All that might not have impinged on my childhood mind had I not had an unfortunate speech defect. This exposed me to teasing at school. 'Lysaght, you speak like a baby,' some boys told me hurtfully. 'Don't mind them,' my father reassured me, 'Winston Churchill also has a lisp and, apart from James Dillon, he is the greatest orator in the world.'

To encourage me, my father got me recordings of Churchill's speeches. I listened to them over and over again, absorbing their rolling rhythm. I learned passages by heart and used phrases from them at school debates. Churchill became my unlikely hero.

I was up at Cambridge when he died in January 1965, aged ninety. All England stood still in the week between his death and funeral. Memories of his heroic life and British triumphs under his leadership were recited endlessly, making it a time of celebration rather than of sorrow. The fulsome enthusiasm of it all was a welcome relief from the mocking mood of self-denigration that had gripped England in that dreary decade of decline.

On the night of Churchill's death, that consummate old stylist Harold Macmillan, the former prime minister, wound up the tributes on television.

He looked even more doleful than usual as he peered out from the screen. 'None of us,' he concluded, 'can be without a sense of personal loss that the greatest heart in England beats no more.'

Almost the only discordant voice came from Ireland. President de Valera said that Churchill might have been a great Englishman but he had been a dangerous enemy of the Irish people. Twelve years previously, in 1953, the two men had met for the first time. Their lunch, held in Downing Street, went well. Afterwards, Churchill told friends how much he liked the man. Dev was less forgiving and his words on the morrow of Churchill's death sounded ungenerous. First reports, happily not fulfilled, were that our government would not even send a minister to the funeral. I decided that I, at least, would keep faith and be there.

I was up at six in the morning to be given a lift to London and join the throngs lining the route of the State funeral. In a biting east wind beneath a steel-grey sky, we waited for hours on Ludgate Hill, just below St Paul's Cathedral. We saw the leaders of one hundred nations mounting the steps to Wren's magnificent building. Most striking was the tall, erect, solemn figure of Charles de Gaulle, President of France. For all their wartime rows, he was the Frenchman whom Churchill esteemed above all others.

Meanwhile, the funeral procession wended its way along the ancient road to St Paul's from Westminster Abbey, where the body had lain in state for three days and four nights. The route was lined with young soldiers, their heads bowed over their rifles in respect. The bands played old military tunes. Each minute we heard the distant echo of the ninety gun salute – one for each year of Churchill's long life. The sailors, soldiers and airmen in all their panoply advanced past us, marching in measured rhythm. Then came the oak coffin borne on an open gun carriage pulled along by a phalanx of naval cadets. The chief male mourners and pall-bearers attired in top hats followed, led by Churchill's ailing son Randolph, struggling uphill on foot. So quiet was the crowd about us at that moment that one heard only the crunching footsteps of the naval escort on the sanded road as they marched in step beside the gun carriage. In the awe and emotion it expressed, the hushed silence was more eloquent than any words, and certainly more moving than the applause which has become commonplace at modern funerals. I shall never forget it.

The tension subsided as Churchill's widow, his beloved Clemmie, and other female mourners followed in horse-drawn carriages. The silence was broken in our party when one of the girls turned to me excitedly and said, 'It makes you proud to be English, doesn't it?' As an Irishman, I could not be quite that, but I was and remain to this day mighty proud to have been there.

MERLIN PARK MIRACLE

Liam Lally

I turned seventy a while ago. For most people nowadays, reaching seventy is not that significant, but for me, having spent a lot of my childhood in hospital, it was akin to a minor miracle.

From about the age of four, I could not digest solid food, and frequently woke up at night with a pain in my belly, calling to my mother for a hot drink. Only when I became a parent myself did I realise and appreciate the effort it took for her to meet my impatient demands – getting out of bed, warming milk on a dormant turf fire, adding a pinch of soda. This frothy mixture eased my pain, but the underlying condition persisted.

Travellers from Belmullet to Castlebar know only too well that the R312 was – and is still – a mere tarmacked, meandering sheep track. I first experienced this road in the back of an ambulance in the early 1950s, bouncing up and down from pothole to pothole, lurching from side to side like a drunken giraffe.

Going from farm and turf fire smells to the chloroform-laden air of the County Hospital was a sickening shock to my system. Worse still was the fear generated by the rattle of the medicine trolley, which the nurses wheeled round the ward every morning and evening. My fists would unclench and my heart would stop racing only when that noisy horse passed my bed without stopping. In those days, an injection needle was a fearsome object, more suitable for equine use than inserting into the thin thigh of an emaciated six-year-old boy.

Merlin Park hospital in Galway was my home for much of the next six years. The combined efforts of our gifted GP, Dr Tom Kelly, and his friend, the skilled surgeon Mr Kneafsey, correctly diagnosed my problem: a collapsing oesophagus. Their solution was innovative – replace the faulty section of my oesophagus with a piece of my colon. Great in theory, but such an operation had never been done before in Ireland. And I was too small and weak for such major surgery.

Undeterred, Mr Kneafsey came up with an ingenious interim plan. He would insert a solid tube down my oesophagus every morning to open it and allow food travel down into my stomach. He did this while placing me under mild sedation for a couple of weeks. Then he moved to the next stage – do it without sedation.

Surgical notes made at the time describe 'the patient' – that's me – as being 'uncooperative' during this procedure! Coincidentally, my father came to visit me after the first attempt, and he was informed by a junior doctor that I had bitten his finger that morning.

Mr Kneafsey and his junior doctor persisted, and after some weeks I was allowed home with this wonder-weapon – a solid, flexible tube about 30 inches long which, by now, I had learned to push down my throat every morning. I became so proficient at this manoeuvre that it could have become my circus act.

I spent some Christmases in hospital. Missing my family was eased considerably by visits from the hospital Santa, who seemed to have access to a wider range of gifts than the Belmullet version.

And there were fun times too. At supper time, the nurses allowed me to 'drive' the snack trolley from ward to ward at a speed that nearly turned the milk into butter.

Beside each bed was a four-wheeled trolley. One ward had a large open space in the middle, ideal for trolley races. New patients didn't stand a chance against me, the veteran Formula 1 trolley driver. Some minor injuries were added to our underlying conditions.

There were no children's wards in Merlin Park. Sometimes I was on the orthopaedic corridor where, in those days, patients were often confined to bed for long periods. I became their messenger boy, fetching drinks and sharing newspapers and cigarettes – yes, cigarettes! My reward for this service was to help them reduce the hill of grapes on their bedside lockers.

In those years, parents seldom visited children in hospital. It was believed that such visits could be too upsetting for both parents and children.

Furthermore, bad roads meant that travelling from Belmullet to Galway was as daunting for the older generation as a round-the-world trip might be today. Thus, I became the happily adopted child of patients, nurses, and ancillary staff.

After about a year at home, performing my 'circus act' with the magic tube every morning and gaining weight and strength, I was recalled to Merlin Park, where Mr Kneafsey successfully performed his ground-breaking operation.

Now, more than sixty years later, I begin each meal with a silent 'thank you' to Dr Kelly, Mr Kneafsey, and all the unsung heroes of the medical professions, both then and now.

EL GRECO, 1971

Michael O'Connor

At the end of the night when all bills had been paid,
Frixos, the owner, would come from the tiny bar
and play the bouzouki for the diners who lingered
over their Cona coffee and brandy. Sometimes
he opened a bottle of Commandaria
dessert wine and treated whoever was there. He
gave me a bottle that Christmas, which we liked, but
nobody at home liked the Retsina which he
also gave me. He sang too, and his voice was mellow.
On nights when there was no band, we put a record
player on the stage and played the soundtrack of *Zorba
the Greek*. It was scratchy and made Anthony Quinn's
voice even rougher than it was in reality.
But what's reality, when this all happened long
ago, and only a few remember it?
Well, Frixos was real, and Vassos was real,
and the bowl of water with cubes of butter that
I rolled into intricately carved spheres for every
table in the restaurant: that bowl was real;
and the night I spilled peas over Mr Apple
while easing the meat off the skewer of his kebab:
that was real. There is so much more, of course:
the smoke of our cigarettes behind the curtain
that hid us from the diners; the long drags we took

before emerging to clear a plate, reset a
table or answer a polite request: they were
real. And the foundation stones on the ground floor
– black marble – each with the name of a Burton's partner,
they were real too, but far below El Greco,
which was up a red carpet, on the first floor.

FEBRUARY

THE MORNING RUSH HOUR

Katrina Bruna

These days the bus to Dublin city centre is always late. Every day I leave the house at 8 a.m. sharp and meet the postman on my way out. Waking up before sunrise doesn't really get easier. Just a few years back I could never have imagined myself like this. I'm making my own way in this world, this country, and it's clumsy and awkward and fatigue seeps deep into my bones, along with the rain.

The bus smells like hot-pressed cotton fabric, sweat, disturbed sleep and obligation. The sun is just starting to rise, faint light barely coming through fogged-up windows on the upper deck.

The first rule with public transport is that you will always, somehow, end up on the most crowded bus. The second rule is that the collective annoyance of the passengers will do nothing to speed up the bus; most of the time it has the exact opposite effect. These are three hours every day of sweaty second-hand air that none of us will never get back, so even though all that irritated energy is very potent, ultimately it has no aim.

I drift in and out of consciousness, head falling forward. Just to look more put together, I pretend to check the time on my wristwatch now and again – for whose benefit, I really don't know.

It's always a crawl along the M50, stretching from the outskirts of Northside Dublin. People speak on their phones in hushed tones. Nobody's first language is English, nobody on this bus was born here. And neither was I. My name is written and pronounced in distorted ways, and I have long given up on trying to correct it.

There are too many languages I understand but can't speak. Some days English comes to me naturally, easily, almost like breathing, and some days my native language pokes through more noticeably, and I choose to keep silent. Having an accent feels like failure; not having one feels like betrayal.

I watch the people around me and I think that some of the ghosts that cling to us are only there because we let them, we leave our front doors open for them in a quiet invitation, or maybe we simply don't ask them to leave. We carry the people that our lives have been intertwined with.

I have my father's face and my mother's tired ambition. The sound of my silver rings clicking together is a distant childhood memory, a lot of unsaid words and too-cold rooms in November. I push up my sleeves the same way my middle school friend used to, the friend who now lives on the other side of the world. The way I absentmindedly play with my pen is a shadow of another someone who used to be my best friend. Muscle memory is basic, instinctive, primal – it doesn't make out the difference between burned bridges and newly built ones. I wonder if the woman opposite me raises her eyebrows like her grandmother did. I wonder if the man drawing circles around his thumb with a nervous urgency has picked the habit up from a colleague.

When I came to live in Ireland, the only book I could bring with me was a collection of essays by a Latvian writer. In one of those essays, he writes about the gravity that things have – how they feel in the body. The distance we are from the centre of something affects the gravitational force that it has on us. But there are other forms of gravity acting upon us at all times.

The gravity of emotion. The gravity of success. The gravity of failure. In its natural form happiness is not weightless, but it is not heavy either. It has a healthy, natural type of weight. In the same way a person feels their physical being having mass. Happiness has a comfortable weight. A comfort in knowing that you're really there.

All that gravity comes together in the passengers of this morning rush-hour bus, and I have to use all the strength I have not to be pulled down by it.

These days I'm learning to live with the fact that every bit of grief and anger I hold has to coexist in the same space as my peace and my joy. People constantly apologise to each other for things that they didn't cause and have no control over. We all get up in the morning, drink our coffee out of habit and just before leaving the house, we tuck all the grief we have in the inside pocket of our raincoats along with a set of scratched-up keys. And just like that we all get on the bus together and hope we'll make it on time for work.

The door opens and I get off a few minutes too late: the same every day. The rest of my fellow passengers and their stories drift off and disappear into the city rush-hour traffic.

WILD WORDS FROM THE DINGLE PENINSULA

Manchán Magan

Seachtain na Gaeilge … Seachtain na Gaeilge … What should we do for *Seachtain na Gaeilge?*

As if there's anything … Like, what could you possibly do for a language that's two or three thousand years old in a *seachtain*, a mere *seacht lá*. Seven days. Even if *Seachtain na Gaeilge* does now last for *sé lá dheag* actually. But I only have *sé* or *seacht nóiméad* here, six or seven minutes. A minute for every four centuries of its existence.

What I'd love to do is to give you some words. Some West Kerry words, from Corca Dhuibhne. You know Corca Dhuibhne? *Corca,* meaning the lands or the territory of, and *Dhuibhne,* of the clan named Daoine or Duibhne – the relations of Diarmuid Ó Duibhne who stole the beautiful Gráinne from Fionn Mac Cumhaill. (Although, of course, it was she who lured *him* away … she didn't want to be stuck with cranky, decrepit old Fionn Mac Cumhaill when such a fine specimen of West Kerry manhood as Diarmuid was available.)

Anyway, I want to share some of the words that Diarmuid and his people would have used aeons ago and that are still being used on Leithinis Daingean Uí Chúis, on the Dingle Peninsula today. They are from a book called *Cnuasach Focal ón gCom* – a gathering of words from the area, by Dáithí ó Luineacháin.

Let's start off easy with an easy one*: ina phaidir aidir* – which means to know something off by heart. So, '*Tá sé ina phaidir aidir agam.*' Phaidir means prayer but aidir means nothing really, yet together they convey the sense of 'off by heart'.

Or how about *aililiú pililiú* –weeping and crying? '*Bhí gach aon aililiú pililiú aici nuair a chuala sí*' – she was weeping and crying when she heard. *Aililiú* on its own means goodness gracious, or maybe hallelujah, and *pililiú* means nothing, except maybe hullabaloo, but put them together and they evoke whining and whinging and moaning.

Then there's *aimhleogaíocht*: foolishness, uselessness, usually said, I'm afraid to say, about a woman by a man. '*B'é a haimleogaíocht féin fé ndeara é*' – it happened because of her uselessness.

Now, don't be expecting to find these words in your dictionary. They're not dictionary words. These ones are wild ones – never been tamed or pinned down by a lexicographer. They're the pure drop.

Aililiú pililiú, ina phaidir aidir – and then there's *deoráil maidine*. *Deoráil maidine* – the appearance of rain in the morning as a result of dew during the night.

Yeah, that's how we like our words in West Kerry. Specific, a little bit quirky and somewhat magical. *Deoráil maidine*.

Or how about *alltach mná*? *Alltach mná* refers to a travelling wisewoman who was feared because of her sorcery. *Alltach mná*. Specific, a little bit quirky and somewhat magical. Get your child to put that one in a school essay and just see what happens.

Or, if he or she has no interest in the language, tell them, *baidhte seile* or *baidhte smuga* – a huge spittle or a gob of snot. They'll like that – but maybe don't get them to put that into their essay.

It's the sheer specificity of the words that I love most. Like *mílcheard* – *mílcheard* is a circular sore spot from walking barefoot on the sole of your foot. A *mílcheard* – it'll often have a little black spot at the centre of it. It's not quite a blister and not quite a bruise, it's a *mílcheard*.

You'll see it particularly on people with *bálpóga*. Any guesses what *bálpóga* are? Don't bother. You'll never get it. *Bálpóga* are flat feet. '*Féach na bálpóga atá fé*' – will you look at his flat feet. *Bálpóg* is the singular. In case you ever need it. *Bálpóg*: flat foot.

What about *cócsaileoram*? *Cócsaileoram*. Now, we're getting there. This is the good stuff. The 100 per cent proof. *Cócsaileoram* means a love potion, an aphrodisiac. '*Tá an cócsaileoram aige*' – he has what it takes – the John Travolta stare, the John Wayne swagger, the George Clooney smirk. It works for women too. '*Thug sí an cócsaileoram dó*' – she put the come-hither on him.

There were specific potions and herbal mixes that could be used as a *cócsaileoram*. A well-known was *draoib na buaile*. It was said, '*Chur draoib na buaile ar dheoch an fhir agus beidh sé meallta go hiomlán aici.*' Now, you won't understand the first bit, *chur draoib na buaile*. But what about *ar dheoch an fhir* – it means into the man's drink. Into his *tae, nó bainne, nó pórtar*.

Agus beidh sé meallta go hiomlán aici – and he'll be totally besotted by her.

But what is this *draoib na buaile* that you put into the drink? Well, according to a dictionary it means the scum of the dung heap, but as I say we're far from the realm of dictionaries here. We're well off-piste.

Draoib na buaile in the context of a *cócsaileoram*, or an aphrodisiac, is a metaphor for a woman's menses. Put a few drops of that into his drink and he'll be smitten. Maybe that's how Gráinne got Diarmuid. He was willing to commit treachery on his beloved leader Fionn Mac Cumhail and elope with her because of the *cócsaileoram*.

Sin atá uainn don Gaelinn – that's what we need for Irish – some form of *cócsaileoram* to make us fall in love with her all over again.

ETERNITY ALONG THE STRAND
Fionn Ó Marcaigh

'Am I walking into eternity along Sandymount Strand?'

This is a question Stephen Dedalus asks himself in the 'Proteus' episode of *Ulysses*, as he wanders on the sand and traps himself in his own thoughts. It's easy to see what he meant when you walk on the strand at low tide, on what looks like a never-ending flat expanse. You see it especially on overcast days, when everywhere you look is grey: silver-grey puddled sand below you, iron-grey Irish Sea before you (or snotgreen sea, as Joyce saw it), and the sky above you grey like willow catkins. I feel this slightly desolate starkness is what defines a strand, as opposed to a beach. Being beached is a problem only for ships and whales; when a person is trapped beyond all help, we say they are stranded.

I've seen a lot of overcast early mornings on Sandymount Strand, as well as cold, bright ones and gusty, faltering ones and every other kind of morning Dublin Bay has to offer. It's all in service of the Irish Wetland Bird Survey, or I-WeBS for short, when volunteer birdwatchers such as myself flock to the strands and beaches and other assorted wet places of Ireland to count the waterbirds seeking the shelter of our mild winters. Usually occurring one Saturday a month between September and March, these efforts are coordinated by BirdWatch Ireland and supported by the National Parks and Wildlife Service, and they help to inform Irish and EU policy.

Their subjects are waders and geese, ducks and gulls: tough birds for whom a spell on the strand might as well be a sun holiday. Every autumn, tens of millions of birds fly south from their summer breeding sites in places like Iceland, Greenland and Canada, along what ornithologists call the 'East

Atlantic Flyway'. Ireland is an important stop along this flyway, visited by hundreds of thousands of birds annually; some will stay here until the spring, while others venture on to southern Europe or even Africa. Tens of thousands opt to come to Sandymount Strand and other parts of Dublin Bay. The bay is a site of international importance to the light-bellied brent goose, the black-tailed godwit, and the bar-tailed godwit, meaning that for these species, Dublin Bay supports more than 1 per cent of the whole East Atlantic population.

Dublin Bay's importance to these migrating birds draws the binoculars and telescopes of our Sandymount survey team, meeting every month at the Martello tower and setting out in two groups. There aren't many things that could bring me out of my bed before dawn on a wet winter Saturday. This morning, as every other, the birds are worth it. It's always a joy to survey them, even when the rain spatters my lenses and my cold fingers can barely work the focus wheel. Hardened travellers, they appear nonchalant as they work the cold sand and huddle in gossipy looking crowds by the surf. Like Darwin's finches, they've divided the spoils of the habitat according to their bill shape. The tiny white sanderlings running at the water's edge look like seafoam given life, with stout black beaks for seizing small crustaceans. A shelduck raises his elegant green head above the others, like an officer inspecting the ranks – his red bill not just a status symbol but a tool for filtering tiny snails from the water. My favourite is the almost impossibly long and curved bill of the curlew, which can reach the deep burrows of worms and give voice to the curlew's hauntingly lonely call. In Irish they are called crotach, a word for crook-backed which can also serve as a form of cruthúil, meaning shapely or beautiful. It fits them well.

When you're standing on an infinite strand and recording the steady passage of the birds, you are tempted to feel that it is all eternal and unbreakable. These birds were part of Dublin Bay before us birdwatchers, before Dedalus and Joyce, before the Pigeon House chimneys or the piers of Dún Laoghaire. But still, they are vulnerable. Results from the I-WeBS surveys were published in a 2019 report authored by Lesley Lewis and colleagues, and they paint a stark picture. The total estimated population of Ireland's wintering waterbirds has dropped by 15 per cent over the past fifteen years. The worst affected species are the scaup, the goldeneye and the pochard, which have declined by over 80 per cent. The report, available online, highlights climate change among a list of threats facing the waterbirds of the East Atlantic.

Tides come in and out, seasons change, and every year the birds return to Sandymount Strand. Long may they continue walking, flying, and swimming into eternity. You can keep your golden beaches.

DANIEL O'CONNELL IN NOTRE-DAME

Grace Neville

Over the centuries, the bells of Notre-Dame on the Île de la Cité in the heart of Paris have rung out to mark important events: revolutions, coronations, the ending of wars. Last year, early in the evening of 17 April, two days to the minute after a disastrous fire ripped through the age-old building, the bells of over a hundred churches and cathedrals across France rang out in solidarity with their silent sister. A century and a half earlier, in 1848, Notre-Dame's bells also tolled to mark a now largely-forgotten event that links Notre-Dame and Ireland. That year, on 10 February, in front of a packed congregation, Henri-Dominique Lacordaire, arguably the greatest preacher in nineteenth-century France, delivered a funeral oration on the Liberator, Daniel O'Connell, who had died in Genoa the previous May.

O'Connell had become a near-household name in France and beyond during his lifetime. The great writer Balzac once declared that O'Connell was one of the three people he would have most liked to meet. Educated partly in Douai and Saint Omer in northern France, O'Connell maintained strong professional and personal links with France all his life, as his voluminous correspondence makes clear.

The 1848 event in Notre-Dame was reported extensively in the French newspapers, often on the front page. We read that people began to 'lay siege' to Notre-Dame from six o'clock in the morning. By midday, the cathedral was full, 'despite the high price of admission'. The congregation included the Liberator's son (probably John), the Papal Nuncio, numerous politicians, clerics and aristocrats, the entire community of the Irish College in Paris, and many students from elsewhere. One journalist was struck by the large number of women in the congregation. The ceremony started at one o'clock, a full seven hours after people had commenced queuing. The Archbishop of Paris took his place, and Lacordaire, wearing his Dominican habit, climbed into the pulpit. His voice was weak and could not be widely heard. Despite this, considerable funds for '*les pauvres d'Irlande*' were donated by members of the congregation as they left the cathedral.

A thirty-five-page version of Lacordaire's sermon was later put on sale. It resounds with rhetorical flourishes and rolling crescendos. Lacordaire presents O'Connell first and foremost as a man 'hungry and thirsty for justice'. On the one side is despotism, oppression, pride, tyranny, violence and corruption; on the other is O'Connell. This *simple citoyen* or 'mere citizen' is more powerful than kings and conquerors. He joins Moses, Constantine and Charlemagne in a long list of liberators. By achieving Catholic Emancipation, the Liberator had freed not just the Irish but 120 million people throughout the British Empire, and was a model for the rest of the world for all times to come.

Lacordaire, a lawyer's grandson, had studied and practised law before becoming a priest. His interest in O'Connell the lawyer informs his sermon. For Lacordaire, God and man are inseparable: religious rights are human rights. For him, O'Connell embodies the arguably secular 'French idea of freedom of conscience' nourished in France, especially from the eighteenth century. Thus, Notre-Dame opens its doors to O'Connell, a soulmate, albeit a foreigner. Lacordaire reminds the young people listening that O'Connell was just twenty-five years old when he embarked on almost five decades of public service, without ever causing a drop of blood to be spilt. Describing Ireland as a country overwhelmed by famine, war and destitution, he stresses that after achieving Catholic Emancipation, far from opting for a quieter life, O'Connell laboured to his dying days to help his country. In conclusion, he assures his congregation that God speaks to them through O'Connell.

Lacordaire was not the only rockstar preacher to climb into a pulpit to address Irish matters in nineteenth century Paris. In the 1860s, Ireland was again struck by famine. On 25 March 1861, in l'Église Saint Roch in central Paris, the Bishop of Orléans, Félix Dupanloup, preached a two and a half hour sermon on behalf of the starving Irish to a congregation of between 4,000 and 5,000 people; twice that number were turned away for lack of space. Reaction to his sermon was intense: 'strong men were seen to shed tears [...] there was hardly a dry eye in the entire church'. Again, the following year, on 22 May 1862, in the Église Sainte-Clothilde, just off the Boulevard Saint-Germain, the Bishop of Lausanne and Geneva, future cardinal Gaspard Mermillod, delivered a similar sermon; this one was shorter, lasting a mere one and a half hours! O'Connell features prominently in these sermons, which were later printed and sold to help impoverished Irish Catholics. Both events were organised by the Paris *beau monde* which included aristocratic women like the wife of the future French President, Patrice de MacMahon.

Notre-Dame is being slowly coaxed back to life after last year's fire: its stones are being tested one by one, its wooden beams analysed, its glorious stained glass windows, which miraculously survived the blaze, scrutinised. Its bells will, one day, once more ring out over Paris, over the Île de la Cité, across the Louvre and down the Rue de Rivoli where in 1847 the Liberator, now dying, stayed on his doomed journey south. As for the ideals that shaped his life, so vividly captured by Lacordaire, they have lost none of their power despite all the passing years.

FAMILIAR STRANGER
Blanaid Behan

The Gaiety Theatre, Dublin, late 1970s. I was fourteen. As the lights dimmed, actor Niall Tóibín shuffled onto the stage. He paused, hands deep in his pockets, and turned to look out over the audience. In the seat next to me, I heard my mother Beatrice's sharp intake of breath.

When the show was over and we were backstage with a drink, she explained her reaction. 'It's just frightening, the way he has Brendan's mannerisms so perfectly. It shocks me every time he walks onto the stage. It's like Brendan has come back to us.'

The play was *Borstal Boy*, my father Brendan Behan's autobiographical account of his arrest in Liverpool at the age of sixteen, while on a doomed IRA mission to blow up Cammell Laird shipyards. The three-year sentence he served in Hollesley Bay Borstal was to shape his future. His writing talent was nurtured by the governor, and he later used to say he'd attended the 'poor man's public school'.

Brendan married my mother Beatrice in 1955, having met her five years earlier at her parents' house. My grandfather, the painter Cecil Ffrench Salkeld, used to 'collect' artists and writers at the various Dublin pubs he frequented, and bring them back to the family home in Donnybrook, much to the bemusement of my strict German grandmother, Irma, who disapproved of alcohol.

By the late 1950s, Brendan was the toast of both Broadway and the West End of London, with his plays *The Quare Fellow* and *The Hostage*. But by the time I was born in 1963, my father was seriously ill – a victim of his own success. He died aged just forty-one from a combination of diabetes and alcoholism, when I was six months old.

Growing up, I gradually became aware of his legacy and shadowy presence in our lives. When I made my First Communion, my white veiled face stared back at me from the front page of the Evening Press. 'Blanaid's Day', proclaimed the headline.

A few years later, his short story *The Confirmation Suit* was on the curriculum at school. I don't recall either my fellow pupils or teachers ever mentioning my connection, but I loved the story, and I was proud of my father.

At rare gatherings with my father's side of the family, old Dublin ladies would pat me on the head and say sadly, 'God love you child, sure you lost your da, and he was awful young.' To me at the age of seven or eight, forty-one seemed ancient! 'Sure, doesn't everyone die at forty-one?' I wondered. Photographs of my father and me together are rare, and in those we have, I'm usually crying. His special name for me was 'Miss Mouse'. In the final weeks of his life he spent more time away than at home. When he returned to our house in Anglesea Road, after the pubs closed, he would usually have an entourage in tow. 'Where's Miss Mouse?' he'd say to my mother. 'Can I show her to the lads?' My mother stood firm. 'Brendan, it's eleven o'clock at night, I'm not waking her up. You can't do that with babies.'

Sometimes, my mother took me to see my grandmother, Brendan's formidable mother Kathleen, in the nursing home where she spent the final months of her long life. She was a widow of the 1918 flu epidemic with two small children when she met and married my grandfather Stephen. They went on to have five more children; Brendan was the second youngest. 'Would you like a drink, Kathleen?' my mother would ask, having smuggled in a naggin of whiskey, such luxuries being forbidden to the over-nineties on health grounds.

'Throw it in to me,' my grandmother would growl from under the covers, and to me, 'And come and give your granny a kiss!'

As I grew older, we attended first nights of plays in Dublin and London, and the unveiling of a plaque in Russell Street, my father's childhood home, although by then, the house was long gone. The Dublin of my youth was very different from the Dublin of his day. Despite the books and the television and radio recordings, he was still a distant figure in my life. Familiar, yet a stranger. I examined photos for any hint of a likeness. Joan Littlewood, the legendary theatre director in whose hands his play *The Hostage* won numerous accolades, told me I had his eyes. My teenage years were erratic and a bit wild. Perhaps some part of me was trying to emulate his lifestyle and hard-drinking reputation.

Eventually, I grew up and, like many of my generation, I took the well-trodden path to England for better opportunities than the Ireland of the 1980s could offer me. It was never my intention to stay, but thirty-odd years later, I'm still here. To people in England, the name Behan means little. After my mother died and our home at Anglesea Road was sold, my visits home became less frequent, and the ghost of my father, so it seemed, hovered less at my shoulder.

But then I had children of my own. And I wanted them to understand their heritage. Once again I felt the tug of connection with my past, stronger now.

Coming up to the fiftieth anniversary of my father's death in 2014, we encouraged our sons to write to An Post to ask if they would consider issuing a stamp in my father's honour. At the launch several months later, elderly Dubliners came up to shake my hand and tell me stories of meeting my father in a pub back in the day.

Today when people ask what I miss most about Ireland, the thing that springs to mind is the sea. It dawned on me some time ago that if there was something I inherited from my father, it was, ironically perhaps, a love of water. In *Borstal Boy*, my father sings, 'The sea, oh the sea, is grá geal mo chroí.' There are photographs of him at the Forty Foot, Seapoint, Donegal and Connemara. He had no fear of the sea, he even swam with basking sharks, telling my mother afterwards that 'their skin was like sandpaper'.

So, a hundred years after his birth, perhaps it's when I'm out there, heading out through the waves, that I'm closest to him. I've never swum with basking sharks myself, but I wouldn't rule it out.

THE TWO AMYS

Conor Horgan

Amy moved in at the start of the year. She was dark, petite, and very pretty. For the first while our only significant interaction was her hissing furiously at me from the shadows at the top of the stairs. Which gave me quite a start, last thing at night. The rest of the time she spent hiding under the new lodger's bed. After a while I asked Mariana, the lodger, what was the story with the cat. It turned out that she, Mariana, was slightly allergic to Amy, the cat, and so rarely petted her. We didn't get into why she then had a cat in the first place, but nevertheless, there we were. I spent time getting to know Amy, mainly by feeding her and gently reaching through the banisters to pet her whenever she'd appear at the top of the stairs. It worked a treat, and within a couple of months she was following me around the house, demanding attention. I felt no small amount of pride thinking to myself if I have done nothing else in this life, at least I have habituated one cat.

Then Mariana announced she was moving to a bigger, more central apartment, one that unfortunately couldn't accommodate a cat. She reassured me that it would only take a week or two for her to find a new home for Amy. That was six months ago, so I guess I have a cat now. I'd often thought about getting one, but figured that as I travelled so much for work it would be impractical. Then the Great Unpleasantness began and I found myself not travelling at all, and anyway, isn't it nice to have a cat.

I was heading to the airport recently, on my way to visit family in Canada, when I got a frantic call from another Amy – this one a writer friend from Paris, who writes wonderfully gruesome horror novels for young adults. It turned out she was also heading to the airport, and the friends she was going to stay with in Dublin had all just come down with Covid, and could she possibly sleep on my couch? No, no, not at all, I said, she could have the whole house as long as she didn't mind feeding the cat. I explained there was a kind of a robot feeder thing that clicked open with a serving of dry food every morning, and all she'd have to do was feed her in the evenings and let her in and out. Amy the writer was tickled to hear the cat had the same name as her, and was black as night, like a true witch's familiar.

It was only quite a bit later that I learned what had happened the next morning. I'd neglected to mention that the robot feeder thing had a feature where a brief snippet of the owner's voice could be recorded, then played back three times to alert the cat that breakfast was served. That morning while Amy the writer was still half-asleep, coming to in a strange bed in a new house, she was suddenly jolted fully awake when she heard an odd noise downstairs, followed by my distinctive voice calling:

'Amy, Amy, Amy ...'

She didn't know what was happening – had I suddenly returned from Montreal? Did I have some kind of international intercom set up? Or the worst possible option – had my plane gone down overnight and was she now somehow hearing my voice coming from a watery grave?

It didn't take her that long to figure out what was going on, but up until that point it seems that between us, my cat and I had managed to absolutely terrify the queen of teen scream.

TOWNIE FARMER

Joe Whelan

'You're only an oul' farmer, Whelan!' Billy Bunburger shouted to me across the schoolyard. In 1977, being called a farmer was the biggest insult you could make to any fourteen-year-old Clonmel townie.

'I'm no farmer,' I said, as if I'd been caught with a sheep up my jumper. But Billy wasn't wrong. I had farmers' blood in me, but I kept it very much to myself. My parents came from Harney's Cross, four miles up Tickincor hill at the foot of the Comeraghs. They came from neighbouring farms, and from around the age of five, I spent all my school holidays between both farms.

Under the watchful eye of my grandfather, I became a part-time shepherd. I'd check for lambs on wet spring mornings, ire rash from friction burning my calves, as wellingtons and short pants were a bad mix. In the summer, I raddled sheep during shearings, or stood in gaps when required. I held lambs for my grandfather while he cut their tails with the kitchen knife, and thought nothing of it when Nanny would use the same knife to cut bread for our tea, giving it just a casual wipe on her housecoat.

I worked on both farms, but I was more drawn to my father's home place where his brother, Davie, kept sheep, horses and cows. Davie was the coolest man I knew. He was rough and gentle in equal measure, and he wore a wide-brimmed hat like a real cowboy. When I was with him, I imagined I was a cowboy too. I had the whole Sioux nation of nettles and thistles to fight, and I chopped and slayed enemies for days. When I went to bed, a candle lit the way: dark shadows and burning candle grease, pleasure and fear mixed.

Then one day, everything changed. I was fourteen, and after a long summer stay, I arranged to go back into Clonmel for the weekend. I met my friends, Hogg and Mucky. While I'd been busy fighting thistles and cutting lambs' tails, Hogg and Mucky had been chasing girls and cultivating flowers of their own. One such beauty was Sheila. She had shiny hair and deep red lips, and I wondered how I might impress her. I decided to hit her with my best shot. I told her all of my uncle Davie's best yarns and risqué jokes – I even told her the one about the two nuns on the bicycle. She looked shocked, but I could tell she enjoyed them and more importantly she was listening to me.

I was in love. The farm was a world away. But as quick as it began, my weekend was over. I found myself back up the hill again. All the things I had loved about the place now irritated me. I cursed the backwardness of the place, the lack of electricity, the dimness of the flickering candles. I cursed the hot wax that burned on my hands. I thought of all the lads in Clonmel, having fun with all the girls, but mostly I thought of Sheila and the way she laughed at my yarns. I couldn't wait to get back to town.

As it turned out, I didn't have too long to wait. The next day I was helping Davie to dose sheep, but my head was back in town. I left a pen gate open. Davie shouted at me for letting sheep get loose, and I cursed at him. I'd never sworn at an adult before and immediately regretted it, but Davie just laughed. This made everything worse. I stormed off before he saw me crying.

When the dust settled, I demanded to be brought home. Unfortunately, the only lift was with Davie. The trip to town was quiet, Davie hardly spoke. I thought about Sheila's black hair and wondered what my mountainy bachelor uncle knew of love. I didn't know it then but it would be years before I'd be back in Harney's Cross.

I hung around with the lads for the rest of the holidays. I did eventually pluck up the courage to ask Sheila out; I even stole a kiss from those dark red lips. But as the summer ended, so did the romance. I didn't have much to follow up Davie's jokes and she found someone else to make her laugh.

Years passed and I grew up. Harney's Cross changed too. In time, my grandparents passed away, but my uncle Davie, true to his cowboy roots, stayed the same, wide-brim hat and all.

I used to call to him occasionally and help him with the sheep. He was getting older but could still tell a great yarn. Then one day, with the jobs done, we were sitting by the fire.

He looked at me. 'Would you take over this place when I'm gone?' he asked.

Well, that's where I am now. I'm back up the hill with my own family, along with two hundred ewes and a sheepdog. I wear long pants now so no ire on the backs of my legs.

From time to time, I think of the old schoolyard in Clonmel and Billy Bunburger's jibe, and I think, Yeah Billy, you were right. I *am* an oul' farmer!

VALENTINE

Rosaleen McDonagh

We just went into the second-hand shop to browse, with no intention of buying. But a horseshoe buckle on a brown leather belt caught your eye. You picked it up to hold it, guessing at its authenticity. You spent ten minutes bartering. Spinning a yarn about your grandfather owning a similar belt, long since lost on the road. The owner was intrigued. The starting price was sixty euro. I was listening in, taking note, giggling with embarrassment, hoping your shenanigans wouldn't get us thrown out of the shop, half wanting the owner not to give into your nonsense. If the haggling ended badly, my plan was to buy the belt as a surprise for your birthday.

The grin on your face, not giving in. A tenner lower, and then a fiver. The haggling ended at thirty euro. Half its original.

The background music was jazz. The conversation between you and the owner moved on to sulky horse racing, tinsmithing and general men's chat. Both of you laughing, correcting and explaining. Hearing sporadic names of our people and counties being mentioned, you were in your element.

I meandered around the shop in my chair. Bumping into mannequins. Feeling happy, almost smug. Knowing your eyes were furtively on me. I foraged through the magpie's nest of trinkets in the corner of the shop. Bracelets, earrings, brooches: kitsch, loud and gaudy. I held them, felt their weight, fidgeted with the clasps, secretly wanting to bite into one.

I moved on, past beautiful box handbags on display, skirts and tops. Then, hidden in the corner, plain and simple, the ultimate classic dress: it seemed timeless. You saw me hold the dress up against my body, move towards the mirror. Testing different angles, stretching the fabric across my hips. Green cashmere, subtle and discreet. You took note. The low-cut back echoed that horseshoe shape, the emblem, the symbol that we both love. It hung on my shoulders and for a moment I felt beautiful. But I knew my bartering skills were nowhere near as good as yours. I found the price tag, and put the dress back on the hanger; it was beyond my budget.

A burst of laughter behind me: your deal was done. The belt was in the bag. There was a handshake. I watched you tap your card at the till.

A week later the dress was next to my pillow. Vintage, you said, insisting it was top style. The morning of your brother's wedding, twirling and modelling in it, I realised the length was wrong. My panic was rising. Then you loosened that brown belt from your waist. Wrapping it around my waist, you hitched the dress above my knees. We laughed and danced at the wedding. Ignoring my warnings about messing up my hair and makeup, you boldly whispered things in my ear, tracing your finger on my bare back.

Then came the second lockdown. Early in the romance we'd agreed a conventional relationship was not for us. We were too old, too well-practised to live together, we'd decided. We were also the vulnerable, we were the high risk, we were those words, but mostly we were the scared. Our impairments meant we were immuno-suppressed. We needed to separate, keep a distance: we couldn't have physical contact.

We made efforts on Zoom. But somewhere along the way the intensity lessened. Ordering a takeaway for one held no excitement. No pulling faces at each other's bad choices, no picking at each other's food, eating the leftovers together for breakfast. The internet offered private glimpses, but somehow without intimacy. Occasionally you'd lift the laptop to another room, giving a new view. I'd see your jeans and my favourite T-shirt strewn on the floor. I'd see tissues on your desk and wonder was your sneeze a cold or something worse? The record player, my last gift. Chosen online and delivered by a stranger in gloves and a mask. Our lives felt sanitised and empty. The days, the weeks, the months, vanishing away.

Listless, I'd sustain myself by remembering. I took to opening the cap of your aftershave, Rosewood and Amber, and inhaling. The first time we held hands, our fingers plaited together, you took delight in my aubergine fingernails. Now, on Zoom, my nails were bare. I'd stopped bothering to paint them. You noticed the first time, you said you loved my nail polish.

When we went back into the world, we were both nervous. My jewel-green dress was out of shape from too many washes. I wore it anyway. Waiting for me at the agreed meeting point, you were wearing the belt with the horseshoe buckle, now pulled to the third notch. We gazed at each other, we cried, we moved closer, we blocked the entrance to the shop; finally, we kissed.

BY INVITATION ONLY

Jackie Lynam

I had adored the band Hothouse Flowers since their song 'Don't Go' took over the Irish airwaves in the late 1980s. My homework journal and bedroom walls were plastered in posters of the band, and as well as shop-bought records, I had stacks of bootleg cassettes and video recordings.

I joined their fan club and talked about them non-stop to anyone who would listen. I was so obsessed with them that one winter, screeching cat-like sounds reverberated through my house, as I attempted to teach myself the tin whistle – just so I could play along with the Hothouse Flowers' version of 'Sí Do Mhamo Í'. To my family's relief, I quickly realised my musical prowess was confined to turning the stereo on and off.

My dream was to interview the band for my school magazine. But how? I was a teenager without any media contacts – this was long before social media would allow easy interaction between musicians and their fans.

But I was a voracious reader of newspapers, which is how I found out, in March 1991, that the Hothouse Flowers were to play at the official launch of Dublin as the European City of Culture at the National Concert Hall.

I decided to write to the Lord Mayor of Dublin, Michael Donnelly, to ask if I, as the band's biggest fan, could attend along with the invited councillors.

I checked the post every morning, but – nothing.

But I was young and determined.

On the morning of the event, my friend Sorcha and I headed early into town, where celebrations were underway to mark the designation, including the release of 1,991 balloons into the sky at St Stephen's Green. It was a

Saturday morning so there was a large crowd looking on as the Lord Mayor made his way in style from the Mansion House to the Concert Hall in the ornate Lord Mayor's carriage.

We followed him on foot and stood awkwardly outside the railings, hoping to spot one of the band members going in. The taoiseach, Charles Haughey, arrived, as did several European culture ministers. This was a proper official do, so it was starting to look unlikely we would get anywhere near the band.

But when one of the city councillors came out to have a smoke we got chatting and quizzed him. 'What's it like in there?' we asked. 'Have the Hothouse Flowers played yet? Did you see them?' Maybe he was impressed with our devotion to the band. Or maybe he just felt sorry for us as we shivered in the cold, but right away he said 'Come on, I'll get you in, there are loads of spare seats.' He ushered us inside, then pointed at the side of the stage.

'See over there?' he said. 'When the event is over you go through that door and that's where the band will be. Best of luck!'

We were in! The Salute to Dublin ceremony was beautiful and finished with a wonderful performance of 'Christchurch Bells' and 'The Older We Get' by the Hothouse Flowers. We then brazenly followed our friendly councillor's instructions and found ourselves in a backstage area chatting to the band's bass player, Peter O'Toole. He loved our story of how we'd managed to get in to see them. He gave me the number of the place they rehearsed and told me to give him a ring to organise a day and a time for me to interview them. It was that easy!

And so a few weeks and one phone call later we turned up at The Factory rehearsal studio near the Grand Canal. When we got inside, the group's saxophone player, Leo Barnes, was the only member of the band there, and even though he knew nothing about it, he kindly agreed to be interviewed by me.

Peter arrived with Liam Ó Maonlaí and Fiachna Ó Braonáin a little later. We were quite starstruck. Sorcha was hardly able to speak. But over tea and biscuits, they put us at ease and answered all my questions with good humour and patience. Fiachna mentioned his newborn twins were keeping him up at night, yet his tiredness didn't show. Leo said he didn't have many good memories of his schooldays, which he spent in an orphanage in Kilkenny, although he did enjoy playing hurling. Peter told me he left school early and got a job delivering bread, which left him with the afternoon free to hang around with his friends in St Stephen's Green.

Before we finished, Liam mentioned that the original name for the band had been Goose Stomp 75. 'We said we'd open a book on a certain page,' he told us: the page was 75 and it had the word 'Goose Stomp' written on it. The world was nearly saved from all those flower-related headlines – blossoming and wilting and so on. Then they brought us into their studio and played us two new songs from their next album – a world exclusive! They also had fun looking through my scrapbook of newspaper cuttings about them that I had collated over the previous three years.

It felt like a dream to me. They were, at that time, considered the biggest band in Ireland after U2, and yet they gave us, a couple of ordinary teenagers, two hours out of their busy schedule for my school magazine article, as if we were well-known journalists with *Hot Press* or *NME*.

A few days after the City of Culture launch, I received a letter from the Lord Mayor apologetically explaining that the event wasn't open to the public. I had learned a valuable lesson. If you want something badly enough, don't wait for an official invitation!

THE BALLAD OF FRED AND GINGER

Paula Shields

Someone's cold nose is nudging me, knocking hard against my right hand and arm. Avoiding the gesture only makes him more insistent. Black and white legs are upside down in the air – they may look like they're flailing but the windmilling paws are strategic. Fred is on a mission to supplant the thing I'm ignoring him for – lapdog versus laptop in a contest previous form says he'll win.

For almost ten years, Fred has been herding me around this house – I've only just registered that that's what he's doing, that I'm his unwitting, obedient flock. His sister Ginger lives mostly downstairs – no room up here to chase a ball or a squeaky toy, so why would she bother?

I can barely remember life BC, Before Collie.

Fred and Ginger. He does move like a dancer, on tiptoes – he'd do well in the dressage round at the Dublin Horse Show. He has the black-and-white markings of evening dress, tuxedo-style, a genteel film star of yore, if not Fred Astaire himself, then David Niven perhaps.

Ginger is black and white and tan with a magnificent Elizabethan fur ruff around her neck. She moves like John Wayne, broad-shouldered, with more purpose than grace, especially in pursuit of a ball, throwing her weight forward into heaving shoulders. If show jumping at the RDS is Fred's arena, the Aviva Stadium would be Ginger's. She'd be good in a rugby scrum.

He is all slender elegance as he runs. She keeps her poise for domestic life – not for her his frantic seeking of attention and approval from anything with a pulse. No, she is a regal dog, one who likes her own space, and my best rugs. She's so self-contained and deliberate indoors that to see that comic, clumsy run outside is to witness unexpected, endearing vulnerability.

Both have amber eyes, and the bewitching border collie stare.

As with many of my better ideas, I had little clue what I was taking on when Fred and Ginger arrived in June 2013. I went through a portal new parents know only too well. The elation, the fear, the dopamine hits.

They were tiny bionic fur balls. Fred Velcroed himself to me wherever I went; Ginger, more wary to begin with, would engage only if I threw a ball for her in the back yard, which I did, a lot. I camped out downstairs with them that first summer. Snack, snooze, walk. And repeat.

Eventually, everything I said wouldn't happen on the home front did. The dogs weren't to be allowed on the sofa; they would not be going upstairs, and certainly not on to beds. Friends endured my initial confident declarations and then enjoyed the U-turns. I am not as dogged as collies, it turns out.

Snack, snooze, walk. The walks were – and are – best of all. Following those fluffy ears and jaunty tails out the road. Full of enthusiasm for the exact same paths we'd take day after day. We discovered nearby fields, other dogs and their humans. My tribe. Henry, Cosmo, Winnie, Troy, Milo, Charlie, Russell the Jack Russell. Canine names easier to recall of course than people's. We dog folk talked about dogs, and work. But mostly dogs.

Until Covid. When new resonance was bestowed on your nearest 5 km and who you cross paths with. Then we talked about how eerie it all was, schools closed, streets emptied, the silence, the not knowing, everyone's not knowing – even the experts, to begin with. We greeted each other like comrades in the same disaster movie.

Three years on, the worst of the pandemic over, I know where to find sun and shade on these regular routes; I know where the grandest magnolias and the brightest laburnum live. I've encountered the same trees and hedgerows maybe twice a day, every day, in every season, from early blossom to the spare branches of winter, from light-filled spring greens to mature autumn reds, in sun and wind and rain and snow. I've learned that repetition has its joys, and that change happens anyway, unasked for, even in times of apparent limbo.

Ten years is a considerable span in a dog's life. I don't do the maths.

After those early intense training years – mine as much as theirs – we got into the swing of things, found the measure of each other. I speak Collie now, can tell the meaning of one bark from another. And they don't bark much; in truth, the stare is loud enough.

Life with Fred and Ginger is never still – birds and strangers to chase when they're on home turf, neighbours and strangers to rush up to and greet when we're out and about. Like their humans, they're café dogs. They, like us, are slowing down. It's late in the day. Fred is snoring gently here beside me … Every now and again, a paw shoots out, and catches my arm. I'd better go!

ON THE NUMBER 10 BUS

Frank Kavanagh

'Hold the bar!' I hit the bell twice, ding ding, and off we went. Last-minute runners grabbed the bar as they leapt dangerously onto the platform of the moving, open-backed green bus. Many of these last-minute runners were also anthem runners, the ones who dashed out of the cinema in the space between when the film ended and the national anthem came on – a national sport at that time.

'Fares please.' The leather bag sighed with the weight of coppers, shillings and the odd half-crown, ten-shilling and pound notes sequestered in a slot at the back. Twirl the handle of the ticket machine and out came the wide ticker-tape tickets for stage four and counting. Don't go past your stage or the inspector will get you, just like the goblins your mother threatened you with when you were a child and wouldn't go to sleep. 'Name and address,' the inspector would say, 'the fine will be sent, now get off at the next stop.' Poor creatures, those dodging passengers, but I couldn't do anything about it. I was the conductor and the whole orchestra would collapse if I didn't do my duty.

Having hungry mouths to feed at home, I found myself conducting the Number 10 bus by night and studying intermittently by day in the new UCD library in concrete 'Belfield' – what a misnomer. There was little belle about that suburban field to which the Archbishop had exiled us all from the cosmopolitan Left Bank of Earlsfort Terrace and environs: O'Dwyer's on Leeson Street; Alexandra and Trinity colleges, with all those fine young Protestant women, and Earlsfort Terrace itself, where the Earls did seem still to go forth each night.

But there I was, the captain of the lurching green ship that flew from 'An Lár' to the outer spokes of south Dublin.

Being a full-time third-year English and History student, and bus conductor, demanded a certain degree of balance, robustness and strength of character – especially when the bus went around the corner and I was halfway up the stairs.

But there were many pleasant moments in that time, when all the cool people seemed to be smoking grass, its special smell accompanying them onto the bus. And then there was that faint whiff of patchouli oil as the women in long flowery dresses worked their way up to the upper deck: 'Hold the bar!' Being a recognisable regular of the new restaurant in Belfield, the poor successor to 86 St Stephens Green, I'd have great difficulty collecting fares from people who knew me, as they headed into town for the oases of Grogan's, the Coffee Inn, or other islands of student civilisation. If an inspector got on in such circumstances, the bus would empty of half of its student population at the next available stop.

Like Kavanagh's ghost sitting on the Grand Canal bank as the Number 10 passed Baggot Street Bridge, you also knew 'the secret signs', such as the subtle game of 'polling', the object of which was to follow closely on the bus ahead so that your bus avoided collecting too many passengers. That was long before GPS, and you could see a long line of buses with similar destinations, crawling one after another along Morehampton Road, all stopping dutifully at each stop. The trick was not to be conducting the leading 'car'. The use of this latter word was also one of the secret signs: it meant 'bus' to CIÉ initiates, from the French word autocar.

One of the conductor's tasks was to maintain law and order on the bus. One memorable such occasion was a Saturday night fight on the 46A between Dún Laoghaire and Monkstown Farm. I had to ring the bell three times, which was the emergency signal for the driver to stop the bus and come around to help.

I was valiantly preparing my ticket machine to use as a weapon when a pathetic fighter crawled out from under the pile and said to me, 'It's all right! I'm one of your own!'

This drunk off-duty conductor then called the melée to order. 'These lads want to go home, it's the last car to Donnybrook … good night and good luck,' and off they got at the Farm.

I eventually got my degree and left for another life. I still think fondly of that warm bunch of brave, strong warriors of the road, especially those on the old Number 10.

A CONFESSION

Gerald Dawe

My late mother was of the opinion that her father's people were Scottish because of the way they spoke English. She was both right and wrong. The Bradshaws ultimately had their roots in Scotland going back in time, but when my mother knew them – in the 1920s, 30s and 40s – they were County Antrim people through and through, from places called Ballywatermoy, Craigs, Aughaboy, Killymurris.

Originally carpenters and small farmers, they had, in the shape of my great-grandfather, moved into business, selling household goods through the length and breadth of the northern counties, and doing well enough to set up an establishment just off Belfast's Shaftesbury Square – JR Bradshaw, Wholesale Glass and China Merchants. I recall seeing with a heightened sense of surprise the name above the double-fronted store as a very young boy.

But back to the Scottish business. During the Second World War, her parents now separated, my mother and her brother were evacuated from north Belfast to their father's people in County Antrim, to a place called Creavery. After the initial shock of two city kids readjusting to farm life and country school, they settled down and would welcome their mother's occasional visits, dressed (as always) to the ninety-nines and often accompanied with her friends as well as the current boyfriend as chauffeur.

Decades later, I'd still hear my mother recounting some of the spoken English she'd heard as a teenager at that time, the early 1940s: 'fornenst', 'thole', 'girning'. What she hadn't quite realised was the language of her father's people, and the way they spoke English in the villages and hilly townlands, wasn't Scottish – though it sounded like that to her much-travelled yet young urban ears – but Ulster-Scots. When her parents Ethel and Norman had married they both began moving clear of their different families, with their own separate lexicons and pronunciations, and entering a familiar world of English, inflected by local nuance, of course, but no longer moored to their inherited places. They were forming a vernacular of their own, shaped by lives lived in London, Toronto, and eventually, by the return to Belfast. So, living in the countryside as evacuees must have been a bit of a shock for sure to their two cosmopolitan children.

One day, it must have been about 1960 or 61, I was in town accompanying my mother on a shopping trip; it would have been a Saturday, for sure, and we were in – my memory tells me – the newly-opened C&A store in downtown Belfast. She was perusing the various clothes racks when a woman came up to her and said hello and introduced us to her daughter, before asking my mother how things were.

Ethel, my grandmother, had died recently, and the solicitude was apparent even to the young fella I then was – eight or nine. From their manner of speaking, the comfortably dressed woman and daughter, I soon realised, were relatives from Antrim. They spoke with a calm and intimate inflection, almost an elevated tone too. I wandered off just as the girl was asked to give me a sweet which I took without thinking anything of it. It was, however, distasteful, a lozenge or 'drop' with a bitter, quasi-medical flavour. When the conversation returned to my mother and her recent loss, I magicked the 'sweet' out of my mouth, but, bereft of what to do next, I placed it as unobtrusively as possible within the pocket of a nearby impressive woollen coat, and tried not to think about it ever again.

I don't think we ever met those folks again either; certainly, I have no recollection of visiting houses in the villages of Antrim or the amazing Glens. All I recall of that 'Scottish connection' was the family name above the store in Belfast (now long gone), the remnants of a language caught in the intimacies of familiar words handed down, the tones of voices and, of course, that dire lozenge! Apologies to whoever bought that fine coat sixty-odd years ago; I still shudder to think about how they brought it home only to find that unwelcome, sticky gift dissembling within the pocket of their brand-new winter coat!

UISCE COISRICTHE

Catherine Foley

Tá mé i mo leaba ag dul a chodladh
Istigh sa dorchadas,
Smaointí an lae ag síor-rothlú i mo cheann.
Cloisim a céim ar thairseach an dorais,
Agus tagann sí isteach.

Siúlann sí trasna chugam,
Éadrom mar rinceoir sa bhailé.
Mothaím a méara ar m'aghaidh,
An t-uisce coisricthe
Á chuir ar m'éadan.

Gearrann sí comhartha na croise
Ar phlána mo chraicinn lena h-ordóg.
'Oíche mhaith,' a deir sí
Agus ritheann an t-uisce síos ina shruthlán

Chomh fada le mo mhalaí,
Fuar mar oighear,
Úr mar dhrúcht maidine,
Go dtí go dtitim i mo chodladh.

Agus mé i mo luí ar mo leaba
Is cuimhin liom

Gur dhein sí é sin gach oíche gan teip.
'Oíche mhaith,' a deireadh sí,
Na deora beaga sin á leagadh aice ar m'éadan,
Mar chuid den searmanas teaghlaigh a chleacht sí gach oíche.

Chuir sí an ruaig ar mo bhuarthaí ar fad,
Agus deirinn 'oíche mhaith' ar ais léi
Sula dtitinn i mo chodladh.

An bhfuil marc fágtha
Ag an uisce sin ar m'éadan,
Greanta.

HOLY WATER

I'm in my bed going asleep
In the dark,
The thoughts of the day swirling around in my head.
I hear her step on the threshold
And she comes in.

She walks across to me,
Light like a ballet dancer.
I feel her fingers on my face,
Putting the holy water
On my forehead.

With her thumb she puts the mark of the cross
On my brow.
'Goodnight,' she says.
And the water trickles down in a stream
To my eyebrows,
Cold like ice,
Fresh like morning dew,
Until I fall asleep.

As I lie here in my bed
I remember
That she did that every night without fail.
'Goodnight,' she used to say,

Putting the little drops on my forehead
As part of the familial ritual that she followed every night.

All my worries used to vanish
And I used to say 'goodnight' back to her
Before I fell asleep.

Is the mark of that holy water on my forehead now,
Engraved there?

MARCH

THE LADS THAT WILL NEVER BE OLD

Conall Hamill

The British Army patrol that stopped me on the road between Newry and Poyntzpass sometime in the mid-1980s did most to convey to me the emotional truth of the war poems of writers such as Wilfred Owen and Siegfried Sassoon. I had read them in college, but in common with a lot of the documentaries about world conflicts that I had watched on television as a teenager, they had seemed to belong to the distant past, and felt somehow unreal.

By contrast, the young soldier who was leaning down towards my car window and asking me to show him some form of ID was very much of the present and his rifle looked alarmingly real – and yet he did not conform to anyone's idea of a fearsome enemy. I presume he must have been at least eighteen or nineteen years old, but he could have passed for fifteen. His light, downy moustache looked like something he might have bought in a joke shop and stuck on his upper lip that morning in a valiant, but vain, attempt to appear older; his uniform seemed too large for him and, despite the coolness of the day, beads of perspiration trickled down his forehead from underneath his helmet. He looked like a frightened child – which, I suppose, is pretty much what he was. And I wondered if he was destined to be one of those soldiers, those boys, AE Housman had in mind when he wrote about 'the lads that will die in their glory and never be old'.

The same thought occurred to me over the last few days looking at the heartbreaking images on television and Twitter: those young Ukrainian men bidding farewell to their girlfriends, wives and families as they prepared to leave Ireland to return home and fight for their country. I looked at the teenage volunteers carrying foam ground mats and sleeping bags, described by Jeremy Bowen of the BBC as resembling students going camping but for the fact that they had assault rifles slung over their shoulders; I watched the video that appears to show a young Russian soldier who has surrendered being given food by a group of Ukrainians, and crying as he talks to his mother over the phone, placing a gentle kiss on the screen; I saw the cherub-faced marine engineer who volunteered to detonate explosives on a bridge to slow the Russian advance, knowing that he would also be killed in the explosion. Yeats's phrase, 'the delirium of the brave', came to mind. The awfulness of war takes many forms and while acts of heroism can lift the heart, there is something particularly harrowing about the idealism of youth falling victim to the darker forces of geopolitical manoeuvring.

A few weeks ago, in early February, I went along to Dublin Castle to have a look at the exhibition 'Objects of Love'. This is a very personal collection of family photographs, documents and memorabilia gathered by the Dublin-based art dealer Oliver Sears to record the suffering his Polish family endured during the Second World War. Their crime, as he puts it, was 'the simple crime of being Jewish'. He explains how the pre-war photographs of his family are the hardest for him to look at because they record a time of innocence, 'a time that could not conceive of a plan to eradicate [Jews] industrially, without trace.' He notes that his paternal grandfather lost his parents, his brother, twenty aunts, uncles and their families in Auschwitz and Treblinka and I tried to imagine how it was possible to persuade so many people to behave in such an unspeakable manner to their fellow human. Sears goes some way towards answering this question when he writes, 'I give this account of my family history to describe what happens to ordinary, law-abiding, loving human souls when democracy is dismantled and replaced with fear and diktat. The degradation is incremental and it always starts with words ...'

As I walked around the exhibition and learned how such atrocities mark successive generations of a family – even those who were not directly involved – I foolishly congratulated myself on being fortunate enough to have been born into a Europe that could no longer conceive of a plan to invade another country, a Europe where large-scale conflicts were a thing of the past. About twelve days later, Russia invaded Ukraine.

Most Junior Cert school students today are familiar with Wilfred Owen's powerful poem, *Dulce et Decorum est*, in which he describes in graphic detail the gruesome death of a soldier by mustard gas. Owen, who had first-hand experience of trench warfare, castigates those in power for telling young soldiers, mere children, eager for glory, the old lie that it is sweet and honourable to die for one's country. The title of the poem and its anti-war sentiments are an ironic twist on an ode by the Roman poet Horace, which is essentially a poem in praise of war and self-sacrifice. I re-read the poem the other day and could find comfort only in the last two lines:

> The wicked man advances, but Punishment,
> though lame of foot, has rarely let him escape.

TELEPHONE

Nicole Flattery

My mother has four sisters. Even writing that seems wrong. I consult my own sister – how many sisters does our mother have? We estimate it's somewhere between ten and fifteen. Then we begin to list them: Rita, Mary, we pause. There must be two Marys. No, we decide after a short discussion that there is only one Mary. Betty, Anne, we think, that's it? We've only got to four. That can't be right. Twelve seems like a more satisfying number of sisters. We start again. There are, finally and conclusively, only four.

In Donald Antrim's strange 1997 novel *The Hundred Brothers*, the opening sentence lists the names of all the brothers, all one hundred of them: it's a weaving, endless, almost multiplying sentence. That's what I thought it would be like to name all of my mother's sisters. I thought we would be left confused as to how they all fitted in their house growing up. I thought, at the very least, there would be enough for a camogie team, a game my mother and her sisters used to play. But no, there's really only four, a totally unexceptional number.

The reason it feels like more is, I think, the way I used to see my aunties as a child: pulling their cars haphazardly into our driveway, wearing glamorous clothes and high heels, always carrying with them an air of drama, the faint whiff of the telenovela. Another reason I think there are more is because of the telephone.

It would be impossible to estimate the amount of time my mother has spent on the phone to her sisters, speaking in her low, secretive voice, scrutinising information and gossip. One of the earliest memories of my life is hearing the phrase, 'I'm on the phone.' It's a phrase now lodged concretely in my mind, a phrase that carries with it its own specific set of instructions – don't dare come in, I'm doing something you're not privy to. Now, there's no real need to announce you're on the phone; we're all on our phones all the time. But back then my mother sat against the wall on a dining-room chair, the telephone cord wriggling in her lap as she giggled delightedly at whatever one of her sisters was saying now.

I'd never considered until recently what a release those phone calls must have been for my mother. She worked in an office when I was growing up, where she would have been required to have a professional demeanour, to be careful what she said around her boss and colleagues, to laugh at their jokes regardless of whether or not she found them funny, to exude refinement, to prove herself capable. When she came home, she had a husband and two young daughters to whom she must have felt a sense of personal responsibility – to be nice, to be instructive, to show us how to move through the world as women. What a relief those phone calls must have been; what a momentary liberation. They provided her an opportunity to be funny, to be mean and petty if she felt like it, to show a version of herself that we never saw – the young woman who must have once stayed up all night with her sisters, giddy and manic, talking, talking, talking.

On the American shows I watched as a girl, someone was always picking up the other phone – the extension, as they called it, an impossible item and wild luxury in a rural, nineties, Irish childhood – and finding out things they shouldn't have. So many of the paper-thin plots in these soaps relied on the existence of the phone extension; without the phone extension these shows might not have existed at all. I couldn't imagine picking up another line and listening to my mother's most intimate conversations – even overhearing one side felt too confidential. Of course, they would have discussed their irritations, their daily disappointments, but how many deaths, losses and failures had they guided each other through? And what about those private impulses you sometimes get, the desire to abscond, quit your job, leave your life behind, all these things you might never do, but can confess to wanting to do, over a forgiving phone line. Although the American allure of the extension was strong, I couldn't have ever listened to that and not felt like I was committing a betrayal.

It's well publicised that young people don't like talking on the phone now, that they will go to any lengths to avoid a call. I feel differently – I find video chat too exposing, my hands and facial expressions give too much away. I prefer the secrecy of the phone, where I'm just a voice and I can forget about my body and face. I know it's a trait I've inherited. Years ago when I was studying film in college, my class watched a Pedro Almodóvar film which featured an array of comic aunties playfully giving advice and offering instructions. Like all Almodóvar movies, this one went down a mysterious route. However, it wasn't the lack of straight realism one of my classmates took issue with, but the depiction of the aunties. After a number of scenes of outlandish fantasy this was the film's greatest problem as he saw it. They were too vibrant, he said, they were too ridiculous, they were too involved; they, quite simply, talked too much.

I had to disagree with this. 'But,' I remember saying, 'that's what it's really like.'

LOWERING THE LADDER
Quentin Fottrell

I've been thinking a lot about Marian Finucane since her death. I live 3,000 miles away in New York, and I feel a void. When I participated in her newspaper panel, I loved to watch her flip through her notes and declare, 'And a very good morning to you!' Her voice was soothing, but carried effortless authority. The radio, if you listen carefully enough, doesn't lie.

The first time I took my seat in Marian's studio, I thought, 'I've arrived!' I was there to discuss very important issues of national interest – dinner-party etiquette. I took a deep breath and made sure to enjoy and appreciate the moment.

Over the years I would be invited back to the programme regularly to talk about everything from online dating to the banking crisis and, later, marriage equality. The trajectory of my career seemed to play out in her studio and it continued all the way to New York.

Even before the banking crisis, I was strapped for cash. Marian liked that I still threw a tablecloth over a wallpaper-pasting table for dinner guests. My culinary repertoire consisted of one dish: pasta surprise. It has feta, tomato, spinach, onions, secret spices (that is, whatever is lying around) and lashings of garlic. As one friend noted twenty years after I first served it, 'The only surprise is that you're still making it.'

On another show in the weeks before Christmas, I told Marian that I ruled my dinner parties with an iron fist. She peered at me over her glasses with a quizzical, amused look. Of course I added that being a good guest is just as important as being a good host, but the host must set the tone. On that particular Sunday morning, her producer fielded a call from a disgruntled host who wanted to out me as having cancelled on his dinner party at the last minute. I was about to get roasted, right there live on RTÉ Radio 1. Luckily for me, her producer didn't put him through. It wasn't the first time a female journalist saved my bacon.

Fifteen years ago, I wrote a piece for the *Sunday Tribune* about homophobia in Irish life. On the TV, on the streets, in the classrooms. It was the first time I'd written about this subject; this time I put my own story out there. I felt exposed. My phone rang that Sunday morning. It was Anne Farrell, producer for Marian Finucane. She put me through live to that week's newspaper panel. We wouldn't be talking about dinner-party etiquette today. On that day I found my voice.

Years before, the late Christina Murphy fished my CV out of a pile and offered me an internship at *The Irish Times* a couple of months before I finished my journalism post-grad in Galway. I don't know what direction my career or my life would have taken without that opportunity.

It would turn into a pattern. Caroline Walsh was features editor at *The Irish Times* during that summer internship. One day, she spotted a lost twenty-one-year-old kid sitting forlornly in the canteen on D'Olier Street. She asked me to write a feature about polo. 'Isn't it great now we have Quentin writing that story?' Caroline said to her assistant. I knew that she said it within earshot so I would feel like I had something of value to contribute. Like the magic porridge pot, small acts of kindness keep on giving. Caroline too is gone and that was nearly thirty years ago, but it means as much to me today.

Mary Cummins sat behind me that summer. She had copper hair, blue eyeshadow and cloaks galore. My anxious paper-shuffling attracted her attention. She swivelled around in her chair and offered to go through an article I had written about a dispute involving nuns selling their land. 'We covered this story last year,' she said. 'Check the clippings!'

In my current job in New York, I hire our summer intern. It is the most important thing I do all year.

Mary Holland, a political reporter who like her namesake Mary Cummins died far too young, walked into *The Irish Times* office one day that summer and pinned a rainbow flag on my lapel. She was a smart, intimidating and no-nonsense woman with a demeanour of warm steel who broke stories about secret peace contact between the British Government and the IRA.

I looked down at my lapel and back at Mary. It was 24 June 1993, the day Ireland officially passed legislation that finally decriminalised homosexuality. I didn't feel out of place that day. I felt seen. Nobody else noticed what she did. It took a moment and it was done. But she may as well have wrapped a warm blanket around me.

A decade later, women journalists still had my back. At the *Sunday Tribune* Christmas party at McGrattans bar and restaurant in Dublin, Nuala O'Faolain worried about me walking home alone in my flashy fur coat. 'You might get beaten up!' she said. I gave it serious thought – after all, I was a pint-sized, fur-clad social columnist who had dodged trouble perhaps one too many times. Would tonight be the night I ended up in the gutter? I wore the coat home, but I kept my eyes peeled. Then, as now, such vigilance goes with the territory.

I've had four full-time writing jobs in my life: two in London, one in Dublin and one in New York. In all of them, without exception, I was hired by women.

Christina Murphy, Caroline Walsh, Mary Cummins, Mary Holland. That generation of feminists paved the way for today's crop. I wish they were still with us, to see so many things they fought for coming into being.

And Marian? She never quite showed her hand on the social and political issues of the day. Perhaps staying above the fray enhanced her status as one of the most celebrated broadcasters of her generation. She shone a light on stories that might otherwise have gone ignored. She, and her sisters in arms, helped lay the foundations for modern Ireland.

But they all made sure to leave the ladder behind for those who came after them.

MY MOTHER WAS A SCRUBBER

Brian Farrell

'She's only a scrubber.' That's what my mate said to me when, at thirteen, I admired a young girl on the street. I was a bit surprised. Not only that he said it, but that it was meant as such a terrible insult. Because the truth was, my mother was a scrubber, and so was his. They scrubbed cuffs and collars to get the daily grime from their husbands' shirts. But more than that, in the evening when the perfumed workers left their offices to return to their families, our mothers left their children in Finglas for the city, where they dusted and polished and scrubbed, room after room, office after office, floor after floor. They weren't always scrubbers. Sometimes they joined the assembly lines in the Ashtown Tin Box Company, or the Gateaux Bakery, or the beast of Jamestown Road, Unidare itself. The young mothers took any job to supplement the family income and keep up their employment stamps.

Often, during the 1960s when seasonal work was going strong, the women would travel en masse to the factories, pulling up their bicycles at the houses of their friends and collecting them on the way.

They would cycle in a circle outside our home as they waited for my mother to get on her coat and scarf and then, after adding to their numbers, like a murmuration they would weave and swerve and follow each other down the long road, chatting and laughing and looking back every now and again to wave goodbye to the children they left behind, until finally they rounded a corner and were out of sight.

When the seasonal work finished, we'd have our mother home again for a while to bring warmth to our evenings, but we knew deep down that it was only a temporary reprieve until something else would drag her away.

On one occasion, I remember her break was cut short by the delivery of a dreaded 'unexpected invitation to a wedding'. Christenings, communions and confirmations could invariably be saved for, but we needed the Lord's own protection from the 'unexpected invitation to a wedding'.

It began with the postman dropping a handwritten envelope through the letterbox and it not even Christmas. My mother and we children stood around in a circle looking down at this imposter as it lay on the yet unpaid-for lino in the hall, our faces full of shock and horror as if we'd just discovered an unexploded Second World War bomb in the middle of our happy home.

Before we called for the bomb squad we desperately grasped at straws, trying to convince my mother that it might just be a letter. We tried to identify the handwriting. 'Is it Auntie Joan in Roscommon?' we asked, without lifting the letter from the floor. 'Maybe it's the nuns in South Africa?' (Even though it had an Irish stamp.) 'It's Uncle Bill. Uncle Bill has a lovely hand.' 'So has Uncle Paddy. It could be Uncle Paddy.' 'It's not Uncle Bill, and it's not Uncle Paddy and it's not Auntie Joan,' my mother said in a defeated tone. 'And flip whoever it is. Flip them anyway.'

I offered to run down the road with the bomb before it exploded and drop it in through Chrissie O'Riordan's door. let her deal with it, but no one even graced me with a reply. That was that, God had no mercy.

It was an 'unexpected invitation to a wedding' and my mother would soon be heading back to scrubbing the city offices. Not that her meagre earnings would pay for the suit or the dress or the present or the rounds of drinks or the taxi home, but the earnings would help pay off the moneylender's loan for the suit or the dress or the present or whatever the unexpected event would cost us. So it was back to the scrubbing and returning home late at night with hardened, blackened knees to be washed in a basin by the fire.

One day while I was walking down the quays with my father, he pointed out the Sunlight Chambers building. Standing on the corner of Parliament Street and Essex Quay, it opened in 1902 as the Irish headquarters of Lever Brothers, the makers of Sunlight soap. He told me it was his favourite building in Dublin and it was all because of the two horizontal decorative bands running along its three sides at the base of the first and second floors. These beautifully ornate, colourful friezes pay homage, in storyboard style, to the men and woman who toil. Shiny figures of men ploughing, women sowing seed, children playing, workers reaping and harvesting, building and sweating, all apparently in the process of gathering the ingredients for Sunlight soap.

Right in there, in the middle of it all, are the scrubbers: cleansing all so production can start again and the circle of life and toil and earning can be completed.

So forget about Gandon's Four Courts and Custom House or Trinity's Corinthian columns. The next time you're taking a bus down the quays to Heuston Station or crossing Parliament Street Bridge for City Hall, raise your eyes and feast them on the frieze where someone was decent enough to celebrate the work of the much-maligned scrubbers, because as we all know, they were always so much more than that.

ADA SUE

Clare Monnelly

She came into the world early. Impatient, raring to go. It was a fittingly dramatic affair. Her dad was due to be on stage that evening. Twice that evening, to be precise. In Galway. On the opposite coast. We'd later learn that the gang waited in the pub from the afternoon on for an update on Her. Causing trouble before She even got here.

I was on the massage table in the salon when I finally accepted what was happening. I was too polite to interrupt the masseuse's work despite the growing pain and the diminishing time between contractions – because yes, Clare, that's what that is. You are in labour.

I still paid for my massage, mind.

I could hear the disbelief in my husband's voice. Okay. Call your sister, call the midwife, then call me back.

The contractions were two and half minutes apart now. And they were definitely real.

By the time I got to the back of my sister's car who had gotten to me in record time, I thought She'd be born there.

He was on his way. The company knew and the shows would be cancelled and boy would I be in trouble if this was a false alarm. But She was coming. And She seemed in quite the hurry.

Maternity hospital staff are calm angels. Nothing fazes them. He was through Enfield, flooring it, no doubt. My sister told him to put his hazards on and drive on the hard shoulder.

The midwife told me not to be holding on for Dad now – this baby was coming and I was to tell her if I needed to push. They didn't think he'd make it.

He arrived just as the pain relief kicked in. *He* was the real relief. We put on Christmas FM and all was calm. I pushed. And pushed. And pushed. The doctor thought I'd need help, but my angel midwife – real-life angels they are – she thought I could do it. She asked for a couple more minutes. And she was right. And She was here. And immediately – I knew Her. Till that very moment the whole thing had been so abstract. Yes, I could feel Her moving around in there. Yes, we'd bought the bits and pieces and done the online classes and in theory, I knew She was coming. But in that moment – I knew Her. I recognised her presence. She felt so very familiar to me. I have yet to find the words to describe the wave that came over me – not love, as people say, but … I felt certain. Sure She was ours and that although I didn't know what I was doing yet, I'd figure it out. Utter calm.

But She was little. So She had to go. Away from me. He could go with her, but I had to go to surgery, complications, I had to go away from Her, and is that completely necessary? Yes.

Okay. Whatever She needs. He got to go with Her and I was glad of that.

And when I got out of theatre he got to come back to me, but then neither of us were with Her and no one was with the dog and my blood pressure and where are Her clothes and when can I see Her again and can I get that tea and toast now that everyone goes on about and I have a picture of him with it you know, the tea and toast and the moustache that he had for the show and an angel nurse told me I could see her once I could walk again, I should sleep a little and she would come and get me at 5 a.m. on the dot and she did and she brought me to Her and there She was. Toasty and warm and tiny and mine. She got to come back to me soon after and I don't remember what we did exactly but I didn't sleep for days. I sat watching Her, because I was so tired that if I slept maybe I wouldn't hear Her and the less I slept the more tired I got so the riskier it was to sleep and so I just didn't. For about eight months.

Her name is Ada Sue.

GROWING UP IN MILTOWN

John Hurley

I had the good fortune to grow up overhead a newspaper shop in Miltown Malbay. Long before it became famous for the Willie Clancy Festival, it was home for me, and to this day gives me a sense of place.

Before opinion polls existed, we knew a person's voting intentions by the newspapers they bought. *Irish Press* – solid Fianna Fáil. *Irish Independent* – certain Fine Gael. A Fianna Fáiler would never buy the *Independent* and vice versa. Sales of *Cork Examiner*s depended on whether we had a 'blow-in' guard or bank official. We sold two *Irish Times*, one to the Protestant minister and one to the resident lapsed Catholic. This man fell out with the fiery curate at Mass one Sunday morning; I was an altar boy at the time. The man had refused to come up from the back of the church. The curate insisted; he refused and eventually left the church, swearing he'd never darken its doors again. The following day he came in and placed an order with my mother for the 'Protestant' paper. For years afterwards he marched up the town with *The Irish Times* under his arm, the masthead clearly visible.

I collected the *Press*es and *Herald*s from the West Clare train every evening. I'd find them buried underneath exhaust pipes, Matterson's bacon and day-old chicks. Sadly some of the chicks didn't survive the trip from Limerick, and regularly, some of our papers didn't survive either! Some smart aleck in Ennistymon or Corofin got the free read, fair play to them. And they were good at removing the papers they wanted from the bundle too, because we never knew they were missing until we counted them.

Every October the Christmas annuals were delivered. *Topper*s, *Beano*s, *Dandy*s stacked up in the sitting room above the shop. I spent endless hours in the company of Desperate Dan, Korky the Cat and the Bash Street Kids. I ignored *Bunty* and *Girl's Crystal*, all that was sissy stuff as I saw it. The sixty-four-page cowboy and war comics were firm favourites. Walter Mitty-like, I imagined myself as a rear gunner on a Spitfire pursued by the Luftwaffe. For years I repeated 'Achtung, Achtung, Donner und Blitzen' and 'Gott im Himmel' in my childish games, having no idea what they meant.

In my aunt's pub, The Blondes, my love for traditional music was born. The effortlessly natural music coming from the locals and visitors became part of my DNA. It was there, on The Blondes' record player, that I first heard Bridie Gallagher's 'Boys from the County Armagh'. To this day, whenever I hear the opening two signature piano notes, I immediately recognise the Kilfenora and remember Kitty Linnane.

Christy Moore lived in Miltown for a few years and was a welcome visitor to our shop. Luke Kelly wandered in one morning and bought the copy of Edward de Bono's *Lateral Thinking*, which had strayed in somehow and was languishing among the Mills & Boons and Zane Greys. We thought we'd never get rid of it! I recall seeing Séamus Ennis nursing a mug of strong tea in the kitchen one morning when he was a bit the worse for wear. He had fingers as long as Clarke's tin whistles – an essential asset for uilleann pipers, I later found out.

Tommy Makem came in another time and bought a tin whistle. My mother didn't recognise him and, along with his change, she handed him the self-tutor manual *How to play Down by the Salley Gardens*. When she later found out who he was, unabashed, she said, 'He was as entitled to the manual as well as anyone else. You never know, he might even learn a new tune!'

Willie Clancy was both a *Sunday Press* and a *News of the World* man. Some Sundays, he wouldn't make it up to the shop because of a late session. His 'messenger' would call in to us instead. Willie had left strict instructions with us that on those occasions we were to hold back the *News of the World* and just give out the *Sunday Press*. But one time, my brother forgot, and out of habit, handed over Willie's usual order. The messenger was outraged. Back flew the *News of the World* across the counter with the words, 'You can keep your British filth to yourself, thank you very much!'

GRANDDADDY

Kathleen Murphy

When my grandmother on my father's side died suddenly in 2011, I was grief-stricken. We'd been very close. She understood me. She saw me for who I am and didn't want or expect me to change.

Grief is a strange thing. She was no longer in my world, yet everything reminded me of her presence.

Then came the regrets. Why didn't I visit more? I should have told her more that I loved her. And so on, until all I could remember for a while were my regrets.

So I made it my business to spend more time with my granddaddy. At first, I did it for selfish reasons. I didn't want to be consumed by the same regrets I had with Grandmommy. I wanted to spend time for the sake of spending time.

Maybe that's not the best reason to spend time with someone you love.

I wanted to be closer to him, like I was, and am, with my other grandfather, but I didn't know how. Granddaddy was a strict, serious, funny man who only used the number of words required and not one more than necessary. I guess that is where Daddy gets it from. Growing up I respected and loved Granddaddy, but I didn't know how to talk to him. Despite the fact that we both spoke English, we might as well have been speaking two different languages. Compared with his use of language, my words spill out of my mouth with abandon as I try to relay stories and tales using my imagination to conjure images of the past, present and future in my listener.

I would often go to visit him. The house was usually full of sons and daughters or grandchildren. The mixture of voices intermingling creating a calming white noise that would propel me back to my childhood. Despite this, I struggled to find the right words that would allow conversation to flow easily between us.

Around this time I had also started doing the genealogy of my family. I wanted to see where we had come from and how far I could go back into the past.

One day while chatting about it in Granddaddy's house, he took an interest in what I was saying. As he answered my questions, he began to weave his own stories about his past, his upbringing, his life on the road and our culture. Through his stories, his experience came alive to me. The beauty of travelling from town to town selling goods at different markets, bartering with local farmers for food in exchange for the tinkering of pots and pans or other work on the farm, and the tragedy of seeing loved ones buried long before their time.

He began asking questions of his own about what I had found and who. We would have long conversations about the family tree, and I saw the pride in him when he talked about his own.

Suddenly we had found a common language.

From then on, whenever I would go to visit, we would chat about our family tree. But we expanded our common language in time. We'd talk about the movies we enjoyed like the old Westerns starring John Wayne, or black-and-white films from a bygone era, and whatever else came to mind. Over the years I would fill him in on what I was up to and while at times I didn't visit as often as I should, when I did visit, I was glad I did. I began to see a different side of him, the young man he had been, the husband, the father and then the grandfather he had become.

In 2017 I went to America for the summer as part of a leadership programme, the first Irish Traveller to ever be on the programme in its history. Before I went, I told my grandfather all about it. 'America!' he said. 'Won't you make sure and come home now?'

While I was gone, Granddaddy's health took a turn for the worse and he had to have surgery due to complications from his diabetes. When I returned, he wasn't the same. He'd become more frail and was using a wheelchair. Over the following months his health went downhill, and he was in and out of hospital.

In late February of 2018 before heading away to Clare for work, I called in to see him. We chatted for a while and when I left, I told him I loved him and would see him soon.

While in Clare, I kept getting this awful sense of foreboding. It had begun to snow really badly and to my relief our team left Clare early. We arrived home on the evening of 28 February.

On the morning of 1 March 2018, the first anniversary of Traveller ethnicity being recognised in Ireland, we got news that Granddaddy had only a few days to live. I sat in my apartment hoping he would last out the storm so I could go and visit him. Around three that day, something told me I needed to get into the car and go and see him. Twenty minutes later, Granddaddy died peacefully at home surrounded by all of us family.

While I was devastated by the loss, I have no regrets. I am lucky. I got to know my grandfather twice, once as a child and the second time as an adult.

THE DAY LUKE KELLY CAME COURTIN'

Emer O'Kelly

Luke Kelly died, almost unbelievably, thirty-five years ago. For those who knew him, his vivid, funny, profane presence, as well as his awesome musical talent, burn undimmed. And now, he looks across two works of art across Dublin streets, one north, one south, at a city he would be unlikely to recognise. Vera Klute's massive head is in Sheriff Street near where Luke was born; John Coll's graceful full figure-bronze is close to the entrance of Stephen's Green, not very far from where Phil Lynott, himself a devoted Dubliners fan, has held court for years.

Ireland, and Dublin, have changed almost beyond belief since Luke and the Dubliners held sway in O'Donoghue's pub on Merrion Row, promoted initially by the laconic and still – happily – very much with us Noel Pearson. Dublin, despite their mischievous presence, was still a fairly prudish and closed society in 1984, the year Luke died. Official Ireland was still suspicious of outside cultural influences, along the lines of the then quite recent claim in the Dáil by the Laois-Offaly TD, Oliver J Flanagan, that there was no sex in Ireland before RTÉ.

Many frowned censoriously at the worldwide fame achieved by Luke, John, Ronnie, Barney and Ciarán. Happy to laud their music, maybe, but some people lamented their freewheeling ways. The music might be a great advertisement for Irish culture and a visible boost to our tourist trade, but what about our reputation as an island of saints and scholars, they wondered. Did the Dubliners fit that?

For the rest of us, the Dubliners were that. They were unpretentiously learned and of course gloriously talented in all aspects of folk music. But there was always joy in the Dubliners' music. It was never self-conscious, never overtly political, never defensive, just real, warm, and soaringly musical. Mean-minded condemnation of lack of national purity never bothered them; they weren't in the business of saving Ireland from itself. And they dropped traditional rebel songs from their repertoire when the conflict in Northern Ireland escalated.

Luke Kelly, Ronnie Drew, John Sheahan (still happily with us), Ciarán Bourke, and Barney McKenna were the original Dubliners. Ciarán, sadly, was the first to go: he had to leave the group, his health after a brain haemorrhage unable to stand the pace of touring. Jim McCann of the cherubic countenance and impish smile joined later, followed even later by Eamonn Campbell and Paddy Reilly. Ronnie came and went. And there were others as the years passed.

The music played on, but the soul went out of things when Luke died. He was only forty-four, but he had lived as hard as he had worked, and had been diagnosed with a brain tumour in 1980.

I am proud to this day that he personally taught me my party piece. I have no illusions about my talents: I'm an audience, not a performer. But Luke apparently thought I could do a rendition of 'Maids When You're Young Never Wed an Old Man', also known as 'For He's Got No Faloorum …'

'There's an imp in that face of yours,' he told me.

I remember the day clearly, and looking back, the shadow of the illness that would take him might well have been hanging over him already. Walking in Grafton Street, I ran into Luke. 'Are you coming to Grogan's for a pint?' he asked. With Luke? Of course I was, even though it was only four thirty in the afternoon. It was freezing cold, the atmosphere was dank, and Luke's cloud of fiery curls shone like a burnished halo.

He was interestingly clad: the inside seam of a pair of green trousers was ripped from top to bottom, providing a flapping, one-sided skirt effect. Fair enough, if chilly on a November afternoon. But Luke wasn't wearing underclothes, to use the most polite term. Perched on a stool in Grogan's, he smiled pleasurably into a creamy pint, remembering only from time to time to sweep his trouser-skirt across his, em, family jewels, to use another polite term.

And he did that only after I'd overcome my convent education enough to point my finger meaningfully in their direction.

Then, mercifully, we got on to the repertoire. That was when he demanded I produce paper and pen so he could write out the verses of the song, underlining the emphasis he wanted, marking the pauses, and circling the bits to be drawn out. 'That'll do you now,' he beamed, handing it to me.

Sadly, the paper has not survived the years, although his notations are still in my head. 'That was great craic,' he said outside the pub, giving me a smacking kiss, and disappearing into the damp darkness, his green train flowing regally behind him, as befitting a musical king.

MY FATHER, SAINT PATRICK
Kate Carty

I met my father on the road the other day. He was behind me on the cycle path in his old jalopy of a Jeep. I was cycling back towards Westport when I heard the horn pipping me. I was on the lane through his fields, so I stopped and hitched my bike into the ditch to let him pass. There was a slow whistle as the window descended and he was there beside me chewing on a piece of straw. Of course, he wasn't my father; he's been dead nine years this January. But this man was the cut of him. The woollen black hat pulled down, skimming his ears.

'I shouldn't have beeped you,' he said. A smile played on his lips.

'It's okay, it was better than running me down.'

'No, I wouldn't do that. Still, I shouldn't have beeped you.'

'You're all right,' I said.

'Where are ye from yerself?' he said.

'Nottingham originally, now I'm over the other side of town. Parents both Irish, home every summer on holiday. You know the story.'

'I do, I do,' he said, his eyes straying over to the sheep.

'My father was a farmer too,' I said.

'Was he now?'

'Well, he was a builder, but as soon as he got the chance he bought some land and a house beside it on the edge of Nottingham.'

'Had he cattle?'

'He managed to buy thirty acres,' I said, 'and then he rented nearly a hundred and so he had a big herd of Charolais.'

'That's mighty.'

'It was,' I said. 'I think it was like a piece of home for him over there. He had donkeys and miniature horses he bought carriages for at farm sales, then he'd drive the grandchildren around in them whenever he got the chance.'

'Mighty, he sounds mighty.'

He shifted around in his seat and I saw him wince as he moved his hip. Dad was the same sometimes. He often walked like a magpie carrying an apple in his beak.

'Well, I best get going,' I said, 'the rain's coming.'

'It surely is. Good luck'.

With an abrupt nod of his head, he saluted me and drove off down the lane.

I pushed down hard on the pedals but I felt the grief rising in my chest. It was as though for a few minutes my father had been there beside me. I ached to be back in his farmhouse kitchen in Trowell warming my bottom against the red Aga. Making tea for himself and Larry Quinn, once they've had a sip of poteen to put some warmth back into themselves after another winter Saturday spent chasing cattle that had broken out into the neighbouring fields.

Then they'd do the feeding and foddering of the menagerie of horses and donkeys, and the flock of sheep he minded for Father Kearney whose Bulwell parish had no pasture.

I'd give anything to stand again looking out of his back window at his turkeys, the one-eyed goose, the ducks and the hens. I long to hear Quentin's melancholic braying at dusk, calling for a mate, more soulful than any pining lover. Quentin was a handsome Poitou mule, another bargain from a farm sale whose pedigree turned out to be flawed, but Dad kept him anyway.

Nearing Carraholly on my bike, I can see Croagh Patrick standing tall over Clew Bay. I'm reminded of Dad wearing the ceremonial mitre and green and gold vestments on permanent loan to him from Bishop McGuinness. He wore the mitre low on his high forehead as he strode out with his staff, leading the Nottingham parade every 17th of March. He was one of the founders of the Nottingham Irish Club in the 1950s, and he was never prouder than when he was asked to be Saint Patrick in the annual parade. Prouder even than of his role in the purchase of the new premises for the club on Wilford Street in the 1970s, where he did most of the building work to create the dance hall with the sprung floor, the restaurant and Stable bar. I was only fourteen or fifteen and I was his brick hodder that long hot summer.

It was quite a spectacle when he led the parade through the centre of Nottingham, all the traffic stopped, the crowds waving little Irish flags and all of them looking at him. He became an annual feature in the *Evening Post*. Meanwhile, I led the procession of floats in his old Land Rover, towing the big model Irish cottage that himself and John Dermody had built and thatched. Dad kept the saint's robes on long after the parade, and in the pubs everyone was dying to buy Saint Patrick a Guinness.

I feel such pride now for that shy lad who left Charlestown in 1949 with a fiver and two pairs of socks in his pocket. Yet for years I was mortified by his antics, saintly and not so saintly. After he died, I found his Saint Patrick regalia – the alb, chasuble and mitre still hanging in the wardrobe, and not a snake to be seen anywhere.

I HAVE NOTHING TO WEAR

Barbara Scully

I have, over the years, spent many hours of my life standing in front of my wardrobe, in my dressing gown, moaning, most usually to my husband, that I have nothing to wear. This usually occurs when we are going out. Not to somewhere fancy mind you, because then I definitely wouldn't have something to wear and that fact would be of no surprise to anyone. And so I'd have planned accordingly and bought something.

But no, this moaning is reserved for when we are just going out maybe to the pub or for a meal with friends. In desperation I stare into the abyss that is my wardrobe and lament that I have absolutely nothing to wear. My husband looks from me to the wardrobe full of clothes, clearly thinking, 'are you mad, woman?' But having been married to me forever, he rarely articulates this thought. And so he will mutter something fairly innocuous that he thinks won't make me explode.

Well, a few weeks into this new pandemic world, I can categorically state that I truly HAVE NOTHING TO WEAR. And this time I'm not going anywhere. But I don't have a wardrobe for this new life. How could I? This new life came out of nowhere. We weren't given time to adequately prepare. All right, we knew this virus was coming but nowhere did I see, or hear a mention of the general public needing special clothes in order to cope with this enforced springtime hibernation. No. No warning, nothing at all.

And yes, I know my wardrobe malfunction is emphatically not a real problem in the greater scheme of things, but giving our attention to the small practicalities of life is how many of us are getting through this strange time.

And on that, let me be clear about two things. Firstly, I am not what my dear mother would call 'a fashion plate'. No, I am a middle-aged woman.

And like most middle-aged women – actually no, like most women, I suspect, I like to be well turned out, but I also like to be comfortable. And just now I can't find where that comfort is.

Okay, so I know I could stay in my PJs all day. But that's not very hygienic, is it, especially now. Also, I'm not a slob. So PJs, they're not the answer. We may not be going out much but we have to venture out for a walk every day and even under the latest restrictions we occasionally need to visit a shop or the chemist. Leggings and a sweatshirt are appropriate for the walking. But seriously, how many people over forty-five do you know who look good in Lycra, even when coupled with a huge sweatshirt? I don't feel at my best in public with all my lumps and bumps on show when I am not obviously engaged in an activity aimed at reducing those lumpy bits. Jeans are my usual casual attire but you can't lounge on the sofa in jeans. And yes, of course my jeans are stretchy but they still aren't that comfortable when one is reclined horizontally.

What we need and need urgently is a range of good-quality but very cheap lounge wear that, to use fashion parlance, could take us from sofa to home office to the supermarket and back, allowing us to feel comfortable and at our best in a relaxed and informal way. And just as that realisation set in, what happened? The non-essential shops had to close, including the very places where we might actually have had some hope of finding such garments at prices we could afford. So, it looks like for the coming weeks, or even months, I am reduced to changing my clothes twice or even three times a day, as I attempt not to completely let myself go.

But I worry that I'm already on that slippery slope. My poor nails are wearing shellac that is well over a month old and has started to crack and chip. I'm no fashionista, but I've always been allergic to the sight of chipped nail varnish.

And don't get me started on my hair. Without the miraculous ministrations of my local hair salon, the grey is appearing at an alarming rate. Hairdressers have instructed us not to even consider doing a desperation 'box colour' ourselves as the damage we inflict on our barnets might take years to sort out. Use one of those root sprays, they advise. Grand, except root sprays are now as rare as flour and liquid soap in the supermarkets.

So, I am well on my way to a full-on bag lady in my Lycra leggings, chipped nails and greying hair. If you see me on my daily regulation excursion close to my home, you can feel free to ignore me, although I'm fairly confident that, looking how I do at present, it's highly unlikely you'll recognise me.

HAPPY MOTHER'S DAY

Claire Garvey

The road into the Bessborough Mother and Baby Home stretched out long and grey before me when I arrived there in August 1985. Flanked on either side by fields where cows grazed, the old house had sweeping views over the Douglas Estuary, and had once been the home of a prominent Cork Quaker family. In 1922, it was bought by the Sisters of the Sacred Heart order of nuns and became one of the first of the new state's institutional answers to the perceived problem of unmarried mothers.

The nun who admitted me asked what name I wanted to have. It transpired that the girls in Bessborough were assigned house names, as we worked on a first-name basis only, but I asked if I could keep mine, as no one else had the same one.

I soon discovered that everything was cloaked in secrecy. For the sake of the neighbours, the Dublin girls were 'doing a course in London' and the Kerry girls were 'doing a course in Dublin'. Nuns took letters and had them posted in England to add authenticity to this story.

I was just six miles from home and I was confused.

We settled in and we formed a bond, our little group of 'fallen women' – as some, no doubt, would have regarded us. We worked in the convent and in the nursery, some of us studied for our Leaving Cert, we scrubbed floors and at night we knitted. We adapted without question to the strange ways of the Home and the strange people who lived there. Just a few girls passing through, but there were others who had come and never left. Old women now, who were institutionalised, and screamed in the night.

It was a strange time, the 1980s. Ireland felt like it was caught between worlds. While we scrubbed floors in a Mother and Baby Home, we also did an AnCO pottery course, listening to Elton John on the radio. We went to Mass in the chapel and then afterwards tried to play pool – which is difficult with a bump!

And we chatted all the time, but not about where we came from or giving away any details that would identify our families. Deep down, we all knew none of us would be leaving there with our babies, but we still sat on each other's beds and talked and fantasised about a different future where we would just walk out with our babies and go home.

The few grainy Polaroids I have of the time show rosy-cheeked women sitting on beds – no Instagram posing here – all looking so young. Young mothers.

Autumn was beautiful that year, with coloured leaves and mist settling on the far hills that I could see from my window. All the time I was growing and cradling my bump and wanting time to stop because my baby was with me, and part of me. My art teacher from school brought me in paint and paper and I tried to capture the colours and stop time.

But nothing stops the tide, and I couldn't suspend time.

My baby was born in December, a shock of black hair and perfect in every way.

I stared, mesmerised.

I was a mother.

This was a fundamental change. Tectonic plates had shifted and life would never be the same. And when I left the Home and left my baby to be adopted, the changes travelled with me. To boarding school in West Cork, to college, to working abroad, to settling down, to a new family. The notion that any of us would be able to 'put it all behind' us was laughable, unthinkable, impossible.

It would be another two decades before my child and I found each other again. Achingly alike.

And I often wonder about those women, whose real names I don't know, and where they are now. Young women who must have returned, white-faced, to their families and communities around Ireland, side-stepping awkward questions about their absences, their fictional courses. 'How did you get on in London?'

Or did everyone know? Did everyone just play along with the line they were spun? Young mothers who kept their secret and were denied the recognition of that most seismic change that had occurred.

But still mothers.

And so, today, I salute the girls I knew only as 'Rose' from Tralee, 'Sheila' from Killarney, 'Jane' from Dublin and 'Claire' from Cork, and I wish you all a Happy Mother's Day.

APRIL

GHOSTS IN GREEN AND WHITE

John O'Donnell

It begins with joy, the surge of exultation you get when your team wins. The winning players, cavorting in delight around the field; the beaten side collapsing to their knees. Then the speeches, and the presentation – the trophy raised on high to cheers from the faithful – followed by the lap of honour, new energy flowing through tired limbs as the victors thank their loyal fans.

And there are the celebrations, the crowded bars toasting the team's achievement. Like a long-awaited new arrival, the trophy is paraded on tour; later, pictures will emerge of the silverware gleaming in old haunts, as well as in other unexpected places, festooned with the winners' colours.

Green and white. The Ireland rugby team's recent Grand Slam, won at home in Dublin in front of ecstatic fans on St Patrick's Day weekend, surely made even the most cynical citizen briefly proud to be Irish. It wasn't just the fact of the success, but the style with which they won, a swashbuckling abandon that seemed to hark back to an earlier, more carefree time. The media are always quick to emphasise the historic nature of any big win, so it's appropriate to remember the teams that came before, the players that did – and didn't – make it, so many of them since becoming shades, as James Joyce – surely the number 10 on any Irish writer's rugby team – would put it: Jack Kyle, Tom Kiernan, Ray McLoughlin, Barry Bresnihan.

Green and white. My old school, Gonzaga College, wears the same colours as the Irish team. We were always ribbed mercilessly for this; rugby was its main sport, but for many years the school achieved absolutely nothing except the dubious distinction of being the butt of endless jokes. Gonzaga conceding a pushover try from its own scrummaging machine. Gonzaga losing in a game of unopposed. No wonder other schools struggled to take us seriously – confused by what exactly was meant by the requirement to wear 'boots', I played my first rugby game in Wellingtons. Another contemporary, now no longer with us, turned out on the pitch wearing a scarf and gloves.

If there was a rich comedy in our ineptitude, there was sometimes tragedy as well. Here is another shade, the ghost of Michael Brennan, the boy who died fifty years ago this year, on the main pitch, aged sixteen, while playing for Gonzaga. How did the teachers, the coaches, explain to us, a small community of boys numbed by shock and grief, that rugby is still only a game?

It's hard not to feel sorry in other ways for some of our earlier coaches over the years. They were an idiosyncratic bunch: Mr McCarthy, the Cork hurler who had never handled an oval ball before he became our trainer; Mr Whirdy, the taciturn Northern Ireland soccer fan doing his best to inject us with a bit of Ulster steeliness; and Father Brennan, teaching us how to pass, the ball held reverently like a ciborium in his two hands while we stood on that tussocky back pitch, knock-kneed, shivering in pristine shirts and shorts as yet unsullied by the horror of mud and grass.

Notorious for producing legions of lawyers, maybe some of the school's alumni occasionally seem a bit too pleased with themselves. Perhaps the reputation for being ... er, self-assured, comes in part from Gonzaga's much-derided interest in the Classics: it was said to be the only school in Ireland where the line-out calls were in Latin and Greek. Now I hear a voice calling out of my own past: our old Greek teacher, the late John Wilson, an All-Ireland medal winner for Cavan back in their 1947 victory in New York's Polo Grounds.

I am back in class, and he is dangling my untidy, ink-stained copybook between finger and thumb. '*Deipnon kounos*', he says with disdain, '*deipnon kounos*. A dog's dinner.' Which was also a fair description of the kind of mess we'd made of many of the games our school had played in – until that same recent Grand Slam March weekend, on St Patrick's Day, when Mr Wilson's grandson Paul Wilson lifted the Leinster School's Senior Cup on behalf of Gonzaga College for the first time ever, after beating Blackrock College, the bluebloods of the schools' game.

There are still plenty of jokes. One WhatsApp message says, 'There won't be a cow milked – or an avocado peeled – in Ranelagh.' Another wonders if the lads will now be speaking Latin in Coppers.

Like their senior Irish colleagues, in time they will move on. But already they seem immortal, these young men, their day of triumph already fading into the mists of the past as they, too, become ghost-heroes in green and white.

LELAND AT HOME

Brian Leyden

In its sheltered cutting, the late writer Leland Bardwell's cottage stood on the brink of the Atlantic. She'd bought the coastal property in 1992 for twelve thousand pounds. 'It's usually the other way around,' Leland once told me. 'I borrowed three hundred pounds from my children, and the rest was an arts award.'

The seller lived in America. When Leland sent the money, a big, rusted, old-world key arrived in the post, the transaction done entirely on trust. No deed of title changed hands. If she occupied the house for fourteen years, she could apply to have new deeds drawn up in her name. It was the first property she'd ever truly owned. Even at that, she had to live to be eighty-four before she could rightfully call the cottage her home.

Born on 25 February 1922, Leland liked to say, 'I'm as old as the State.' A professional writer who did nothing but write – not teaching, no ties to dollar-rich American universities. She wrote and she read. Arriving home with a new book, she often couldn't wait to enter her house and instead sat in her metallic gold Renault Clio and read by the light outdoors.

Early one spring morning in 2011, when Leland was eighty-nine, I arrived at her cottage to find the back door open as usual. 'Are you up and about, Leland?'

'Up, anyhow,' she called back to me.

Inside, I heard her footling in her bedroom. Then, in the quiet, her radio sounded out of tune.

It was a cause of consternation and confoundment when Leland meant to adjust the volume and changed the tuning by mistake. Before she appeared,

I turned the knob ever so slightly, because my intentions were good, but she wouldn't appreciate me meddling.

On her kitchen table a big adjustable spanner rested on a sheaf of newspaper. I turned and lifted the lid of a large stockpot on the stove and found a hulking boiled-red lobster. The spanner presumably intended to bash open the luckless crustacean.

'Where did you get the lobster?'

'Somebody left it on my doorstep,' Leland said from the depths of her bedroom.

I transferred the lobster onto a plate to bring it to the fridge that held a mini-yogurt carton and the last crumbs of Madeira cake.

'Did your home help come this morning?'

'The one who calls to see if I'm dead?'

'The one who's meant to see you've had breakfast.'

'It's all rather awkward, actually,' Leland said, her steady gaze on me when she entered the kitchen. 'She kept moving things around on me, and got into a terrible tizz when I told her stop.'

Leland would've been the one in the terrible tizz, but I passed no remarks. She was big on kindness, but short on tolerance. Only people who knew her understood that Leland's apparent ferocity masked her lifelong shyness. The unencouraged child who'd buried her head in books to escape the belief, heartlessly engrained in her by her mother, that she was ungainly, unbeautiful, unloved.

Leland put on the kettle and we pulled our chairs up to the kitchen table. Her short story collection *Different Kinds of Love* had been reissued. And I'd had a call from Leland the night before to tell me she'd won the Turkish PEN organisation's Dede Korkut Short Story Award. Could I help her write an acceptance speech on the blasted new computer?

We worked until we had a serviceable draft, the gist of which said there was a general feeling that all Celtic peoples were the same, but we Irish were in fact proud of our individuality and didn't want to be 'of the one tribe'. As Leland saw it, we had ended up living on the edges of society 'as though we had invited the stronger, more practical and therefore more powerful to brush us away'. Which made us quick thinkers, she said, 'drawn to the quicker art-form of the short story'. In this we were like children at the circus, 'pushing our way to the front' through a crowd that wanted rid of us.

When a news bulletin replaced the classical music on her radio, I suggested we take a break. I opened the knapsack I'd brought and produced a packed lunch. Leland clapped her hands delightedly and treated my forward thinking – that we might need to eat – as an act of genius.

At the end of the day I found it hard to say farewell. Before I left I made certain her fire was banked up and the lobster's hard protective shell had been peeled away, its tender innards plated for supper. The speech got a further polish, and I read back the result. Leland listened attentively, paused and said, 'I'm losing words – and I've always loved words.'

MINDFULNESS

Maurice Crowe

The first time I witnessed mindfulness meditation was in a cowshed in West Clare. I'd heard of the practice of being in the moment, and I'd even read some of the teachings of Jon Kabat-Zinn and Thích Nhất Hạnh but still I struggled with the concept. Then one very wet evening by the estuary, where the Atlantic Ocean and the Shannon and Fergus rivers begin to socialise, the idea of being in the moment was explained. Outside the cowshed I squelched and dripped, moving like a robot in restricting raingear, trying to make myself useful, as humans sometimes need to do, even in the most ludicrous conditions. Inside the shed stood four donkeys, gazing softly, as mindfulness practice would suggest, out the door.

Because they weren't looking at me, I joined them in the shed, my need not so much to be present, as to be in their presence. The donkeys ignored my soaking-wet intrusion, deep in the stillness of their meditation. I stood amongst them, seeking attention. When none was offered, I lay an arm over the animal to either side of me. The rise and fall of their bodies was grace-filled, gentle. They looked out at the teeming rain, as it cross-stitched into the estuary waters, a basket of grey thread above, below, and beyond. The rhythm of the rain on the corrugated roof was ornamented by the gush from the gullies and the eaves. If they saw what I saw, they didn't react, but seemed to accept each moment, each raindrop, without judgement, watching it dissolve as the coming moment replaced it.

Elvis, the tall grey jack donkey, was on my right. Because of his wicked sense of humour, I was surprised by his ability to stay so still for so long. His partner Priscilla was on my other side. Her mindfulness practice was no surprise, as she always seemed serene. Their two daughters, Star and Macushla, practised as I imagined veterans would.

Ease and containment seemed to emanate from their breaths. As the five of us stood together I began to understand the suggestion of 'Being in the moment'.

Priscilla was four years old when I went to Roscommon to collect her. Down another small road a man asked me what I had in the horsebox. When he heard what my cargo was, he pleaded with me to take a young jack donkey that was a scourge to him, that it would be an ease to him. I thought it would be an ease to the grey gangly animal too, as he was spancelled with rope and a block of timber. When I brought the two of them home, a neighbour asked me what was Elvis, stating that if he was a jack then all his apparel hadn't arrived from Roscommon. In time his package arrived and when he found his voice, he and Priscilla set about the language of the heart. Star was their first born, meeting the world from a field of buttercups, as summer blazed the estuary in light taken from an Aegean ideal. Two years later Macushla gave the world her delicate presence. Both foals were brown like their mother, with none of the garishness of their Jack-the-lad father.

The day could be timed by their movements. They spent each night and early morning in the big meadow, and gradually, lazily moved through the eastern bane, the Orchard Field, to Gorna Hill where they stayed until nightfall. They were wonderful watchdogs, alert to each and every paw and footfall in their realm. Four sets of ears would point to a field corner, tracing a fox or evening badger. They would bray when the gate latch clicked. They would delight in human visitors, the three females attracted to brightly coloured clothes and carrots, Elvis trying to bite a hand or leg, or pushing his weight against the fragile human.

After their initial lesson in mindfulness practice I sought their company for subsequent teachings. They taught me the importance of noticing the changes in the day and season, of seeking shelter or shade, and that gaining their trust, for a human, is something hard won but easily lost. They had their individual moments of practice each day but I never found them in collective meditation as intense as that wonderful wet evening.

Since that day, Elvis, sadly, has left the building, while Macushla followed her father's spirit and is now buried on Gorna Hill. Priscilla had one more son, Flop, while Star had her own son, Flip. Today Priscilla, Star, Flip and Flop, course the same route each day and night. They remain watchful for each movement and change, noticing not judging, accepting not reacting, except when humans impose change that usually is not necessary. They continue to teach, if the lesson is sought, and continue doing with ease what can be so difficult to do: breathing in, breathing out; breathing in, breathing out.

A HARD TIME TO DIE

Mary Jane Boland

In memory of Dr Michael Boland, 1948–2020

People say we do death well in Ireland.

When my husband's father died suddenly five years ago, the local community rallied around his family. His body was laid out in the front room, friends brought casseroles, people drove from all over the country for the funeral. Memories were shared, tears were shed.

This is not an unusual story. In fact it describes every death in Ireland I've ever experienced. We do death well, not because we cling to archaic traditions of wailing women and waked corpses, but because even now, in the twenty-first century, it is a ritual.

We come together for the 'removal'. We shake hands. We hug the members of the family we know well; we offer words of comfort, however shyly or awkwardly, to the ones we don't. We walk the coffin to the graveyard. We drink, we sing, we remember.

My father died last week. After thirteen long years he succumbed to a disease that slowly stripped him of his identity, of his wit, of his recognition, and eventually of his ability to live.

Grief is something different to everyone, but with Alzheimer's, it happens slowly and constantly.

I remember the beginning, when my father had enough awareness to notice that those he loved were treating him differently; he was now a patient, not a peer.

I remember the day I asked him to sign a birthday card for my mother and he sat for ten minutes staring at the pen, wondering at its function. That was the middle.

And then there was the end, when life delivered him back to his earliest state: a seventy-year-old man who needed the care of a newborn. Just as vulnerable, just as reliant, just as devoid of understanding.

My family has lived with this chronic grief for my entire adult life. It has had an impact on the smallest aspects of our daily living and our broadest life choices.

I thought when the time eventually came we would finally be allowed to share our grief with others. We would come together with people we know and some we don't, in that act of ritual we Irish do so well at a funeral. Something to put a full stop at the end of this drawn-out story.

But these are not usual times. We are living through a moment in which no one will have the collective grief or the funerals they deserve, neither the dead nor the living.

Families across the world will have to carry their loss within themselves. This virus is reducing lives to mere numbers and we are in danger of doing the same ourselves.

When every day brings more deaths, the numbers climb to a point that seems incomprehensible and it is hard to feel like anything is really … real.

So let me tell you that it is. We must not get complacent about life. But for anyone losing a loved one at the moment – whether it was a long life, lived well or a short life, ended abruptly – these strange times don't make their departure from this world any less heart-breaking.

It is a cruel irony that my father, a man who was denied the act of remembering in life, was not memorialised in a way wanted or needed in death. It is something my family will live with and indeed share with others over the coming months.

In many ways I think my dad would be glad about the way things ended – seeing a golden opportunity to slip out the back door without anyone noticing. A very Irish way to leave the party.

Behind masks, behind doors, behind windows, I will remember and celebrate him. I know others will too. I hope one day we will do so together.

EASTER 1916, HEDY LAMARR AND MOBILE TECHNOLOGY

John McDonald

On a grey day in November 2016, a small group gathered outside the Kingfisher restaurant on Parnell Street. They came from near and far to re-enact a moment from just over a century before: the surrender by the leaders of the Easter 1916 uprising to the British armed forces. This group were the descendants of those pictured in a photograph documenting the surrender, on the same street corner, of Padraig Pearse to Major Lowe, the British officer charged with suppressing the 1916 uprising.

The moment of surrender, from just over a hundred years ago, is captured in a series of grainy black-and-white photographs. It is fascinating to compare these two groups now, on the very same spot of ground occupied in widely different circumstances, a hundred years apart. In one of the 1916 images, standing beside Pearse is Nurse Elizabeth O'Farrell, who had remained with the wounded men in the GPO throughout Easter week. She supports Pearse in surrendering, although she is barely glimpsed behind him. For almost a century, her presence and bravery were all but unknown. Recently she has emerged from Pearse's shadow to own her place in this moment.

Also in one of the photographs, standing beside his father Major Lowe, is a tall, gangly young man in uniform. John Lowe was on a break from the fighting on the front in France when the Rising erupted in Dublin. Doubtless caught unawares, he was enlisted by his father to assist in the surrender process. He is only eighteen, which may account for his louche posture in the photographs. He seems casual, indifferent, as interested in his cigarette as he is in the formal events that are unfolding around him.

Had I come along that day in 2016, when these descendants gathered to commemorate the surrender a hundred years previously, no doubt I would have taken out my phone, photographed the event, and shared it on social media. If I had, there would have been an intriguing connection between the phone in my hand, the technology that allows me to do this and the people gathered outside the Kingfisher restaurant.

Young John Lowe's life would not follow the example of his father Major Lowe. Twenty-seven years after the events of Easter 1916, he is living in California. It is 1943, and John Lowe, now renamed John Loder, is a leading man in film, a Hitchcock star, and is about to marry another European emigrée, Austrian movie star Hedy Lamarr. It is a third marriage for both of them and it is their son and his own son who will stand with the group on Parnell Street in 2016. Their mother and grandmother, Hedy Lamarr, was known as 'the most beautiful woman in the world'. A heavy crown to carry, especially when you are also intelligent, talented and an early version of what we would now refer to as a tech geek.

Hedy, at twenty-seven, had already led several lives. She had escaped an earlier marriage to one of Europe's top ammunition manufacturers: as a young trophy wife she had entertained military leaders such as Mussolini and perhaps even Hitler. She absorbed much of what she heard discussed around her at various dinner parties. Unable to reconcile herself to what she saw happening in Europe, Hedy fled her native Austria in the late 1930s, via London, for Los Angeles.

As America entered the war, she was intent on helping the Allied forces. An inventor as well as an actress, she put her knowledge of wireless communication to use. In California she instigated a collaboration with the composer George Antheil, best known for his ability to remotely synchronise sixteen pianos to play in unison. Together they created a technique for scrambling the wireless device that guided torpedoes to their final destinations. Their goal was to halt the devastation to transatlantic shipping which was then crippling the Allies.

By 1942, they had patented their invention. Hedy understood that if they were to succeed, her fame and gender might prohibit their ideas being taken seriously, so Antheil went to Washington alone. As she feared, upon finding out who they were, the Navy did not take them seriously and their patent was shelved. Hedy was advised to go to work selling kisses on war bond tours – which she did, raising millions of dollars.

However, by the time of the Cuban Missile Crisis, twenty years later, their ideas had resurfaced, and subsequently were developed successfully. This idea of frequency hopping, the ability to send a message wirelessly over many frequencies – a message that is secure and can survive various interferences as it travels to its destination – emerged from the military, and is the basis for our mobile phone technology today.

Hedy and George Antheil never enjoyed any acknowledgements or benefits from their efforts, as their patent had expired by the 1960s. Like Nurse Elizabeth O'Farrell, Hedy spent most of her time with perhaps her most important contribution going unrecognised. But by the time she died in 2000, a new generation had come to understand the significance of their collaboration, and films like the recent documentary *Bombshell* continue to bring her story to new audiences. Like Nurse O'Farrell emerging from Pearse's shadow on that corner a hundred years ago, Hedy Lamarr is finally gaining the recognition she deserves.

Consider this, next time you're on Parnell Street looking up something on your phone, checking your messages or asking Siri for directions.

A CERTAIN HEROISM

Neil Hegarty

In a museum in Derry, a collection of portraits hangs clustered together. Striking portraits, in closeup. Female portraits, by the visual artist Friz. The exhibition is entitled 'Peace Heroines', and it has been touring venues for some months now, as time ticks on and on, down and down. Soon, twenty-five years will have passed since the signing of the Good Friday Agreement.

It's good to take stock. To pause, and draw a breath, and look at our history – at how it has been represented, painted, portrayed. I pass among these powerful portraits, and I feel this history, a collective history, undergoing a most necessary correction. There are the trade unionists Inez McCormack and Saidie Patterson, and the community organisers May Blood and Linda Ervine, and there's Mo Mowlam, who took off her wig when negotiations were getting fraught, and whom certain men could not stand. I explore the context provided: look, there are the Derry Girls, their lives in the 1990s threaded both with the mundane and the unspeakably weird. And look, there's Bernadette Devlin's famous line, unmissable in this exhibition: *It's not that women get written out of history, they never get written in.*

And there's Pat Hume.

I know the most about Pat Hume, whose face everyone knew in Derry, but whose voice was almost never heard in public. Who held everything together in private, who kept the show on the road. While John Hume was in Strasbourg or Dublin or London or Washington, outlining a vision for the future – and wouldn't he be proved right by history? – Pat was at home in Derry, answering the phones, keeping the office and family running, calling the glazier when the windows of the family home were broken; the repair shop when the front door was scorched by petrol poured through the letterbox and set alight.

Who'd have wanted to be in Pat's shoes?

Yes, there's Pat Hume, holding her grace.

After I tour the exhibition, I cross the Guildhall Square: spruce and handsome today, how times change – its multiple little fountains are playing and gurgling, and children are running in and out of the water. Into the Guildhall itself, with its smoothly polished wood, its cool terrazzo floors, and its outsize statue of Queen Victoria in the atrium. Upstairs, passing the great sheets of shining stained glass commemorating the building of the city walls, and the colonial link with London's merchant companies – and there at the entrance to the Great Hall, a smaller exhibition has just been installed. John Hume's Nobel Peace Prize from 1998, the medal and citation. Alongside it, two more peace awards: the 1999 Martin Luther King Award from the United States, and the 2001 Gandhi Award, from India.

I appreciate the extraordinary layers of context surrounding this small exhibition: Queen Victoria, colonial Londonderry behind its walls, Gandhi, Martin Luther King, the Humes, all within a few feet of one another. And although this morning's two exhibitions have surely not been planned together, I am pleased to see Pat Hume's life's work honoured here in the Guildhall alongside that of her husband. Equal billing, equal footing, the proximity of the Nobel Peace Prize, and a quotation from President Higgins to encapsulate a life grounded in the 1960s vision of civil rights for all: 'The life of Pat Hume,' Michael D. observes, 'was one of total commitment to community, to the possibilities of peace, to the measures of non-violence that were necessary to assert, vindicate, and achieve the results of civil rights.'

Again, a necessary correction of history, augmenting the language that has gone on in front of the cameras by adding more substance, more grit. I leave the Guildhall and sit in the sun on the steps of the building for a few moments, and watch the fountains at play. I'm surprised by the emotional impact that these combined exhibitions have had on me. At the door, a member of the staff has murmured, 'Powerful, isn't it?' and has gestured across the square to the museum, and added, 'Have you seen the other exhibition running across the way? Powerful too,' and I've nodded, and agreed.

Powerful. Powerful is the very word. So much of the work, the patient, silent work of building a future – and recasting the past, too – goes on away from the cameras, behind the scenes. It is thankless work for the most part: literally thankless, because it's unsung. And heroic, yes, this is the very epitome of heroism.

EGGS AND FISH

Alan Finnegan

I went for a long-overdue haircut to my local barber shop in Dún Laoghaire recently, which, given the current circumstances, was fortuitous, as I'd have otherwise been coming out of the crisis we now face looking like a balding hippy. As I waited my turn, I watched the owner empty his fish tank with a siphon which he sucked on periodically to ensure a decent flow. The fish seemed happy enough, even if the water appeared to have the colour and consistency of a good chicken stock. He complained about the filter and its efficiency, assuring myself and the mother of the boy getting a blade one all over that he had only cleaned it out a week previously. I didn't doubt him. As I said, the fish seemed perfectly content and it so happens that I'm an expert of sorts on just how easy it is to kill a tank full of healthy tropical fish.

One Easter many years ago, when I was about ten, my parents came home from a holiday with a Toblerone egg for me about as big as a medium-sized dog. For the entirety of Holy Week, I looked at it with desire as it sat on the table in the good room, trying to imagine the thickness of the chocolate, what the egg might contain inside, and how quickly I could eat it before my six older siblings took notice.

Sunday arrived and I didn't even make it halfway back upstairs with my egg before being intercepted by my mother. Under no circumstances was I allowed near that egg until after 12.30 Mass, she told me. Thus chastened, I grudgingly put down the egg, which by this stage I'd already opened, on the nearest flat surface, which happened to be the cover of my brother Paul's fish tank.

Sharing a room with a brother six years your senior is, I've always suspected, like sharing a prison cell with an organised-crime boss. While a certain degree of benevolence was shown – mainly due to the fact I knew most of his secrets, such as where he hid his fags – I was never under any illusion as to whose room it really was. The record player, the records, the shelf space, even the walls with their posters of AC/DC and Kim Wilde, were his. More importantly, the aquarium, three feet long and filled with more than fifty tropical fish, from guppies and neons to long-whiskered suckers, was most definitely his.

With the same attention to detail he later brought to cooking in his career as a chef, my brother would tend to his shoal lovingly and meticulously. He monitored the water levels, he installed the correct bulbs in the tank's lid, he cleaned the filters and pumps regularly. There was even a primitive kind of feng shui at work in his positioning of a plastic pirate ship and palm trees to further enhance the fishes' living conditions in our bedroom. He carefully fed them their breakfast and dinner of fish flakes each day, never too much, he explained with authority, as overfeeding would kill them. I often gazed at the tank from my lower bunk, wondering what would happen if I tipped in the whole tub of flakes. Would they slowly expand until they suddenly exploded or would they just get fat like our two dogs?

But the dietary habits of sucker fish wasn't what preoccupied my mind that Easter Sunday morning at the back of the Church of the Assumption, Dalkey, but rather the two pounds of Swiss chocolate I planned to stuff my face with as soon as I got out of there. Hymns finished, I sprinted home ahead of everyone else and made straight for the bedroom.

I was confronted with a crime scene. The egg had disappeared from where it had stood on top of the fish tank, leaving only a crumpled mess of golden tinfoil in its place. Closer inspection revealed a brown mess oozing down the sides of the lid, but I still hadn't comprehended the true nature of the crime until my brother entered the room a few moments later.

Trapped beneath a slab of solidified chocolate, all fifty-plus of his treasured tropical fish floated dead in the tank. Who knew an Easter egg left on an aquarium lid in which were embedded several super-heated light bulbs would melt in less than an hour, perfectly covering every square inch of surface area, and depriving the fish of oxygen? Who knew fish needed oxygen to survive? Not me anyway.

How I survived to recount this story and get my €8 haircut nearly forty years later owes much to my mother's prompt arrival home from Mass before my brother could properly strangle me. And while my memory of the subsequent weeks is hazy, we continued to share that room for a number of years after that and in due course the fish tank was replenished.

Some days after my trip to the barber I arrived home from work to be greeted by my wife and youngest daughter excitedly ordering me to close my eyes and follow them into the kitchen. After walking me intentionally into a door and table, they finally let me open my eyes to discover their secret. A small fish tank with a plastic palm tree and a single, shining goldfish.

GOODBYE, FURBALL

Niall McArdle

Charlotte and I found him on Darcy Avenue in Toronto, that's why we called him Darcy. When I spotted him, he was huddled and quaking under a car, a tiny white furball with a black Gorbachev smudge on his forehead and a plump black tail finished off with a shock of white.

We dutifully did the rounds of the houses on the street, asking if this kitten belonged here. People shook their heads and apologetically smiled 'no' in a way that indicated that we were going to be stuck with him.

I didn't realise then that he would become one of the most significant parts of my life, in spite of the fact that – to put it mildly – he never really liked me.

We thought he was only a few weeks old, he was so small. It turned out he was almost five months; he must have lost his mother quite early. As a result, he had little in the way of feline skills. He was scared of birds. He was scared of squirrels. The sight of wildlife in the garden induced a panicked hiss and a full-on, all-paws, three-foot-high cartoonish leap into the air. Snow – and bear in mind this is Canada, where snow covers the land five months of the year – bewildered him, and he would grumble and growl his way through it, lost in its whiteness save for that black periscopic tail.

He never learned how to retract his claws, and getting stuck in the furniture provoked panic in him. The vet suggested we put him on a drug to calm him down, in the hope that he'd eventually figure out how to get unstuck. This is how, to my knowledge, he was the only kitten in the world with a prescription for Prozac.

It didn't really work, but he did learn to live with his disability. Many's the time we'd come home to discover him stuck to the side of the couch and asleep, having given up the struggle to be free.

On that day we first found him, on the drive home he lay in my lap in the passenger seat curled up in an old T-shirt. That, it turned out, was the closest he and I would ever get. Shortly after, I came back to Ireland for an extended visit to see family and friends, and upon my return to Canada, there was a definite change in the house. Darcy was a one-person cat, and that one person was Charlotte. I was a usurper, my presence resented on the couch and in bed. It's a lovely thing, we think, to have a cat curl up next to a person, but when that curling up involves the cat actively pushing the other human on the couch away, it's somewhat less endearing. It's quite a thing to watch a gap growing between you and your spouse, getting ever bigger and ever furrier.

It wasn't just that he preferred her to me. He actually seemed to hate me. He had a contemptuous facial expression reserved just for my benefit. He would push books off the nightstand – mine, of course, never Charlotte's, and mugs of coffee off the kitchen table – mine, of course, never Charlotte's. Once, he peed in the laundry basket ... somehow targeting only my clothes.

He used to claw and bite as I passed, and of course only a fool would try to pick him up, resulting in a spray of arterial blood that wouldn't be out of place in a Sam Peckinpah Western.

I held my ground where I could. Darcy was a big cat – thirteen pounds – with broad shoulders and a large backside. The polite term for his frame is 'Rubenesque'. When he walked up and down the stairs, there was a gentle undulation to his steps, his back end swinging like a pendulum. I called him Waddlebum.

Years after Darcy bulldozed his way into our lives, our marriage ended: Charlotte left the country, and the cat realised grimly that it was now just the two of us. He had to learn to tolerate me, the way you do an annoying but necessary flatmate. We would have to actually get on. It took him some time to readjust to the new way of things. His meow – previously an aloof whine of general contempt at my temerity in so much as looking at him – became a baffled, weary sigh, as if to say, 'Oh, you're *still* here?', but now he deigned to spare my books, mugs and laundry. The scratching too became less vicious, almost playful, and, usually, bloodless.

He still slept on the bed – as far from me as possible, naturally, at first, but eventually he started curling up next to me, and after time he granted me permission to stroke him, resulting in the satisfactory rumbling engine noise called purring that all cat owners know and crave.

Later, in the revolving door of our post-divorce friendship, I was the one who was going out – back to Dublin – while Charlotte returned, and the cat was noticeably happier with this new, old arrangement.

A while ago Charlotte called to say she'd had to have Darcy put to sleep. He had become sick in his old age – he was sixteen, a fair age for a cat. She said he was cuddly with her all the way to the end. Of course he was.

I'd like to think that if I had been there, he'd have let us both hold him as he drifted off into an eternal slumber. I know of course that it would have been a disaster, that the vet would probably have had to perform emergency surgery on me.

Still, I often think of – and in spite of everything, miss – that fat furry blob, curled up by my side, paws gently, but firmly, pushing me away.

CATHARSIS

Oliver Sears

The invasion of Ukraine came a week after my mother Monika's eighty-third birthday, which I had celebrated with her in Chile, where she lives with her husband Carlos, who is almost eighty-eight. The war had punctuated an unusual week of reflection, coming at the end of an exhibition I had mounted, with my wife, Catherine.

'The Objects of Love', presented at Dublin Castle, had been years in the planning, and its launch was delayed a further twelve months by Covid. Comprising a precious collection of objects, photographs and documents, the exhibition tells the story of a Jewish family before, during and after Nazi occupation in Poland. The family, of course, is mine; my mother, who survived the Warsaw Ghetto and numerous other reckless encounters with mortality, was observing the unfolding reaction to the exhibition with revolving sentiments. What impact would this exhibition have on an audience coming to this history with little or no connection? How does the public presentation, the laying bare of her entire life, through the prism of her youngest son's eyes, contribute to her own understanding of the war and its aftermath?

The images and reports coming from Ukraine seemed unimaginable, crashing into my own post-mortem of the exhibition. The bombing, accidentally or deliberately, of the site of Babyn Yar, a ravine where thousands of Jews had been executed by the Nazis in 1941 over two days, had a particularly disturbing resonance – a kind of Holocaust redux – as though killing the victims in the pit a second time, with a backdrop of millions of refugees whose lives had suddenly been upended or torn apart by one individual's monomaniacal vision. The pain for my mother, to witness this human carnage in Europe again, is especially harrowing, although she keeps the details of this new anguish private; she doesn't need fresh horror to kettle her memories into an inescapable corner. Not now.

A few days before the end of my visit, Monika began to articulate her feelings around the exhibition at Dublin Castle, first to Catherine and then, more confidently, to me. Certain words bubbled up to the surface: relief, pride, gratitude. But she was insistent that gratitude did not really come close to expressing how she felt, implicit though it was in her feelings. And then she settled with self-assurance on the word that best described her emotions: catharsis. A well-worn word perhaps, that has its ancient origins as a medical term for menstruation, but was adopted for dramatic effect in Aristotle's *Poetics*, to describe the purging effect that can happen after tragedy. Much later, Sigmund Freud embraced catharsis into his own concept of psychoanalysis. For Monika, catharsis came in two separate guises. She explained that seeing the arc of her life as a complete event, she now no longer felt any survivor guilt. This is a phenomenon that many Holocaust survivors experienced. It seems counterintuitive, but it's a syndrome that's well documented. She recounts so vividly returning, aged six, with her mother to her hometown of Lodz in Poland at the end of the war where the glare of incredulous adults, especially mothers, singled her out. How and why had she survived when their child had not?

The second catharsis related to her impossibly complicated relationship with her own mother: saviour, heroine, manipulator, tormentor. Protecting a child in such stressful circumstances left an indelible imprint; hidden identities, broken hearts and the casual near misses where death visits in an instant. War often turns the innocent into the implicated. Liberation may never mean freedom, not in the emotional sense. Her mother expected the kind of gratitude that no child should ever give to a parent. Monika said that she now no longer felt any guilt about her relationship with her. The exhibition had allowed her to see her life on her terms, as an individual with her own entitlements; an individual no longer responsible for her mother's happiness. And this moment came thirty-seven years after her mother's death. Two landmark moments in Monika's emotional geography, whose contours I could simply never have located, let alone imagined shaping.

But catharsis was to have a third and unexpected hearing at the end of our trip. Ten minutes after depositing us at the airport, Monika and Carlos were carjacked at gunpoint. Four young thugs attempted to force them out of the car. Monika, who was driving, baited the assailant on her side. 'Shoot me, kill me,' she said, in the Spanish that she had acquired late in life, as he tried to prevent her from reaching down to press the engine starter. He shouted to his colleagues to get the old woman out of the car. On Carlos's side, his assailant was trying to free him from the seatbelt. Carlos took out his retractable pencil with its steel tip and stabbed him … pointedly. Meanwhile, as Monika's attacker made another lunge for her hand, she sank her teeth deep into his arm and he recoiled. At that moment, with both doors open wide, she fired up the engine and floored the accelerator. They had escaped. The attackers had picked on the wrong two octogenarians. Not being lightweight, in any sense of the word, their generous girth made them very difficult to pull out of their seats, especially with their belts attached. They also have a long experience of the world and are not easily intimidated. My mother's instinct for survival operates at a different level. Fear, if it appears at all, comes after the event.

Monika was delighted that both her and Carlos's pacemakers had worked perfectly, especially as she had just had her own adjusted the week before. But she expressed outrage at being referred to as 'the old woman' and when I asked her what her attackers were like, she replied, 'Very ugly. The one I bit probably has food poisoning now. Besides, the gun looked like an imitation.'

PAULINE, I THINK YOU'RE STILL ON MUTE

Pauline Shanahan

'Pauline, I think you're still on mute' is the phrase that best sums up the past two years for me. On Zoom calls, I often forgot to turn on my microphone, so while I thought I was being funny or making a powerful point, I was just waving my arms around in silence whilst everyone felt a bit sorry for me.

As everyone knows, people regularly freeze on Zoom – mid-sentence, they just freeze. There was a time when this was the most exciting thing to happen all week. Eventually a brave soul would ask, Can you hear us Mary? Mary, can you hear us? Like a doctor in a hospital drama.

The strangest thing I've done on Zoom is stand-up comedy. Comedians are a wily bunch; it didn't take long for us to figure out we could continue gigging online. For an art form that's dependent on shared laughter and timing, it seemed like the obvious fit.

The first few gigs, all the mics were left on. It'd be nice to hear the audience laughing, we told each other. We did hear the audience laughing. We also heard them shouting at their kids, cooking dinner and doing the hoovering. I remember one woman chuckling away while cleaning out a cutlery drawer.

So, from then on, all the audience mics were muted. That proved to be a new challenge. I would sit in my living room talking into a screen, telling well-timed jokes, to complete silence. But watching the screen closely, you could still kind of tell if the gig was going well. You could see when people laughed and you could see when they didn't laugh. You could also see how and where they were watching you. Sometimes you'd be carried from room to room. Sometimes you'd be in bed with the person as they lay on their side chuckling away. Sometimes it was a blank screen with the name of the person, or a still photo of them, doing one of two things: being active outdoors, or looking professional.

It was strange not to hear the audience's laugher, but stranger still was reading the audience's laugher. They would write 'ha ha' and 'lol' in the chat box.

Sometimes they would write things that were related to my material – which at the time was a lot about my cat – but by the time I'd notice them, the moment would be gone. *Oh, you have a cat too, Seán? Excellent!* If I spoke to someone directly, it would take them a moment to realise, and then they would reply, and then I would say, 'Oh, I think you're still on mute,' and then they would unmute themselves and repeat what they'd just said. So let's just say they weren't the most spontaneous of interactions. I found it best to stick to my material and give the audience as little to do as possible.

I get very nervous before gigs and online gigs were no different. I would be pacing around my living room trying to quell my nerves, listening to the pre-show music coming from my laptop. After a live gig, you have time to decompress by chatting to fellow comedians or members of the audience. But after my first Zoom gig I sat alone, fizzing with post-show energy, silence ringing in my ears. I walked to my kitchen, made myself some tea and watched my cat Doris wash her face.

Whatever this was it was, at times it felt like the exact opposite of a comedy club. But both audience and comedians were desperate for connection, so it worked. Sort of. Which is the essence of the Zoom experience: it works. Sort of.

Maybe there'll come a time when we'll be nostalgic about Zoom, and Teams, and the rest of it. Like we are about Chopper bikes and leg warmers and Tamagotchis and MySpace; time, by then, having erased how much we all now hate it.

Thankfully, theatres are open and live comedy has returned. But Zoom still has its role to play. It seems perfect for this twilight world, where we need to connect but can't always do so in person. Where we are emerging into a different reality. Where we are all still, slightly, on mute.

THE END OF THE SARAJEVO LOCKDOWN

Mark Brennock

I was there to see the end of another lockdown. One night in early September 1995, the streets of Sarajevo filled up as people came outside to listen to the sounds that signalled their liberation at last. Loud explosions in the mountains all around this beautiful, devastated city were caused by NATO bombs, falling on the army whose siege of the city had kept these people frightened, without heat and often without water, for four years.

I was a journalist then, sent to cover the beginning of the end of the horrible Bosnian war. On the main pedestrianised street, Ferhadija, light shone from shops and bars that had been dark for so long. Young people strolled up and down, laughing, calling to each other, some groups in a line linking arms, cheering each bomb as it landed.

For those previous four years, the people of Sarajevo had lived under lockdown because the Bosnian Serb army had surrounded the city, putting it under siege, cutting it off from the outside world. The enemy sat in the mountains, firing missiles into the city. Snipers picked off civilians who made themselves visible for too long. Fifteen thousand people were killed.

But that September night, the people of Sarajevo walked up and down their own main street again, without fear, listening to the final defeat of those who had terrorised them for so long and killed their family members and friends. Their faces were lit up with the thrill and the joy of it all.

And despite four years living in the dark, in basements and in apartments whose glass windows were long destroyed by the war, most of the women were dressed as if they had just emerged from homes in fashionable Paris or Milan instead of war-torn Sarajevo. They didn't look like survivors of a long military onslaught. They could have been on Grafton Street on a normal Christmas Eve. There were women in smart clothes and make-up and good coats and good shoes. I stopped some of them and asked questions, and some gathered around to talk to the foreigner with the notebook. I asked them how, after living lives of such hardship for so long, they were able to come onto the streets looking so well. They told me they had carefully minded these possessions through the dark days, and that they were not trivial things. They were the items that made them feel human. They marked a refusal to accept the position that their attackers had chosen for them. One young woman, Alma, told me, 'All we have is our pride, our make-up, and our dresses.'

Throughout the siege, the people held film screenings and musicals in basements, sometimes taking their lives in their hands in order to attend. Some simple gestures of defiance had huge power. In February 1994, a mortar round landed in a downtown Sarajevo marketplace, killing twenty-two people. The cellist Vedran Smailovic responded by performing a very mournful piece, Albinoni's 'Adagio in G Minor', at the site, for twenty-two consecutive days, one for each death. Every day, people gathered to watch him defying horror with beauty. He played his cello at funerals, and in ruined buildings, refusing to let his city's dignity be taken away.

Fourteen months into the siege, the Miss Besieged Sarajevo contest was held in a basement. On stage the contestants stood in a line in their cocktail dresses holding a banner for the world's media which read, 'Don't let them kill us'. The moment inspired U2's song, 'Miss Sarajevo', which they sang with Luciano Pavarotti.

I revisited Sarajevo twelve months later to write about the first post-war elections. The shops were open, rebuilding was underway, young people sat at pavement cafés. A group of international athletes came to the city at the same time for an athletics meeting as a gesture of solidarity, and I went along. Mangled tower blocks overlooked the stadium that had hosted the Winter Olympics just a decade earlier. Behind them were the hills from which Bosnian Serb gunners had pounded the city, including this stadium, close to ruin. Beside the stadium was a large graveyard, the old gravestones vastly outnumbered by hundreds of simple white crosses marking the graves of some of those who had died during the siege.

And after a couple of political speeches, a group of more than a hundred four- and five-year-old girls and boys emerged at the sideline and ran to the centre of the stadium. These children had been born during the siege. They had been minded and protected and nurtured as war raged outside their doors. Now they danced unselfconsciously and safely as we all clapped and cheered. There was time for a fuller life again.

EROICA

Eva Bourke

Concert in aid of Ukraine, conducted by Daniel Barenboim, March 2022

Many of us are crowded into the Berlin opera house
this Sunday morning, not one of the red velvet seats
is empty. We've come to this three-tiered golden hall
for the consolation of music, our hearts
are heavy with the news of war.

It is back on all our screens, in all our minds,
detailed as a medieval canvas painted
in the bleak colours of soot, blood and rust.

We've come from all parts of the city
whose streets and houses could tell us about it,
if they could speak: bombs, alarms, the park in flames
and thousands dying among the rubble
or running for their lives, backlit by fires.

We've come to listen to Beethoven's 'Eroica'
in the hope that the music, the instruments,
the clarinets or violins will reassure us.

The old conductor is in pain, weighed down
with his task. He can hardly lift the baton.
Sometimes he directs the musicians with his eyes only.

We move closer together, we sit in a circle
of golden light, safe and fearful. We are no heroes
but somewhere not far from us heroes are made.
A poet once said: Pity the country
that needs heroes, and we do with all our hearts.

How can music drown out the uproar of cannons?
And yet it does again and again, the violins
tremble in despair, the oboe sings,
the sweetness of the cello solo lifts us up,

all of us as we sit there, the older man next to me
with his walking stick, the woman in front
who wept throughout the funeral march,
and the first violinist with her delicate face
who is working the bow at breakneck speed.

MAY

DAWN CHORUS

Grace Wells

It was the first bird
that called me

her one note
like a waking bell.

Mist was down, leaching
the garden white.

I made my way by memory
and sound,

for they were all calling me then,
singing a path to the trees

where I lay on my back
beneath their canopy of song,

an orchestra of throats,
woodwind of pigeon,

and the small birds
in a high chorus.

I lay on the ground until they had finished,
and I had grown quite cold,

then I got up, and
stepped back into my tongue.

GRANTED: ONE PHONE CALL

Peter Trant

My friend Liam telephoned from Twickenham recently. 'They're taking your phone box down,' he said, 'I thought you should know.' And why would the removal of a phone box from a London street be of interest to me?

Well, over thirty years ago, I revealed to him that every time I passed this phone box I felt a strong urge to bless myself. Had I witnessed an apparition there? was his droll response. No, I hadn't but I assured him that something miraculous had occurred there just the same. And I explained that when I landed in London in the early 1970s, I had drifted in and out of jobs in bars and building sites, basically rootless and heading nowhere. But I'd always harboured the ambition of becoming a teacher. A friend from home had managed it by availing of a government grant. Back then in England, funding for full-time courses was awarded to eligible candidates. However, due to a shortfall in my tax contributions, my attempts over two years to acquire a grant had been justifiably refused. Hardly Al Capone territory but enough to deny me just the same.

The following year, still not meeting the conditions of the awarding authority, I tried my luck by applying again anyway, and this time I followed up with monthly letters. And, just to be on the safe side, I telephoned every week as well – frequently to the exasperated response of, 'Oh no, it's that Irish bloke again. Will you take it?' So, no luck.

On my third year of trying I decided to put the cart before the horse: I applied for, and was offered, a place in a college, St Mary's, Strawberry Hill, and despite having no money to pay the fees or to support myself, I enrolled on the first day of term. A phone call to the authority on my way home would decide whether or not I'd be returning the following day. So after registration I headed for the nearest phone box and, fumbling coins into the slot, I offered up a heartfelt prayer.

A softly spoken voice on the other end of the line informed me that she had my paperwork in front of her. She remarked that it was one of the thickest files she had ever come across. 'Well, that's hardly surprising,' I snapped petulantly, 'I've been writing to you every month for the last three years.'

The voice, firmer now, informed me that she had seen grants awarded too many times to people who dropped out after only a month or two.

'Well,' I spluttered, 'I think that file in front of you tells you I am not one of those. Would I be wasting everybody's time if I was going to drop out?'

'I agree,' the voice said.

In my astonishment I swayed backwards, the cast-iron and glass framework of the kiosk cool against my damp shirt.

'I'm sorry,' I said, 'but what did you say?'

'I don't think you are like them,' she said, 'looking at your correspondence. But,' she added, 'you still fall short of the requirements necessary for a bursary.'

Rejected again. I nearly put the receiver down, but she continued, 'However, because I believe you won't drop out, I'm approving your application. I'm not giving you my name so there's no need for any more letters or calls to this department. Do you understand?'

'Yes, I do,' I mumbled. 'Thank you. You don't know what that this means to me.'

'I think I do,' she said. And with a hushed, 'Congratulations. Don't let me down,' there was a click, she was gone and my life had changed forever.

Respecting her wishes, I never tried to discover the identity of this stranger, who went out on a limb to give a young man of little means an opportunity to better himself, and maybe do some good in the world. Why did she help me?

Perhaps my perseverance had paid off, and maybe that prayer did no harm either. 'One thing I am certain of,' I said to Liam, the day I explained about my phone box, 'is that an angel answered my call that day.' And we stood looking at the kiosk which was now transformed into something less ordinary for him too, which is why years later he felt its passing had to be acknowledged.

In these trying times, the opportunity to worship in the traditional way has been considerably curtailed, but you don't need to be in an elaborate

146

edifice to commune with the spirit. Any structure will do. Even an iconic red telephone box. Indeed, it may be better suited than most for the purpose, for if ever there was a man who knew about places of worship, it was its designer, Sir Giles Gilbert Scott. He was also the architect responsible for the construction of many chapels, churches and cathedrals, including Liverpool's Anglican cathedral.

Is it too fanciful then to suggest that the spirit imbued in those hallowed buildings is no less present in his humble telephone box?

One more thing. Did I let my anonymous benefactor down by dropping out? I did not. It wasn't until almost forty years after that fateful call that my career in education drew to a close. In that time, it's been my privilege to have taught several generations of young people – always inspired by my faith in the transformative power of education.

TIEDE AND ELISABETH

Frank Shouldice

The man picking me up at the railway station in Arnhem was impeccably dressed. Looking trim and fit in his mid-seventies, he welcomed me in Dutch-accented English and walked me to his car.

The man's name was Dr Tiede Herrema, a household name in Ireland after being kidnapped by the Provisional IRA in October 1975. And if you don't count a well-known racehorse, he was, you could say, our most famous hostage.

I went to see him in Arnhem in 2001 with the idea of making a television documentary. There were elements to the story that I felt were yet untold. And I thought the twenty-six-year gap might offer fresh perspectives.

The good doctor's ordeal began when he was abducted on his way to work at the huge Ferenka wire factory in Limerick on 3 October. He was put up as a bargaining chip for three IRA prisoners. No deal was done and three weeks later gardaí tracked him down to a council house in Monasterevin, County Kildare.

There, his captors, Eddie Gallagher and Marion Coyle, held out for eighteen days before giving up on 7 November, leaving their hostage with an unusual souvenir, a bullet with his name on it.

Tiede Herrema was whisked away to the Dutch embassy in Dublin. He was resting there when his wife Elisabeth arrived. Seeing him for the first time after thirty-six harrowing days, she stood at the doorway. Tiede sat up. 'Hello,' he said. Elisabeth smiled back and went downstairs, telling embassy staff not to worry, her husband was fine.

Arriving at their apartment in Arnhem I was warmly greeted by the same Elisabeth. Her once dark hair had lightened to white. She set a tray with sandwiches. As I watched her make coffee in the kitchen, I remembered her famous television address during the siege. She didn't break down and cry, like many expected. Instead, from behind thick black glasses, she told the kidnappers quite plainly there was nothing to be gained by taking her husband. When asked by reporters if the government should pay a £2 million ransom to secure his release, Elisabeth replied categorically: 'No.'

I had previously visited St Evan's Park in Monasterevin to see for myself the council estate that had flashed around the world, international reporters standing under dreary streetlights on a local green in the wintry fog of 1970s Ireland. The idea for the documentary was so far advanced in my head that I already had a title, 'Disturbance at Number 1410'.

The hostage drama outlasted the media's appetite for fresh angles. But every kidnap has a silver lining: in this case, a bonanza for the Hazel Hotel, improbably booked out in late October with steady business at the residents' bar. They came, they saw, they drank. And then after eighteen days, the siege came to an end, thankfully without any loss of life.

I was amazed to find out that during the war years, Tiede Herrema had been pulled out of the Dutch resistance and interrogated by the Nazis before being despatched to a labour camp in Silesia. You learn how to survive, he said simply, adding that studies in philosophy and psychology can gave you inner strength, whether in a Nazi labour camp, or bound and blindfolded in the boot of a car somewhere between Castletroy and Mountmellick. He remembered that he cried just once in captivity, thinking of his youngest son, a boy named Harm. He gathered himself, banishing from that moment on all thoughts of home, of family, of Elisabeth to keep at bay anything that might weaken his resolve.

Eddie Gallagher was sentenced to twenty years in prison, and Marion Coyle, fifteen. Remarkably, the Herremas both spoke out against the severity of these terms.

They recalled this over coffee, quiet pauses between lucid memories. The former hostage was a little bemused that anyone should be interested in the story twenty-six years later. Fuss, I could see, was not his thing.

I asked Elisabeth how concerned she was about him at the time. 'I mean, it was a terrible situation,' she said. 'But I knew Tiede would be able to handle it. The kidnappers had no idea who they had taken on.'

She was not given to exaggeration and proved herself unflappable under extreme pressure. When I asked how they'd met, Elisabeth said it was January

149

1946, shortly after the war. She was with a few pals at the ice rink in Utrecht. Through the crowd she saw a solitary figure skating, poised and free. 'Who is that?' she asked aloud, before declaring, 'That's the man I'm going to spend the rest of my life with.' One of her friends offered to set up an introduction. 'No, no,' replied Elisabeth, already making her way. 'I'll introduce myself.'

Tiede nodded with a smile at the memory of this young woman's confident, direct approach across the ice.

Tiede drove me back to Arnhem station. He said he'd consider my proposal, but I could tell his heart wasn't really in it. The following week I got a letter penned in neat handwriting. He said he enjoyed our meeting. Elisabeth was in favour of doing the documentary, he wrote, but he was against. Less for him and Elisabeth, more for their four sons. He wanted family life to move on, to grow and stretch beyond the reach of long shadows.

I met the couple once more, many years later when they visited Dublin. They were older but just as familiar. Sharp, warm and engaging, pleased to be named honorary citizens of this country.

In April I heard that Elisabeth Herrema had passed away, aged ninety-four. Then came the news that Tiede, five years older, had also died just one day after burying his beloved. How fitting that it should be so. The loss of two independent thinkers, their lives separate but connected, one neither leading nor following the other but as ever travelling, somehow, in the same direction.

FROM INIS MÓR TO ISTANBUL: CARRYING THE SONGS

Alannah Robins

I'm going to tell you a story.

Once upon a time a warrior was sent on a mission to collect a chest full of wonderful treasures. He knew he needed to find not just brave and strong individuals to come with him, but people who were happy and content within themselves, because this was going to be a particularly long and hard journey.

He gathered a group. Off they went, singing their songs. The spirits of their ancestors and their gods were coming with them and they made great progress.

They entered into new lands, where the vegetation and geology were different. But they were still singing their songs and their ancestors were still with them.

One day they started to slow down, seeming to sink into some kind of trance state within themselves, and the warrior was impatient. He said to the elder of the group, 'We were making such great progress. Now what's happening?'

The elder slowly spoke. 'We have moved so far, so fast that we must now sit down and wait for our souls to catch up.'

This was a story told, *as Gaeilge*, by the young storyteller Liam Ó Flaithearta to his father, Gearóid, on Inis Mór, in March 2020. It was the start of a project I had been cooking up for some years called 'Carrying the Songs', after Moya Cannon's poem of the same name. The idea was to send a story into the world, Chinese whispers style, and to see how it could travel. The project was ambitious and the logistics were eluding me until the coronavirus came along. When we were all under lockdown I realised that people were only just waiting to reach out to one another. I launched myself feet first into coordinating a journey which would take the story from Inis

Mór to Istanbul, via Zoom, through the mouths of more than four hundred people. I set up meeting after meeting in which one person would tell the story to another, who would then tell it to another (hereto waiting in the now very familiar waiting room). So, Gearóid told the story of the warrior to Aisling, who told it to Cyril, and it had started its journey ... but did it stay the same?

Well, before it was out of Connemara it had been replaced with a love triangle and stories of the *bean rua*, a redheaded woman with an ill-fated effect on fishermen. It continued to gradually adapt itself, with a force that was almost magnetic, towards its next destination.

When seanchaí Pap O Murchú heard the story in north Mayo, he said: 'This is very exciting, I haven't heard this story since the 1940s. When I tell it to Treasa in Carrowteige tomorrow, it will be going home.'

In Sligo, a young art student described in vivid detail the layout of the floats and nets on the sea, and the play of light on the water. These details were not given to her, neither was she elaborating gratuitously, but this was the picture she saw in her mind's eye.

In this way, passed through the lens of each individual's own experience, the story was constantly evolving.

Robert the Bruce's inspirational spider came into the story near Belfast and while the strong coastal connections were gone, the story remained about the sea or water, until it reached Istanbul, thirty-four weeks after the first story was told. In Scotland one man heard the story of his own childhood told to him by a total stranger. In Wales, what went into Welsh as 'oars', came out of Welsh as 'spades': this poor lad was rowing around in circles on the sea with one spade until he happened upon a second spade. He met the love of his life, they had a spade each and they rowed off into the sunset!

The story suffered badly from a dreadful internet connection in Brittany, and in France it became the story of a fisherman who became a fisherwoman. As it moved north through Germany, the story became longer, more flowery and more romantic.

Then an old friend of mine in Duisberg declared himself allergic to this 'romantic rubbish', and he swore to tell the story in three sentences, which he did! I looked on in horror as he pretty much decimated my treasured storytelling project.

Yet it only gave the story a chance to develop fresh growth.

My friend had converted the mermaid of the story into a suicidal young woman hurling herself into the sea. But the next woman to hear the story from my friend confided in me, 'I didn't like his suicide, so I made her a mermaid.' This was really amazing, as each person only hears the story once, but the trope of the mermaid is clearly very strong in Germany.

In Denmark and Sweden, the story concerned a man who found a figurine of a mermaid in a dusty attic. He put the figurine in his pocket, and rowed a boat out onto the middle of the lake. A storm blew up and capsized the boat. As he sank down he felt himself being borne up, until he was landed on the shore, by the mermaid. She was returning him to his right element, as he had done to her.

In the most northern tip of Norway, the story suffered again, when the person who was meant to hear the Sami shaman's version didn't turn up. A woman with a limited understanding of Sami bore the fragments of the story forward.

In Finland, an old fisherman found himself in a repetitive spiral of stormy capsizings, near drownings, rescuing by fair maidens, promised fidelity to the same fair maidens, and being caught out when the last one turned up … back to our old love triangle!

The story mutated to a polyamorous relationship between the three protagonists and then remained pretty consistent throughout Estonia, Latvia, Lithuania, Poland, the Czech Republic, Slovakia, Hungary, Slovenia and Austria.

It dipped in and out of more poetic and symbolic meaning and at one point, the bright or light woman was the sky and the dark woman the sea.

In November 2020, after a journey through twenty-nine countries and fifty languages, Maral Perk told the last version of the story in Istanbul. And here it is:

A small girl from a small village was taking a walk on the beach when she stumbled upon a conch shell. She listened to the shell, ran back to the village, and invited the other villagers to listen. Those who listened felt a restlessness, a longing for the sea and for the unknown. Using their doors, curtains and furniture, they made a boat. The whole village sailed for three days and three nights, passing the shell around.

Soon they found themselves in a violent storm. When the storm settled and the sun came out, they found themselves on familiar shores, but nothing was the same. The old village was gone and the place transformed.

They turned on the girl in anger. She threw the shell back in the sea and a spirit swirled out of it. 'I am the witch of the seven seas,' it said. 'I am your mother. I have cradled you and called you home. If you stay with me six moons, I'll return everything to you ...'

THE HEYSEL STADIUM DISASTER

Michael Hamell

The 1985 Heysel Stadium disaster is a far off, almost forgotten tragedy. But for those directly affected, it casts long shadows.

Brussels in the mid-1980s was a cosmopolitan city, mesmerising in its linguistic complexities but relaxed, at ease with itself. The Irish community was small. We had a Gaelic club which played occasional matches, and a soccer team in the Brussels Embassy league. Through this rather loose connection, ten of us got tickets for that year's European Cup Final at Heysel Stadium on 29 May — unexpected but very exciting.

Liverpool were facing Juventus and our tickets were for the 'neutral' terrace.

The day itself was hot, steamy and sticky. Ahead of the game, fans gathered and drank strong Belgian beer in the many bars around the Grand-Place.

We went directly from work by metro from Schuman, beside the European Commission headquarters – our suits left at the office, T-shirts and jeans more in keeping with our anticipation of a great game between Europe's leading clubs.

Getting into the ground presented few difficulties. Local policemen surveyed the good-humoured crowd. Around us on the neutral terrace were many Belgian-born Italians; most of them sons of migrant workers who had come to work in the mines after the war.

The first hints of trouble were fairly mild. Some Liverpool fans started chanting from their terrace, only divided from us neutrals by some flimsy barriers and a handful of policemen. But chanting is normal enough. Attention turned towards the match, just twenty minutes from kick-off.

Then some Liverpool fans started tossing things at us: oranges, apples, tomatoes. The people around us became restless, like a herd sensing predators.

What happened next was much more sinister. Harder missiles began to come our way. Some Liverpool supporters, thugs, not supporters, in truth, were now hurling bottles at us, and stones. They were swarming the little barriers. Now they were over them, brushing the hapless policemen aside, and charging us, brandishing poles which, moments earlier, had carried proud Liverpool colours.

We were in the midst of a panicking crowd, and quickly, in the crush, I was separated from my companions. Some of the crowd were running back up the terrace towards the exits, some pushing down towards the pitch. I decided going down wasn't good and going up wasn't great either, so I tried to hold my ground. Those running back were wisest, I later discovered, for they escaped the imminent mayhem but for the odd slap of a stick or loss of a shoe. Those pushing or being pushed downwards squeezed into others further down, who fell and were crushed against the crumbling wall protecting the pitch. Such was the pressure, there was little chance to climb the wall and reach the pitch: even if your arms were free, the rest of you was trapped in the crowd.

I tried to hold on, but the crowd eventually forced me down. I fell and those beside me did likewise until we were a human heap like a landslide slowly rolling down the terrace. I managed to wriggle to a crowd barrier which afforded some slight protection and lay there trying to free my shoulders and breathe while being pinned down by falling and fallen bodies.

I remember thinking, this is absurd – I've played hurling all my life, I've been in every big stadium watching GAA and rugby – and now I'm going to die at a football match because of hooliganism!

But in six or seven minutes perhaps, I began to feel the pressure on my back ease and I could sense the crowd beginning to stand up behind me. The thugs seemed to be in retreat. I unsteadily began to stand up, but the two men who had been pressing down on my arms did not. They were motionless, either worn out by their efforts to stay alive, or possibly already dead.

Shaking, I looked around for help. I could see police reinforcements coming across the terrace. At the terrace walls, there were piles of people still unable to move, trapped just inches from the pitch and safety. Further up the terrace, bodies lay strewn where they fell.

A Red Cross volunteer appeared beside me. Her colleagues would look after the injured, she told me. She helped me to the pitch and I walked unsteadily to the far end, trousers and shirt ripped, face, arms and hands scratched and bloodied, to rest a while in safety.

The pitch was slowly cleared of human casualties and, incredibly, the match went ahead. This was afterwards explained as a way to reduce the risk of more crowd trouble. I stood in a daze for a while, then managed to get out, onto a metro and back to Schuman to join my girlfriend and other friends and seek out news of those who had not yet returned from Heysel. It was a long night of waiting and wondering, until two or three in the morning, when we were able to confirm that all our friends were safe.

I was also trying to phone home, fully aware that the tragedy had been shown live on television, unfolding as the TV audience waited for the match to begin.

When I finally got through to my parents it was half eleven, as the lines had been blocked for hours. I could hear the relief and uncharacteristic emotion in my father's voice when he said, 'We're so delighted you're all right.'

Next day, we woke up to a shocking toll of death and destruction. Among the thirty-nine dead – all from the neutral terrace – were thirty-two Italians, four French, two Belgians and a man from Belfast. About 600 people had been injured and treated by the emergency services or in hospitals across Belgium.

There was much debate as to responsibility. Certainly, the stadium was run-down and unsuitable by the standards of the time. The placing of Liverpool fans was thoughtless, not least given the growing reputation of a small cohort of English fans for causing trouble, and their lack of distinction between neutrals and opposing fans.

Security was far from perfect, and policing within the stadium was almost totally lacking. In fact, it seems preparation by all concerned was hopelessly inadequate, with the important exception of the medical services.

But not one of these inadequacies justifies the appalling behaviour of the perpetrators who had love of violence as their motive, and certainly not love of football.

The wheels of justice turned slowly. Almost five years later some thugs were convicted of manslaughter and received very short sentences for the part they played in the disaster. As far as I was concerned, the message that violent hooliganism is not subject to proportionate justice could not have been clearer.

I've never forgotten that day. Thirty-five years on, I still think about those young men on the terrace around me who never came home. Husbands, brothers, sons; children unborn, dreams unfulfilled. All because of a tragedy that should never have happened.

THE DAY MY SISTER MET THE QUEEN

Roslyn Dee

When she was here back in 2011, she certainly smiled a lot, and seemed keen to talk to everyone, and wore various shades of green, and threw in the few words of Irish in her speech up in the Castle ... But did Queen Elizabeth *really* have a good time when she made her first visit to these shores?

Well, yes, she did. How do I know this? Because shortly after that visit, that's precisely what she told my sister. At Buckingham Palace. When she pinned an OBE on her jacket.

They were all chat, the pair of them. And then the Irish question arose when Pauline buttonholed her about the recent visit.

'Well,' said Her Maj, in that quiet but extraordinarily posh voice, 'it was *most* enjoyable.'

So there you have it – straight from the horse's mouth. Elizabeth Windsor had a ball in Ireland.

It was a great occasion at Buckingham Palace on that June day, and the culmination of a series of events that began on a snowy evening the previous December as my family gathered to celebrate a milestone birthday for my father.

There was something else to mark as well, said Alan, my brother-in-law. Pauline was up for an OBE in the New Year's Honours List.

'Yeah, yeah, yeah,' we all said, laughing. 'No, really,' he said. We all looked at Pauline. It was true.

And so it began.

When would it happen? Between January and July. How many guests could she bring? Three. Actually into Buckingham Palace, into that grand ballroom to watch her getting the yoke pinned onto her jacket? Yes, three. So that was Alan, her husband, Steph, her only child, and moi, her only sibling. Could I set aside my anti-monarchy instincts for just one day, my sister couldn't resist asking? Could I what!

And so it was that the day itself arrived.

Ah, yes. The day itself.

I woke in my hotel room at 5 a.m. It was a spectacular June morning, complete with a clear, azure-blue sky. So I got up and sat at the window, watching, transfixed, as the city came alive.

'Earth has not anything to show more fair,' wrote William Wordsworth in the opening lines of *Composed Upon Westminster Bridge, September 3, 1802*, his beautiful sonnet about London. 'This City now doth, like a garment, wear / The beauty of the morning ...'

As indeed it did.

And so, four hours after my literary musings, we happy few were taxiing down the Mall, dressed in our finery and clutching our passports and bright-yellow invitations – the golden tickets to give us entry to the inner sanctum.

Tourists were heaving outside the palace as we approached the gate. A quick flash of our invites and passports at the friendly bobby and, hey presto, we were in.

Across the front apron of the grounds we traipsed, into the quadrangle beyond, then up the red-carpeted steps and into the palace.

With the star of our show gone off to join her fellow VIPs, we three headed for the ballroom, and were amazed to find ourselves escorted to the very front row. We couldn't believe our luck.

Posh frocks and hats dominated the roomscape. Oil paintings hung around the walls. Red, velvet-covered banquette seating lined the sides of the room and an orchestra played somewhere towards the rear.

We looked at our watches. 'Still over an hour to kick-off,' Steph said. But then up stepped an elegant-looking palace official to talk us through proceedings: applause etiquette, if you don't mind; when to stand for the Queen; what to do at the end. That sort of thing.

Before we knew it, the witching hour of 11 a.m. arrived, a door opened to our right and in came the Queen herself, escorted by two Gurkha soldiers and five Yeomen of the Guard, resplendent in their red regalia.

First impressions? That she was tiny, and that her silk frock with ivory background and tiny splashes of colour in green and yellow was both understated and extremely elegant. Hooked over her arm, meanwhile, in exactly the same way that my granny used to carry hers, was an oversized black patent handbag.

She walked to the slightly raised platform in front of us, set down the bag, and proceedings began.

We three were a bit on edge, looking to our left all the time as the queue snaked forward, nervously waiting for that first glimpse. And suddenly, there she was. Our Pauline. About to meet the Queen of England and to be acknowledged for all her wonderful work. She moved forward – from first base at the door, to second base beside a 'minder', just a few feet from the Queen.

'Pauline, Mrs Pendlebury,' boomed the man-with-the-voice announcing each recipient: 'for services to education'.

My sister walked forward, curtseyed subtly (no need to lose the run of yourself when you're Irish) and approached the Queen, who leaned forward and pinned the coral-ribboned medal on her jacket.

And then they chatted. And chatted. About all sorts, apparently, including the visit to Ireland.

Then, finally, the Queen shook my sister's hand, Pauline backed away, turned, caught our eyes, walked past us, and out of the ballroom.

The rest of the ceremony was a bit of a blur and then, all done and dusted, we stood for the national anthem (instrumental only, no singing allowed) as the Queen gathered up the handbag and exited, stage right.

We rushed to find my sister. 'Where's the yoke?' we asked her, expecting to see the medal gleaming on her jacket. She had it in its box.

And that's where it stayed for the rest of the day, while we wandered the corridors of the palace to find the loo (four-star, old-fashioned hotel standard, a bit like Buswells in Dublin), mingled in the quad for photos, sat in the sunshine in Green Park as Pauline Pendlebury OBE spoke to our proud parents back at home, and while we drank prosecco in Franco's on Jermyn Street, where we were joined by the rest of the sister's lunch party, all of whom had travelled from far and wide to help her celebrate in style.

It was some day.

But then, why wouldn't it be? For, as a friend back in Dublin texted me later that afternoon: 'She's some woman.'

And no, she didn't mean the Queen.

RIVERKEEPER

Kerry Neville

Most days in Limerick, my temporary and beloved home, I was inside grey skies, a grid of buildings, and strangers under hoods and umbrellas who could be friends but were not yet. We rushed by in our haste to get warm and dry, to get food and drink, to get drunk and flirt with someone, anyone. I also lived across the street from the Shannon river, so wandered the boardwalk with a vagabond's hope for a heron or swan to claim me, swooping me up across the water. The Shannon is a tidal river, surging at four knots on the ebb. High tides can reach seventeen feet under a full moon and high winds. I tracked its rise and fall, and its current, quiet or quick, and understood in my riverkeeping the predictable metaphor: time was a current.

But this current was more than a metaphor.

People lost and at their ends – booze, drugs, unemployment, heartbreak – and feeling forgotten in this post-Celtic Tiger Ireland – men, mostly men, and mostly young, took their own lives in the Shannon. Two men in one month right in front of my house. My landlady explained that for a few years, right after the 2008 crash, it was particularly bad. 'It's gotten better,' she said. 'Not as many, not as often, but what is "better" when it comes to suicide?'

One morning while I was drinking tea in bed, still holding on to the night's warmth, a helicopter churned loud and low over the river. Boats and fire trucks raced into view. News flashed on my feed: 'Emergency services have been deployed to a river rescue following the report of an individual entering the River Shannon this morning.'

I watched at the window, hands pressed to the cold pane –

– and remembered, as I prayed, a long-ago November night in college when I jumped into a half-frozen lake and was saved by campus security. How I swam away from their dinghy, how I fought their hands and kindness, how I longed to disappear underwater, to stay alone in my aloneness, how a burly officer dived in and hooked his arm around my neck as if catching the saddest, angriest sea monster.

'No,' I said. 'NoNoNo.'

'Yes,' he said. 'YesYesYes.'

When we reached the shore, I shivered with a sudden tooth-chattering violence, but felt, too, how I was being returned to the world. I remember the moon, so bright and distant in that dark sky, and the officer whispering, 'We'll get you warm. Help is coming.'

And the odd flash of recognition when I walked alone at night along the Shannon, a keening towards that old despair: how easy to jump into that current. I searched, instead, for the swans paddling in the moonlight, as if my searching for them mattered.

One late night, I walked around the river, crossing over its bridges, circling the dark, circling my ordinary loneliness, circling my way to compromise: keep moving don't stop keep moving don't stop. I leaned against the river railing and watched a swan paddle through the dark water. Ghost bird.

A man and woman on bicycles and wearing bright-yellow vests pedalled up and stopped. Quiet, gentle smiles. The Limerick Suicide Watch.

'How's your evening?' the man asked.

'Grand,' I said. 'Just watching the swans.'

'You okay out here by yourself?' the woman asked.

'Oh,' I said, 'just walking.'

The answer was no and the answer was yes and I knew I'd keep walking and would be in bed soon, would not be in the river because I could see that was what they feared because the man was searching my face and the woman seemed to be watching my hands that gripped the railing.

'It's just that we noticed you've been walking around the river for a while now so ...' the man said.

How many people had they missed? How many people had they found who might have been thinking this this this now now now, and how many had they saved? And could I be a counterweight to the many they had not?

164

I saw their worry and decided not to worry them unnecessarily.

'Thank you,' I said. 'It's a lovely night, no rain. But now I'm on my way back home to bed.'

They smiled, waiting on their bikes and I saw they were hoping I'd walk on and so I did.

MY MOTHER LOVED ME IN RED

Rita Ann Higgins

I saw my mother's grave
from the top of the bus recently,
She died in 1971.
I only saw her grave
from this angle a few days ago.

I was a great one for the buses years ago.
I even wrote a poem about it.
Then we got the Arts Council bursary car
and that was the end of the buses for me.

Now that I have the bus pass,
I'd be inclined to use the bus more often –
plus, I can see my mother's grave
from the upper deck.

I say nothing to the other passengers
as we pass the graveyard.
Much as I want to shout –
Inside that wall,
four graves in to the left
lies a good woman –
Margaret Mary Higgins,
who died aged fifty-five.

She gave birth to twelve.
One died at six months,
Joachim Mary had a hole in his heart.

My mother loved me in red,
she would say,
'Red is lovely on you.'
She told me this, not often
but as often as she could –
while the other ten were out of earshot –
which in truth was as likely
as a lunar eclipse,
a ghost rainbow,
or meeting a natterjack on the run.

REMEMBERING MARY MAHER

Séamus Dooley

Mary Maher never just turned up. She arrived, bustling with ideas, lists, demands and questions, bright, curious eyes sparking as she filled the room with energy.

You'd almost feel sorry for Mother Mary Ignatius of the Holy Child who was one of the first to encounter Mary's relentless questioning in a Chicago classroom, while encouraging a group of ten-year-olds to pray for the conversion of Godless Russia.

As the Cold War raged, Mother Mary Ignatius explained that the deprived children of communist Russia had no personal property of their own, all property was shared.

Mary Maher shot up her hand.

'What's wrong with that?' she asked. 'Do the Holy Child nuns do not make a song and dance about living in a community? Why is sharing wrong in Russia but right for the nuns in Chicago? And don't all the Irish families share hand-me-down clothes?'

Mother Mary Ignatius told her to sit down.

On graduating from university, Mary Maher worked for three years in the *Chicago Tribune* but the arch-Republican newspaper was not a comfortable home for her.

On a visit to Dublin in the early sixties, she met the irrepressible news editor of *The Irish Times*, Dónal Foley, who was impressed by her intelligence.

They struck up an immediate friendship. He asked her what she thought of the Kennedys. Mary said she disagreed with the hagiography surrounding them, and the jury was still out on their legacy.

She could have played it safe, but that honest answer was to mark the beginning of four decades as a journalist at *The Irish Times*.

Mary Maher, who died in St Vincent's Hospital in November 2021, was born on 9 November, 1940, to Bonnie Burns and James Maher, a lawyer.

As a journalist, trade unionist and founder member of the Irish Women's Liberation Movement, she made a profound impact on Irish journalism.

I remember talking to Paddy Behan, one of the residents of Mountjoy Square, about Mary's visit to his home during the Dublin Housing Action Committee's campaign against slum conditions.

'Some journalists came up and had a look. Mary Maher stayed and listened,' recalled Paddy.

That ability to listen was reflected in her work on *The Irish Times* Women's Page.

Mary Maher was the first Women's Page editor – even thought she had initially opposed the idea of a segregated page.

Donal Foley changed her mind. The proposal was not merely to reproduce the kind of fluffy stories she had flown across the Atlantic to avoid. 'Why not have a women's page with serious articles?' he asked her. How could she refuse?

Her first comrades on the Women's Page were Maeve Binchy, Maher's lifelong collaborator and friend, and Renagh Holohan, an accomplished reporter with a strong news sense.

Maeve and Mary set to the task with relentless energy.

The marriage ban, contraception, unmarried mothers, deserted wives, family law, children's courts, prison conditions, Travellers' rights – all these became hot topics for public debate.

In her own life she broke through a myriad of glass ceilings: she was the first married woman to return to work in *The Irish Times*; the first woman to take paid maternity leave at the paper; the first woman to lead the NUJ at *The Irish Times*.

When she retired in 2001, she was the first NUJ member in Irish newspaper history – and the first woman – accorded a knock down, a noisy, exuberant, tribute traditionally reserved for (male) printers.

Throughout her life Mary loved music and song. She sometimes claimed that while she found a career in Dublin, she really stayed for the music. She was a founder member of the Clé Club and a regular contributor to their singing sessions with her distinctive, melodic voice.

Her own musical tastes were catholic: she was reared on the music of John McCormack, and at the drop of a hat or the clink of a wine glass could burst into one of the songs her father and mother loved: 'Molly Brannigan', 'Teaching McFadden to Waltz' or 'The Minstrel Boy' before moving on to 'Bread and Roses', 'Buddy Can You Spare a Dime' or 'If You Miss Me at the Back of the Bus'.

Coming to live in Ireland opened up the world of Irish traditional music, songs and ballads.

Her friends all have their own memories of her voice as she sang songs like Frank Harte's 'Johnny Doyle' with the magical description of Ringsend which she loved – 'the jewel that sparkled by the Dodder', or 'When Two Lovers Meet', which she'd picked up from the singing of Dolly McMahon.

She has left us a rich store of memories of sessions at the Merriman School in Clare, in Liberty Hall, in the Teachers Club and in conference halls the length and breadth of Ireland and beyond.

Mary donated her body to medical research and left orders to be remembered with an evening of music and song.

Last Sunday, on May Day, we honoured her wishes in the Mansion House in music, song and story and later in the Teachers Club on Dublin's Parnell Square, where Mary herself loved to sing of 'Bread and Roses'; of love, and loss, of struggle and strife.

Her voice may be silent, but she leaves a remarkable legacy.

HIDING IN THE GRAIN

Sharon Hogan

It is hard to watch the short autobiographical film *Hiding in the Grain*, made by the Czech filmmaker and recent NCAD graduate Bara Palcik, without being reminded of all that is unfolding in Ukraine today. Watching her film, I think of the stunned faces of small children, walking through the night towards unfamiliar borders, arriving in unknown countries, holding mothers close while fathers dissolve into the darkness of war, and I wonder: how will those small children make peace with such events? How will they be in years to come, when this time of upheaval and uncertainty has been absorbed into their deepest sense of themselves and their world?

Palcik, who now lives in Ireland, was born in the former communist Czechoslovakia, a homeland which changed its name three times, split into two halves, then separated completely, all before she was eleven years old. Inspired by the autobiographical filmmaker Mark Lecky's use of images culled from the internet, Palcik wondered if watching footage of Czechoslovakia in the 1980s and 90s might help her to understand more clearly her own persisting sense of loss, and what in her earliest experiences still influences the adult she is today.

Her film, shown at NCAD's recent graduate show, opens with a sepia-toned view through the window of a train moving away from a Czech city.

'I lived there,' she says, and asks, 'Have you ever felt a peculiar emotion going through your ... whole body while travelling from the place you called home?' This emotion was one she knew well: not belonging. 'Belonging' was something she sensed others felt, but she did not.

A stream of found images then evoke her earliest memories: sunlight flickers through netting on a hammock; an old wooden cuckoo clock tick-tock-ticks.

And then: a core memory. Nineteen eighty-six. Chernobyl. Its explosion mirrored in the iris of her own eye, she remembers sitting in the kitchen the morning after the disaster; her mother telling her and her sister that they could die; the television warning that the poison that could kill them had neither smell nor colour, but sometimes had the scratch-and-crackle voice of a radiation counter. On that day, she experienced what she calls her 'very first fear'. From that day, she knew that her mother could die. Every time her mother was late, she thought, 'This is it.' She was four.

The found footage that revived that memory opens out into grainy images – children playing with gas masks:

'It felt like a game,' her voice whispers, 'I was six.'

Distant echoes of Czech words, shadowy laughter hovering, somehow, on the edge of tears; her own footage of friends dancing, playing pool, intimacy and farewell shimmering in the dim light even as they laugh and flirt with each other. In the act of filming, in the moment of trying to catch and hold them all together, there is a sense of loss.

'Gone,' Palcik's voice says, as the images fade.

Her later footage in Ireland is more lush and fertile, but Palcik remains preoccupied with what is 'gone'. Her lens explores the interior of an old stone cottage overgrown with nature and time, searching for hints of what she calls 'the invisible yet so present past'.

'Who lived here?' she asks; 'What was their story?'

'Gone,' her own voice answers.

Yet, of Ireland, she finally feels able to say, 'This is it: homeland.' Somehow, in revisiting her earliest losses, in 'touching the memories' as she puts it, something has settled in her and opened a capacity to realise a sense of home. Her film closes as it opened, looking through the window of a train travelling from city into countryside and beyond; but now, instead of feeling that something is being left behind, Palcik seems to be taking her memories with her as she travels out into the world.

The closing words of the film are of another reclaimed memory, of playing hide-and-seek in her grandmother's garden. She has slipped into the garage where a large barrel of chicken seed is stored. She climbs into the barrel, sinks into the warmth of the grain, feels it gather around her, fragrant, comforting, and she remembers the feeling that everything was all right: that she and the whole world were safe and held in that barrel.

'I am five,' her voice says. 'It's summer. At my granny's garden. Covered in the seed in the barrel ... I'm home. Hiding in the grain.'

I think of those bewildered children crossing the Ukraine border into countries they barely know the names of, and hope that they, like Palcik, carry a memory deep in their being of a moment in a granny's garden, a memory so redolent with warmth and safety that it can be called up to challenge whatever today's traumas leave behind. I hope that some day, today's experiences of fear and loss may be eased by the warmth of even deeper experiences of love.

WONDERFUL PARTIES

John Banville

I can't remember how I came to be invited to join the Arts Council. I suppose I must have had a letter, or even a phone call, from the taoiseach of the day, Garret FitzGerald. I'm sure I was expected to be flattered; instead, I was extremely reluctant. It was the early 1980s, I was young, or youngish, I was in the throes of writing a difficult novel, and I couldn't see myself becoming a part of what we lazily think of as the Establishment.

I consulted my family, and my friends. All, I could see, were having a hard time of it not to laugh. Someone, keeping a straight face, asked if I would be required to wear a suit and tie, and attend State banquets, and brush up on my schoolboy Irish.

No, I thought, no, the thing is impossible – me, a member of the Arts Council?

Then I met the archaeologist Máire de Paor, at some reception or other. 'Oh but you must,' she said, 'you must join.' She had been a member for many years – she may have been the first woman on the Council – and she could assure me that it was a Good Thing. She told me how many struggling writers were kept going by the odd bursary, how many pictures by living artists were purchased, how many small publishers were funded – and besides, she said, we have great parties.

That was the clincher.

I'm sure I turned up for the first meeting in flares and a floral shirt with a floppy collar – I did say that this was the eighties. Adrian Munnelly was the director – one of the best there has ever been – and Mairtín McCullough was a very diligent and punctilious chairman – in those days the chairman was still the chairman. The morning dragged, though there were moments of interest and even levity. I was very conscious that this was a State board, though the director was insistent on our autonomy and freedom from political interference. My fellow members were impressive, with one or two exceptions. And anyway, it would soon be lunchtime.

At lunch, I found to my consternation that no wine was served. This, it was patiently explained to me, was because there would be another session in the afternoon. I could see Máire de Paor, seated opposite me, registering my dismay with a glint of amusement.

'Yes,' she said, 'and that's when the real work is done.'

And she was right. As the hours dragged on towards evening, I found myself voting on the distribution of pitifully small amounts of money to a vast range of organisations, most of which I had never heard of before. Couldn't these decisions be left to the staff, who I could see were formidable people, with far more knowledge of the world of the arts than I possessed?

'Ah, no,' I was assured, 'only the executive has executive powers – the staff are merely there to advise.'

My heart sank. Was I to spend a day like this at the beginning of every month, doling out a few bob here and a few bob there, to frame a few pictures for an exhibition, or purchase a new fiddle for a promising soloist, or to buy ballet shoes for aspiring baby ballerinas? I recalled what Máire had said: this was, indeed, the real work, and on it, a great many real people, in the real world, pinned their hopes and aspirations.

Was there wine served after the meeting, or did we go to the pub? We had a drink, I know that, and certainly I welcomed it.

'Well,' Máire asked me, 'how did you find your first day?'

I wonder what answer I gave her?

We did have gay times. I recall a particularly convivial weekend at the Tyrone Guthrie Centre at Annaghmakerrig in County Monaghan. We had our annual general meeting there, spread over two days, and then we relaxed. Indeed, many of us relaxed to the point of stupor. Máire had the best stories, all of them funny.

There was, for instance, the one that turned on the name of the Hungarian composer, Zoltán Kodály. A tenor had gone into a Dublin music shop, McCullough Piggots, jointly run for many generations by our chairman's family, and ordered the sheet music of a nineteenth-century Russian ballad,

'Could I but Express in Song'. Returning a week later to enquire if the score had arrived, he was informed that prolonged and diligent searches had failed to turn up the number he had requested – Kodály's Buttocks-Pressing song.

'It's true,' Máire said, 'honestly, I know the singer!'

She was a dear heart, and I miss her still. Her sense of humour sustained her to the end. When she was diagnosed with oesophageal cancer, I took her to lunch in Cooke's Café, of blessed memory. Over our caprese salads I spoke, at length, of the poet Philip Larkin, lately dead. Máire let me wax on for some time, then looked at me with a wry smile and said, 'You do know what he died of, don't you?' Too late, I did – cancer of the oesophagus.

I don't know if my time on the Arts Council did some service to the State – I hope it did, however negligible. Certainly it did me the service of allowing me to come to know the most delightful woman. Wonderful parties, indeed.

KEEPING THE FAITH

Marina Carr

When I think about the Arts Council, I think about it as the financial saviour of my youth. I'm talking about my early twenties when I was writing my first slew of plays and I'm talking about three people in particular I always associate with the Arts Council: Tom MacIntyre, Phelim Donlon and Lar Cassidy.

I didn't know the Arts Council existed until Tom MacIntyre said to me one day, you should apply for a bursary from the Arts Council. I said, you mean, someone will give me money to write? He said, raise your sights a little. I was on the dole at the time, living in a bedsit in Rathmines and three days out of seven I was literally penniless. Tom, very much an outsider and a wild soul, was generous to me in those days. Generous with his praise of a fledgling playwright, and generous with his time. I was often invited to his dinner table. He once cooked me a rabbit, there was always lashings of red wine and mad talk and beautiful poetry recited and savoured along with the cheese and the wine. Tom taught me how to live as a writer, how to keep the faith in the word: you take care of your sentences and the world will take care of the rest.

Around that time I had the good fortune to meet Phelim Donlon, who was head of Theatre at the Arts Council, and through Phelim I met Lar Cassidy who was head of Literature. Both were kind men and both were interested in my writing and took me seriously when many didn't, including myself. There is so much doubt in a young writer. The bar is high and you wonder if you have it, can you keep going, will you ever write anything worth reading. These two men seemed to think I had something worth investing in.

Those were the days when you could just turn up at Merrion Square and ask to speak to Phelim or Lar. I don't remember ever making an appointment. Once I showed up to weep about a play I had written, *Ullaloo*, it was on at the Peacock and had been savaged by the critics and then swiftly taken off in my absence, without my knowing. I was in Romania, supposed to be translating a play by Marin Sorescu; I don't know what I was doing there without a word of Romanian, and Sorescu's wife was deeply suspicious of me. God knows I was suspicious of myself. Anyway, I turned up at Phelim Donlon's office and he took me in like a distraught daughter and listened to my rant and made me tea, and when I had calmed down he asked me about my next play and what it was about. You go a long way to find that sort of decency in this world.

Young writers need someone at their back and when I look back now, I realise how lucky I was that my paths crossed with these three men. All family men, all had daughters and I suppose being older and wiser they knew how difficult it was going to be for me because at that time the theatre was a boy's game, and in my innocence I didn't even realise that. But they did and they kept me upright and kept me writing.

The other memory I associate with the Arts Council is Lar Cassidy's funeral. He died young, leaving small children, and it was a terribly sad affair. The church was packed with family, friends, relatives but also with poets, playwrights, novelists, artists, painters, musicians, composers. I couldn't say I knew Lar Cassidy very well but on the occasions I was in his company he was always kind to me. The year before, he had taken a bunch of writers and poets and musicians to a festival in Germany, Frankfurt I think it was, the Book Fair, with Lar as the ringleader. It was my first trip away with other writers and that was an eye-opener in itself. But I remember Lar and his kindness and his encouragement to me and the other younger writers on the jaunt. So here we were at his funeral, to pay our respects and to acknowledge the passing of one of our own tribe who believed passionately in the arts and who, through his work and dedication and wide-ranging knowledge, touched so many lives and helped so many artists on their journey.

WOLF SONG

Mary O'Malley

In memory of Eavan Boland

Sit still now. Take up your pen.
In this space before noise begins
Tigers are visiting the cities
And a white leopard sits

On a lawn in Suburbia.
A wolf is walking along
An empty beach in California
A poet sings his traces.

Now she too is becoming history.
Already her first slow movement
Of the strings is parting the silence.
This is the point in the story

When shadows thin as blades
Take over the April sky.
You can see the wolf through them.
Soon he too will be gone, forgotten.

This long free walk by the sea a detour.
The sea will remember him.
When he licked my hand at the hawthorn
His eyes sharpened the salt air.

JUNE

COME HERE YOU

Rachael Hegarty

'Come here you – what poems are coming up on the Junior and the Leaving?'
And this is where it started. I'm in our local supermarket in Finglas and one
of me ma's pals, Mrs Buckley, thinks I might have some inside info on the
State exams – she has one child doing the Junior and another doing the
Leaving. Word had gone around our estate: the youngest Hego girl is doing
a Masters in Poetry at Trinity. Poetry, I ask you? But it's exam season and the
parents of Finglas examinees are just as desperate for help as any. Poetry –
turns out the youngest Hego girl might be good for something. I tell Mrs
Buckley the truth, that I have no idea what poems are coming up on the
Junior or the Leaving. Her face looks crestfallen, so I offer to do a free grind
on the elements of poetry.

'Come here you – what poems are coming up on the Junior and the
Leaving?' And so began my now twenty-year habit of offering free poetry
grinds of a June bank holiday. Since then, I've had a date with any and every
Leaving or Junior Certer who wants to stall by and get a free grind. And by
Jaysus, they come. Cars pull up outside our house in Raheny and parents
march kids up to our doorstep. Our garden wall becomes a bike rack for
those kids brave enough to knock on the door themselves. The dog barks
and then wags her tail as teenager after teenager gets a welcome through the
hall door and into the kitchen.

When it comes to teenagers, trough, as we call it in my house, is the
key. My older nieces and nephews were enticed to come and get the poetry
grind by a promise of chocolate pancakes. I learned that trick from me ma
and da: with kids it's best to feed-feed first, and they'll talk-talk later. So,

everybody is offered a cuppa and some pancakes and then we get down to talking about the elements of poetry: form, metre, images, symbols, line-end rhymes, internal chimes, half rhymes and how a whole world of wonder is possible when words are crafted into a poem. For those who can't be bothered with poetry I ask them to tell me the name of their favourite song in the charts. We look up the lyrics. Lo and behold – even Stormzy uses metre, form, images, symbols, line-end rhymes, internal chimes and half rhymes.

Our eldest son did his Junior Cert in 2019 and he insisted that himself and his best mate get their own private grind on account of the 'scarlet for your ma' factor. I was fool enough to ask him why he's morto of his ma and the look he gave me reminded me of the look I'm sure I once gave me own mother. However, I relented and gave the eldest and his best pal a private lesson before I did two sessions of the free poetry grinds. That year we had ten Junior Certers in the morning and twelve Leaving Certers in the afternoon. Word had spread among the Mammy Mafia and there were even a couple of kids from the Southside.

But last year, there were no free poetry grinds. The June bank holiday came and went in a blur of Covid shock and sadness. Who cares if there is no Leaving Cert or Junior Cert when you can't be with your mates, play a match, dance in a field to real loud music with thousands of others, kiss a yonwan or yonfella and worst of all – not hug your nanny or your grandad for fear of more Covid deaths? As a neighbour's kid said – give me the Leaving Cert any day!

And this year? Well, our youngest won't be doing his Junior Cert and he's okay with that. He's already finished his summer tests and his junior cycle of secondary school grades will be based on previous exams, classroom-based assessments and other learnings. However, he shared my elements of poetry online with his classmates and other pals.

As for the Leaving Certers – well, the Mammy Mafia has awoken out of its pandemic stupor and kicked into gear. Now, me free grinds have moved online and moved beyond Dublin. I have Leaving Certers from Limerick, Galway, Cork and Kilkenny using me poetry worksheets.

'Come here you – what poems are coming up on the Junior and Leaving Certs?' I still don't know. But I know a poem has form, metre, images, symbols, line-end rhymes, internal chimes, half rhymes, and a word glimpse of wonder. And this Wednesday, the class of 2021 will have the choice to do their Leaving Cert English and other exams in the coming weeks. The first Wednesday in June, and the exams begin. Some kind of lovely normal is returning, and that, that is pure poetry.

THE LONGEST EMBRACE

Antonia Gunko Karelina

After a year's break, I finally went to a tango night. I haven't tangoed since the invasion, finding it difficult to allow myself to feel alive, when every day brings death and suffering to my homeland.

The tango night was a birthday party, held in Waterford, for the oldest tango dancer in Ireland. Jim McManus had turned 103, the same age as Ireland's independence. Prior to coming to Waterford, I had read a couple of articles about him and found out he was a Second World War veteran.

I gave Jim a Ukrainian flag as a birthday gift. He genuinely thanked me, saying that he'd display the flag in his window. And he made everyone laugh with his birthday speech in which he said, 'Tango is very important. It's the most important thing in the world.'

But as for me, when it came to the dancing, overwhelmed by the stress of war-related events and after a prolonged period without any practice, I felt awkward and clumsy. I danced with a couple of people but felt pretty much nothing, as if my senses couldn't un-numb.

Then I received an invitation from another dancer and noticed how different his embrace was. My tango teacher in Kyiv repeatedly emphasised the need to stand on my own feet, to use the floor as a prop. This dancer's embrace, however, was very tight, as if my partner was inviting me to lean on him, to forget about whatever weighed me down and just dance. It was in this embrace that my senses started to revive, and I was even able to feel playful.

I later described Jim's birthday tango as part of a Fighting Words writing project for Ukrainian refugees, trying to convey the idea that if a 103-year-old dancer and Second World War veteran is able to find joy on the dance floor, then maybe I could too.

The day before St Patrick's Day, I received an email from a photographer who was creating images based on the stories of the project participants. His initial idea was to capture Jim and myself dancing together, but after learning that I was significantly taller than Jim, the photographer changed his plan. He wrote, 'Maybe we could cast another man who is the same height or taller than you.'

'I love the way the two bodies support each other in tango,' he continued, describing photo samples he had attached to the email, 'there is something very poetic about it, to me at least.'

'There is something liberating about it, to me at least,' I echoed him in my mind.

The day after St Patrick's Day, I went to Bray for my second tango event in Ireland. Someone asked me up to dance. He said he remembered me from the Waterford party.

'I thought you lived there,' the man said.

'No. I live in Cavan. I made that trip just to attend the birthday party.' I told him. I wasn't sure I remembered him at all, but then ...

'... NOW I remember,' I said, as we started the dance in an embrace that felt so secure. He told me his name was Michael.

In the meantime, the photographer was making plans with a Dublin tango teacher for the photo shoot. He emailed to tell me that I was to come to the city on a Friday night. On my bus ride I followed a thread of emails and noticed that the tango teacher couldn't make it. The photographer wrote to me reassuring me that it was okay because 'we have Michael coming (a tango-dancing Irish man)'.

'I hope Michael looks 103-ish.' I attempted to be humorous.

'Well Michael is in his forties, but he'll serve as a symbolic representation of Ireland,' the photographer said, promptly changing the concept of the photo shoot.

'It has to be that Michael,' I thought, 'somebody who was willing to let me lean on him so that I could enjoy the dance.'

I came into the community centre and the first thing I heard was tango music. I met the photographer, his assistant and Michael – the right Michael!

'Did you know it would be me?' I asked him.

'No. I knew nothing about this project. That teacher just asked me if I could volunteer for a tango photo session. Did you know it would be me?' he replied.

'I didn't have any specific information about which Michael was coming, but I knew it would be you. I mean, how many dancers named Michael are there?'

'There are quite a few,' he smiled.

'There may be other Michaels in Ireland, but only some of them are willing to share the burden of a Ukrainian refugee,' I thought.

For the next couple of hours the photographer asked us to pose in a tango embrace. We tried a few dance moves but then stopped and obediently stood still. It was the longest tango embrace I ever shared with anyone. It had only a few variations according to the photographer's instructions – like me leaning on the partner more, or standing face to face as if before the dance. But for the most part we were just holding each other.

'If you knew that you would be representing Ireland, would you still have agreed to do this?' I asked Michael while we were taking a short break.

'Probably not,' he laughed, 'that's an intimidating task!' And he immediately stepped back to resume the embrace and to patiently hold my weight in an 'off-axis' tango position.

'You would,' I thought, 'because you are very Irish. Your people and your embrace have proven more than once that you are willing to share the burden of those who, just now, can't stand on their own feet.'

Since coming to Ireland, I've met Michaels, Patricias, Clodaghs, Orans, Orlas, Rosemaries, Stephens, Denises, Alans, Aidans, Fionas, Aideens, Briedges, Hughs, Liams, Nollaigs, Gabriels, Ians and many others. All of these people have helped Ukrainians by sharing our burdens and allowing us to enjoy life at a time when we are struggling to stand on our own feet. This indeed is the longest embrace I've ever had – it started when I arrived here and has been lasting since.

HOW DUKE THE DOG BECAME AN ITALIAN CITIZEN

Tom Clonan

Our son Eoghan had spinal surgery during his school's Transition Year. A History and Classics fanatic, he missed the school trip to the Colosseum in Rome. So that summer – in the time before Covid – we pack him, his wheelchair and his assistance dog, Duke, into the family car, a brand-new, specially adapted passenger van. Packed to the roof with four teenagers, a large golden retriever, suitcases, laptops, iPads, smartphones, and two large ten-kilo bags of dog food, we head to Dublin Port on our odyssey.

Two ferries and several UK motorways, French autoroutes and Italian autostradas later, we arrive in Rome on Tuesday 23 July. Teeming with tourists, the Eternal City bakes in 38 degrees of heat. In insane traffic, we navigate our way towards the Colosseum. As luck would have it, we find a disabled parking bay close by, near Via Marco Aurelio.

In brilliant sunshine, we queue at the Palatine Hill for entry to the Forum. Some Italian policewomen approach us. Gesturing at Eoghan's wheelchair and Duke the dog, they lead us to the top of the queue and usher us through the turnstiles. Eoghan gets VIP treatment.

He insists we see everything. I manhandle him and his chair into and around temples: Vesta, Romulus, Augustus, Julius, across cobbled streets and into the arena of the Colosseum itself. Eventually, exhausted, we retrace our steps and arrive back at the disabled parking bay.

But it's empty.

I approach a policeman and in broken Italian, inform him that our car appears to have been 'towed'. He places his arm around my shoulders.

'No, Signor, it is not towed, it is stolen. It happens every day in Roma.'

The teens pop out their ear pods. 'What did he say?'

The car's been stolen. Everything is gone. Suitcases, laptops, iPads, ten-kilo bags of dog food and our passports. We are shocked into complete silence. Two thousand five hundred kilometres from home. All we have is the clothes we are standing in. All I can hear is my own heartbeat and the relentless whirring of crickets in the surrounding trees. The silence is finally broken when Eoghan makes two fists and curses loudly. Duke pants and wags his tail at the elegantly dressed policeman.

Dario – the most philosophical police officer in Rome – studies our faces and says,

'Okay, okay, *tranquillo*, you are all safe, all together.'

He walks us to the police station, Questura di Roma – the grandly titled Commissario di P.S. Sezionale 'Esquilino' on Via Petrarca. The police stare at our forlorn family through the bulletproof glass in Reception. A buzzer sounds, a door clicks and they welcome us into the air-conditioned office area. Cops and detectives gather around us, 'la famiglia irlandese'. A very tall policewoman – the boss – pushes her way towards us, and in perfect English, directs us into her office.

The cops bring bottles of Coke for the teens. One detective with mirror sunglasses has a handgun shoved down the waistband at the front of his trousers. Rossa, the youngest, whispers to me, 'If that gun fires, it'll blow his pants off.' I think this is one of my lesser worries.

We fill in a report. The boss tells me to listen carefully to her. 'Your car is gone forever. It will not be recovered. You must plan now to get home to Ireland. I will call the Irish embassy and then, we will take you to Termini train station to hire another car.'

A few phone calls later, we've informed the insurance company of our predicament and have an appointment at the Villa Spada, the Irish embassy, for temporary travel documents, the next day. We book a flight home, check into our accommodation and have a dejected dinner that evening in Trastevere. Eoghan looks at my long face from his wheelchair. Grinning, he launches into the chorus of Joe Dolce's 'Shaddap Your Face' to cheer me up. We all burst into laughter. The words of Dario, the cop philosopher, return to me once more: 'You are all safe, all together.'

The following day, we drive across town to the Irish embassy on Via Giacomo Medici, close to the Vatican. The ambassador greets us with coffee and dolci. He tells us the history of the Villa Spada. Unfortunately, he can do nothing for Duke, who must get his own passport from the Italian authorities. Without an official pet passport, Duke will go into enforced quarantine. Eoghan will lose his working dog, his partner – his world, our world, will fall apart. A frantic Google search reveals that we must travel out of Rome to get the necessary travel documents. The clock is ticking.

We race up the autostrada to Siena, where the Department of Agriculture, Veterinary Section is located. Our clothes are getting dirtier. I have not shaved since the theft of – well, everything.

When we get there, they're already pulling down the shutters for the day. I lift Eoghan out of the rental and the entire family, wheelchair and golden retriever make it through the door of the building ... just.

Initially, the Italian vets tell us they can't help; they say that they have no 'jurisdiction' over an Irish dog.

'No, wait!' I say. I start to tell them, with the help of Google Translate, of the theft or our family car in Roma, and what it will mean for us if we can't get Duke home. The vets fall silent. They confer in hushed staccato whispers – staring all the while at the dishevelled Irish family. Understanding of our predicament suddenly dawns on them and the atmosphere in the room changes in an instant.

'*Mamma mia!*' They hug Eoghan, '*tesoro mio*,' and each of us in turn. Duke gets a hug too.

Duke is photographed. His chip is scanned. His Italian passport is produced. The fee is waived. They ask me his name. 'Duke', I say. '*Il Duce*,' they laugh as they enter his name into his new documents.

Two days later, we fly home. Exhausted. Filthy. But despite everything, elated. The Aer Lingus staff pat Duke on the head and assist Eoghan off the plane at Terminal Two. Cool, wet Dublin.

As we leave the terminal, we face one last trial, when we're stopped at Customs and the officers demand to see Duke's papers.

'Why are you bringing an Italian dog into Ireland?'

'Well, now!' I start to tell them the story. They wave us through.

In the taxi home, Eoghan and the teens say, 'That was so cool,' and even, 'Can we do that again?' We are all safe. We are all together. *Il Duce* wags his tail.

AND I NEARLY SAID I LOVED HIM

Larry McCluskey

In a poem, Seamus Heaney tells us he phoned his friend, the playwright Brian Friel. Anne, Brian's wife, answered and said, 'Hold on, I'll just run out and get him – the weather here's so good, he took the chance to do a bit of weeding.'

That poem always reminds me of my father, also a keen gardener. One Saturday morning in May 1955, he and I were driving through heavy rain to Carrickmacross for me to sit the entrance exam of the Patrician High School there. I was eager, confident, but I sensed an anxiety in my father.

The Primary Cert exam that year had been something of a disaster. It was 'the year of the French' – not Tom Flanagan's, but '*Na Francaigh*'! On the Irish paper, I had answered the questions as if *Na Francaigh* of the comprehension passage had been rats, rather than the French expeditionary force of 1798. The local secondary-school scholarship exams were an opportunity for recovery of academic reputation. And, anyway, money was scarce – few could afford boarding-school fees in the 1950s.

Recognised among teacher colleagues as a good mathematician, my father was setting me some mental tests in the car.

'An isosceles triangle has an external angle of 120 degrees – what's the size of the apex angle?'

'Sixty degrees,' I answered promptly. 'And it's not an isosceles triangle – it's an equilateral triangle!'

'Very good,' he said, laughing as our eyes met. I vividly remember that moment of father–son conviviality.

The entrance exams had three functions – to assess applicants' ability, to exclude likely failures (who were thus diverted to the local tech), and to enrol bright students, attracted by the half-scholarships on offer, who would 'bring honour' to the school at Leaving Cert level. (The universities are at the same lark today!)

In the end, I won a half-scholarship to St Pat's in Cavan. My brother and I arrived there in the same big Austin10, ZD 8629, father driving, mother fussing over our appearance. We were happy, excited at new adventure shared by a few classmates from Cootehill – Kevin Blessing, John Boyle, Michael Shields. To the chapel for reading of the rules: 'no undue familiarity with domestic staff'; 'within the precincts of the college'; 'seniors not to fraternise with junior students' – unfamiliar Latinisms, major emphasis on crimes and punishments; this and that 'subject to disciplinary action' or, in extremis, 'expulsion from the college'. Terrifying images!

Then, exploration. The College walks: 'the Half', 'the Whole'; Handball Alley; Bishop's House and Walk; Front Avenue with lunchtime-walk of priests, six or seven abreast, like bishops in Maynooth or cardinals in Rome. The first term night-time ritual 'stuffings' – Seniors forcing grass down the trousers of Juniors (whatever that was about) and 'duckings', junior heads forced under cold taps. Primitive rites of passage!

In the second term, there was a long form to be filled in – outdated references to TB sickness and length of stays in the Infirmary. One question caught my attention: 'Do you receive extras in the Refectory?' What? – by then, to us, college life was perpetual hunger.

'Certainly not,' I wrote. A few days later, I was summoned to the Bursar's Office. 'What do you mean by this?' Lamely, I read out my answer, balloon deflated now.

'Do you know that your father hasn't paid last term's fees yet?' I didn't. 'Go back to class – and no more smart-aleckry out of you.'

'Yes, Father.'

I hadn't yet learned the words for humiliation, but I felt wronged. More hurt than I was by the beatings – once for robbing the Bishop's orchard (we sold surplus apples to fellow students); the Dean's binoculars, detective-like, on his window ledge as we joined the queue outside his door for bedtime caning; or clattering down the stairs, shoes untied, late for morning Mass, to meet him, black-cassocked, silver hair impeccably coiffed, bamboo cane in hand – four or six of the best for Matins. Oh, the pain!

Boarding school, even for the brightest – I excelled in both its academic and sporting life – can be a cruel place. While on the whole I enjoyed it, liked most of my teachers and got on well, I don't hold with those who say it toughens you for life. I'm more with Heaney when he called his St Columb's schooldays, 'my first of many exiles'.

As Heaney waited for Friel to come to the phone that day, he heard the grave ticking of hall clocks in far-off Donegal, and when Brian spoke, Seamus tells us: 'I nearly said I loved him.'

Travelling the wet, winding road from Shercock to Carrick that May morning in 1955, our time was ticking, too, but what I heard was the smooth, steady thrum of the Austin's powerful engine under the big black bonnet, my anxious father driving at his careful, schoolmasterly steady pace. Whenever I recall the intimacy of that journey, I know exactly how Heaney felt when, suddenly, Brian Friel said hello.

ADOPTED MOMENTS

Zainab Boladale

I loved to learn. The early morning wake-up call on each school day did not disturb me, my daily destination Scoil Chríost Rí, a small school community in the heart of Cloughleigh, in Ennis, its yellow walls warm and welcoming.

The school's student population spilled out from the main building into prefabs which formed a square enclosure.

Many years later, I would return to the school as an adult to meet again the teachers that shaped my school days, and I would find that the old building was no more. It had stretched and stretched till it could stretch no more, and Scoil Chríost Rí had been granted the luxury of a modern building.

Back then and even now, Scoil Chriost Rí was known for the extra effort its staff put in, developing their students further by introducing their students to the world in a way that textbooks could not. This was the case in 2008, ahead of National Grandparent Day.

I was in Sixth Class at the time, feeling grown up at the idea of being the oldest in a school I'd been attending since I was small.

The teachers had organised for some of the elderly people within the community to come in to talk to those of us without grandparents in Ireland.

If you've lived in Ennis long enough, you'll realise a few things. In this small town, things are kept simple and sweet, locals have a sense of pride of place and most people are obliging when it comes to giving their time to school students. As the saying goes, 'It takes a village to raise a child.' Strangers to us at the time, these grandparents we knew nothing of would visit regularly and tell us stories of when they were young and what life was like.

It's funny how generational differences melt away when it comes to storytelling. My 'adopted' grandparent was a man named Paddy. What I remember most clearly about him is his calmness and curiosity. When he came in, questions would go back and forth like a ping-pong ball.

I talked to Paddy about my little sister (this was before my brother was born), and we exchanged stories about our school days. Paddy had gone to Kilmihil primary school and became a teacher in later life. He'd lived lots of places – Cork, Donegal, Tipperary – before coming back to Ennis, where he taught at Kilrush Tech till retirement.

I knew what it was like to move from place to place too, having moved from Lagos to Clare when I was small.

Paddy and I found that we were surprisingly similar, both blessed with the gift of the gab but equally interested in listening to each other.

As for my own grandparents, my mom's mother passed away in Nigeria in 2011. But I would speak with my dad's mother over the phone now and then. She showered me with prayers, speaking Yoruba with a whipped, undiluted tongue I barely understood. I met her as an adult only two years ago on a trip back to Nigeria, after a gap of over ten years.

I never met either of my grandfathers. Both passed away before I was born. So, the time I spent with Paddy, my adopted grandfather, was special to me.

November 2019. I'm sitting in the living room of my rented Dublin home reviewing my social notifications and I notice a Facebook message from a few days ago. It's from Paddy's daughter. She was an SNA teacher and had worked in Scoil Chríost Rí. She tells me that Paddy had passed away some years before. Her reason for messaging me, though, is not to tell me that. She and her mother had recently come across a booklet that I had gifted Paddy on our last encounter.

A distant memory of mine finds its way to the present. As a way to thank our adopted grandparent, we had been tasked with making something for them. Confident in my moulding skills, I had created a candleholder and made the booklet; I think others did the same.

Miss Lynch had sent a picture of my booklet.

I chuckled at my handwriting, big and bubble-like, with inconsistencies in how my letters curved. Telltale signs of youth, depicting the excitement of someone who had just started using a pen. It read:

196

Dear Paddy,

Thank you for coming in and being my adopted grandparent and sharing all your wonderful stories. I really appreciate you coming in. Have a very Merry Christmas and have a great 2009.

From, Zainab.

At the bottom of the booklet in printed font, it read:

This booklet was completed by Grandparents Mr & Mrs Lynch and Grandchild Zainab Boladale.

All my memories of my time in the classroom exchanging stories with Paddy came flooding back. I'm amazed and touched that after all these years, this booklet still exists. The things we experience as children and the people we meet never truly leave us. They shape us into who we are as adults. No moment is too small to matter to young minds.

Unknown to her, Paddy's daughter, Miss Lynch, had written the final chapter of my adopted-grandparent story.

FATHER'S DAY

Chris McHallem

My dad didn't have a clue, but I never blamed him.

I must have been twelve, and he was what? About forty-five or something. Ancient.

By that time, a man couldn't remember what twelve was like.

I tried sometimes to picture him as a child, to imagine his dreams and ambitions, but whatever youthful plans he'd once made, he'd ended up here, living above a pub in Fulham with a twelve-year-old to entertain, every second Sunday.

We tried museums for a couple of weeks, but the crowds got on his nerves.

I was always fearful that all those chirpy families with their Thermos flasks poring over their guidebooks would make him feel like he'd messed up, so when he suggested we 'give something else a go', I was more than happy.

We went to the football, but I knew from the start that his heart wasn't in that either.

He was what today we would call 'old school'.

He respected the players as athletes and applauded the abolition of the maximum wage, but deep down inside, he still felt that a player couldn't properly represent Huddersfield if he wasn't from Huddersfield. Or Ipswich. Or Tottenham. Or Crystal Palace.

We watched an uneventful cup tie between Fulham and Someone, and as we went towards my train he asked if next time we might try 'the pictures'.

'Yes,' I said.

And we did.

And for the next two years or so, that was it.

He'd meet me at the station and we'd go to the cinema by way of his flat, or to be more precise, by way of the pub under his flat.

I was too young to go inside, so he'd stand at the bar with a group of regulars, and I'd sit outside drinking ginger beer and eating crisps. Even as it was happening, I realised that this was the epitome of poor parenting, but to be honest, I loved it. I could eat and drink my fill, read Sunday newspapers which my mother wouldn't have allowed through the letterbox, and watch grown-ups behaving like kids.

The cinema was round the corner and had clearly been chosen more because of its location than its repertoire.

Hardly any of the films were in English.

They were nearly all black and white, and the vast majority of them were, according to the man in the ticket booth, 'pre-war'.

He didn't say which war.

My dad liked the films because they were quiet and slow and after four or five pints, no man wants bright lights or excitement.

And I liked the films because they were filled with philosophical thieves and actresses with expressive hands and dark, kohl-pencilled eyes.

If the film was dull or incomprehensible, and often they were, then I would leave him to doze, but sometimes a film would grab me and hold me tight from the start and, thinking that my father might enjoy it too, I'd launch into a routine of nudges and coughs designed to give him a chance to wake up and watch it with me.

And so, on Monday mornings, as my classmates talked about *Ice Station Zebra* or *Kelly's Heroes*, I would fill them in on *La Femme du Boulanger*, *Pépé le Moko* or perhaps Luis Buñuel's *Land Without Bread*.

*

I didn't go to his funeral.

Our lives had diverged long before he died. He was in some university town that I'd never visited, while I was in Ireland with a family of my own.

But a few days after he'd gone, I saw that *Bicycle Thieves* was showing on TV.

This was one of the films which I'd woken him to watch and convinced as ever of Vittorio De Sica's genius, I grabbed my five-year-old, told him how

199

I'd first seen this film with the grandfather he'd never meet, and convinced him to watch it with me.

It opens with shots of war-torn Rome. A man too thin for his suit has got a job as a poster hanger, and we watch as his wife pawns her bedsheets to get him the bike he needs. It's a hard film: all the faces are hungry, and the sunlight is unforgiving. But when the man gets his bike, his smile is like rain in a desert. I looked across at the child, wondering whether he could be caught by the film as I had been almost forty years before.

He was, of course, deeply asleep.

CROSSING THE BORDER

John Kelly

Growing up in Newry just inside the North of Ireland border, we were subject to fairly hard food rationing during the Second World War, and for some years afterwards.

This rationing extended right across the United Kingdom, which of course included the six counties of the North, and it covered such items as tea, butter, sugar and most other groceries. But what concerned me most as a young wee fellow, not yet in his teenage years, was the strict rationing on sweets.

Each of us children in our large family had his or her own sweetie coupons which we would deposit in Petie Loughran's sweetie shop in nearby Queen Street (later renamed Dominic Street).

Having got our pocket money on the Saturday, next morning on our way to Mass in the local Dominican church we'd call into Petie's shop to buy our weekly ration of sweets. I'd usually choose Dolly Mixtures, Bull's Eyes and Spangles. Now, Petie, being the good Catholic, always reminded us to keep the fast and not to eat the sweets until after the Mass, which of course we dutifully obeyed. The rationing was strictly enforced, and Petie had no latitude whatsoever to give us any more than our coupons clearly allowed us.

During those war rationing years, my mammy had an informal smuggling arrangement with our elderly aunt, Mary Anne, who lived in the village of Blacklion in County Cavan on the Free State side of the border. Auntie Mary Anne, carrying the shopping, mostly butter and sugar as requested by my mammy, would cross the few hundred yards over to the village of Belcoo in County Fermanagh – always with a friendly wave and hello to the British custom house men on the bridge – and post the smuggled shopping to Mammy in Newry.

But the routine changed dramatically on my tenth birthday when I received the magnificent present of my first bicycle. I remember every detail of it still; it was a beauty. It was a Raleigh and had a three-speed gear arrangement so that I could switch into low gear when climbing a hill. This was great on the steep part of the Dublin Road whenever I was cycling home from school, when everyone else had to dismount and push their bikes up the hill, and I could continue cycling.

After that, instead of putting in her request to Auntie Mary Anne, my mammy would give me her shopping list and the appropriate money, and send me to Dundalk in the Free State. I'd cycle the six miles or so to the border, on the far side of which were sweetie and other shops in the Free State, where they knew nothing about rationing or coupons.

I still remember every curve on that road. There was a plethora of shops that greeted you as you entered that side of Dundalk, and after doing Mammy's shopping in the grocer's, butcher's and dairy shop, I naturally gravitated to the sweet shops for my own purchases.

Before turning for home, I used to put the bag of tea inside my shirt, and the packed pound of butter down one of my thick woollen socks. I remember well that in those days, the butter on our table in Newry often had the fine profile of my calf muscle.

Though still in short trousers, I was never stopped by the customs men. They got to know me and say hello as I cycled through their road barrier. Except the once, and that once was probably my last venture at smuggling.

That day, when I crossed the border on my way home, a new customs man on duty whom I hadn't seen before waved me to stop. He asked me what I had inside my stocking, as it was sort of obvious there was something there. I showed him the butter, saying that it was butter for my mammy. He was smiling, and would probably have let me go – he seemed a nice man – but I had other ideas. I noticed just beside me under the customs' roofing, Mrs John Henry Collins, a formidable but friendly neighbour from our Dublin Road. She'd just been cleared by the customs and was about to get back into her car to drive off down the road to Newry.

Abandoning my customs man, I ran across to her with the butter in my hand. As her car was moving off slowly, I pushed my pound of butter through her open window and said, 'Hello Mrs Collins! Would you ever please give this butter to my mammy?' To her great and eternal credit, she grabbed the butter from my outstretched hand, pressed down on her accelerator, and headed off down the road to Newry.

To his credit, too, the customs man just threw his hands up in the air, turned his back on me, and walked away back into his custom house. And I cycled off down the road home.

With the advent of Brexit, it looks like the border between Newry and Dundalk may have a very unwelcome rebirth, and I sometimes wonder if I should establish a smuggling consultancy advisory firm? My expertise is unique, and the business should be good, especially if Boris Johnson brings back the sweetie coupons.

FATHER FOR A DAY
Barry McCrea

When I started teaching *Ulysses*, as a doctoral student in my mid-twenties, I was just a few years older than the 22-year-old Stephen Dedalus. Now, at forty-four, I am six years older than its other main protagonist, Leopold Bloom. The age gap between the two men is central to the basic plot of *Ulysses*. It's a very simple story: a talented but clueless young man, Stephen Dedalus, is abandoned by his friends during an unhappy drinking binge; he runs into an acquaintance of his father's, Leopold Bloom, who takes Stephen back to his house to sober him up and have a chat. We know nothing about what happens to the characters after this encounter. The novel opens and closes with that one day, 16 June 1904. As the Irish expression goes, *níl ann ach lá dár saol* – all it is is a day in the life.

The novel hints that Stephen is somehow in need of a father, while Bloom is looking for a son. What does this mean? In a literal sense, Bloom is already a father: although his son died in infancy, he has a daughter. And while Stephen is traumatised by the recent death of his mother, his father, Simon Dedalus, is very much alive.

Simon Dedalus is in a way one of the villains of *Ulysses*, a vainglorious, self-centred lout who spends his time carousing with his cronies while his hungry children boil shoe-leather for soup. But the novel is also saturated with him – his singing voice bewitches the whole company in the Ormond Hotel, and his quick wit and sparkling vernacular energy give the novel much of its humour and tone. He may be, as Stephen says about him in *A Portrait*, 'a bankrupt ... a praiser of his own past', but the attention devoted to Simon Dedalus in *Ulysses* – to his songs, turns of phrase, to his ability to tell a story – betrays a deep, loving fascination on Joyce's part with the world of his own Cork father.

No matter what kind of father you have, parents contain the mystery of our own origins, and their world before they had children is often a source of special, magical curiosity for their offspring. You see this especially in people whose parents are dead or far away.

'As my father would have said,' people say, trying to find a way to make the lost or absent parent speak again. When I think of my own father – a father mercifully as different from Simon Dedalus as it is possible to imagine – his boyhood playing cowboys and Indians on the banks of the Suck in the 1950s seems to me a sort of enchanted landscape.

Now that my own childhood on a housing estate in the 1980s begins to take on increasingly sepia tones, I find myself ever more aware that, since I do not have children, no one will ever have that kind of fascination for my early life. My memories of tip-the-can and BMXs and cola bottles will pass away with me, unscrutinised and uncelebrated by any son or daughter.

I feel no tragic regret at not having children, but I do notice that my daily emotional life is increasingly haunted by the ghost of the father I will never be. In teaching, for example, mini-versions of the overwhelming feelings parents must have for their children project themselves onto my students. I find myself terrified by their vulnerability in what seems like a harsh world; I feel envious of their youthful energy and afraid that it will find me aged and irrelevant; I am overcome with curiosity and concern as to what they will become in the world outside my classroom.

In my semester-long course on *Ulysses*, by the time Stephen and Bloom finally meet and talk over cocoa in Eccles Street, the students, someone else's daughters and sons, are getting ready for the summer. Most of them, when they walk out of the classroom, will also walk out of my life forever, and as I get older I feel ashamed of the intensity of the melancholy this departure incites in me; it feels very *childless*, a pale, pitiful substitute for the great adventure of parental love, a kind of mourning by a mind or even body that is surprised not to find itself a parent at forty-four.

After their conversation in the kitchen, Stephen refuses Bloom's offer of a bed for the night, and he steps out into the dawn, never to be seen again, at least not by us, the readers. That one day is all we will ever know of the characters; the meaning of the encounter between the younger man and the older man resides entirely in the passing impulses and instincts that, however briefly, bound them to one another on 16 June.

What I take from the meeting between Bloom and Stephen is that parenthood is not only a long-term investment that will ultimately offer emotional pay-off. It can also express itself as a short-lived, ephemeral flow of feeling from the older to the younger: a passing desire to protect or connect; to open the door and offer respite to those who have lost their networks of comfort and support; to those who need temporary material or psychological refuge; to those who are orphaned in all the many ways that this is possible in an unequal, war-torn world. These feelings for other people's children, as it were, may not be merely substitutes for the real thing, but something rich and even valuable, even if they only flare up briefly, even if *níl ann ach lá dár saol.*

VINO ROSSO PRONTO, PER FAVORE!

John Egan

We had just been shown to our table and the waiter was about to get some menus when my travelling companion piped up with the first and only words of Italian I would hear her speak: '*Vino rosso pronto, per favore!*' It was clear that no menu would ever be perused before a calming glass of house wine had been administered.

My companion and new best friend was the renowned journalist, civil rights campaigner and feminist Nell McCafferty. We had been sent to Italy to cover Ireland's pivotal World Cup game against Romania for *The Pat Kenny Radio Show*. Like most people in Ireland thirty years ago, I knew Nell by reputation only, so when we met at Dublin Airport, I was a little taken aback to see that her luggage comprised two T-shirts, assorted underwear and a toothbrush, which she carried in a squashed-up plastic shopping bag.

'What more do I need?' Nell said, 'Sure we'll only be away for two days.'

Now while a trip to Italy might appear to be a dishy assignment, the catch was that we'd been asked to travel at less than twenty-four hours' notice. We had no hotel bookings, no match tickets, no Italian lire, but I had managed to find us rooms in a modest hotel about 30 kilometres south of Genoa. By the time we sat down in that friendly trattoria, we were both completely whacked out, and famished. We'd been living on our wits since leaving Dublin that morning, but now at least we had a roof over our heads and a vague promise of tickets for the following day's match.

Nell McCafferty and myself were unlikely candidates for this World Cup assignment. Between us we only had a passing knowledge of any of the Irish soccer players. But in a way, that was the genius of sending us to cover Italia 90. We were like the majority of people in Ireland that summer, when the country got swept along on a tsunami of excitement and optimism, in support of Jack Charlton and the Boys in Green.

Monday 25 June 1990 was a swelteringly hot day. Nell and I had breakfast and sipped strong espressos on a shady terrace overlooking the small fishing harbour of Camogli, considering our travel options. While trains, buses and taxi services were readily available, I felt our approach to the city should be more in keeping with Genoa's maritime history. After all, it was the birthplace of Christopher Columbus.

It took an hour of my limited and very broken Italian, lots of hand waving and gesticulations, as well as some serious haggling, before I found a speedboat owner who was willing to ferry us up the coast – about the same distance as Greystones to O'Connell Bridge.

For more than an hour we bounced over the azure blue waves of the Mediterranean, cooled by a sea breeze and salt spray. Our water taxi delivered us into a luxury yacht marina which was jam-packed with squillion-dollar pleasure boats, the likes of which you'd only ever see in James Bond movies.

With our feet firmly back on dry land, we regained our equilibrium and discovered that it was just a short walk to the stadium. With three hours to go before kick-off, the concourse around Stadio Luigi Ferraris was already heaving with thousands of Irish soccer fans, brimful of anticipation. Jack Charlton's travelling army had won the hearts of the Italian people for their bonhomie, irrepressible singing and insanely optimistic ambitions for the tournament.

Here, Nell's status as a national icon came into its own. As she mingled among the waiting fans, she was instantly recognised and very warmly greeted. Grown men shared incredible stories with her of abandoning good jobs and raising credit union loans to be there, as if she were a long-lost, much-loved family relative.

And there was the intrepid granny from Tallaght, who had joined her son and his mates as they drove a camper van from Dublin to Cagliari and onwards to Palermo before finally ending up in this stadium car park in the northern tip of Italy. No, she wasn't interested in attending the match itself, she told us. She had just washed the lads' sweaty clothes and hung them on a makeshift washing line, because there was great drying out that day.

The match itself is imprinted on our collective unconsciousness: nil–all after extra time, it went to a penalty shoot-out, which Ireland won 5–4, after a stunning, arms-outstretched save by Packie Bonner and an ice-cool tap from David O'Leary into the back of the Romanian net. The stadium went Vesuvius … as did everyone back home.

Ninety minutes later, Nell and myself had inveigled ourselves onto the media bus, which was travelling in convoy to the Irish team's hotel. On arrival, we walked nonchalantly, eyes always forward, straight into the dining room to join the team and their families for the post-match celebration.

We bagged a couple of spare seats at one table but our lack of football knowledge quickly became apparent as it took me until dessert to realise that we were deep in conversation with none other than Ronnie Whelan and his family. I wrote his name on the back of a napkin which I slipped over to Nell.

After dinner, we crowded around Big Jack and had our photo taken with him. In the photos, he's beaming with his magnificent trademark smile.

As midnight approached, Nell and myself headed back into the centre of Genoa to commune with the hordes of delirious Irish supporters, many of whom were still chanting *Olés* and cooling their jets in the medieval fountain of the Piazza De Ferrari.

Already these fans' thoughts had turned to the Stadio Olimpico in Rome, where Ireland would surely conquer the host nation Italy, five days later, for a place in the World Cup semi-finals.

At 4 a.m. I escorted Nell back to our hotel in Camogli, and I had her up again a few hours later and sitting in a radio studio talking to Pat Kenny about our journey to Genoa. Eyes closed, she regaled listeners with a fantastical tale of our match day wanderings, recounted in an almost Joycean stream of consciousness. She ended that broadcast with a plea for RTÉ bosses to send out more money and fresh knickers.

And so we made our way on to Rome, where we managed to attend a team training session. Chatting to Packie Bonner, I was astonished to see just how lean and athletic he was – rippling with the energy of a racehorse.

We also joined the team for a special audience with Pope John Paul II, after which I lost Nell for about an hour. She'd gone walkabout in some

209

out-of-bounds part of the Vatican, and had been taken in charge by the Swiss Guard, who escorted her back out to St Peter's Square.

Our extraordinary Italia 90 odyssey lasted another week. We spent our days meeting and chatting to Irish fans everywhere, then sharing their tales with Pat Kenny and, vicariously, with an entranced nation of radio listeners.

Every evening, exhausted but exhilarated, we would find an affordable trattoria, and sink into our seats to take stock of the day. And before ever looking at a menu, Nell would order up a carafe of '*vino rosso pronto, per favore!*'

THE HUNTING OF THE OCTOPUS

William Wall

I was once hunted by an octopus. I was standing knee-deep in the crystal-clear water of the little stony beach of San Fruttuoso on the Portofino Peninsula when I noticed that what I took to be a stone was, in fact, moving steadily towards me and had arms – or legs. Eight of them.

I had time to count before it lunged at me.

I stepped back, the octopus lunged again, I took another step, he followed, and so on. Finally, I was standing on dry land and the octopus was still coming for me. He, or she – it's difficult to know with an octopus unless you're an expert – stopped half-out of the water and fixed a beady eye on me. He was clearly waiting for me to make the next move. And when I didn't react he moved back out to deep water, but not before I got a photo to prove it.

I have often wondered why, of all the people swimming and paddling there that day, the octopus chose me. Did I give off some exotic Irish scent when my feet combined with salt water? Was he fed up with eating Italians? Was he a deranged octopus who lost the run of himself one day? And if so, are there a lot of them about, and should we be worried? And what was he doing in two feet of water anyway? Wasn't he supposed to be lurking offshore?

Finally, after years of scientific investigation I am in a position to answer one question – the 'why me' mystery may be solved. The answer is whiteness. There is nothing quite so white as an Irishman on an Italian beach. Even after two or three days of constant exposure to sunlight, your average Irishman never gets beyond a state of iridescent pinkness that is frankly embarrassing as a suntan. It's not even recognised as such by most of the rest of the world's population.

But it's important to understand that the octopus is attracted to white things.

My friend Salvatore, who fishes for octopus, explained the whole thing to me.

In the old days, he told me, they worked a two-man boat. One rowed and one fished. They used a box with a glass bottom – *lo specchio*, they called it in Neapolitan, which means the mirror, though it is not a mirror, more of a looking-glass. With *lo specchio*, you can see the bottom.

Before ever I see the octopus, he said, I see his house and his garden. The octopus always has a garden.

If at this point you are reminded of a song by The Beatles, do not be surprised. I am making my small contribution to the vast literature devoted to the analysis of the cosmic lyrics of Ringo Starr.

The hideaway of the octopus will always be a cave or a crevice in the rocks. In front of his house will be an area of the seabed that the octopus sweeps clean and fills with ornaments that attract his attention. This is what Salvatore calls *il giardino del polipo*, the octopus's garden. All of the ornaments will be white, especially white stones. Which perhaps explains why my friend from San Fruttuoso was attracted to my palely gleaming feet.

How they catch the octopus is interesting too. The fisherman dangles a white-painted hook, more like a small grappling iron, in the octopus's garden. The octopus thinks it's a fish or a garden ornament and reaches out to embrace it. Although well provided in the tentacle department, the octopus is remarkably short on discernment. As soon as he grabs the hook the fisherman jerks it upwards very hard and fast. If he does not strike quickly, the octopus gets a chance to brace himself and he will not be dislodged. The only way they can get him out now is to repeatedly batter his rock home with a heavy iron which they slide down the same line as the hook. Hopefully the iron will break the stones that he's hiding in, and they can pull him out. Otherwise, they must cut the line and start again with a new one, a substantial loss when one considers the exchange value of an octopus vis-a-vis that of an iron hook and rope.

But how does a pair of Irish feet rate as a garden ornament in the suburban octopus's garden?

My guess is: on the lower end of the scale between a one-armed Venus and a garden gnome.

WHY I TRAVEL ALONE

Rory Gleeson

Noko or Simon or Beano had a plastic bag of Subway dangling down by his bare leg, letting the warmth of it dab at his skin as it swung towards and away from him. The train was getting going in the early morning sun. We were somewhere between Germany, Austria, Switzerland, Hungary, Croatia.

We were sweaty and underwashed, tired, muggy, luxuriating in our own filth. Our clothes were damp and rotting with sweat, bundled up in our rucksacks on the racks over our heads. There was too little water between the six of us. Someone was wearing the same T-shirt for the third day in a row. There'd been an argument about where to go next, about what city was the right one to go to. The train shook and shook as I thought, I hate every person in this booth.

I told them I was going to sit somewhere else on the train and read. Ignoring the bits of half-glances to each other, I left, going down the other end of the train to find an empty booth. I'd been utilising this tactic more and more as we'd gone into the later weeks of our trip. Generally, I appreciate a certain amount of time to myself, and like to avoid people if I myself am in a bad mood. This was not part of the group ethos, which was that we should always, as much as possible, stick together. People would get snippy with each other, exasperated, and yet remain in the same room, arguing through their moods. I preferred to bail and come back when tempers had calmed.

When I stepped off the train at our destination, the other lads were already walking away hurriedly down the platform, seeming almost to have forgotten my existence. When I caught up to them, they maintained a sharp silence. Were they that offended that I'd left, preferring to spend a two-hour

213

train journey by myself? I followed, confused for a bit, then sensed that something else had happened in my absence.

Later on, I learned exactly what had happened.

After I'd left our compartment, a beautiful young Australian woman had slid open the rattling carriage door. Blonde and fresh and cool. They looked up at her.

'Sorry, guys,' she'd said in unmistakeable Australian wide-mouthed vowels. 'Do you mind if I take that seat?' Pointing at the seat I'd just vacated.

The answer was, of course, 'Please do!' They could barely, barely believe their luck. She stowed her rucksack beside their bags on the rack above them and swung into the empty seat beside the window. They pretended not to look at her. She was well used to the situation, and instead of waiting to see which one of them would talk at her first, find her name, find where her hostel was, make contact, establish rapport, get contact info, she just breezed into it.

'So where are you guys from?' she asked.

'How long have you been on the road?'

'Where are you going next?'

They answered, someway or how, in an incredibly friendly and inclusive manner. But she was a mirage, she wasn't real. A gorgeous woman didn't just slide into your life, occupying the seat some long-forgotten ginger mate had left, and start making small talk. Usually there were more hurdles to get over – icy friends, protective males, her own standards. This didn't just happen, not like this.

There was a lull in the conversation, as each young man struggled to plot their strategy ahead.

Noting the brief silence, the Australian girl turned her head and looked out the window.

Then she stood up.

'Sorry, guys,' she said. 'I can't do this.'

She took her rucksack down from the rack.

'It's not personal,' she said. 'It's just … guys, it stinks in here.'

She left, sliding the door firmly shut after her. They watched her go, away off down the carriage to find another compartment that didn't reek of reused socks, wet towel, warm Subway sandwich, too much Lynx, not enough soap, sweaty T-shirts, cigarettes, old burps, new farts, beer breath, hair grease, garlic cheesy chips, pull my finger, mayonnaise, kebabs, kebabs, kebabs.

214

When I rejoined them on the train platform, a long, hard silence was on the group.

They checked into the hostel, brought the bags to their bunks. Then the sound of water gushing in the shower rooms.

It would be a long while before they told me about their humiliation. Even longer still before they recovered. There's that image you have of yourself when young and on the move. Well-travelled, soiled but in a charming way. Martin Sheen in *Badlands*, old T-shirt, young body, grubby but romantic.

Then there's the reality. A carriage full of smelly, smelly young men scaring off a gorgeous young backpacker.

And that, more or less, is why I travel alone.

SMALL GIRL, RED FLOWERS
Sarah Moore Fitzgerald

It was on an Italian beach in the summer of 2002, under the dangerous blaze of the afternoon sun that, for a short time, our daughter got lost. A month away from her fourth birthday, I still have a technicolour image of that version of her: the small swimsuit with a low-waisted frill and a red flower print. Her pale skin slathered in sunscreen, a little hat shading her face, her small, strong, stocky legs, always running.

Viareggio is a seaside town on the Ligurian coast: Art Deco fronts, glimmering ocean, great marble mountains to the north; rows and rows of waterside umbrellas in coloured stripes, vividly flapping in the wind. In high summer the beach has a glorious soundtrack. Tanned, T-shirted salesmen with creaking baskets slung over their shoulders sell hot pastries filled with pistachio cream or molten chocolate. Deft women in pale tunics and wide-brimmed hats walk among the sunbeds and deck chairs, offering the soothing magic of massage. There's something of the town crier about these vendors. Their announcements –'*Bombolone!*' '*Massaggio!*' – must be loud and showy to compete with the other noises in the air: children laughing, parents calling, teenagers showing off, music rising from speakers, the roll and fizz of the sea.

In the instant when we could not find our daughter, all those sounds grew muffled, the rising of our fear seeming to silence any possibility of sunny normality. Her father and I shouted for her, hurrying to the places we thought she might be. As there continued to be no sign of her, quickly we became more frantic.

In the anguish, most of our fragile Italian vocabulary was lost to us as we tried to ask for help. Sensing the situation, kind families and café staff gathered, willing to support, but even the smallest pieces of information felt impossible to articulate. I did not have the words for flowery swimsuit or pale skin or curly hair. All I could muster again and again was '*Piccola regazza. Fiori rossi!*' How unhelpful it must have been for the locals to hear me clumsily repeating 'Small girl. Red flowers' at them, like a contestant in a hellish game of charades whose confidence has failed her and whose already limited resources have been exhausted.

I remember a gleaming young lifeguard of about twenty sternly addressing me: '*calma, Signora, calma*'. In hindsight I forgive him, but at the time if I'd had the Italian that was so badly failing me, I'd have told him: 'My child is lost. There is no *calma*.'

In reality, it can't have been more than fifteen minutes or so, proof that there are times when life plays havoc with any ordered sense of logic or time. All at once those minutes seemed to warp and stretch and stand still. By the time our distress was at its chaotic peak and the crowd had thickened, a gap appeared, and in it a woman – or rather a Botticelli angel – with our daughter in her arms.

Our girl was hiccupping with sobs, but otherwise fine. She reached for me and we clung to each other while my normally less demonstrative husband fell to his knees in front of our startled saviour and embraced the woman around her legs in an operatic gesture of relief and gratitude.

I see the comedy of that moment clearly still: laughter all around us and in us – the privilege of comfort after danger. Our girl is a grown-up now. No longer small. Still an adventurer. We don't often talk about it, and when we do, it's with the memory of the mirth that concluded it. But we carry the darker ghost of that long-ago afternoon with us still, when for a brief time, like a jagged rip appearing in the sky, an unthinkable possibility opened in front of us and almost as quickly zipped itself up again, returning us to the cheery noises of the beach, the sunshine, the music, the sweet pastries.

JULY

MY VOICE

Mary Kate O Flanagan

I opened my mouth and nothing came out. This had been happening a lot lately – I kept losing my voice. I was reduced to whispering until I went to see an ear, nose and throat specialist who scolded me, 'Whispering is the very worst thing you can do, it puts a terrible strain on your vocal cords.' He prescribed complete voice rest. Now I was twenty-two and I was mute, on doctor's orders. I couldn't do my job, I couldn't socialise, I couldn't even complete simple tasks like shopping or buying a train ticket without a notebook and pen. I couldn't chat, which is in the top three of my favourite things to do.

The specialist sent me to a speech therapist, who took one look at my name on the form (this was in London) and said,

'Mary Kate O' Flanagan – convent girl? Yeah, I see a lot of you. The nuns teach you good manners but also to suppress your rage'. She continued, 'The voice is closely linked to emotions. I can give you exercises to do to release the tension you're holding in your throat but until you go to therapy, this is going to keep happening.'

I didn't want to go to therapy. I didn't want to look at myself. I was afraid the reason my voice was failing was tied up with the reason I had a chaotic love life, but I needed my voice to function in the world, and so I committed to therapy.

Now, talk therapy is a slow and painful process, especially when the reason you're doing it is because you can't talk. And at first it can feel like things are getting worse, not better, because you have to unpack the junk you don't want to look at. But I persisted with it, and I knew it was helping.

Still, after a while, I lamented to a friend that I just wanted someone to magically heal me. And she said, 'Oh honey, you can't heal your soul with just talk therapy. You should try reiki.'

So I tried reiki. I lay there while a woman ran her hands over the air a few inches above my body, and I remembered how my sisters and I laughed ourselves sick when a friend of ours paid to have her aura massaged. But I felt suffused with an undeniable sense of wellbeing which kept me coming back. And then reiki led to acupuncture, which took place in an alternative health centre, and there I learned of many other healing modalities. Soon I was dedicating more and more of my spare time to drumming circles and vision boards, yoga weekends and tantric workshops.

At one stage, chatting with my sisters, I said, 'My rebirther says that every feeling, fully experienced, inevitably turns to joy,' and my sister Rachel said, 'We'll unpack the rest of that sentence in a minute, but let's start with this – you have a rebirther?'

It was at a Heal Your Life workshop based on the book by Louise Hay that I confided to a fellow participant that I wished I could find the thing that would mean I was fixed. And she asked me, 'Why do you think you haven't?'

'Because if I had,' I said, 'I would be able to sustain a romantic relationship for more than a minute and a half.'

She said, 'What if your life is exactly how it's supposed to be?'

The answer came with a clang of clarity. If I had been granted my heart's desire when I was twenty-two, to meet someone and fall in love and live happily ever after, I never would have had the experience of feeling serenity in the aftermath of climbing to the top of the Boboli Gardens in Florence, or done yoga on a beach in Thailand, or hugged the baobab trees in the Okavango Delta of Botswana. And more, I wouldn't have witnessed the courage of battered spirits persisting, day after day. I could have missed meeting the fellow travellers seeking solace in sacred spaces.

If I had been granted my wish, I might never have had the time to develop what I think could be my superpower, making friends.

My wild and wonderful life has grown around my ancient scars, like a pearl around a grain of sand, beautiful not despite it but because of it. What a gift.

So I wasn't seeking anything at all when I struck up a conversation with a nun at a luggage carousel in Copenhagen airport. As we chatted, I realised that she was Sister Breege, who is world-renowned for her healing gifts.

As we were parting, she produced from under her robes a bracelet of turquoise wooden beads and said, 'I'm a matchmaker too,' as she slipped it onto my wrist. It was a rosary bracelet and I was delighted with it, although I thought it was a strange gift to give to a middle-aged woman. Especially as I've worn a wedding ring for years, a trick known to female solo travellers, giving the impression of a male protector about to appear.

And yet as if by magic, not long after that, a tall, dark handsome man took me by the hand, then into his arms and into his heart. And after all those gurus, shamans and voodoo priestesses, it was a good, old-fashioned Irish nun who finally broke the spell and granted my wish.

And as you can hear, I found my voice, too.

BOB SHEPPARD: VOICE OF THE YANKEES

Jonathan White

In September 1968, a colleague of my father's, working for Bord Fáilte in New York, did me perhaps the greatest favour of my life. He brought me to my first baseball game.

I was ten years old, and a passion was born that autumn evening that has lasted me to this day. I had never experienced anything like the sensory overload that awaited me. The jostling crowds making their way into this New World cathedral, the pungent smells of hot dogs and popcorn being prepared, the dazzling emerald that grew larger in front of us as we emerged from a dark tunnel to gape at the floodlit field stretched out in front of us. And almost immediately, echoing around us, a voice for which the adjective 'stentorian' could have been coined, a voice frequently referred to as 'The Voice of God':

'Good evening ... ladies and gentlemen, welcome ... to Yankee Stadium.'

That voice, the voice of Bob Sheppard, had been a fixture in that place since 1951. His first game had also marked the debut of the great Mickey Mantle and was the final opening day of Joe DiMaggio's career. And for fifty-six years, until ill health forced him to step aside from the microphone in September 2007, Bob Sheppard's measured tone and meticulous enunciation contributed significantly to the aura and majesty that surrounded the New York Yankees and their big ballpark in the Bronx. He was very clear, however, on the priorities and limitations of his role as a public address announcer, albeit the best-known one in America.

'A public address announcer,' he said, 'should be clear, concise, correct. He should not be colourful, cute or comic.'

His job consisted of welcoming patrons to the ballpark, announcing the starting line-ups prior to the game and, as each player came to bat, intoning his name and number. He took great pride in giving equal measure to each name, whether a majestic star or a minor player. He also made it his business to check with visitors or Yankee newcomers if he had the correct pronunciation of their names. He revelled in the ever-expanding melting pot from which the game drew its players, as first Hispanic and then Asian names were added to his repertoire. He took particular delight in the likes of Salomé Barojas and Shigetoshi Hasegawa. On the other hand, he maintained that 'Anglo-Saxon names are not very euphonious. What can I do with Steve Sax? What can I do with Mickey Klutts?' His visits to the clubhouse to check a pronunciation were legendary. Pitcher Mike Mussina was asked if it was 'Moosina' or 'Mewsina'. Stunned, he replied, 'Whichever you like.' Sheppard retorted, 'It's not what I like, young man. It's your name.'

Though he was fond of pointing out that 'Most men go to *work*, but I go to a *game*,' nonetheless part of his routine was his meticulous preparation at the end of every contest which allowed him – even at an advanced age – to make a speedy exit, thus allowing him to beat the crowds on his way home to Baldwin, New Jersey.

For his 'other' life was, if anything, more important to Bob Sheppard. A devoted family man, professor of speech at his alma mater, St John's University in New York, a devout Catholic who served as lector not only in his own parish but also, when the Yankees had a Sunday home game, in a makeshift chapel underneath the stands where the congregation consisted of ushers, vendors, reporters and coaches and players from the Yankees and their opponents.

He never retired and cherished the hope that his health would allow him to return, especially when 'his' Yankee Stadium closed at the end of the 2008 season to be replaced by a lavish, updated replica across the street. Bob recorded the Yankee line-up for the final game at the old place, as well as a message for the fans which was accorded one of the biggest ovations on an emotional last night. And there was even more emotion in Yankee hearts like mine when news came through on Sunday 11 July 2010 that Bob Sheppard had passed away, three months short of his one hundredth birthday. Although that was ten years ago, his voice still opens the broadcast of every Yankee game.

In the months and years after 9/11, a feature of all significant Yankee contests was a stirring rendition of 'God Bless America' by the Irish tenor Ronan Tynan. Sheppard – mindful of Tynan's medical qualification in addition to his singing prowess – would always refer in his introduction to 'Doctor Tynan'. Ronan Tynan returned the favour at Bob's funeral by singing 'On Eagle's Wings' and 'Panis Angelicus'.

On the day of his father's death, Paul Sheppard said, 'If you're lucky enough to go to heaven, you'll be greeted by a voice, saying: "Good afternoon, ladies and gentlemen. Welcome to heaven!"'

TEDDY'S IRISH BARDS

Daniel Mulhall

When you have lived abroad for as long as I have, you tend to find echoes of Ireland in the most unusual places. That was the case last summer when I spent a short holiday in the Dakotas, two huge, sparsely populated western American states. Even today they are hard to get to and are often among the last of the fifty US states visited by enthusiastic travellers seeking to see all of America. In the late nineteenth century, they were remote frontier societies that attracted the ambitious and the adventurous.

Theodore Roosevelt, who had a privileged upbringing in New York, fled to the Badlands of North Dakota in the 1880s to seek solace on the American frontier, following the death on the same day of his wife and his mother. When I found myself in the North Dakotan town of Medora, I stayed at the Rough Riders Hotel where the memory of Teddy Roosevelt's two-year spell in the area is richly celebrated.

The hotel lobby boasts an extensive library of books related to Roosevelt and his many interests. I opened a volume of his collected works devoted to literary criticism and, to my amazement, hit upon an intriguing essay on Irish sagas published by Roosevelt in January 1907, while he was President of the United States. It's hard to imagine any serving US president, or Irish taoiseach of recent vintage, having the time or the inclination to undertake such an ambitious scholarly venture.

Roosevelt did not have any ancestral connection with Ireland, and indeed had made his career as a reformer pushing back against Irish-American dominance of New York politics.

In his 1907 essay, Roosevelt lauded early Irish poetry which, he thought, had some 'unique beauties' that were not to be found elsewhere. He drew a politician's conclusion that the Anglo-Norman invasion had had ruinous effects on the growth of national life in Ireland, a sentiment with which I am sure many of us would readily concur.

While he was busy delving into Ireland's antique literature, Roosevelt hosted a distinguished Irish visitor, Douglas Hyde, later Ireland's first president, who was on a seven-month tour of America raising money for the Gaelic League. He travelled to Washington in the winter of 1906 and met with the president at the White House. During a convivial conversation over a simple lunch washed down with a cup of tea and a glass of sherry, Roosevelt revealed that he had been raised by Irish nursemaids from whom he had first heard the legendary names of Cúchulainn and Fionn MacCumhaill. Hyde was impressed by his host's knowledge of Irish and Norse mythology. The president told Hyde that he planned to write to American universities urging them to appoint Irish language professors so as to capture all that was good in Irish life and make it part of America.

Hyde was not the only Irish writer to encounter President Roosevelt during his seven years in high office. During his first visit to America in 1903, W.B. Yeats was invited to the White House to meet the President, who was already an admirer of the Irish Literary Revival. Yeats, who would write approvingly of Constance Markiewicz, when as a young woman she 'rode to harriers', was warned in Washington not to accept an invitation to go horseriding with the president, who was a notoriously vigorous horseman.

While he was president, Roosevelt had the habit of inviting ambassadors to ride with him at pace through Washington's Rock Creek Park, which must have been a bracing experience. Riding the range in the Dakotas as Roosevelt had done for two years would have been a far cry from Yeats's image of the Galway races where:

> Delight makes all of the one mind,
> The riders upon the galloping horses,
> The crowd that closes in behind.

The fact that a famously active American president was willing to make time to meet with two visiting Irish writers highlights the fact that Irish literature was causing quite a stir in those early years of the twentieth century. After he left the presidency, Roosevelt retained an attachment to Irish writing and especially to Lady Gregory, whose work he greatly admired. He sided with the Abbey Theatre against its Irish-American critics of Synge's *Playboy of the Western World* when the Abbey toured the play in America in 1911.

Roosevelt credited the Abbey with having brought about a revival of the ancient Irish spirit, which is precisely how Yeats and Lady Gregory would have seen it. In Roosevelt's view, the Abbey had succeeded because its plays 'spring from the soil' and evoke the heart of the Irish people.

In today's Washington, Roosevelt, who inspired the original teddy bear, is remembered chiefly for his involvement in a mock race against effigies of George Washington, Thomas Jefferson and Abraham Lincoln that takes place every time the city's baseball team plays a home game. It is a contest in which, for some reason, the Roosevelt effigy is always an also ran. Now that would never happen to Cúchulainn, or Fionn MacCumhaill, or to the 'hard-riding country gentlemen' of Yeats's imagination!

GAME, SET AND MATCH

Joe Ó Muircheartaigh

For my brother, my friends and me, when we let our imaginations loose, it was always our sporting daydreams that featured most prominently.

The dreams changed weekly, monthly and yearly.

It could be the World Cup or the Olympics, when we could kick ball like Johan Cruyff or run laps like Lasse Virén, even if the reality was very different.

Every September we were hurlers and footballers, kicking or pucking the winning scores in the All-Ireland with the cheers in our ears.

In April, footballs were kicked to touch, hurleys were downed and golf clubs were picked up and we were storming Augusta National like the young matador Seve Ballesteros en route to winning the Masters.

But no sooner was that over than cues replaced clubs and we were tearing around the snooker table like Alex Higgins, and potting balls for fun.

Meanwhile, those of us in Dublin who had the 'piped television', as it was called, never let a winter pass without plaguing our parents to bring us to the artificial ski slope in Kilternan.

The Dublin Mountains were higher than the Alps, as far as we were concerned. After watching *Ski Sunday*, we knew, given a chance, we could be the next Franz Klammer or Alberto Tomba.

That we were right to dream was brought home to me from mid-March onwards – all those days and nights, weeks and months of no sport, when all we had was our dreams.

These weeks should be Wimbledon's, those weeks where a strange kind of glory comes over all of us. We're not really a tennis nation and never have been, but even if you don't know a tennis racquet from a squash racquet it doesn't matter when it comes to Wimbledon. It sucks you in, seduces you, has you craving strawberries and cream.

Forty years ago, at this time of year, myself and my brother were Bjorn Borg and John McEnroe; we were in Dingle at the start of our summer holidays.

Borg, brooding and beautiful, with the flowing blond locks that seemed more a homage to the Summer of Love or Woodstock than 1980s coiffure.

McEnroe, the brash young New Yorker and as much a Raging Bull as boxer Jake LaMotta ever was, whose hair was more Keith Richards than Flower Power. Both wearing headbands. We wanted those bands badly – but with no Amazon or eBay back in 1980, we improvised with our elasticated nylon football socks.

Racquets in hand, off we went to our Centre Court, a couple of miles east of Dingle to Dúnsíon Strand.

Ours was the first Wimbledon final that depended totally on tidal conditions. It had to be out long enough for the sand to be compacted and hard.

Rain was never going to stop play, but soft sand could.

We mapped out our court with the precision of cartographers charting territory. We'd no nets; we'd no wigs either to complete our carbon-copy looks, but we did have an umpire – my first cousin from up the road, who called us to arms like we were going to war.

And we were. Across a little inlet on Kinard was where patriot Thomas Ashe used to play his pipes. They were the war pipes to us, so we were in the right place.

Borg won the real final in five sets. But ours never got that far, because in acting out the part of McEnroe to perfection, my brother fired more expletives than aces and disputed so many line calls that the umpire was soon swimming off in the direction of the headland where Ashe played his pipes.

We didn't mind, though. Youth was ours, and we were playing out our dreams, just like our contemporaries on beaches and in gardens up and down the country were. Like they might be this week.

As a reminder of what we're missing and what we want back, want back badly. Sport, any sport will do!

MARCHING

Anne Delaney

The Irish have long been marchers; it was a way of life for the ancient Gaels who engaged in constant battles with their neighbours over cattle or territory. Their modus operandi was to march at lightning speed over rough terrain, strike hard and fast, then decamp rapidly with their spoils.

I was reminded last year of the Irish legacy of marching when I visited Donegal Castle. Built in 1494 by the O'Donnell clan, it's an evocative place, with its fifteenth-century cobblestones and its deliberately uneven spiral staircase, cunningly designed to trip invaders, and curving to the right to facilitate the right-handed O'Donnells.

The visit revived schoolday memories of the Battle of Kinsale, when the marching feet of thousands of Donegal men smashed an incredible 300-mile path through a country largely without roads, and gripped by a freeze of epic proportions, to bring aid to their besieged allies in Kinsale.

That marathon march was a stunning achievement, for Ireland was locked in the icy clench of a mini Ice Age in the winter of 1601.

Red Hugh and his army left Donegal on 23 October of that year, banners flying, just as winter was closing in. It's said that the foot soldiers of O'Donnell travelled thirty miles that first day.

They stopped off at the O'Donnell Castle in Ballymote to pick up reinforcements, then marched through Roscommon and Galway and crossed the Shannon to reach Tipperary. There they were blocked by the English Commander George Carew at the head of an army of 4,000.

O'Donnell didn't want to engage prematurely so, to evade Carew, he flung his army on a desperate march through the treacherous bogs of the Slieve Felim mountain passes, under cover of night.

O'Donnell's army must have been a startling sight as they moved by torchlight through a hazardous mountain pass which would normally have been impassable for an army with baggage.

The gamble paid off; the ground was frozen solid that November and so took the weight of the marching army. O'Donnell's exhausted soldiers, calling on an endurance built up over generations, marched non-stop through the night, covering forty bitter miles over rough and dangerous terrain. It's said that Carew, the English commander they foiled with this manoeuvre and a hardened veteran, afterwards admiringly described that nightmare trek as 'the greatest night-march in military history'.

Some months after that visit to Donegal Castle, when my husband and I took a short break in County Antrim, I was reminded that people from this island are still marching. We had set out early on the morning of our holiday, keen to explore a part of the island we had never visited. It was a hot day, so we decided to stop off for refreshments in the small village of Dervock. We had just parked our car when an explosive, powerfully assertive rap of sound made us jump. It didn't take us long to realise its significance.

We had never witnessed an Orange march before that day. But we soon realised that we were to be initiated, for the Dervock Young Defenders Flute Band, self-described as a Blood and Thunder Flute Band, was on parade that afternoon.

The atmosphere in the village made us slightly uneasy but we were drawn in by the pageantry of it all. I was particularly fascinated by the Lambeg drummer, who seemed to be the focal point of the parade. He was in constant motion, gliding from side to side with a kind of prancing grace as, elbows flailing, he pounded on an enormous drum.

I learned afterwards that the skill of Lambeg drumming probably came to Ireland with the Plantations of the seventeenth century. The art has been passed down through generations of Orange marchers. The drum is usually made of oak and tightly cinched goatskin, so that it emits a fierce punching beat. It is a sound designed to instil fear, and we became a little unsettled that day in Dervock, and soon made an unobtrusive exit.

Later that evening, we reflected on our lack of insight into the traditions of those who live so near to us. We had, of course, known of the famous marches of 12 July and 12 August. But we were totally unaware that thousands of smaller Orange marches routinely take place all over Northern Ireland every year, starting around late spring, and continuing till late September.

I can still remember the effortless, relentless gait of those marchers in Dervock – wave after wave of people who looked as if they could march forever. Is it possible that the tradition of Orange marching is somehow linked in to those other powerful Ulster marchers from a different culture and a different time?

I sometimes wonder about that.

CONFESSOR TO THE KING

John Hedigan

On 21 January 1793, as he faced the guillotine, Louis XVI, King of France, was attended by an Irish-born priest, Henry Edgeworth, known in France as Abbé Edgeworth de Firmont.

Henry Essex Edgeworth was born in St John's Rectory in Edgeworthstown, County Longford in 1745, but raised in Toulouse in France, to where his father, the Church of Ireland rector of Edgeworthstown, was obliged to move his family following his rather sensational decision to convert to Catholicism. Young Henry studied for the priesthood and was ordained as a Catholic priest in Paris. At this time, he adopted the addition of de Firmont to his name, Firmount being the name of an estate in Ireland that the family owned.

Over the following twenty years he devoted himself to a ministry of the poor in the slums of Paris. His reputation grew such that on the recommendation of the Archbishop of Paris, he was chosen by the King's sister, Elizabeth of France, as her confessor. He thus became a frequent visitor to the Tuileries palace and this role led to his part in one of the most important events in the French Revolution.

A full account of the heroic part he played in those chaotic days in French history is provided for us by Abbé Edgeworth's own memoir of the last hours of King Louis's life, written after his almost miraculous escape from France.

On the eve of his execution, the doomed King requested, on the suggestion of his sister, that the Abbé attend him. The Minister of Justice himself carried the request to the priest and accompanied him to the Temple prison where the King was held. They arrived at a scene that was almost apocalyptic. Drunken guards of fearsome demeanour at times blocked their way. It was, recalled the Abbé, horrible beyond description.

After some time, they were led up a narrow, winding stairway into the presence of the King. The Minister of Justice read the Decree of Execution, fixed for the following morning. The King was calm – the only calm person present, according to the Abbé. When he saw the priest, the King ushered all out of the room and closed the door himself.

Over the following hours, priest and King prayed and conversed deeply and intimately. Much of what transpired, the Abbé did not reveal. What he did describe was a scene of great sadness but resignation on the part of the King, and a determination to meet his end with dignity. He witnessed, at some slight remove, the heart-rending farewells the King was allowed with his wife and children.

Astonishingly, Abbé Edgeworth persuaded the King's captors to allow him to celebrate Mass in the King's cell. To their protests that they could not find a priest or the things necessary to celebrate a Mass, the Abbé replied,

'The priest is found, I am he; the nearest church will supply all that is required.'

Thus, he put his own head on the block. Revolutionaries were hunting priests all over France.

The following morning, in the King's chamber, the Abbé found an altar, perfectly prepared with everything required – more even than he had asked. King and confessor celebrated Mass together.

At eight o'clock the King, accompanied by a large guard of soldiers, departed the Temple for the place of execution. To the surprise of both King and priest, the Abbé was allowed to accompany him in the carriage. The journey was at a snail's pace through crowded streets, with military present to forestall any rescue attempt. The King read from the priest's breviary.

Just after ten o'clock, they arrived at Place de la Révolution, today's Place de la Concorde. A vast crowd was gathered there, contained by apparently endless massed ranks of soldiers. The King alighted from the carriage and insisted on removing his scarf and jacket himself. The executioners produced a rope to tie his hands. The King shrank back in horror.

'Do what you have been ordered, but you shall never bind me,' he said.

The Abbé recalled this as probably the most terrible moment of that dreadful morning. The King stared in desperation at him, his only friend present. It seemed the men would lay hands upon the King, which was unthinkable. They explained to the Abbé that it was necessary to bind the King's hands to prevent their interfering with the falling blade. A terrible impasse seemed inevitable. The King continued to look desperately at the priest for guidance. And then the Abbé spoke.

'Sire, in this latest outrage, I see only the last trace of resemblance between your Majesty and the God who is about to reward you.'

This brilliant piece of emotional intelligence gave the poor King the ability to see himself as Christ bound and led to the slaughter. He raised his eyes to heaven and said,

'Surely nothing less than His example could make me submit to a similar affront. Do what you will. I will drink from this chalice even to the dregs.'

His hands were then bound, though not with rope. The chief executioner, thinking the King's objection was to a rope, took off his own scarf and bound the King's hands with it.

King and confessor, arm in arm, climbed the steps of the scaffold. As he reached it, the King stepped firmly forward and addressed the crowd in a strong and resonant voice.

'I die innocent of all the crimes laid at my charge; I pardon those who have occasioned my death; and I pray to God, that the blood you are now going to shed may never be visited on France.'

He would have continued but the drums were ordered to be beaten to drown out anything further he might say. He was then bundled quickly under the guillotine.

As the blade descended, the Abbé Edgeworth de Firmont fell to his knees upon the scaffold, his final words to the dying King heard by everyone around:

'*Fils de Saint Louis, montez au ciel.*' 'Son of Saint Louis, ascend to heaven.'

NO REGRETS

Frank Keegan

When I eased back on the control column, the nose of the Boeing 737 lifted slowly over the end of the runway and above the glittering yellow lights of the Eternal City of Rome. Having overflown the city, I engaged the Boeing's automatic pilot and set course on the 2,500-kilometre flight to Dublin.

We had been delayed in Rome Ciampino airport, and it was in the wee small hours of the morning that I climbed the Boeing along the coast of the Tyrrhenian Sea. Back in the cabin, almost 200 passengers settled down with a snack, drinks or snuggled into their blankets. The cabin crew dimmed the lights for sleep.

Shortly afterwards we crossed over the French coast at Nice and tracked the necklace of lights stretching ahead along the Rhône Valley. We now bade *arrivederci* to Rome air traffic control, and switched over to French radar in Paris.

The French controller welcomed us with typical Gallic nonchalance.

My co-pilot on this trip was a very new, very affable, and very enthusiastic young 25-year-old. Besides being an excellent pilot, he also happened to enjoy making radio calls. This is a common condition with all new pilots and generally lasts until the flying hours build up and the novelty wears off a little bit.

Now, a very important aviation radio procedure consists in checking in with air traffic control every ten minutes. During normal hours this isn't needed, because there's so much traffic, radio calls are taking place constantly anyway. But tonight, unusually, we were the only aircraft operating in that part of the night sky. Therefore, my co-pilot set his timer running and every ten minutes on the dot he called the French controller.

The radio patter sounded something like this:

'Paris control, Ryanair 242, flight level 400, radio check.'

'Uhhmmm. Ryanair 242, reading you strength 5.' (Strength 5 is radio shorthand for reading you loud and clear.)

'Ryanair 242, Roger. Strength 5.'

As we routed towards the east of Paris my co-pilot made these identical radio checks religiously every ten minutes, and all with the same air traffic controller.

In my mind's eye, I visualised the controller almost alone in a vast ATC centre, watching a single green dot representing our radar signature, blipping very slowly across his screen. I imagined him puffing on a Gauloise with an overflowing ashtray and a plastic cup of tepid coffee on his desk, his reverie rudely interrupted every ten minutes by an Irish voice from 40,000 feet, calling for another identical radio check.

As our flight progressed and the number of radio checks totted up, I vaguely detected a declining enthusiasm in his response. However, it was a beautiful night for flying and I didn't want to disrupt the soothing ambience of this very peaceful star-flight.

Our flight plan took us to a navigation beacon close to the old rugby stadium at Colomiers, a place well known to Irish rugby fans of a certain vintage. After Colomiers, we turned towards the Channel coast at Boulogne.

Now, with the shimmering lights of Paris glowing on my left, my co-pilot requested the radio check, once again.

Silence ensued for about ten seconds and then the radio crackled into life:

'Uhhmmm. Are you feeling lonely up there tonight, Ryanair? Would you like me to sing you a little song?'

It took a couple of seconds for this surprising reply to register. My co-pilot glanced over at me, wide-eyed and stuck for words. Perhaps subconsciously commenting on his career choice of late-night air traffic controlling, with little or no thought I keyed my microphone:

'How about Edith Piaf and "No Regrets?"'

After a few seconds' pause, our French friend replied with a hearty laugh and we three joined together in a moment of air to ground laughter, spanning an arc of hundreds of nautical miles across the airwaves.

Some ten minutes later as we approached the coast at Boulogne, our ATC friend called us for the final time and bid us '*Au revoir ... merci!*'

My co-pilot bid him farewell with, '*Merci* and *slán leat.*'

A double click from the controller's microphone wrapped up this very human exchange within the normally high-tech and businesslike world of aviation.

With the sun now rising behind us and the yellow lights of London glowing over the nose of the cockpit, we crossed over the English Channel towards Dublin and home.

STEAMBOAT

Andrew Doherty

'Steamboat …!'

The call rang out across the estuary, and fishermen in every small punt within earshot jerked their heads around. Our small open wooden punts were ranged across the river on an afternoon flood tide.

Overhead, the sun beat down on a wonderful July afternoon ashore but a south-westerly wind meant that a jumper and oilskin were essential kit on the water. Downriver, the estuary widened, creating the shorelines of Waterford and Wexford, which guided the three sister rivers of the Barrow, Nore and Suir to the sea. The sisters met at Cheekpoint and it was also the junction for the ports of Waterford and New Ross, a busy shipping area that presented additional challenges for fishermen. Now, a huge ship was surging up the estuary, the bow opening up on Buttermilk Castle on the Wexford shore. Her speed was apparent in the progress she made and soon the entire length of the ship was obvious as the white superstructure appeared astern, where a pilot advised her captain on the channel.

'Steambooooat …!'

A more theatrical cry, further up the estuary, and within moments every punt, from Mourne's Poles, Mount Quay, Cheekpoint and the Rookery was on alert. Some took little notice, secure in the knowledge that because of where their nets were currently drifting, they were outside the onrushing ship's reach. Others had more precarious positions to assess. These were just off the main channel and could with some degree of certainty leave the nets as they were, but perhaps they might lower the outboard engine and steam out to stand by the outer end, better to mark their position. Several, however, were like us: drifting across the channel and needing to haul the nets aboard; the drift was gone and they were cursing their luck.

Paul Duffin and myself were in our early twenties, but already seasoned salmon fishermen from the village of Cheekpoint. Our tar-hulled punt with green topworks and a white painted band had caught its fair share of salmon that summer using the light-green nylon driftnets that hung in a curtained line in the water, hoping to snare the king of all fish.

Earlier we had come across on the flood tide from the village, our punt jostling with the others on the Shelburne banks, on the Wexford shore. As the black swathe of mud was covered by the incoming tide, it was followed by noisy seabirds who hungrily hunted across it on webbed feet for shellfish. Eventually, we got an opportunity to set our nets in towards the bank and then, with strokes on the oars, we drifted apace, constantly watching for signs of our prey. Later, we would haul the nets aboard, having drifted to Great Island Power Station and then steamed back down against the tide to try to reset once more. It was at that point, with the tide rising high on the mud, that we opted to set half and half: half the nets on the tide, half on the shallow waters with the now covered mud. A good drift, but the risk was that as we dragged off the mud and away into the tide, a ship would come.

Steamboat ... Paul took the cork rope, I took the lead rope and, tensing our muscles, we started to haul, hand over hand.

Steamboat. It was an odd word when you thought about it in this age of oil-fuelled vessels. The first regular coal-burning steamboat in these waters arrived in 1826 when the *Norah Creina* spurned reliance on sail and wind, bringing a greater degree of regularity between Waterford and her ancient trading link of Bristol. Nearly 150 years later in 1962, the last steamer crossed between Waterford and Liverpool: Clyde Shipping's *Rockabill*, although in 1985, one steamer remained in the harbour. She was no danger to fishermen for she was a slow-moving dredger called the *Portlairge* which clung tenaciously to coal and steam. Her skipper was Michael Heffernan, originally from Cheekpoint, and Michael and his crew would no more come near a driftnet than we would go near a water bailiff. No, the shout that warned of ships was just a tradition, and the fishermen of Waterford harbour were nothing if not immersed in traditions.

Paul and I had over half the nets aboard when the steamboat passed. Or in this case, a shiny blue container ship, powered by oil and owned by the

Waterford-based Bell Lines Company. Many of the crew were men from around the harbour and beyond; if they had their way they would try and avoid us too, but their master was on a time schedule and nothing could be allowed to slow his journey into port.

Our drift was done and with our empty nets aboard, we faced a decision. Fish don't ring bells, they say, and maybe the next drift might reward us. But closer to high tide meant more chance of ships! And we dreaded hearing that cry again that day, at least on the same tide ... 'Steamboat!'

BLOODY FRIDAY

Olive Travers

In the summer of 1972, Alice Cooper's hit 'School's Out' captured my mood. With A Levels over, I was heading off to Scotland to work in a fruit-canning factory. After eighteen years on a small farm in rural Fermanagh, Scotland seemed as exotic a destination to me then as Timbuktu. I bought a trendy duffle bag into which I packed my treasured new hot pants, my purple velvet smock, my white tights and my checked Oxford bags.

It was a beautiful day when I met my schoolfriend Margaret in Enniskillen to hitchhike to Belfast. With my duffle bag on my back, I felt myself on the edge of a world of boundless possibilities. With lorry drivers as our knights in shining armour we made good time. Our ferry sailed at midnight; our plan was to spend the day checking out the clothes shops in the city centre.

It was not to be. In Belfast our lorry driver was forced to stop at the top of the Donegall Road. At a checkpoint, young soldiers shouted at us to keep our heads down as someone was shooting at them. Terrified, we crouched down, and the driver swung into Sandy Row, but there, a tartan gang carrying clubs headed towards us. The driver, with an air of calm resignation, told us it was the lorry they wanted, and we would be okay. The same soldiers came to his rescue, but they ordered us out so they could search our bags. They looked no older than us, and when they got a look at us with our flowery bags, off on our big adventure, they chatted and joked with us instead of doing a bag search.

Our shopping plans were back on target, or so we thought, before we walked unsuspectingly into one of the most horrific days of the Troubles Belfast would ever experience.

As was later reported, at least nineteen IRA bombs exploded in the city centre in an eighty-minute period that day; nine people would die, and 130 would be injured.

In the letter I wrote home later, I described my experience.

'Honestly,' I wrote, 'It was really awful. Ambulances and fire brigades screeching, explosions going off and people running everywhere, some with blood streaming down their face. Someone would tell us to run as it was dangerous where we were, so off we would go. We would meet people rushing in the opposite direction and they would shout at us not to go that way. Then we would run another way and be turned back from there. We didn't know what to do. There were explosions all over the place and rubble everywhere.'

I did not say in my letter how I saw my own terror reflected in the eyes of all those running in fear for their lives, and how I would have given anything then to be back in the home I had been so anxious to leave.

Somehow, we made our way to the docks, but we weren't allowed into the ferry terminus. Exhausted and out of options, we sat on the pavement. Soldiers suddenly surrounded us. I asked one if we were safe where we were. His not-very-reassuring reply was that we would be, if the next bomb was less than 20 lb! Where to go? Margaret found the crumpled phone number of a seventeen-year-old boy called Barney whom she'd met in Bundoran. We found a phone box and rang him. Like a miracle, he appeared in a black taxi and brought us to his home in Andersonstown. After his mammy had given us tea and homemade apple tart, we returned to the docks to see the twisted metal of a 50 lb bomb which had destroyed the Liverpool Bar, strewn over the same pavement where we'd been sitting.

I only made contact with home by letter when we eventually got to the factory in Scotland two days later, as my parents didn't have a telephone. I didn't know that until they got my letter, they were frantic with worry, having seen on television the shocking images of mutilated bodies being swept up and collected in black plastic bags. The impact of the bombs was so horrific that for several days it was believed that the death toll was much higher than nine, and my parents had no way of knowing that I was not among the dead.

My mother kept my letter, and I have it now. There is something unusual about it.

My mother always opened letters carefully with a paper knife, but this envelope is roughly torn open. Its jagged, uneven edges bring a whole new realisation to me of her relief when the letter arrived.

Today, as I do every year on 21 July, I remember the victims of that day known as Bloody Friday, and the families for whom no letter arrived.

A DOG BARKING IN THE DARKNESS

JM Dolan

The 29th of July 1958 was a warm, sunny day in Dublin. He went to seven o'clock Mass as usual in Church Street, or could it have been John's Lane? We don't know, but we do know that he helped Mrs Mulhall remove the heavy wooden shutters from her shop front window at number – well, we're not quite sure, North King Street. He would have been travelling by bike, a bike he had christened 'Trigger'. He was our father and we would never see him again.

Back home in Manor Street in Stoneybatter we had risen to a beautiful summer's morning. By the time I was up, my brother Matt, six years older than me, had already mixed a bucket of whitewash using water and Reckitt's Blue, all done under the watchful eye of our mother. who was always encouraging, but might have added a harmless criticism such as 'Darling, you're not doing it right,' and then retrieve it all with an, 'Oh to be young!' The reason for the whitewash was that our house had a backyard and the wall that faced on to the kitchen was used as a trap to reflect sunlight into a very dark room.

It was the sound of the new doorbell that stopped the work. My father had just installed it a few days previous. It had a luminous red light at its centre. *Bzzzz.* I stood in the back hall and watched as my father's bike 'Trigger' and my brother Shay's bike 'Topper' were led in, but both of them were being led by strangers. I can still feel that midsummer heat and smell the floor polish on the lino floor. I can still see the blanched face of my mother as she opened the door.

'Which of them is it?'

She knew right away that either her husband or her son had been killed, she just didn't know which one.

Soon the house was crammed with people: family, neighbours, priests, nuns, while aunts in flowery aprons made sandwiches and pots of tea. Hushed groups whispered in corners.

'Ten children, Lord save us.'

'They say the good die young.'

'Oh, you're right there, Jack.' An uncle put his hand on my head, 'God help ye, ye poor gosson.'

A neighbour gave me a shilling. My ashen-faced grandmother, in a black shawl, mouthed silent prayers with rosary beads clasped in her gnarled fingers. My mother sat surrounded in the parlour streamed in sunlight, shaken and distraught, like a little bird with a broken wing. The two bicycles leaned against the wall in the hall and two uneaten packed lunches rested on the hall table.

Later in the afternoon my brothers and I were sent to our Aunt Peggy, who lived on Carnew Street. Our cousins invited us to play football with the other lads in the back lane. The game was very competitive and suddenly the day became normal again. A couple of hours later we were called in for tea. At the back gate of the house a group of kids stood around a dead cat. One of them poked it with a stick, another rolled his bicycle wheel over its stomach. My brother Matt looked at me and said, 'Daddy's dead.'

'I know,' I said, pretending I hadn't forgotten.

After tea we all went for a walk in the Phoenix Park. Although it was evening time the heat was becoming even more intense, and ominous clouds filled the skies over Dublin. We decided to head home and were passing Aughrim Street Chapel when a sheet of lightning followed by the roar of thunder stopped us in our tracks. The heavens opened, and we ran into the church porch for refuge. From there we could see the life-sized crucifixion scene with hail and rain lashing against the face of the dead Christ. I said to my brothers, 'Is this the end of the world?' They both just laughed.

Later, lying in bed, I looked out the window at the night sky, now calm, silvery and starry. I spent the night tossing and turning, trying to make some sense of it all. At the back of my mind was the nagging thought that maybe I was in some way the cause of what had happened. Dawn was breaking and the Angelus bell was ringing in Stanhope Street Convent when I finally fell asleep. I dreamt that I saw him walking along the Bull Wall; he was playing his harmonica. He was far in the distance, and I called to him, 'Daddy, Daddy, you're alive, you're alive!' But he couldn't hear me and didn't look back, he just kept playing his harmonica, walking slowly towards the sea until I couldn't see him any more.

The earliest memory I have of my father is of being brought down to the small back room when I was sick and being given an Aspro. I'd had a nightmare. My father was lighting his pipe; the name of the tobacco was 'Friendly' and it came in a bar wrapped in cellophane. He struck a match, and it seemed like silver stars glowed on the ceiling as he inhaled. My mother held me in her arms, and I fell asleep as my father smoked his pipe, and that safe, beautiful feeling will live with me forever.

My father was a carpenter and on the day that he died, he was installing sash windows on the fourth floor of a block of flats that was being constructed in Summerhill. My eldest brother Shay, who was only eighteen at the time, was working with him; years later he told me exactly what had happened. My father was on the scaffolding, which was made of timber, and Shay was inside the building. He was having a problem holding a very heavy concrete lintel and my father told him to pass it through the window to him, whereupon the scaffold plank broke in two; he fell forty feet and was killed instantly.

I also learned from my mother that a few weeks before he was killed he told her that some of the scaffolding planks were rotten. This still haunts me. The fact that he knew of the danger but was willing to take the risk for the sake of his family.

It was only when I was grown up that she started talking to me about him again. She told me he was afraid of the dark ever since he was a child when, during the War of Independence, the British Army raided the house in the middle of the night and put a gun to his father's head.

And she spoke of their last night together in 81 Manor Street. She said they heard a dog barking all night, and ever since then she hated that sound. I can see them in my mind's eye, holding each other close in the bed in the small room, not knowing that this would be their last night together, listening to a dog barking in the darkness.

249

SHAKING GOD'S HAND

Joe Kearney

Some time ago I found God. He was standing beside me at a lunch counter in Kilkenny City. I'd probably have failed to notice him if it wasn't for the special attention and smiles he was getting from the waiting staff. We stood side by side, shuffling along with our food trays and it was only when he turned to leave the counter that I caught sight of Brian Cody's unmistakable face. Without thinking, I leaned towards him and stuck out my hand. He hesitated for the briefest of seconds, balanced his food tray against his hip and extended his own hand in greeting. I mumbled some obsequious inanity as we awkwardly pressed flesh. Although I can't recall what I said, I do remember that handshake. It was warm and firm, yet slightly yielding, somewhat like a loaf of crusty bread fresh from the oven. Those are the hands he will spit into and rub together today, for all the world like a man preparing to split wood or drive a pickaxe into unyielding ground.

Ironically, the café where we met was within a sliotar puc of Kilkenny Castle. And in his day Cody could have easily bent, lifted and struck the small ball high over its crenellated walls and into the grounds. It was there in 1366 that the English Lord Lieutenant summoned a parliament to pass a number of statutes buttressing the Crown's position in Ireland. The Anglo-Irish were forbidden to use the Irish language. They could not sell horses or armour to the natives and they were expressly forbidden from playing hurling. When you think about it, this latter restrictive statute could perhaps be understood. Hurling has long had a martial history. It is known to have evolved as a form of battle training for Irish warriors. In the eighth century, under the Brehon laws, it was used as a mechanism to solve disputes between neighbouring communities. The laws went as far as setting out a scale of compensation for the families of anyone killed in these spirited sporting encounters.

There is a saying that boasts, 'The men of Ireland were hurling when the Gods of Greece were young.' This claim may be true.

The Annals of the Four Masters record a mythological battle between the Tuatha de Danaan and the Fir Bolg in 1272 BC. The encounter is claimed to have lasted four days and approximately 4,000 warriors were slaughtered in the encounter. In the days preceding the battle, a great hurling match was played. The finest warriors from the opposing sides lined up, twenty-seven on each team. This was a warm-up to the main event, a little limbering up before the battle, just to get the adrenalin flowing. Records are confused regarding the outcome of the hurling match, with some accounts stating that the Fir Bolg won and immediately killed all twenty-seven of the opposing team. If this was the case it proved a little rash, as the Tuatha were victorious in the ensuing battle.

In pre-Famine times, during periods of political unrest, hurling games were often used as a smokescreen for political rallies. There are multiple reports of these events, many taking place in Kilkenny. In 1765, several thousand people assembled at a bog in Mooncoin for a Sunday game that had little to do with hurling but much to do with injustice and the Penal Laws. In January 1831, so-called hurlers assembled at Callan. This time, tithe gathering was at the centre of the unrest. Once more, agitation overtook the beautiful game. It is recorded that for appearance's sake, they once or twice threw the sliotar into the air and took a few harmless swings, but their hearts and motives were elsewhere. On these occasions, as can be understood, tempers were known to boil over. In that same town of Callan, local diarist Humphrey O'Sullivan recorded an entry for 29 June 1827:

'Feast of Saint Peter and Paul, a holiday ... hurling on the green ... the sticks were being brandished like swords. Hurling is a war-like game. You could hear them striking from one end of the field to the other.'

He goes on: 'I was knocked down by a young brat, but it was nothing to be ashamed of, as I brought him down as well.'

Humphrey's observations from the nineteenth century are nothing new. When I was growing up in that town, I recall overhearing my Uncle Jimmy explaining how he had stopped bringing my Auntie Agnes to club hurling games. He claimed he was fed up finishing the sideline fights she was inclined to start.

Many times, we have heard the great GAA commentator Mícheál Ó Muircheartaigh crooning how hurling is a game for the gods, played by gods. Whatever today's outcome, win or lose, I will feel my right hand tingle and know that on one perfectly ordinary lunchtime in Kilkenny I once shook the hand of God.

REEK SUNDAY

Bernard Dunleavy

My father's first job was as a cashier in Bank of Ireland. There wasn't officially a level of employment more junior than cashier, but if there had been a tier beneath this entry grade, it was those cashiers who were assigned to what was known as 'relief staff'. As a relief cashier, my father travelled all around the country providing cover wherever there was a vacancy in a branch which was not yet filled.

It was a hardship posting, a sort of Russian Front of the banking world. A transitory existence where the men – and they were only men in those days – put in their time hoping for a final posting of some permanence and perhaps the chance of promotion. Nobody wanted to stay on relief staff: nobody that is, except my father. He loved it!

The place he was sent that he liked best of all was Westport. He had grown up in Paulstown in County Kilkenny, far from the sea, and the sense of possibility which came with proximity to the limitless Atlantic gave him a thrill which lasted a lifetime.

Westport is a town which sits in the shadow of Croagh Patrick, or the Reek as the locals call it. My father lived in digs where his landlady had, as a young girl, climbed the mountain each day to bring lunch to the twelve men who worked on the construction of the church at the summit during 1905. Years later, when he had moved a long way from Westport and when recalling that story reminded him of how much he missed the place, he bought himself a special climbing stick, curved at the top and with a sharp metal point at the bottom – what the Germans call an Alpenstock – and we spoke about how we'd get to the top together some day.

My father's sudden death meant that we never did get to climb the mountain, and for several years afterwards I forgot all about that plan.

However, I kept my father's old Alpenstock after he died. I didn't have a use for it, but it reminded me of him.

'I'm going on a pilgrimage,' I said to my eldest daughter six years ago. 'I'm going to climb a mountain.' I didn't really ask her if she would join me and she didn't really say that she would, but in that way where things that are only mentioned as possibilities move towards things that are accepted as eventualities, we found ourselves on the road to Mayo one Saturday afternoon. Nothing – nothing that is except a brief stop in Supermac's in Ballinalack as a concession to my travelling companion – could deflect us from our path towards Westport. We arrived in the town on the eve of Reek Sunday, the last Sunday in July, and the annual pilgrimage up the mountain. Except there wasn't any pilgrimage that year. The following day, for the first time in a millennium, the pilgrimage was cancelled. A freak hurricane had struck the mountain overnight and stormy conditions had made the climb treacherous.

Nobody told us.

When we woke up, we didn't bother turning on the news. We saw the miserable conditions but no one in our hotel enquired where we were going. By the time we got to Croagh Patrick we were so late that the stewards and marshals who might have warned us off the mountain had melted away with the rain. Before we started to climb, I took my father's stick out of the back of the car and tucked it under my arm.

We met pensioners in bare muddy feet. We met two mothers who carried children up the mountain in their arms through the rain. We met cheerful groups of young Traveller men who told us a prayer at the top would release a soul from purgatory. 'Safe up,' everyone said as we passed.

All of this was a welcome distraction, because Croagh Patrick is a hard climb. That year the climb was measured not in hours but in chocolate bars, as I tried to coax my eight-year-old daughter up the slope. Just when I thought that I had estimated a Mars Bar too few to get us to the summit, suddenly there was the simple church in front of us. My left fist was closed over my daughter's hand to keep it warm. In my right hand was my father's stick. Kneeling around us were pilgrims whose reasons for climbing were as individual as our own. We said a prayer for my father and then we slipped and slid back the way we had come. Safe down.

We were both quiet for a long time on the road back to Dublin and eventually I asked my daughter what she was thinking. There was a long pause that stretched on as she seemed to struggle to put all she had seen and experienced on the mountain into words.

'Dad' she said, 'if we go next year ...'

'Yes ...?'

'... I hope we get to stop for burgers in Ballinalack again.'

ISLAND DEVOTIONS

Geraldine Mitchell

Islands wear collars crocheted
from waves, necklets of glitter,
beaches like bolts of raw silk.

They hear silence
nibbled by wind,
water dribbling in ditches,

a tatter of gulls round a currach
out to haul pots,
its faint putter.

They're puckered appliqué,
patches sewn to a bucking sea
tethered to the mainland by ferries.

Islanders keep their islands
pinned to their hearts,
secular scapulars.

AUGUST

MY FRIEND, THE DUKE

Paddy Murray

It was the summer of 1974. I was a young reporter in my first year with the *Evening Herald*.

Every day back then, mid-morning would always see an exodus from the newsroom once the first edition was gone. Most of the reporters went for tea or coffee; one or two headed for their first pint of the day.

I was the cubbest of cub reporters, so I stayed behind. One morning, as the others left, my news editor took a call. He hung up and looked around for a reporter. And there I was.

'Young fella,' he called. 'Go up to the Gresham Hotel. Someone says John Wayne is there.' It was not much more than twenty years since the release of *The Quiet Man*, the film which made John Wayne a hero, and a legend in Ireland. This was pretty big news. So why did a cub reporter get the job?

I suspect it was largely because the whole thing seemed unlikely. Big movie stars didn't show up in Dublin hotels and give an interview to the first reporter who asked, did they? So send the cub. At least it'll get him out of the office for a while.

I strolled up to the Gresham with our photographer, the late Eamonn Gilligan. We headed straight to the dining-room, having been told that John Wayne was having breakfast there.

And so he was.

There was no security, no minders, no handlers. Nor was there any point in beating about the bush. Either he'd talk to us or he wouldn't. And so I walked over and said, 'Excuse me, Mr Wayne. My name is Paddy Murray and I'm with the *Evening Herald* newspaper. I was wondering if I could have a word?'

He looked up and smiled. 'Sit down young feller,' he said, 'and have breakfast with me.' And I did, and so did Eamonn.

'So, I guess you're a reporter,' he said. 'And who do you work for?'

'The *Evening Herald*,' I reminded him.

'And do you like working for them?' he asked me. I told him I did, as it became clear that it was he who was interviewing me. He asked a few more questions. Did I go to the movies, what movies did I like, to which I of course replied, 'Westerns.'

Eventually I got to ask him about *Brannigan*, the movie he was making in London. It was a part he chose having turned down the role of Dirty Harry, subsequently taken by Clint Eastwood.

He didn't know Dublin had a famous detective called Brannigan known to one and all as Lugs. He laughed. 'If I had known that I might have called myself Lugs in the movie,' he said.

We chatted about *The Quiet Man* and his memories of making that classic movie in the West. 'Ireland is the most beautiful country in the world for making films,' he said. 'I would dearly like to make another film here. But it would have to be personal, and those scripts are hard to find.' He reminded me that his ancestors came from somewhere in County Cork.

We talked, too, of his admiration for Richard Nixon. A fine American, he said. He had ended the Vietnam War when two other popular presidents couldn't. A man who had done nothing wrong, he said – just weeks, as it happens, before the disgraced president quit.

What had him in Dublin, I wondered.

He had come, he told me, to meet his 'good friend Lord Killanin'.

'And when are you meeting him?'

'I'm not,' he replied. 'Turns out he's in Zurich.'

So on we chatted as he tucked into two fried eggs, half a dozen rashers, a few sausages, tea and toast. He was a thorough gentleman, and made sure there was tea and toast for us too.

As I stood to thank him – deadlines, you know, we could have chatted all day otherwise – he asked me where he might get a 'báinín hat and a blackthorn stick'.

Just up from the main door of the Gresham back then, where Toddy's Bar is now, there was a souvenir shop, and so John and I – he told me he didn't mind me calling him John – walked together up O'Connell Street, to the astonishment of the city's citizens.

Eamonn snapped away with his camera, taking photographs of the movie star and the cub reporter as wide-eyed Dubliners looked, stared and stepped forward to shake the hand of a man who was then, and is forever, a movie legend.

And while John managed to get his souvenirs, I have none. Because I have no idea where the picture of the two of us on O'Connell Street is now. The photograph of John Wayne and a group of Dublin admirers appeared in the paper, but not the one of him and me together.

Sadly, John never got to make another movie in Ireland. He died less than five years after that day we met in the Gresham.

But at least I have the memory. And so, if the name of John Wayne ever comes up in conversation and I'm asked did I ever meet him, I can reply smugly, 'Meet him? Of course I did. Sure, we had breakfast together.'

THE NON-WEDDING PHOTO

Farah Abushwesha

There are no wedding photos of our parents. They got married in Granada, Spain, each in a clean pair of jeans.

But recently I restored a hazy 1970s photo of them in Tripoli's Martyrs' Square. I'm missing from this period of my parents' life, as I'm in Dublin with my Irish grandparents. It's one of few photos we have of them together, and was taken shortly before Dad was placed under house arrest.

My parents seem so glamorous, standing in front of a white car, dusk-lit palm trees in the background. Him, a writer, in dark jeans, open, blue-striped shirt, buckled leather belt, stubble. Her, an artist, in white jeans and pink shirt, her long dark hair tumbling over her right shoulder. Her hair was the envy and wonder of many, often touched by curious strangers on the Tripoli streets; she'd tie it up with a pen or wash it in the kitchen sink, to the bemusement of her Libyan in-laws.

The reconditioned photo reveals Mom is wearing silver platform sandals – no doubt height-checked: I often recall my parents standing before a mirror to ensure Mom wasn't towering above Dad when she was wearing heels. There's a chain around Dad's neck, and an elephant hair bracelet he wore for luck. He's beaming, an eyebrow slightly raised, and he's leaning for effect on a walking stick. He oozes charm if not a little madness, and he's holding a cigarette.

Mom is wearing sunglasses, yet it's early evening. Her fingers entwined, she's smiling, slightly self-consciously. Her ability to draw fascinated me: pictures at her fingertips. They look in their mid-twenties, but they're already in their early thirties, a decade of an eccentric, tumultuous life together behind them.

They met in McDaid's pub, at a reading of my uncle Macdara Woods's poetry, and first lived together in Ireland before moving to Granada, six months or so before the clean jeans wedding: it's where they made me. Then to London for a time, where we resided with the historian AJP Taylor. We moved next to Azziziha, the small Libyan town Dad grew up in. Mom loved my Libyan granny's Azziziha home, a single light bulb hanging from the ceiling reminding her of her grandmother's farm in Athboy, County Meath in the 1950s. We finally settled in a small terraced house in Tripoli, the last place I knew there as our family home.

My favourite story of Mom and Dad is of them stuck in traffic in the car from the photo. Near this spot is Martyrs' Square. Dad couldn't drive, but he was a terribly bossy passenger seat driver, instructing Mom to 'Turn, Orla, turn, go this way – no, no, that way, Orla, look, Orla, look!' On one occasion, fed up, she opened the car door, got out and walked off, leaving him stranded in a pile-up of traffic, unable to drive away.

We travelled through the square on our way to the family farm, sometimes with Mom driving, and sometimes in a shared people-taxi. There, our big extended, noisy Libyan family would sit on cushioned floors: generations eating, gossiping, combing hair, applying henna tattoos whilst drinking sha'hee; men in one area, women in the other. Before I left Tripoli, when I was seven, my Libyan grandmother intricately hennaed my legs with spirals and flowers. When my Irish granny, a teacher, saw them, she left me soaking in the bath, then tried to scrub the tattoos off: she was fearful of the judgement I'd encounter in my Irish school. 'There's nothing more narrow-minded than a teachers' staff room,' she'd say.

Over the years, my Dad, my sister and I would meet intermittently in Tunisia, but never Libya. But I finally returned to Tripoli in November 2011 for a post-uprising conference, and met my father there. As we walked to the square, people approached Dad, now a renowned writer and painter, and he proudly introduced me as his daughter. During the uprising, Dad communicated with us by text; by then he'd lost his voice to cancer. He had three voices, he said, his own, a pen and a paintbrush. For a while Gaddafi blocked texting – the only time Dad was silent, until now.

That last trip, as I stood in the square near where the photo was taken, I closed my eyes and conjured this image, the symbolic essence of why my sister and I came to be.

Everything about Libya is noisy, but the square is so distinct in its noise – beeping, shouting, traffic, birds, the souq, a cacophony against a bouquet of coffee smells, heat, gasoline, dust mixed with the spices of Libyan food emanating from the restaurants. In the near distance is the waterfront and the Mediterranean Sea. This is where our parents arrived one morning to see for themselves that the rumours were true, that Gaddafi had painted the square green overnight.

My sister and I often walk along Sandymount Strand reminiscing, wondering if we'll ever visit Libya once again – echoing the past of our parents – now that our father no longer walks amongst us. Mom too has a yearning to visit Libya one last time, often speaking of a time when they lived in the White Elephant apartments – what she calls her happiest years with Dad, before the regime and the troubles began. As I look at this photo, I feel him kissing my forehead, something he's done since my childhood, and hear his pre-cancer voice, whispering his beloved Rumi:

'Goodbyes are only for those who love with their eyes. For those who love with heart and soul, there is no such thing as separation.'

NO ONE WRITES LOVE LIKE PUCCINI

Muriel Bolger

The internet was down, and I was contemplating the lake in Annaghmakerrig, County Monaghan. I was listening to *Puccini Without Words*. Words distract me when I'm writing, but the music seeps into my subconscious and transports me to other times and places.

Several swans glided along the far bank, leaving creases on the surface of the water, and I wondered how much inspiration Giacomo Puccini had got from the lake near his house in Torre del Lago in Tuscany.

A few years ago I visited his villa there. I fell into conversation with an elegant lady sitting in the shade of the flower-filled gardens. She told me she was Simonetta, Puccini's granddaughter, his only known living descendant. I didn't know then that she had fought a fifteen-year-long court battle to be recognised as such, a battle which saw her inherit one-third of the composer's considerable estates. With no children by his wife, Giacomo's son Tonio had fathered her outside marriage.

She thanked me for visiting the villa.

Thanked me!

I was on a pilgrimage.

I had reached Mecca.

I had fallen in love with her grandfather's music when I saw *Madama Butterfly* for the first time, and it made me cry.

In search of rustic seclusion, Puccini bought the property at Torre. He gutted it and built the villa when the royalties from *La Bohème* began to roll in. He enjoyed his years there, with his fleet of boats, his fast cars, card games and wild parties. It was here that he wrote most of his operas, too.

And here I was now, about to enter his home and walk through the rooms where he had sat, played, composed, laughed and loved.

For me no one writes love more beautifully than Puccini.

And he had lots of experience.

His wife, Elvira, was married when he met her. Neither State nor Church laws sanctioned divorce so when they had their son Tonio, she had to move away to avoid the scandals and the damage it would do to his career. They could only legalise the union several years later when her husband was shot dead by his married lover's husband!

A plot almost as incredible as some of his operatic ones.

Elvira was a jealous wife. Not in the normal wifely way, but in an insanely obsessive way. Mind you, she had reason to be a bit concerned, as he had a tendency to fall in love with his leading ladies and his correspondence documents at least seven lovers amongst them.

Using the excuse of his artistic needs didn't do much to reassure Elvira. She accused him of having an affair with a housemaid, spread dastardly rumours around the town, slandered the maid to her family and even threatened to drown her in the lake. Devasted and denying such claims, the twenty-three-year-old girl ingested poison and died three painful days later.

The post-mortem, it was reported, showed she had been a virgin.

Elvira was tried and sentenced to five months and five days in prison. Only after much haggling did Puccini manage to buy her a way out of that by offering substantial compensation to the girl's parents.

This too could have been a plot from one of his operas.

The villa is much as it was when he and Elvira lived there. And there's something hauntingly surreal about standing in this, the large room, the faint strains of *La Bohème* playing softly in the background. It's easy to imagine Giacomo sitting there at the upright Förster piano. It had been fitted with a special damper because of his habit of working through the night.

He might even have chewed on one of the pens on the nearby desk where his writing paraphernalia is spread out. There are signed photos of his contemporaries all around: the great Enrico Caruso, Gustav Mahler and Franz Lehar amongst them. There's also one of Maria Jeritza, the Czech soprano whom he claimed was his best Tosca ever. She was one of his lovers, too.

The gun room was not something I had expected to find at Puccini's villa. His guns gleamed in a glass case. Boots of all shapes and sizes were arranged neatly in a row; stuffed water birds kept their beady eyes on me, reminding me that I was an interloper.

I hadn't expected the little chapel between the gun room and the study either. His son had this built after his father died suddenly, following surgery, in 1924. Now his remains rest in the villa where he wrote love, desire, loss and yearning like no one else.

He was later joined by his wife Elvira, daughter-in-law Rita, his son Tonio and, in 2017, by Simonetta herself.

She may have been the last in the line, but as I sit listening to *Puccini Without Words* I know his legacy will go on and on, because nobody wrote love more beautifully than the maestro, and I doubt if anyone ever will again.

GOOD DAY SUNSHINE

Angela Keogh

'Lovely, just lovely,' said the man who was walking towards me. His accent was kindly and unmistakably Liverpudlian. It was a clear, sunny afternoon in Brighton, the late summer of 2002. The blue of the sky and sea reached out to meet each other in the stripe of the horizon. Beach huts lined one side of the promenade and green wrought iron railings ran the length of the other, where the path dropped down to the smooth pebbled beach.

But it wasn't this idyllic holiday scene that the man was talking about. He was referring to my two small girls, speeding along on scooters, laughing, just ahead of me.

Something in his voice and warm, hazel-eyed smile struck a chord in me. The busyness of endless housework and domestic chores that is the treadmill of early motherhood, of having two girls just eleven months apart, was still overwhelming. I hadn't come to terms with the culture shock that parenthood brings and my world hadn't yet settled back onto a relatively steady axis. But the sincere smile of the stranger was full of a kindness that made that busy day seem a little more manageable.

We stood watching the girls, this stranger and I. Watching them spin in circles on the promenade, oblivious to the world and the watchers. Their golden, sun-softened hair and tiny agile bodies gave them an otherworldly appearance as they propelled themselves on their scooters, moving faster than I could ever hope to run. The glare of the sun made halos of their hair. And suddenly I saw the scene through the eyes of the stranger, through the eyes of someone outside the maelstrom of trying to make ends meet and I felt my eyes well up.

I had never expected to find parenthood this hard. At no point in my entire education had anyone, including my friends, ever talked about motherhood and the struggles and uncertainties and fears it brings. The kindness of this stranger's words had caught me off guard.

I returned his smile and sighed, 'They are indeed.' And in that moment I recognised both the voice and the face of the stranger. The self-pity and frustration that had bubbled up gave way to astonishment.

I'd heard that Paul McCartney had bought one of the beach houses near the harbour and was living there with his new wife, Heather Mills, but I had never expected our paths to cross. My voice almost failed, but I managed a 'Thank you.' In an automatic gesture I reached out my hand and shook his. 'Thank you,' I said again. Given time, I might have managed more but a shriek from one of my fleeing children called me away. I withdrew my hand and turned to run. He waved and laughed heartily and his laughter was filled with that language of joy that we all understand. I waved back and sprinted past the beach huts, towards the lagoon where Mairenn, my younger daughter, was crying beside an upturned scooter.

I scooped her into my arms and kissed her small hands and scuffed knee. By the time I looked back, the stranger was close to home and almost out of sight. 'Happy face,' said Katie and the three of us made our biggest smiles.

Later that evening, I would think of all of the things I might have said, the things I might have told him. The music I was so grateful for, how brilliant it was to meet him. But later still I would remember his smile as he looked on at my children. I would radiate in the remembered warmth, and I would see, again, the scene as he did: these glowing girls, this young, fit mother, freely together on a warm blue day by the sea, and that view was more of a gift than all the songs I'd ever heard him play. This one song, the sound of his laughter, was doubtless the one that has mattered most to me.

TWO KILKENNY MEN

Olivia O'Leary

My grandfather, John O'Leary, was a simple and loving old man, tall with a long white beard. He was the town baker in Graiguenamanagh, but his real passion was for local history and archaeology, and old books. On his day off he'd take the bus to Dublin and spend the day wandering around all the second-hand bookshops on the quays. One day when he came home to Graig, he looked a bit shaken and my mother, his daughter-in-law, asked him why. He told her about his day and how he walked up past Trinity College to find somewhere for his lunch. He found a grand clean little place, he said, and he asked for his favourite meal, pink bacon on a blue plate. It was lovely, one of the tastiest dishes he'd ever had. 'But Mary dear,' he said, 'the price of it!' It didn't take my mother too long to work out that Granddaddy had wandered into Dublin's finest restaurant, Jammet's.

His house in Graiguenamanagh backed on to the thirteenth-century Cistercian abbey of Duiske. Indeed, many of the houses on Lower Main Street and along the quay cling to the walls of the abbey like mussels to a rock. When the family were trying to install new ovens for the bakery long ago, they found they had knocked through into the tombs of the old monks. Reverently, they reinstated the wall.

My grandfather, John, and his two cousins, Patrick and William O'Leary, spent their lives collecting bits of local history. They produced a number of booklets, about Duiske Abbey, about Ullard Church and about St Mullins. My grandfather did some of the research and most of the sketches; his cousins, who had a better education, did much of the writing.

They searched out fragments of columns or carved stone which had been removed from the ruins of the old churches to stop a gap in a hedge or ornament a garden. They weren't professional archaeologists, but without their amateur efforts, precious parts of ruins would have been lost and people would have been less aware of these rich reminders of their past.

Hubert Butler, the great essayist from Bennettsbridge, and my grandfather were founder members of the revived Kilkenny Archaeological Society in 1945. My grandfather was its president for the first twelve years, during which time there was a famous row.

Butler, who had attended some of the war crime trials in Yugoslavia after the Second World War, went to a lecture in Dublin given by the editor of the Catholic paper *The Standard* in 1952. The lecturer described at some length how the communist regime of Tito persecuted Catholics. He said nothing, however, about the murderous campaign by the Nazis and their Croatian henchmen during the war to force Orthodox Christians to convert to Catholicism. He said nothing, either, about the failure of the Catholic hierarchy to distance themselves from this campaign. When Hubert Butler stood up at the end of the lecture to make this point, the Papal Nuncio, who was in attendance, walked out.

There was mayhem. 'Insult to Nuncio' screamed one newspaper headline. One forgets how powerful the Catholic Church was then. Local government bodies all over the country condemned Hubert Butler, a Protestant. Butler was shunned. A motion that he should resign from the honorary secretaryship of his beloved Kilkenny Archaeological Society was put, but defeated. Butler, whose motivation in reviving the society was to have a cause on which Catholics and Protestants could unite, resigned voluntarily rather than be a cause of division.

My mother, who gave me Butler's various essays to read, always felt that a great wrong had been done to him. She was right, and various bodies, including Kilkenny County Council, have since apologised for their votes of condemnation. What my grandfather thought, I don't know.

But only a few years ago, Suzanna Crampton, Hubert's granddaughter, gave me a cartoon done by one of Hubert's friends at the time of the controversy. It shows the famous Kilkenny Archaeological Society meeting in stormy progress. All those against Butler have devil's horns on their heads. All those who supported him have halos.

Old John O'Leary, my grandfather, is pictured with half a halo on one side of his head and a devil's horn on the other. As president chairing the meeting, he would have had a casting vote, but the majority in Butler's favour was decisive, so he never had to cast it. He was probably vastly relieved.

Over the years, the two men remained as friendly as their very different social positions then allowed. The society they co-founded promoted new interest in the antiquities of Kilkenny. It saved the beautiful Rothe House from destruction by buying it, a campaign in which members Maureen Hegarty, Cissy de Loughrey, Daisy Phelan and Kitty Lanigan played a large part. Rothe House is one of the finest Irish examples of a sixteenth century merchant's dwelling and that's where the society's archive is now kept. It's a rich heritage, one which brought together two founding members of different creeds, class and education – because they were, above all, proud Kilkenny men.

MAPMAKING

Ian Sherry

I joined the Ordnance Survey in Northern Ireland in 1966. It was an organisation that truly hadn't changed since 1824 when the British Parliament granted £300,000 for Lt Col Thomas Colby to map the entire island at a scale of six inches to one mile, from a perfect 7.89-mile base line on the shores of Lough Foyle – they were by angles only able to cover Ireland with a framework of triangles at a density close enough to be chained.

When I started, they were in the middle of the retriangulation, building pillars on the top of mountains and burying cement block in fields. After a block of months in the office learning to draw with a rule pen and a while training in Ormeau Park, I was assigned to the Trig Section, carrying the gear to the remotest places.

For fifteen days on the trot, we carried a tellurometer and theodolite, lights, thermometers, barometers, car batteries and lunch bags from sea level at Maggie's Leap to the top of Slieve Donard.

As I look back, I find it amazing that the only way we could communicate from one mountain to the other was by Morse code. Hence all the car batteries, for the tellurometer and for the light to flash the Morse code. When you see the profusion of mobile phones now!

Then I was a leveller. No, nothing to do with religion or finance. With a cold chisel I cut benchmarks: crow's feet in stone bridges and walls to be given a height above sea level.

In 1972 I ran a line along the south Armagh border. It's amazing how accustomed we became to 'the Troubles'. On hearing gunfire further up the road, we'd stop for a while, then start again and move on. Old benchmarks cut by the sappers were incorporated in the new work. Outside Crossmaglen I was looking for such a mark, when a man came out and said to me, 'I was waiting for you, you're looking for the crow's foot, aren't you? We had to widen the entrance,' whereupon he took me round to the side of the house where he had, public spiritedly, built the big stone with the mark on it into the wall.

And up in the Mournes above Kilfeaghan, I was cutting marks out on the mountain, drawing a little sketch of each so that a surveyor in a hundred years' time could find and use them.

Dan White was a local shepherd; he too had his own hammer and chisel and took to cutting marks that were more or less identical. Little did I realise that in a short time, with the advent of satnav, Dan's marks would be just as relevant as mine.

It's the field man's job to have a look at anything that may be of archaeological interest. In the corner of a field in Kilfeaghan, I noticed a pile of stones that may have been a souterrain or a cairn. And in the house down below it I went over and spoke through the window to a woman making a griddle of bread.

'Do you know anything about the pile of stones?' I asked.

'I do,' she said. 'Every year on the night of the seventh of August, two teams of small dark men come up from under those stones. They play a game of football in the field, and then they go back down.' She was a sonsy woman with flour up to her elbows and she told me this in such a matter-of-fact way – never deviating from making the bread.

In 1980 I was working in Carrickfergus, and climbed a wall and started measuring in a big garden. Then, thinking the owner might phone the police, I stopped, went back, got the van, and drove up the avenue to where a flight of granite steps led to the mansion's double doors. There I rang the bell and to my alarm two things happened – well, a number of things happened. The door opened a little, and out of the courtyard at the side of the house tore two huge Rottweilers. Instinctively, I shouted 'Goodness me!' or words to that effect, and burst through the door, slamming it behind me. As I did so, I inadvertently bumped into and jostled a portly gentleman in a tartan waistcoat and a red bow tie. He was very shocked, and so was I.

'I'm from the Ordnance Survey,' I blurted – noting the place dripping with antique artefacts and beginning to understand my dancing partner's alarm at this sudden intrusion. In time we both calmed down.

'I could easily have walked up the avenue and been torn to ribbons,' I said.

'Oh, not to worry,' he replied loftily. 'They're trained guard dogs and would have simply shoulder-charged you, knocked you down and held you until I came.'

Well, thank God for that!

LESSONS FROM LEITRIM'S COASTAL FRONTIER

Colin Regan

Not a lot of people outside the northwest know of Leitrim's little three-mile coastline. But for those who live on it, who from it hail, it has helped define who we are.

Tullaghan village is where the county dips its toe into the waters of the Atlantic. It's neither a port nor a fishing village, but still harbours the qualities of a place with one foot planted in rock and the other in water. In its heyday, it shared the casual lawlessness of an island visited only on occasion by a garda whose token appearance is forewarned by the ferryman to all its residents.

Tullaghan also possesses the opportunism of any border place, and the meitheal mentality necessary to any outpost.

In the early 1980s, a phone would ring in the Maguires' house. If the call came from one of my brothers in London or Germany, Mary Maguire would jump in the car and drive the three miles to our townland of Derryloughan to let Mum and Dad know that Barbour or Davy or Jon would call again in half an hour. And so, one of my favourite little adventures was set in motion as we piled into our car and made for Tullaghan and Maguires, home to one of the few house-phones in the area at the time.

There were many elements to such an outing, each sparking my curiosity and illuminating my understanding of the world.

Catching up on the adventures of my older brothers always took precedence: each of us was offered a bare sixty seconds' phone time to quiz them on life and what they might bring home with them on their next visit, usually coinciding with Christmas.

Once this was taken care of, our attention would turn to play. Sean Maguire was nestled in age exactly between myself and my older brother Gordon, and so helped to bridge that four-year gap.

My younger brother and I – numbers eleven and twelve in the family – are Irish twins, Stuart's birthday coming just 361 days after my own. My older sisters Jean and Sandy, Karen and Alison were friends with the Maguire girls Evelyn, Patrice, and DeeDee.

The teenage Maguire girls were dark and exotic creatures with a hint of Spanish Armada about them: old enough to inhabit a different world and, even if I didn't quite know why, beautiful enough to make me want to visit it sometime in the future.

From the Maguires' backyard, you could throw a stone into the sea if the tide was in. In high tide or high wind, their back garden would fill with foam from the waves below, and I always feared that their house might flood, but it never did. There was no boundary at the bottom of the lawn, it just stepped down onto the rocky coast and transitioned into another landscape.

To the right we were bound by the mouth of the Drowes River which also provides the boundary to county Donegal. To the left we rarely ventured beyond Tynte Lodge which looks out over the coast and across to Donegal Bay, its folly stone tower standing like the last sentinel of a forgotten chieftain's army. Even as a child, I was struck by its fading grandeur. It was clear that it belonged to another era, and that it was threatened as much by the indifference of modern Ireland as the eroding coastline below its boundary walls.

As we roamed the coast we would hopscotch the rocks to develop our balance and to beachcomb for anything worthwhile we could find, for it was the rocks that would decide what gifts they might offer to the sure-footed few who first reached their bounty. My most exciting find was a message in a bottle that had made its way from a high school student in Newfoundland in just a matter of months.

I got permission to call the number on the letter, but when I finally got to talk to the girl who'd sent it, I was mightily disappointed – she didn't sound at all that impressed! She told me she'd report where and when it was found to her science teacher, but inexplicably, offered no all-expenses-paid invitation to regale her classmates with the story of my discovery and tales of my far-flung land and its people.

I still have the letter, though, and a love for the coast, and a need for its healing water. Shortly after my brother Gordon died in a car crash in 2002, aged thirty, our family headed together to Tullaghan's coast with our grief draped about our shoulders like seaweed on the rocks. We found the tide had bowed its head and humbly receded to expose Leitrim's little oasis of sand and as we sat on our private beach, the sun came out from behind Tynte Lodge, and I watched as the family's next generation of children laughed and made sandcastles and little plans of their own.

As we walked into the water together, three generations and a fourth soon to follow, I looked back on Tullaghan, knowing that soon the waves would wash away the footprints of my parents and the castles of their grandchildren, and that nothing could turn back that tide. And so, we celebrated a life well lived.

CHRISTY RING, THE FIRST SUPERSTAR

Jim McKeon

I first met Christy Ring when I was eleven. We'd won the under-twelve street league final and we were to go along to the Glen Hall to receive our trophies. It shows how poor a hurler I was that I was placed nineteenth in the waiting queue. One by one my team-mates went up. At last my turn came and, with legs like jelly, I walked up the aisle, head down, hair over my face. As the great man shook my hand, two things stood out. First, his massive wrists. Second, he had the most unusual steel-blue eyes which seemed to have a built-in twinkle. I'll never forget what he said to me:

'Keep your eye on the ball, even when it's in the referee's pocket.'

He presented me with my trophy. That night I floated home.

Not alone was Christy Ring the most charismatic player of all time at his chosen sport, but for a quarter of a century he was outstanding when the standard was at an extraordinary high level. He played with fire in his veins and a pride and passion in his performance. At the age of sixteen I cycled from Cork up to Limerick just to see him play. He was reputed to double the attendance wherever he played. He was the only player in the world I would pay money to see training. He tried the impossible. What other player would practise cutting the ball over the bar from behind the corner flag?

In the 1950s, it seemed to be an annual pilgrimage to Limerick to watch Cork do battle with Tipperary in the Munster final. Tipperary's full-back line – Byrne, Maher and Carey – had an awesome reputation. With Tony Reddan behind them in goal, they were like the Rock of Cashel. Nothing passed.

When Cork did score, I can still see the sliotar sailing over the bar while the Tipp defenders wrapped their hurleys around their unfortunate opponents' necks. Then there was that colossus, John Doyle. It must have been like going through the Berlin Wall to find yourself being flattened by a Russian tank. Even Roy of the Rovers would have had his hands full, yet 'Ringy' got many great goals in those games.

They were six titanic struggles fought out with an intense fervour, and the victors went on to win the All-Ireland title each time.

But will there ever be a more dramatic Munster final than that of 1956 when Cork played Limerick? I was a shy, sensitive *gasún* listening in my aunt's kitchen in Dublin. With ten minutes remaining, Cork were being thrashed by Limerick, and that fine hurler, Donal Broderick, was playing a blinder on Ring. Radio Éireann decided to switch over to the Ulster football decider. What a mistake. With despair in my heart, I sat down and waited for the result. Limerick 3–5, Cork 5–5. I jumped up and, in my excitement, knocked cups and saucers all over the place. My aunt picked up a frying pan and gave me a box across the back, but in my euphoria, I didn't feel a thing.

'Ringy' had the actor's instinct for dramatic timing and his three goals in five minutes in that eventful game were pure genius. In hindsight Limerick didn't stand a chance.

Come September and those giants from Wexford stood between Ring and his ninth All-Ireland medal. Memories from that thrilling game will stay with me forever: Ring's great tussle with Willie Rackard; his solo run and point followed by a goal which electrified the crowd of 83,000; Art Foley's late, important save which got better and better in memory as the years rolled by. I was quite near it, and on the day, I thought it was a very ordinary save. I can still see 'Ringy' charging in on the goalkeeper and the apprehensive Art Foley hopping up and down on his goal line. But the great man just shook his hand and when the final whistle blew, in a lovely gesture of sporting reciprocation, the Wexford backs shouldered him like a king from Croke Park. Sadly, as Cork was to go through a barren ten-year patch after that, it was his last All-Ireland.

My children mock me when I polish my little silver egg cup, which I received from Christy Ring all those years ago in the Glen Hall. I ignore them because, that night, I met my God.

DONNYBROOK FAIR

Ann Marie Durkan

Everyone needs to let their hair down at least once a year. Today we have Longitude, Electric Picnic, the Fleadh Ceoil, the Ploughing Championships and more. In times gone by, Dubliners had Donnybrook Fair, records of which go as far back as 1204.

The fair usually took place towards the end of August and lasted for about two weeks – or until the revellers' money ran out. As with carnivals around the world, Donnybrook Fair offered people an escape from their ordinary lives, music, dancing, entertainment, food, drink, sex, and of course fighting. In fact, the word 'donnybrook' has earned its place in the *Oxford English Dictionary* meaning a scene of uproar and disorder; a heated argument.

Located near where the rugby clubs are in Donnybrook today, the green was filled with marquees providing hospitality and popular entertainment. Vintners and hoteliers from the city set up tents to feed the masses, offering such delights as Wicklow hams, dishes of potatoes and gallons of punch. In the nineteenth century, artists Erskine Nicol and Edward Lees Glew sought to capture the atmosphere of the fair, and their paintings show tents with banners aloft advertising their entertainment, traditional fairground rides and multiple vignettes: people picnicking, young men enjoying a large brawl, two men cutting off another's coattails, a popular prank at the time. An escaped pig runs riot, knocking a woman over and sending her basket flying, and actors from Calvert's Royal Theatre offer all of Shakespeare's plays in twenty minutes.

A close inspection of the painting by Edward Lees Glew also reveals well-known characters such as 'Peggy the Man', a milk seller from Harold's

Cross of uncertain gender; 'Zozimus', composer, street balladeer and raconteur; roulette wheel-spinning 'Sporting Molly' from County Down; blind musician Patrick Byrne, playing the harp in Paddy Kelly's tent; and renowned runner 'Cantering Jack', among others.

Along with local entertainers and musicians, the freakish and grotesque were ever popular: Levi Leach, an American contortionist, performed in 1815, while a 10-foot-tall 'Irish Giant' appeared in 1823.

It was also a time of great carousing. Fathers and brothers were warned to keep an eye on daughters and sisters, who faced ruin if they fell pregnant. It was common for a defrocked clergyman to set himself up in a tent and, for a small fee, marry a couple for the night and legitimise their fleeting pleasures in the eyes of God. The most famous of these was a German by the name of Schultz, from Cullenswood, known as 'The Tack'em'. Sadly, a submission from Police Head Office to the 1834 parliamentary report on intoxication stated that the 'intemperate orgies' at Donnybrook Fair were leading to a fresh supply of young women on Dublin's streets every year.

As with all elements of daily life, animals were there too. From dawn to dusk during fair time, horses and cabs raced to and from Dublin city ferrying people hither and thither at breakneck speed. In 1829, when a Dublin cabman was charged with 'furious driving' in Sackville Street, he begged the magistrate to go easy, saying, 'These is Donnybrook times, and everyone is merry now. If you let me off, I'll be aisy for a week.' The magistrate was unmoved, and the driver was fined a pound.

Performing animals have always drawn the crowds, and Erskine Nicol's 1859 painting of Donnybrook Fair includes a banner promoting 'Living Wonders and Paddy Maguire's Learned Pig Toby who can tell the hours of the day & discourse like a Christian'. Now, the idea of the 'intellectual' animal had been around since at least as early as 1586, when 'Marocco the thinking horse' was exhibited in Europe. Marocco had been trained to walk on two or three legs, play dead and urinate on demand. He could recognise certain colours and identify audience members wearing spectacles and was said to be able to count. Although he never visited Ireland, Marocco toured the Continent, entertaining crowds in Paris, Frankfurt, Lisbon and Rome.

Scotsman Samuel Bisset trained the original 'learned pig' in the 1780s and toured him with great success. Once the cognitive ability of pigs was understood, others began training them and they became a popular spectacle at fairs in Britain and Ireland. 'Toby the Sapient Pig' appeared in London in the early nineteenth century, and after that Toby was adopted as the standard name for all 'learned pigs'. One Toby, exhibited by Nicholas Hoare in London, even went so far as to publish his autobiography: *The Life and Adventures of Toby, the Sapient Pig: with his Opinions on Men and Manners. Written by Himself.*

In Ireland, opposition to the fair on moral grounds had been mounting since the middle of the eighteenth century because of its association with lawlessness and moral depravity. It was finally shut down in 1866; that year, a new Catholic church in Donnybrook, dedicated to the Sacred Heart, was opened on the very same Sunday in August when the fair would have traditionally started.

There was some resistance to the fair's closure. Donnybrook publican Joseph Dillon organised a smaller fair across the River Dodder, but it failed to attract a crowd and wasn't repeated. Virtue had apparently vanquished vice, for the time being at least.

MY PRE-UNIVERSITY, UNIVERSITY CHALLENGE

Jennifer Carey

For years, there's been an unspoken rule in our house that on Monday evenings at 8 p.m., the TV will be switched to BBC2. Dinner eaten, we make a cup of tea and take our places on the sagging couch as the chirpy, convoluted tune of 'College Boy' plays over the title sequence of our favourite show, portraying figures of the past, different inventions and theorems. As the camera pans along, a voice declares, 'University challenge!' and that Jeremy Paxman will be asking the questions. Then, the courteous introductions to the hyper-smart students: preppies, hipsters and the captain, always third from the left.

I would make a split-second judgement, and pick a side. As a secondary school student with the Leaving hovering into view, I tried to imagine what it would be like to sit under the glare of studio lights, having not just to know all this niche information, but to be able to retrieve it at the speed of a finger pressing a button.

When I first started watching the show, I'd sit in wonder as some of the best students from the United Kingdom's universities were grilled on subjects that I had no idea about. The odd time, I was lucky enough to even understand the question being asked. The most I'd take part in was the picture round.

But for the past two series of the show, my attention while watching *University Challenge* was heightened because I'd been set my own challenge by my ultra-competitive dad: to beat him at this, his favourite quiz show. His record was twenty-two correct answers, so he was a formidable opponent, but I had noted that his performance could be inconsistent, week to week.

Surprisingly, this challenge was a welcome distraction from my schoolwork, and at times seemed to even complement it. The bombardment of poems, geographic processes and French verbs coming at me in school all had the potential to crop up as a starter for ten, adding to my arsenal of information. Every Monday I'd join my dad in front of the TV to compete, never mind that I might have two tests the next day, a project due and three essays to be done by the end of the week.

I began to set myself easier challenges by taking my dad on in other shows, such as *Mastermind*. The general knowledge round usually held a fair mix of questions for the pair of us, sparking ever closer battles. His weaknesses were my strengths. I actually understood today's pop culture and distinctly remember leaping out of my seat when I had the opportunity to answer questions on the *Percy Jackson* series, BBC *Sherlock* or *Harry Potter* as my father sat, mute.

And while his answers came sometimes more slowly than before, mine got faster. Knowing that I could complete the English paper 2 for my Junior Cert without a dead hand afterwards, as well as three six-page Leaving Cert history essays in the space of 120 minutes, really boosted my confidence. By the start of Sixth Year, my dad began to realise his days as the self-proclaimed 'king' of *University Challenge* might be numbered.

It wasn't all about the accumulation of precise facts, either. As I got older and sharper, my hunches at answers began to produce results. Over time, patterns emerged. Any question on a German composer? Usually Beethoven or Wagner. British artist? Try Constable. A forefront political figure in Europe in the 1870s? Probably Bismarck. An inexplicably complex-sounding maths question? Best odds are to answer with a number between 0 and 4.

Moreover, I had the upper hand on my father in science. I was doing honours biology; he failed lower-level physics. But he was still holding his own.

Agonisingly, one evening I managed to reach a draw with him yet still did not win. As my study for the Leaving Cert increased, my scores became increasingly erratic and often abysmal. Some nights, I managed merely three correct answers and started to think that maybe my chance had gone.

But then one inauspicious evening, I came home from school, a Sixth Year badly in need of a break. I sat down with my usual cup of tea. But it remained untouched as my fourteen years of schooling culminated in correctly answering an almost unbroken run of questions involving quotes from Gerard Manley Hopkins and *Macbeth*, European tensions in the late nineteenth century, protein synthesis and the physicist Richard Feynman. That evening, my best ever score of sixteen was more than double my dad's pitiful seven. Victory. Vindication.

My dad, defeated, held back a tear of pride. The moment that I had waited for, and then realised he too had waited for, had finally arrived. The competition, the drama all came to an end at the sound of a gong.

But that, and study for the Leaving Cert, are in the past. Last week, my results let me breathe freely for the first time in two years, all the work and all the learning thankfully rewarded. University place accepted, new questions are forming in my mind. In four years' time, will I still hold close the friends I hold so dear now? What will I wear without the uniform I've worn day in, day out for the past six years? Who will I be – a hipster, a preppy, or some horrifying mixture of both? The safety and the security of secondary school now gone, I look to September as, like so many lucky others, I approach one of the greatest challenges I will ever face – university.

MY SEAMUS HEANEY STORY

Denise Blake

Maya Angelou used to say that whenever she was about to give a poetry reading, she brought the spirit of everyone who had ever been kind to her on stage with her in support. She would say to them, 'Come with me. I need your help, I need you now.' And it gave her courage. I try to follow that advice now. I said those words, just before this reading.

Sometimes, during a conversation with friends about poetry, I end up saying, 'Did I ever tell you my Seamus Heaney story? I have a lovely memory of Seamus Heaney.'

The preamble to my story begins years ago, when, as an adult learner, I enrolled for a Foundation Studies course in Magee College, Derry. I was searching for something, a kindling that could spark, even a glimmer. I had stayed at home when our sons were young, but they were growing up and I needed to move forward. The Foundation Studies involved a range of subjects, and luckily for me one of the subjects was English, and it included poetry. And, luckily again for me, the lecturer gave us some Heaney poems to look at. I had never heard of Seamus Heaney before that time.

I held a trepidation when it came to poetry. I thought I needed a teacher to explain a poem to me before I could appreciate it. The first Heaney poem that was put before us was 'Docker'. As I read it, something in me shifted. I understood the poem and could appreciate the word play in his chosen images. I felt a sense of achievement.

Seamus Heaney himself, in conversation with the poet Dennis O'Driscoll, has described first reading contemporary poetry when he was in his twenties. He said it gave him an eagerness, an excitement, a sense of change. A moment of writing gave him a lift, a joy, a reward. That was exactly how I felt on reading

'Docker'. There was a grace for me in discovering his poems. The kindling I had carried into Magee College was set alight and I began writing poetry.

My life took a whole new direction.

So, we move forward in my story to years later, to an evening in west Donegal, a poetry event where I had been asked to compère. I was really looking forward to that evening. I knew I would be introducing each writer and musician, but I would also be reading three of my own poems. And I knew that Seamus Heaney and Marie Heaney were in Donegal and they would be in the audience.

I felt comfortable compèring the event. The hall was full and the audience was warm and appreciative. I was enjoying myself. I introduced several poets and musicians and then it came to my turn to perform as a poet.

I said the title of my first poem, and then I thought, 'Seamus Heaney is listening to me.' The thought began to drumbeat louder and louder within me. 'Seamus Heaney is listening to my poems.' I started to shake, a nervous tremble that started at my toes and moved up my body. I could barely stand up. The nerves were rapidly coming close to strangling my voice. My husband and friends were sitting in the audience. I could see their expression of utter disbelief as they watched me quivering.

When it came to the end of the first poem I thought, 'I will not get through the next two poems unless I own my nerves.' So I said, into the mic, 'It's not easy when you are told, read a few poems, and oh! Seamus Heaney will be in the audience.'

There was a silence for a moment and then, from the back of the darkened hall, a voice rang out: 'You are doing grand, Denise. You are doing grand.' Mr Heaney himself. I started to laugh. The audience laughed. I settled into myself and finished reading my two poems, nerve-free.

Afterwards, at the end of the evening, I went down the hall to Marie and Seamus and I said to them, 'I can always say now that Seamus Heaney heckled me.' Marie laughed and said, 'Ah sure, that wasn't a heckle.' And then Seamus looked at me, in that enriching way that he had, and he said, 'You could read anywhere, at any time, daughter.'

It was that word, daughter, that grounded what he said, made it feel sincere and encouraging. And now, when I'm doing a reading and I feel nerves are about to invade, I hear him, 'You could read anywhere, at any time, daughter,' and my soul settles.

Thank you, Seamus. You were a gentleman.

SEPTEMBER

ZERO DEGREES

Donal Hayes

For two days, the sea has hung grey with rain, under a sky so low that the mast of my boat perforated the soft clouds, recalling the bumper cars of my Crosshaven holidays. The water is glassy and slothful and although the sails hang like loose flannel trousers, I am still making enough way not to have to turn on my engine.

Nothing really dries on a wooden boat. Clothes are a salty damp, sleeping bags are slightly better and matches always hard to light. My chart, although still functioning perfectly, probably hasn't been fully dry for years. A big chart, covering Kenmare river to Cork Harbour, with old trips marked in soft pencil and permanent corrections in violet ink. There are details priceless to the mariner: tides, currents, depths, anchorages, light patterns, wrecks and contours, all designed to make passages safer. I had scribbled a reminder in pencil on the back, 'It's important to know where the rocks are but it is more important to know where they are not.'

My compass points due north and has been like that all morning since I got my bearing from the light on the Old Head. Every lighthouse has a unique pattern and the Old Head flashes twice every ten seconds. If you find a second light, you can calculate where you are. I need to head dead north now, a bearing of zero degrees, going nowhere. Going home.

They say that when sailors are on land, all they want is to be at sea and when they're at sea, all they want is to get the boat safely home. But today it is the close of a long journey and I feel like a schoolboy at the end of August. More than once I questioned what I was doing; more than once I thought of pulling the tiller towards me until my compass pointed one more time to the heat of Bilbao, the reciprocal course of zero degrees, the polar opposite of going home.

I am sailing in the cold fifties of latitude, as far from the warm Equator as Alaska to the west and Holland to the east. The light is scant and watery and it always falls obliquely, even at the height of summer. My GPS cheerfully shows bars and restaurants and even a 'Pizza Truck' waiting ashore. My chart, however, shows Ballymackean, Killowny, Courtaparteen, right across to Preghane. My awkward, huge, pencil-marked chart that I can still pore over for hours.

All the pilot books warn you of the dangers of a West Cork landfall. The Admiralty Pilot cautions those who sail up from the south: 'Fogs, bad weather and the long nights of winter frequently render it impossible to obtain a position … under such circumstances the course steered, the log, the lead and nature of the bottom are the seaman's only guides.'

The floor rolls a little in the swell and the land sinks under the sea again. When it reappears, it rises from the water changed. There is some light in the western sky and the slate grey that surrounded me is lightening and warming. There is a distant smell of garlic coming from the land. The first time I smelled this I was impressed with the vast amounts of garlic used by Kinsale restaurants but found out later that it is the smell of wild garlic that grows profusely along the coast. I start to imagine I can hear the sounds of Kinsale public houses, a clatter of glasses, a call for beer along the bar, but it is the halyards on my mast and seagulls squawking overhead.

The radio crackles me out of my reverie …

This is Cork Coastguard Radio with the Sea Area Forecast. A frontal depression lies over Ireland. A freshening south-easterly airflow will develop during the afternoon and evening as a ridge of high pressure approaches from Bilbao. The low centre will track along the south coast tomorrow and then fade like a distant memory …

… the forecast and my dreams mixing up together one more time.

Out of habit I record it in the log and note the pressure, the course steered and our speed. Finally I put an X on the chart marking my position. I am proud of the straight line of Xs all the way from Bilbao, north. Tonight, there will be a hot shower, clean clothes and sheets. There will be food cooked by somebody else, and beer from a tap. There will be family to love and friends to make me laugh. There may even be singing. There will definitely be singing.

I am home now, but here are still patterns that tell us all where we are, not from a lighthouse but from the tone of voice, the raising of an eyebrow.

There are cardinal marks to let us know how far we have come. There are obstacles and shallows and low tides to be navigated. There are storms to be weathered and doldrums to be sat out. And all to be done without a damp, pencil-marked chart.

There is, however, a strange comfort in going to sleep with the certain knowledge that your bed will not be in collision with an oil tanker. A comfort in not getting up on the hour to look at the horizon. A comfort in being home.

YOUNG TED

Fred Tuite

In October 1972, I returned for my second year to UCD to find the Belfield Arts Block filled with First Year students trying to find their way about. Making my way through this excited throng, I met a friend coming the other way.

'Come with me,' she said.

And so, I followed her into Theatre L, that huge amphitheatre, which was crowded with expectant students, about to have their first lecture in First Year English.

A lanky figure with a shock of black hair, dressed in priestly garb, came and took his place on the podium. A hush descended on the packed hall.

'Good morning students,' he said, 'I'm Father Michael Paul Gallagher, and these lectures will be on Practical Criticism.'

'But that's not Michael Paul Gallagher!' I whispered to my companion.

She put her finger to her lips and motioned for me to listen on.

'Ah yes,' he continued. 'Practical Criticism. I recall a student who went to Professor Donoghue saying, "I have practically criticised this poem." "Yes," he replied, "practically, but not quite." But at the end of this course, you will gain new insights into poetry, new visions and understanding. You will look at a poem like:

> Humpty Dumpty sat on a wall,
> Humpty Dumpty had a great fall,
> All the King's horses and all the King's men
> Couldn't put Humpty together again

and you will see this not as a nursery rhyme but as an existentialist exploration of the situation of modern man, fallen from grace, and searching for meaning in an absurd world ...'

'Who are you?' interrupted a bearded clerical figure who'd now arrived at the podium.

'I'm Father Michael Paul Gallagher,' the lecturer replied.

'No, *I'm* Father Michael Paul Gallagher!'

'Right! Sorry!' the imposter cried, and off he ran to the cheers and groans of the First Year students.

We caught up with him outside. He was flushed and excited from his act, and keen to know how we thought it had gone. This was my first encounter with Dermot Morgan, Second Year student and all-round funny guy. We became good friends, and as we were both doing English, we saw a lot of each other. I was thoroughly entertained by him on every meeting, for he never stopped performing whether on stage or with company. His energy was manic and his comments hilarious and apt. He was liable to turn up anywhere and everywhere in the guise of his latest character. He even showed up at the Tramps' Ball in the Restaurant building, fronting a band called Big Gom and the Imbeciles. But he had to give up that act, he told me, as people were taking it too seriously and missing the satire, wanting to book the group for dances, while all he wanted to do was poke fun at the country music scene with songs like 'Castleblayney Blues', 'I Walk Blacklion' or 'Be Nobody's Darling but Wine.'

After college we drifted apart, but I followed his comedy career through his letters to the early-morning Mike Murphy radio show, and on to *The Live Mike* on television, where Father Brian Trendy, his next priestly incarnation, appeared. This was an altogether smoother priestly character, well-groomed in his leather jacket, smiling at the camera as he gave us his little bit of religion. He advised us to be like the Irish soccer team and 'pick Devine', or act as a fishing rod for God to 'catch a sole and fillet with love'. But again, there was the danger that his bite-sized pieces of religion might be taken for real, and my mother, for one, loved his little sermons.

His next incarnation was as the growling, irritated-sounding Charlie Haughey, in his own radio show *Scrap Saturday*, alongside Gerry Stembridge. This was full of cutting impersonation and biting political satire that to me represents the height of his career. Maybe it was too close to the bone, as after a few seasons, *Scrap Saturday* was scrapped.

He went on to play his third and most famous priestly role, Father Ted, which brought him international fame. Father Ted Crilly dreams of bigger things than the dead-end wilderness of Craggy Island – a parish to match his ambitions: recognition, fame and fortune. But everywhere his projects crumble under the reality of the people he is surrounded by. It was a wonderful farce, extremely well written and well acted by a fantastic cast. But I kept thinking that for all its quality, Dermot Morgan had so much comic ability underused in the series.

The last time I met him was in Kilkenny when he was on a solo tour called Black Magic. He had been in the news recently, having been fined in court for speeding through Mountrath in County Laois, and his comment to his audience on this was as acerbic as ever.

'Did you ever see Mountrath?' he thundered. 'Fifty miles an hour is too bloody slow to go through the place!'

We met and talked after the show, but he had to return to Dublin early, and promised a real UCD reunion at a future time. That reunion never happened, and he died at the height of his fame, playing the vainglorious Father Ted.

Dermot never lost the manic energy and enthusiasm he showed in Belfield where he constantly had us in fits of laugher with his antics. While the world got to know and love him as the farcical Father Ted, it was in UCD in front of those bemused and bewildered First Years that he played the first of those oddball priests that were to bring him so much fame.

ERSATZ KERRYMAN IN DUBLIN

Mark O'Connell

It's just after 5 p.m. on Sunday, 18 September 2011, and I am walking out of Croke Park to take the short walk home to Lindsay Road in Drumcondra. The disappointment I feel is profound. It is a sense of loss from which I really don't think I have recovered, even now. My fellow Dubliners are unable to control their ecstasy. I console myself by saying that their lack of acquaintance with precious metal in Croke Park accounts for the crude greeting they give when they see me in my Kerry jersey.

'You're a traitor, O'Connell!' blasts one happy chap who picks out my sad face from the tense crowd on Clonliffe Road. 'Bet you're sorry you're wearing that jersey now!'

What that fellow doesn't appreciate is that although I was born and bred in the capital city, my heart and soul have always been in Kerry – and in particular in the beautiful environs of Caherdaniel. My late mother, Teresa, was one of the Florries from Castlecove. And while my father, who also sadly left us in the last few years, hailed from the elegant city of Waterford, Kerry was always the dominant county in our Dublin home. Not only were our holidays always spent in Kerry, but our house was regularly host to our lively Kerry relations.

A key moment for me was a clammy Saturday afternoon in August 1975 as I waited on the platform at Killarney station for the train to take me to Dublin. Having spent a few weeks with my cousins in the Kingdom, I was returning to see the youthful charges of Mick O'Dwyer make their debut in Croke Park against a Sligo team in the All-Ireland football semi-final.

A consignment of poitín, masquerading as a bottle of TK white lemonade, was stuffed into the inner reaches of my kit bag by my Auntie Maura.

'If anyone asks you what that is, tell them it's a bottle of Lourdes holy water for your mum and dad,' she said.

As it happened, my secret would be safer than I had hoped, because the entire two panels of the Kerry senior and minor teams were boarding the same train. Only eleven years old – and showing the hard neck that has served me well in life since – I bunked into the same carriage as my heroes. John O'Keeffe, Mickey Ned, Ogie Moran, Mikey Sheehy, the great John Egan, young Pat Spillane and the others adopted this wide-eyed young boy who was allowed pass the long journey to the capital in their unassuming company. But it wasn't just the footballers I was a fan of, it was Kerry itself.

Memories of those endless days spent on the White Strand in Castlecove, fishing mackerel off West Cove and wandering around the complex of wondrous beaches in Derrynane will never leave me, nor the day trips over Cúm a Ciste to Ballinskelligs and the incomparable Valentia Island.

With particular affection, I recall the summer of 1979 when I worked as a kitchen porter with my brother, Fionán, in the Derrynane Hotel. I was fifteen years old and it was in so many ways the most eventful summer of my life. It was the first time I had a job, the first time I caught a lobster, the first time I drank a pint of Guinness and the first time I kissed a girl.

It was also the summer in which I met my dear friend John Fitzgerald from Cork. To this day, he is pulling lobster pots off the Abbey Island, or showing visitors the marvels of the seashore.

If food could be a soundtrack, then it could be said that the taste in our mouths in those days was of fresh mackerel and Burns' black pudding. The latter is precious stuff in our family. Any time a family member is known to be in south Kerry, they are told to bring home some 'Sneem duty-free'. Once exported safely to its fanatical Dublin customers, the black pudding is divvied up, then cut into small slices and consumed with enormous pleasure. Some ground black pepper and/or several drops of Tabasco are recommended embellishments as the taster steps on to a culinary jet plane back to south Kerry.

As the years go by and my life changes, my trips to Caherdaniel have become shorter and less frequent. My wife and four children draw me to other places. But my connection to Kerry is unbreakable. It keeps drawing me back, a pull which I promise this Dub will never resist.

BASIL/βασιλεύς

Mary O'Donnell

For the nuns, life wasn't too short to stuff tomatoes.
The convent was perched within view of cliffs,
the wrinkled sea. We entered the parlour,
then waited for Sister Mercedes,
my father's sister. I was six,
wore new paisley cords.

The doors opened and she, a slim wisp,
wept for joy, but settled, an angular
black butterfly, wimple and veil
her wings at rest as she talked to me.

A special meal, for visitors.
First taste of stuffed tomatoes
ferried silently from the convent kitchen
by an aproned novice.

I cut into a quivering cheese cap,
that interior flesh, savoury crumbs.
And then: Basil, I was told, sweet basil.
Vivid on my tongue, like liquorice.

That quick taste of summer,
Βασιλεύ, I later learned, from Greece
and the spot where St Constantine discovered
the Holy Cross. Forever after,
our Irish summers, later, a hasty wrench
of basil leaves to dash across glistening salads,
whisk with parmesan, sweet oils.

Pungent that day with Sister Mercedes.
Between mouthfuls of stuffed tomatoes and basil,
she unfettered her mothering skills,
fine fingers stroking my shoulders,
my long hair, as we gazed through the convent window
towards the white-laced waves. Before leaving,
my father left a box of Milk Tray from my mother,
pressed rolled banknotes to her palm.
Then jokes and stories at the convent door,
promises to write soon,
as he tried to distract her from crying.

SILVER AT THE PLOUGHING

Fran O'Rourke

The Greek hero Odysseus was ploughing his field on Ithaca when the recruiting sergeant enlisted him for the expedition against the Trojans. Lucius Quinctius, a retired Roman statesman, was following the plough when a delegation from the Senate arrived to plead with him to return to defend the city against the invader. Victory achieved, Quinctius returned to his farm, declining all honours and accolades. He was known by the sobriquet Cincinnatus, 'the curly haired'. He recently became a Google celebrity when name-checked by Boris Johnson. Cincinnatus's reputation for selfless public service was legendary. In 1783 a society was formed by American officers, called the Society of the Cincinnati, whose aim was to preserve the ideals of the American Revolution. In 1790 a town in the Northwest Territory of Ohio was named Cincinnati in honour of the society. Today a sculpture stands prominently in the city, showing the Roman statesman with curly hair and beard, one hand returning the fasces, a bundle of wooden rods which symbolised his power as dictator, the other resting on his plough.

When Irish ploughmen gathered for the National Ploughing Championships in County Laois last week, I was in Cincinnatus's city of Rome. I was, however, able to summon to the inner eye of memory the ploughing fields of Ratheniska, because it was there I spent the happiest of childhood years. Spelled 'Ratheniska' but pronounced 'Rathineska', the Irish name, *Raithín an Uisce*, means 'little rath of the water'.

During the fifties my father was the schoolmaster in Ratheniska. The teacher's house was located between the school and chapel, which stood at a fork where three roads converged. The countryside gently sloped away,

301

presenting a panoramic vista of serene and varied beauty. Irregular fields of every shape and size were framed by a network of ditches and hedgerows; clumps of woodland punctuated the landscape.

The panorama changed with the seasons: the brown earth and rotting winter stubble turned to delicate green in spring and a brighter tone as the harvest ripened. The mood could change hourly as light and shadow played against one another between earth and sky. To the east you could observe a lashing cloudburst, while the sun flashed through rifted clouds in the west. Shadow and sunburst, wind and light, clouds ominous or luminous, the elements fused in dramatic beauty. Rainbows frequently adorned the vaulted expanse; thunderstorms brought fascination and terror.

One of my earliest memories is of our neighbour Denis Drennan ploughing the field below the school at Ratheniska, his giant Clydesdales frothing at the mouth, hooves stamping as they strained against the creaking harness and heaved into the tearing earth. With the reins balancing the stronger horse against the weaker, Denis guided the ploughshare as it sliced the sod into gleaming ridges. At the end of the furrow, he turned on the headland and in an elaborate manoeuvre aligned horses and plough in the opposite direction. By evening the field was a glistening spectacle of perfectly parallel lines.

Free-range children, there were no limits to where we could roam. On Sunday afternoons as my brothers, passionate about our national games, listened to the commentator's screeching on the battery-powered wireless – to me the acme of boredom – I crossed ditches and walked grassy headlands, gathering hazelnuts, sloes, rosehips, vetches and berries. The hedgerows were a self-contained ecology of growth, with blackthorn, ivy, honeysuckle, ash, sycamore, elm and elderberry all tangled and enmeshed. They were home to the speckled wood and orange-tip butterfly, the honeybee and a host of insects. In those days one heard the corncrake, cuckoo and curlew; the countryside buzzed with wildlife.

One of my most pleasant memories from those Sunday evenings is of the Raidio Éireann programme *Ceol do Pháistí*. 'The Shepherd's Song' from Beethoven's Pastoral was frequently played, the perfect mood music for an idyllic rural childhood. By contrast, I have just one unhappy memory from those carefree afternoons. After Mass on a Sunday in mid-June, my godfather's widow, Mrs Rankin, who never forgot my birthday, gave me two half crowns, a small treasure in 1959. It was the first time I had not just one but two of those prized pre-decimal coins exquisitely decorated with a silver horse. After dinner – in the middle of the day – I set out on my usual adventure, through a gap in the fence into the meadow behind our house. I wandered through the budding corn and scraped my way through brambles and briars. Lying on my back in the sun, I put my hand in my trousers to take out and admire again my shiny pair of horses, and the words *leath chorón* in the old Irish spelling. Both pockets were empty. I retraced my steps in vain. The coins with the silver horses are still somewhere in that field.

As they ploughed the field in Ratheniska last week, I wonder did one of the ploughmen catch a fleeting glint of silver perhaps, as he turned a sod?

THE BIG BLACK DOG

Michael O'Loughlin

My uncle took me to visit his uncle
and see the big black dog,
best gun dog in the county.

My uncle's uncle lived in a mud cabin
near the bog of Bohermeen.
He looked like Les Murray
and wore a brown felt hat.

Inside, he showed me the pelt of the otter
they'd shot in the river
one night they were waiting for duck
– the big black dog had retrieved it.
(Years later, I would sit with the uncles
in the Blackwater rushes
waiting for duck in total darkness
except for the manic horizon light
when I felt an otter's weight
shimmy across my rubber boots.)

He reached up the chimney
and pulled down the shotgun.
I put my finger into the barrel

to feel the tiny holes
where pellets had pitted the steel.

The uncles sat by the fire
sipping sweet tea.
They talked about a neighbour
who watched the railway gates
and had The Spanish Shotgun.
We met him on the lane one day
and saw it: sleek and black and deadly
as a painting by Velázquez.

The uncle's uncle was a stone-cutter
in the quarry at Ardbraccan
like all his family before him.
Only one of the cousins
still cuts stone
though that's not quite true:
once a year he flies first class to China
and fills containers with cut stone
which he ships back to Ireland
and chips his neighbours' names on.

In an animated PowerPoint presentation
I see the mud mutate into brick and concrete
with water on tap, and electricity
TV aerials, slated rooves
then come the glass and steel conservatories
the gravelled car parks
where once the scallions and rhubarb grew.

Now my cousins live in new houses
with six bedrooms *ensuite,*
their living room is big as a hotel lounge
– they don't know enough people to fill the sofas

on which they loll watching giant screens
while occasionally glancing out
through the panoramic windows
at the same old green field, where now
their thoroughbred horses graze.

I do not begrudge them anything.
Day in, day out, all day long
they cut the stone
like the men who built the Pyramids
or Newgrange. They harvested the hay,
they brought the turf home,
they dug potatoes in the mud
on their hands and knees in the wind and rain.

I'm conflating all this from childhood memories
and digitalised census archives,
scrolling through their lives
in a cafe on the Rue Soufflot,
attending to the ancestral hubbub.
At other tables the students pore
over spreadsheets and calligraphed notes.
They've been sitting here for hundreds of years
with their legal codes and pearl earrings.

The big black dog
lay on the stones of the yard.
Arthritic and gaunt
he raised himself up like a cormorant
to lick my hand.

TEENAGER

Mia Döring

She has plain brown hair and weighs eleven stone, which she finds repulsive. In her diaries: poetry and drawings. Over blue Bic pen swirls of horses' manes, she has written, over and over, lists of things she must achieve: lose weight, stop eating, get a boyfriend. Be interesting. Nothing is enough. Nothing she can offer is enough. Nothing she has to give is enough.

She helps, she is afraid, she wants to be useful. She hovers. She hopes. She writes gratitude lists. She apologises, she says sorry, she excuses herself. Playing, as a child, she had to be urged by adults to take part. One time, a friend's mother overheard her talking to a doll as if the doll was a real baby. She and the friend's mother made brief, sudden eye contact as the mother smiled her way up the stairs of her home. Shame stung and suffocated, and although she continued playing in that house, she would never let go to that extent again, she would never lose control like that again.

And then the time came for parents to stop organising playdates, and then the time came for street playing to stop, and although she didn't know it then, one summer day she called into neighbours for the last time, she eventually played her last play in the green, cycled her last cycle home.

She makes up fake social activities so she doesn't look like a loser, even though she isn't a loser and isn't even sure what a 'loser' is, anyway. She befriends the outcasts, the unpopular, the unwanted, the laughed at, the excluded. She goes on walks with them at lunchtime and feels sorry for them, like she is a charity worker, and also grateful, so grateful, for them. Her heart aches with empathy and she wishes she wasn't so soft. Such a pushover. So weak. She wishes she had a bit of the edge and harshness some of the Cool Girls have, some of their bite. She will never have their bite. She does have bite, she doesn't realise she has bite. She will get bite eventually. She relinquishes this desire and tries to forge her own identity but finds it hard to know who she is. She has never got to know herself. She doesn't know how to begin. The who of her has never been heard. The sight of her has never been seen.

She maintains a façade that keeps her safe. She orchestrates, she shows off, she humblebrags, she overachieves, she pretends, and she aches, she aches and she works hard, she does her best. She is doing her best and always feels like she is doing her worst. She is funny and puts herself down, but in a funny way, so it's okay.

She carries inexplicable guilt and the weight of it takes the lightness out of her eyes. She takes the blame for unearned misdemeanours in order to alleviate this guilt. She doesn't know why she does that. Her friends are baffled so she makes out like she is a martyr and sacrificing herself and no one can say anything then. She is privileged, and she knows she is, she carries the guilt. She is soft and sensitive and she watches, watches, watches. Her intuition is deep and deft, but she doesn't know it yet, can't separate out sensitivity and intuition. She has friends, she doesn't trust the friendships, she doesn't know what friendship is. At lunch in school, she asks her group, what are we doing at the weekend, and someone replies, who's we? and she doesn't say another thing, doesn't try again to say another thing.

She watches others. She accepts her cues. She knows she is a leader but follows anyway. She knows she is strong but pretends to be weak, steps behind and into shadows out of fear of her own light, for fear of what the power of it could do. She is aware, somewhere, that all this fragmentation and insecurity is normal, just normal, and she knows that many others have it far, far worse. But everywhere she looks she is the odd one, the soft one, the silly one, the stupid one. She is far from stupid.

DUBLIN 9'S DREAM FACTORY

Helen O'Rahilly

It's the fortieth anniversary of my alma mater, Dublin City University or NIHE, as it was when I went there in the early 1980s, then a new, tiny campus attached to the old Albert Agricultural College on the city's Northside.

I'd been offered a place in Trinity to study Science, but this new college, my second choice, was just ten minutes' walk from home. A real buzz was in the air about the innovative degrees on offer: Biotechnology, Analytical Science and something rather nebulous-sounding called Communication Studies. NIHE also had a unique selling point: it set up students with hands-on, paid work placements during its degrees. In the bleak economy of the 1980s, with record levels of unemployment, this sounded good to me. I declined my Trinity place and was offered NIHE instead. I saw my future in forensic science: white-coated, doing important detective work.

But the campus at NIHE, I discovered, was not much more than a windswept concrete yard. The canteen was the noisy hub of the college. A two-storey red-brick building, grandly titled the Henry Grattan, was the teaching centre: cinder-block walls, brown carpets, wood veneer desks: to describe it as utilitarian is being kind. There was no soaring campanile, like in Trinity, no wood-panelled common room, no water feature, let alone a lake, like UCD had. This was Dullsville, Dublin 9.

My brother, a medical doctor now at Oxford, no less, gave me good-natured grief about 'settling for the Ballymun polytechnic'. But it wasn't so much the place that disappointed me, it was Science. I fell out of love with it almost instantly.

I'd come from a white-coated family: Dad, a pharmacist, the doctor brother ... and it dawned on me that I was sleepwalking into the same line of work. Chemistry, biology and physics had been mental disciplines, puzzles I liked to solve, but once the Leaving Cert was over and the points accumulated, all my passion for science was spent.

Unable to turn another page of quadratic equations, I consider quitting in week three. But by mid-October I'd become intrigued by a black-clad, Doc Martined, red-lipsticked gang. Their laughter and witty banter echoed around the canteen as the entire 1200-strong student body, it seemed, wolfed down chips and beans all around us.

I eavesdropped on their conversations.

'*Saussure ... blah blah blah ... Oh, but Lacan! ... Oh no, Berger's the real deal ... Ah no, you've got to buy Benjamin ...*'

I didn't know who they were talking about. I didn't care. Who were these brash loudmouths on this stolid science campus?

'They're from Communication Studies ... bunch of pretentious so-and-sos.'

I longed to be a pretentious so-and-so. So I knocked on the door of the Dean of Communication Studies. What happened next changed my life.

Dr Martin Croghan, a charming man, sat and listened to me for an hour, then said, 'Helen, I don't want to know what subjects you were good at, I want to know what you love.'

I had never thought about my pastimes, my after-school activities as being something at which I could make a living. I was a keen photographer, having learned in Sister Mel's class in the darkroom of our Glasnevin convent. I made goofy comedy and chat shows with my pals with my Panasonic cassette recorder and tinny microphone. Amateur hour, but it was fun picking music tracks and making up characters. I was a bit of a movie buff and also an avid documentary watcher. I knew the TV schedules of RTÉ and BBC inside out.

'I'll make a few calls,' said Dr Croghan.

The next day, back went the science tomes. I walked into Cultural History with lecturer Luke Gibbons holding forth on the layers of meaning within the TV drama *The Ballroom of Romance*. The phrase 'Will you come into the field, Bridie?' stays with me still.

I was instantly hooked. My world expanded as I immersed myself in subjects ending in 'ics': Statistics, Economics, Linguistics.

I met Emer from Raheny, Pat from Kildare, Padraig from Sligo, Valerie from Castlegregory. All sparky, witty, wordy. We roamed Dublin, weighed down with massive U-matic video cameras and with portable tape recorders the size of microwave ovens hanging off our wilting shoulders. I'm reminded of Christy Moore's line in 'Lisdoonvarna' about media people 'makin' tapes, takin' breaks and throwin' shapes'.

We spent evenings in the sanctuary of the Slipper pub where a pint cost a punt. NIHE, back then, didn't even have a student bar. It was so new, the campus used to get letters addressed to the Northern Ireland Housing Executive.

We had to make our own fun. In cramped Santry digs, music was our shared love: The Smiths, Lloyd Cole and the Commotions, Simple Minds, Talking Heads. Crammed into smoke-filled rooms, we'd watch classic films on crackly VHS tapes: John Ford's finest or Kubrick's back catalogue. Any steamy scenes were met with red faces, bar the odd 'Yahoo ya boy ya!' – hardly the stuff of *Normal People*. We were abnormal eighties people. Forget mobile phones, even email wouldn't come for another ten years. We were just on the cusp – oh the excitement! – of using floppy disks.

We had three years of making magic. But after the hard graft, the essays, the assignments, the video, audio and photography projects, where would we get jobs? Step up the NIHE's pioneering INTRA programme – a six-month paid work placement. I got a place in RTÉ, and they hired me when I graduated. A few years later, the BBC beckoned, and I'd spend the next thirty years in London, working my way to the top of BBC television.

Recently returned to live in Ireland, I was given a tour of present-day DCU by its president, Brian McCraith. Multi-tiered buildings, multi-cultural students, multi-disciplinary research and innovation, the biggest concert hall in Ireland; 18,000 students on 85 acres; the original windswept courtyard now dwarfed by canyons of steel and concrete that had risen around it. It was an astonishing transformation. I was in awe of what had happened to our little, local college – but glad to spot that chips and beans are still on the menu in the canteen.

As for my own pioneering gang, you'll spot the odd Emmy, Bafta or MTV award on all our mantelpieces. Our glittering prizes. So, happy birthday NIHE, or DCU, for spotting potential, for letting us run riot with mad ideas, for giving us that critical head start. Dullsville, DCU? No; it was Dublin 9's Dream Factory.

MY BELFIELD

Daisy Onubogu

UCD Belfield. That's where I learned how to speak my mind, both in terms of believing I could have something worth saying, and the ability to say it comprehensively and with style.

UCD was where I learned the world was nowhere near as unfathomable as I'd thought. It's where I learned about the histories and cultural philosophies and institutions that had constructed the world around me, all the way down to the norms that guided the myriad ways people engaged with me: a young, queer Black woman.

It's where I learned Japanese phrases and massage therapy rules of thumb and how to construct a decent crossword puzzle. Perhaps most crucially, it's where I got my first crash course in leadership and working under pressure.

But let me take you back to my first day, standing by the lake in my trendy weave and my Penney's finest, about to become a Law student, feeling terrified that this would be the place I would finally be revealed for the fraud I was sure I was. And at the same time, somehow, deeply certain that this place would be where I'd finally find true friendship, and love and the deep belonging I'd observed in thousands of books, but had never quite experienced for myself in life.

Of course, it was both and neither. By the end of Second Year, I'd made my first real friend, and I'd seen my terror both realised and assuaged. I'd had to debate someone, a seasoned debater, intelligent and so in my mind powerful, who'd shown my case to be a stupid one, and in a roomful of people. I had a panic attack in the bathroom afterwards.

But in the minutes and hours following, nothing changed. I didn't disappear from the earth. And moreover, this had happened at the same time that nearly all the people within that same powerful cohort had been telling me that I was the one who should become the auditor of this ancient, prestigious society, the Literary and Historical Society (L&H).

Much of achievement comes down to realising what you're capable of. I don't think I could have figured it out without UCD, largely because nowhere else seems to have placed anywhere near the same emphasis on student-led activity.

This idea, that the environment and the time were there for you to figure out how to follow your curiosity and passions, and find a community that valued and validated them, has left an indelible mark on me. There's something for everyone and several someones to do it with, and if you can't find the society you need, start it! My something turned out to be debate, discourse and bringing people together, and the L&H let me learn how to do that, and have the best of times and the worst of times doing it. It made me fearless.

As for that campus. Perhaps because I saw it first on a sunny day, perhaps because it represented so much of what I was desperate for that my feelings overlay my vision, or maybe there's an ideal aesthetic balance between the blue waters, the green nature and the various greys of the landmark buildings, and it just works. Whatever the reason, I loved the physical UCD from the start, right until the end (excluding perhaps, the occasional moment, drenched in rain, keyless and scaling the gates of Glenomena Student Residence). It felt like a Pratchett-esque pocket world, with all the complicated, unconventional beauty, history and idiosyncrasies that that would imply. That's what I thought when, almost at the end of my time there, I finally found the secret lake. The very concept of that, a secret lake! So disorderly, unnecessary and *fascinating*.

Five years on, the strongest memories for me are a juxtaposition of the most intensely emotional and the most banal scenes. I find my mind's eye immediately drawn to both those high-energy, high-anxiety moments where I presided over L&H events with hundreds and thousands in the audience, and some globally renowned individual sitting beside me, or indeed the frantic moments before that where inevitably something would have gone wrong and needed urgent fixing. At the same time, I'm beset with memories of the grassy knoll between the O'Reilly building and the lake on a rare sunny day, trying to get from the Newman building to the Student Centre and ending up halting at least four or five times on the concourse to chat with friends.

That was my Belfield. A world of its own, filled with (at one time at least) almost everyone I loved and respected, at once a warm, safe haven, and a ceaselessly challenging terrain.

MAGIC NIGHTS IN THE LOBBY BAR

Aoife Barry

Some of my memories of the Lobby Bar in Cork are hazy now. What I remember comes in snatches: the painstakingly put together collages of photographs hanging on the yellow walls; the narrow stairs at the back of the bar which led to the venue on the first floor, and the energy of the queues that would form there before each show; the view upstairs out the tall windows to the city and the buildings beyond.

I began going to the Lobby just before I started college in UCC, at the turn of the millennium. As a music-loving teenager, I'd heard tales about this brilliant venue on a corner across from the City Hall. It was the kind of place that attracted well-known names like Christy Moore and Will Oldham, as well as local stalwarts like John Spillane and Sinéad Lohan, and up-and-comers from home and abroad. It was the kind of place I needed to go to.

The venue ended up becoming one of my music teachers, introducing me to another brilliant artist each time I visited. Even if I didn't get to go to a gig, just seeing the band's name on a poster was enough to pique my curiosity about new music. We were lucky, those of us who went to the Lobby, although how lucky only became obvious after it closed. The Irish music scene was going through an intense singer-songwriter phase when I was at the height of my Lobby-going days. So I got to see people like Damien Rice play their first gigs at the venue.

One of my favourite musicians at that time was the American singer Elliott Smith. I loved how his music had a sense of fragility to it. He wrote simmery pop songs that could break your heart, his voice was tender and his melodies sugary sweet, but he was never afraid to sing about the dark sides of life. I played his albums until I knew every note and every drumbeat by heart.

He had never played a gig in Cork, though when I was in secondary school he'd played in Dublin. But sadly, no amount of asking would get me the parental permission I needed to go see him. So I entertained dreams, instead, of one day seeing his name on a poster with 'Live at the Lobby Bar' written under it.

On 21 October 2003, Elliott Smith died tragically in the US. As a heartbroken fan in the months that followed, I wanted to do something to remember him by. So, although I felt a bit of an imposter, I decided to put on a gig in tribute to him on the anniversary of his death, in the Lobby Bar.

Between college lectures, I'd go to the computer lab in UCC to send emails to musicians from Cork and beyond, asking them if they'd like to play the Elliott Smith tribute night. I had no budget and had never booked a gig before, but people said yes.

The reason why people loved performing at the Lobby was obvious: it was the ultimate 'intimate venue'. The musicians stood on a small, curved stage in the corner of the room, inches from the audience. Behind them were large windows overlooking Union Quay, beyond which you could see the moon glint off the River Lee. To sit on a stool at one of the round tables and absorb the music was as great a treat as anything.

As the day of the Elliot Smith tribute gig dawned in October 2004, heavy rain began to fall on Cork. The worst flooding in years came in a deluge onto the city centre, and the Lobby was right next to Parnell Bridge, just feet from the River Lee. I was away from the city centre in UCC all day, relying on phone calls and hourly radio news updates about the rising tide. As the afternoon came, I heard that the water level had reached over three feet high on the South Mall, just across the bridge from the Lobby. I went home from college, preparing for the worst. This was in the days before iPhones and Twitter, and I was still in the dark about what was happening in the venue. I pictured musicians stuck in cars and buses unable to make it to the city centre. In my mind, the Lobby was surrounded by water, and no one would make it through the door. Surely, I thought, the tribute gig would have to be cancelled.

Then, an hour or so before the doors were to open, came a phone call from a friend: Come in, Aoife! By some sort of strange luck, the Lobby Bar stood dry. The venue had stayed open and people were starting to turn up, ignoring the warnings to stay out of the city. The gig was still on.

Despite it all, sixty people braved it out to hear the musicians pay tribute to Elliott Smith that soaking wet night, some who had travelled all the way down to Cork from Northern Ireland. It showed me what people are willing to do for the sake of the music they love.

The Lobby Bar closed in 2005, seventeen years after its first gig. I'd managed to get there just a handful of years before it shut its doors.

On the night of the Elliott Smith tribute, I headed home right after the musicians finished up. Overwhelmed as I was with how it had gone, it never occurred to me to stay, to soak up the atmosphere after such a precious gig. I didn't even take one photograph. All I have to rely on are these hazy memories.

I still think about that night. I imagine the moonlight shining on the swelling Lee which had over-spilled onto the streets, the sharing of memories of a musician tragically gone, the pints supped and glasses clinked, the new friendships made. I picture these moments in my mind as though I had stayed for the whole thing. Despite everything, the event had come together. Perhaps it was down to, as the musician John Spillane would put it in his song about the treasured spot, the magic of nights in the Lobby Bar.

THE PLANS FOR UL

Mae Leonard

Hard to believe it. UL – the University of Limerick – is fifty years old this year. Solid, sprawling, and serene by the Shannon. A regal seat of learning to be proud of.

I remember the big push in the 1960s to gain recognition for the need for a university for Limerick. There were marches and campaigns through the city in the drive to make the dream come true. I was on their side, of course, but when everything was on the brink of approval, I almost scuppered the whole effort. Let me tell you the story.

During the 1960s I was working as receptionist in Limerick Corporation. I manned an enquiries hatch for the public, but that was a bit difficult for me. My chair was low down and I had to stand up to reach the bolt to open it. It was the city accountant who sorted that. He brought me four huge old ledgers and piled them on my office chair, and they raised me up.

There was a constant stream of people through my office on business with the city manager. Visitors waited with me until he was free to see them. I met local politicians, government ministers, corporation officials and heads of departments.

Every evening at closing time, all the post was left with me. It was my duty to list each item and put it into the big leather postbag and fasten the big buckles. The messenger boy came in for it and attached it to the bag crossbar of his bike, before delivering it to the GPO in Limerick.

The then Minister for Education, Donogh O'Malley, was a frequent visitor. A university for Limerick was his primary project at the time. Oozing charisma, he swept through the building on a cloud of Old Spice aftershave, and everything he touched confirmed his presence in the building. He was formidable and exacting, and his driver had his ministerial car engine running right outside the front door. The entire staff breathed a sigh of relief every time he left the building.

One Monday morning, there was a bit of commotion. The city manager and the town clerk were all of a dither. Phones were ringing in every office. The Minister for Education left the building with blue smoke coming out his ears, as someone put it.

Gradually the story filtered down to me. The architectural plans for the university were missing. They had been posted from our offices to Government Offices in Dublin but never arrived. There was consternation, and no wonder. A deadline had to be met. It was a time before photocopying or personal computers or digital anything. Those plans had been drawn up by the city architect and painstakingly copied by draftsmen. The work had taken weeks, and now the plans were missing.

As he left the building that Monday morning the Minister for Education flung a few fiery words over his shoulder, all of which meant 'incompetence'. The plans had to be redrawn instantly. Staff worked throughout the night and the following day, until everything was completed and a staff member was dispatched by train to Dublin to deliver the precious drawings and documents.

It took weeks for the dust to settle.

Some months later, as I reached up to close the enquiries hatch, my chair tilted with the amount of weight on it. The four big ledgers toppled onto the floor, carrying me with them. I wasn't hurt, but there, on the floor, between the spread-out books was a big envelope. I looked at it and recognised it immediately. Then it dawned on me. Oh, horror. The envelope was so big that it was too thick to fit into the postbag that day and I had put it under the books on my chair to flatten it, and forgotten all about it. The disaster that had caused such bother. It was me. I was the one responsible.

What could I do? In a panic I consulted with my closest colleague.

'Burn it,' she said.

But no. I had to own up. I was transferred to the City Library for a month until my incompetence was almost forgiven, and life went back to normal again.

Hard to believe it. Despite all my effort in stalling it, UL – the University of Limerick – is now fifty years old. Solid, sprawling, and serene by the lordly Shannon. A regal seat of learning to be proud of.

THE MASTER

Nuala Hayes

August 1980. We had packed the car with clothes, books, games, footballs and food. Our sons Oisín and Eoin were seven and four, and excited for this adventure. We headed north, through Meath and Monaghan and across the border at the army checkpoint at Aughnacloy, County Tyrone. The boys stared in fascination at the young British soldiers armed with real guns.

Identification and purpose of visit to Northern Ireland?

We were heading to Derry, we said, to work on a production of a new play by Brian Friel.

A new play by the Master, Brian Friel, created a buzz of excitement for anyone interested in theatre at that time. His plays belonged in places like the Abbey or the Gate or the West End in London. So why was his new play, *Translations*, set in a hedge school in a village in Donegal in 1833 as British soldiers convert Irish placenames to English, having its world premiere at the Guildhall in Derry in September 1980?

Field Day Theatre Company had been set up by Brian and the actor Stephen Rea to produce this play. It was a courageous and daring 'enterprise', as Brian used to call it: to find a new audience outside the established theatres, and to explore a new context for his work.

They had invited my husband Art Ó Briain, a theatre director with a background in community arts activism in Dublin and Derry, to join them in the 'enterprise'.

Art was aware from his work in Derry that the City Council, which by that time included both nationalists and unionists, would be open to the idea of a kickstart for a renewal of cultural life in the city which had been ravaged by years of war.

They were welcomed with open arms and after much discussion of suitable venues, the historic Guildhall was chosen, which wasn't a theatre at all. It had recently been restored and reopened after bomb damage. But it was a symbolic building, and had been the setting for a previous, controversial Friel play, *The Freedom of the City*, about the atrocity of Bloody Sunday.

So there we found ourselves, settling into a house in Drumahoe, on the Waterside, on the outskirts of Derry. The big house had a large garden, and from outside its walls you could hear the Orange bands with their pipes and drums practising along the roads. The Apprentice Boys were preparing for their annual march. As we unpacked the car, Oisín, full of pent-up energy, managed to find a small tricolour in the boot, left over from the St Patrick's Day parade. He charged around the garden, waving the tricolour, innocently marking out his territory. Hard to explain to a seven-year-old from Dublin that this might not be a good idea.

We shared an apartment in the house with Mick and Peige Lally, who had arrived on the bus to Derry with their baby daughter Saileog. Together we formed a little family group, a bubble, you could say. The house was full of love and the Irish language, as both Mick and Peige – who came from Inis Meáin on the Aran islands – were native speakers, and Art and I were attempting to raise our boys bilingually.

Translations is a play about language. Mick was playing Manus; I was playing Máire, who speaks no English, and falls in love with Yolland, a British soldier who speaks no Irish.

I have a memory of the entire cast and crew of that first production of *Translations*, sitting around a big mahogany table in the rehearsal room of the Guildhall for the first read-through of the play, always a tense moment for everyone. Brian sat at the top of the table and Art at the other end.

When the reading was ended there was spontaneous applause. All of us – cast and crew – realised then that the script was as perfectly composed as a piece of music. Our job was to deliver it to an audience in four weeks' time.

Brian was with us throughout the rehearsal period, a focused, witty and benign presence. I'm sure there must have been problems behind the scenes, but if there were, they don't figure in my memory.

The opening night. The rich Donegal tones of the voice of actor Ray MacAnally speaking the last lines of the play, as the lights faded to black. Silence.

Applause erupted, the lights came up and the cast appeared for a well-rehearsed bow. The applause continued, so we returned again and again. The playwright joined us on stage to cheers of approval. He said something about a prophecy of Saint Colmcille coming true. Did he really say that Colmcille prophesied that a theatre company called Field Day would take Derry by storm on 23 September 1980? What a night that was. The aliveness of it all!

The play went on to tour the small towns and halls of Northern Ireland as planned, and then to Belfast, Dublin and Cork. Then other productions opened in London and Broadway, and forty years on it has become a classic of world theatre.

There were many other plays, including a huge success ten years later with *Dancing at Lughnasa*. Field Day Theatre Company toured throughout Ireland for another ten years.

Five years after the death of the playwright I think of his work and his legacy. I think of love and death and memory, which are strong themes in all his plays.

I remember how Brian's much-loved wife Anne, who was his rock, and the entire Friel family supported and welcomed us all to their home with such warm hospitality.

I remember the cast travelling the dark roads of the North in a van back to our lodgings, exhilarated after a performance to a packed hall in Carrickmore or Magherafelt or Armagh, where it seemed the entire town had turned out. Singing on the bus, ignoring soldiers with guns cocked, hunched down behind bushes in dark corners.

My own lasting memory is the music of words. In the doomed love affair between Máire, the character I played, and Yolland, the British soldier, their only shared language is the place names of Donegal.

Bun na hAbhann? Druim Dubh? Poll na gCaorach. Lis Maol. Lis na nGall … Lis na nGradh. Carraig an Phoill … Carraig na Rí. Loch na n'Éan … Mullach. Port … Tár … Leag … I wish to God you could understand me!

TAKE AWAY

AM Cousins

First, the seafood platter:
mackerel morsels, wild crab,
oak-smoked salmon
and a great prawn with beady eyes
and a hipster moustache,
arranged and garnished
with slivers of tomato,
red onion and mashed potato,
all for ten euro,
to eat on the spot
or take away for supper.
Afterwards, we follow the guide
from the famine-relief pier
to the Forlorn Point,
to stand on the last remaining plates
of avalonian rock
alongside the Garden of Remembrance.
Listen:
once, the sea
came up to Ballyteigue
and the Normans planted rabbits
to graze the Burrow;
later, a canal was dug
with pick and shovel

and starving men loaded wheelbarrows,
cradled the shafts on upturned elbows,
ran down the hill, gathering speed
to propel them up the ramp.
They glided – almost flew –
on thruppence a week
and a mugful of yellow meal
to take away for supper.

OCTOBER

REDISCOVERING CARMEN BUSTAMANTE

Colm Tóibín

In 'The Dead' by James Joyce, Aunt Kate, in a discussion about singers, announces that for her there was only one tenor. 'To please me, I mean. But I suppose none of you ever heard of him.' His name, she said, 'was Parkinson. I heard him when he was in his prime and I think he had then the purest tenor voice that was ever put into a man's throat.'

But the others in the company have never heard of him.

Scholars have suggested that this is Joyce's way of showing that Aunt Kate's memory is fading, one writing, for example, that 'it seems unlikely that such a group of aficionados would have known nothing of so remarkable a tenor voice as that evoked by Aunt Kate.'

But I think I know what Aunt Kate might have meant. In 1977, in the Palau de la Música, the main concert hall in Barcelona, there was a Beethoven marathon, a whole day dedicated to Beethoven's music. Lasting eight hours, it included a piano concerto and chamber music and ended with the Ninth Symphony.

But what stood out for me was when, in the late afternoon, a soprano came onto the stage and sang a single song called 'The Elfin Fairies', one of Beethoven's Irish songs. It could not have lasted more than three minutes.

I thought the singer had the most delicate, expressive and exquisite voice. Even now, forty-five years later, I can remember how she balanced the lilting tone in the arrangement against the soaring notes in the melody. She was supremely confident. Her name was Carmen Bustamante and she must have been in her thirties then.

But when I asked about her, no one seemed to recognize her name. I wondered why she was not as famous as other singers in Barcelona then, such as Monserrat Caballé and Victoria de los Ángeles.

And then I met someone who explained. Carmen Bustamante was a famous singing teacher. While she did sometimes perform, she did not tour much and had made no recordings. Like Veronica Dunne in Ireland, the quality of her voice was known only to a few. But she inspired several generations of students. She became my Parkinson. She was the soprano who had pleased me. But I had only heard her once: just one song.

Recently, I went back to that concert hall in Barcelona to give a talk about music in the city in the 1970s and I thought I should check, in the age of the internet, to see if there was any more information about Carmen Bustamante. And I found, to my delight, that she had made a number of CDs and I could now, after all the years, listen to her voice again.

Like other Catalan singers, she had made a CD of Catalan folk songs that, in complex arrangements, had almost become art songs as performed by, say, Victoria de los Ángeles or José Carreras.

In these songs, Carmen Bustamante's voice was as confident and exquisite as I remembered. But, like the other two singers, she had also worked with the songs of a number of Catalan composers who had thrived at the beginning of the twentieth century, whose songs had become part of the Catalan repertoire but were hardly known outside Catalonia. Composers like Frederic Mompou, Xavier Montsalvatge and Eduard Toldrà.

There was one song by Toldrà, a setting of a poem by the Catalan poet Josep Carner, whose work has been translated by the Irish poet Pearse Hutchinson, that I started to listen to over and over.

After all the years, here was the voice again – Carmen Bustamante – delicate, intimate, haunting, the control and timing perfect.

It is, nonetheless, hard to explain why this was the voice for me. Perhaps something in the mixture of modesty and a striving for perfection, simplicity combined with technical perfection. Perhaps an understated sense of yearning. Perhaps because she was more at home with delicate art songs than large operatic parts.

I don't know.

Before the lecture in Barcelona, I sent the people there the text and, since it contained so many dates and facts, they decided to check in case I had got something wrong.

Who now remembered a Beethoven marathon in Barcelona in 1977? Who remembered Montserrat Caballé singing Wagner in 1978? And who remembered Carmen Bustamante?

In the office that day, when the fact-checker asked his colleagues if anyone knew her name, they all shook their heads except one. He said that Carmen Bustamante was a neighbour of a friend of his. When they found a number for her and phoned her, she said she was indeed the singer. And yes, she had sung that Beethoven song in the Palau de la Música in that concert in 1977.

A week later, as I spoke in the concert hall about what it meant to hear her then, and what it had meant for all the years to carry the memory of her voice, knowing that this memory was not generally shared, I knew that Carmen Bustamante, a sprightly eighty-four, was in the front row.

So that the audience would know what her voice, at its height, had been like, we played, in her presence, a recording of that Toldrà song. It is called 'Cançó Incerta'.

OPENING NIGHTS

Dominic Dromgoole

It seemed inevitable once I decided to write a book on history's most seismic first nights, that my first port of call should be Dublin. Few cities have packed in as many premieres of mayhem and magic as Dublin, and few countries have funnelled their tensions and rages through the theatre as greatly as Ireland.

Maud Gonne's memorable entrance in a doorway in Yeats and Lady Gregory's *Cathleen ni Houlihan* is one of the all-time first night moments – the argument and dreams of its authors, the hunger and need of its audience, and the expressive capacity of a charismatic figure all coming together in one stark image. The first Abbey was a cockpit of fantastic imagining and bitter truth, and within its wooden clatter were played out the passions of the emerging nation state. Here *Playboy* fireworked into life, roared along by a brawl confected by Yeats, who had invited a group of drunken Trinity students along to make mischief. Yeats was at the centre again fifteen years later when *The Plough and the Stars* opened, and he stood on stage and barked at a seething mob, 'You have disgraced yourselves again'. Yeats could be said to be a connoisseur of the riotous first night, having attended the legendary brouhaha of Alfred Jarry's *Ubu Roi* in Paris. He clearly had a taste for chaos.

My initial weekend of research in Dublin was spent in discussion with a number of academics talking about why the city had a propensity for concocting the broth that boils over and spills out onto the grate. My last conversation was with the theatre scholar Chris Morash. At the end of our delightful chat in the National Library, he pressed into my hands his book *A History of Irish Theatre*. I read it and discovered that on *Cathleen* and *The*

Playboy and *The Plough*, he had got there first and unimprovably, his overall narrative studded with short chapters summoning up the excitement and the drama of each first night. I was, in literary terms, gazumped.

Happily he had left Handel's *Messiah*, a first night which survives into my book. Or rather a first mid-day, since the oratorio began in Fishamble Street at twelve to leave the audience time for a gargantuan Augustan supper afterwards. Nine hundred folk crammed in to the Great Music Hall, a number only possible after an advertisement was published requesting the ladies to appear without their hoops, and the gentlemen without their swords: a request which throws up any number of Freudian interpretations.

In discussing Dublin's propensity for the volcanic premiere, each academic offered a different historical or linguistic or sociological theory. All brilliant and acute. But I kept being brought back to an observation I had once heard.

By a stroke of immense good fortune, when I was young I acquired an extra mother and father in Maeve Binchy and Gordon Snell. They were our *Wahlfamilie* as the Germans phrase it, in one of their encompassing compound words – chosen family to go alongside given family. Maeve used to define one of the characteristics of Dublin and its population as always being 'on the verge'. Sometimes she felt everyone she met was on the verge. Whether of falling in love or of marital break-up, of going down with something nasty or rising back up to glorious health, of a tremendous breakthrough or a calamitous collapse, whichever didn't matter much, what mattered was that they were on a precipice, with something huge about to happen. A whole city on the verge.

Of course there are few moments we manufacture for ourselves more precipitously 'on the verge' than a world premiere. The adrenalin beforehand pumping through artists and spectators, the focus which the attention of so many sharpens, the terror of failure or the exhilaration of success swimming before everyone's eyes, all these factors combine to pump electricity into the air around you. Maybe there is just a natural fit between the temperament of Dublin and the natural temperament of these nights. Maybe they heighten each other to fresh cliff heights of 'on the verge'.

My mind passed over the many first nights I had attended and been involved with in Ireland. The vividness of Declan Hughes's *Digging for Fire* in the Project, which rampantly proclaimed a new, sexy and young Ireland, shucking off the griefs and sorrows of the past. Our transfer of Billy Roche's *Wexford Trilogy* to the Opera House of his home town, where it seemed the entire population had crammed themselves into the beautiful auditorium to witness themselves being related and understood. And the mesmeric powers of Sebastian Barry's *White Woman Street*, which we transferred to the Peacock, where the actors' grizzled faces and Sebastian's weather-beaten words were enough to transport the audience to a Wild West landscape, a suspension of disbelief, which somehow survived one entire bit of scenery falling over.

And I remembered the first night of my production of *Philadelphia Here I Come* in the Gaiety in 2010. An encounter backstage between Maeve and Brian Friel came sharply to mind. Down a long corridor they inched towards each other, Maeve stooping and Brian shuffling. As they approached one another they pulled themselves a little upright …

'We're doing all right, aren't we, Brian?' said Maeve cheerily.

'Maeve, we're both [and then an extremely rude word],' rasped Brian.

It would be hard to imagine a better summary of their different world views.

And after every first night of exemplary exhilaration, much drinking in the bar, then mayhem in the Trocadero restaurant, then retiring to some unfortunate's home, then all spilling out at dawn to dissipate energy and excitement in lonely walks into a sea breeze. There are few places that know how to engender and enjoy a memorable first night like Dublin.

'TWILL SHORTEN THE WINTER

Margaret Galvin

It was always agreed in Wexford that 'the festival shortens the winter for us'. Not only did the festival imbue us with that sense of anticipation and excitement that did indeed 'shorten the winter', it ensured that Wexford was way ahead of other Irish towns in accepting that men from foreign places would arrive amongst us for those glorious October weeks and walk the streets of our place, holding hands.

'Are them lads back again this year?' the locals would enquire, decades ago, and long before any liberal attitude prevailed elsewhere. We learned not only how to live and let live but to positively delight in that which was different, unexpected and never seen at other times. The lads were indeed back, quietly demonstrative in their affection, wrapping long knitted scarves around their necks, protection against the weather they evidently found harsh. Because I worked in a little leather shop on the quay, I used to take particular note of the beautiful leather bags that hung from their shoulders, tan leather, so soft and tactile. We knew nothing then of man bags and we wondered what exotic contents might spill from these pouches. What could these striking strangers be carrying with them?

My hope that one day they'd come into that little leather shop where I worked was never realised. Many strangers did indeed frequent that sitting-room-sized emporium where bags and belts hung from hooks on the ceiling. One customer, in particular, has stayed with me for many decades. I picked up on her disconsolate demeanour as I unhooked a tumble of merchandise for her. Her gaze was unfocused and distracted as she fingered the ware, adding item after item to the pile she intended to purchase.

The selection was random: wallets, a glasses case, an elegant and very expensive clutch bag, a music case and a satchel that made her look like a schoolgirl as she tried it on crossbody style in front of the shop mirror. When I told her this, it brought a wan smile to her lips. 'I'm no schoolgirl,' she intoned, her voice melancholy and wistful, 'and I'm not sure I've learned a hell of a whole lot either.' As I wrapped up the purchases she said 'would do for Christmas presents', she told me that she was from Limerick. Neighbours had inveigled her to come with them for a few days of the opera festival. 'I don't feel well,' she mumbled vaguely, 'they said the change would give me a lift.'

I was too young then to understand the import of the words spoken by a woman who was in her sixties, the age I am now. I wondered at the disillusionment of a woman who could hand over a fistful of notes for an array of luxury goods, a woman who carried the weight of her unknown grief like a boulder, a boulder she left down for a while as she sought a bit of respite amongst the shades of tan and mottled, oxblood and cognac.

I can only hope that the festival did indeed give her the promised 'lift'. I hope that she found it in her heavy heart to join the heaving throngs on the quay-front for 'fireworks night', that exploding pyrotechnic sensation when the lit-up sky caused our hearts to thump and our eyes to shine with the wonder life might hold. No matter what darkness lodged heavy in her soul, the evidence that life could burn with coloured flames in explosive shades of red, orange, purple and silver couldn't but heal with redemptive grace. I hope she lifted her shining eyes to the heavens to delight in showers of falling stars, fountains of light, peony-roses, chrysanthemums and Catherine wheels as they crackled and burst over us, bright with wonder. She came, dispirited and sad to our festival town. I hope that as the fireworks took her out of herself, she too hummed along with all of us, reaching back into memory for 'La donna è mobile' or 'O mio babbino caro'. I hope 'the lads' were there too, the exotic strangers in their knitted scarves, the men who were blessed with love.

LIKE A BIRD ON A BEAM

Tom Mooney

The night the birds gate-crashed the Opera House has entered Wexford folklore. I remember it all too well because I was there, on the eve of the new millennium.

It was the grand opening of the annual Wexford Opera Festival, and not just another night at the opera.

Aficionados throughout the world have flocked in their thousands to Wexford every October since 1951 for the rare chance to see little-known works by famous composers.

The seven hundred or so tickets for the premiere at the Theatre Royal, High Street, in 1999, much like any other year, were like gold dust, having sold out months in advance.

The tiny Opera House was squeezed between terraced housing like the Rover's Return in Coronation Street.

For broadcasting purposes, the premiere is an occasion primed to run like clockwork: the opera starts at 8 p.m. sharp; latecomers are not admitted.

One of the best vantage points for the backstage staff of the theatre to see the spectacular fireworks which launched the Wexford Festival, half an hour before curtain up, was from the roof of the Opera House which rose over the harbour town. They gained access via a door which was left ajar. But they were not alone.

Roosting among the nooks and crannies of the old nineteenth-century roof were the town's starlings, black as ink and invisible in the darkness. Nobody had forewarned them about the fireworks which erupted like Vesuvius half an hour before the cast of *The Queen of Sheba* took to the stage.

The explosions in the night sky were greeted by a tremendous roar from the thousands of men, women and children assembled on the quay front.

Startled, the starlings scrambled like a flying squadron, and took refuge in the Theatre Royal, which they accessed through the door left open on the roof.

Inside, they would have discovered that the ceiling of the old Theatre Royal was conveniently crisscrossed by four wooden beams, a perfect place to perch above the stalls.

The beams were high and warm and dry and out of harm's reach from the fireworks. And the starlings, because it was way past their bedtime, were so unobtrusive that nobody in the theatre below, which was beginning slowly to fill up, knew they were there.

Best of all, they had – literally – a bird's eye view of the stage, directly below.

Before long, conductor Claude Schnitzler assumed his position above the orchestra in the sunken pit. The lights were abruptly dimmed and a hush settled upon the theatre.

After a rousing 'Amhrán na bhFiann' by the RTÉ National Symphony Orchestra, the overture to *The Queen of Sheba* came and went.

So far, so quiet, until midway through the first aria by Cornelia Helfricht, the starlings stirred and behaved the way all garden birds do when they hear singing.

They sang back.

It is not commonly known that starlings are related to mynah birds, which means they are gifted at mimicry.

A cacophony of warbling and shrills, quite beautiful in starling language, began to rain down from on high. There was too, the occasional deposit – bird confetti you might say – which in some cultures is supposed to bring good luck. The audience, well-versed in sitting motionless through hour upon hour of opera, braved the chirping, and whenever the starlings let loose they continued to sit with a combination of indifference and commendable stiff upper lip.

There was naturally the odd chuckle, and eyes raised to the heavens.

Schnitzler ploughed gamely on in the best traditions of show business, but it couldn't have been easy for a conductor whose regular haunt was Opéra National de Paris.

The birds expressed a bias for Ms Helfricht, the German mezzo soprano making her Wexford debut in the title role in front of the world's most unforgiving opera critics. When an aria finished, they chirruped enthusiastically. There was no let-up for the entire four acts of the opera. The starlings interrupted the score at will, all the while dispensing good luck onto the shoulders of expensive gowns and black-tie attire, a hundred feet below.

Finally, after the Queen of Sheba's paramour took an age to expire in the sandstorm, the opera was over. The singing, however, wasn't. The starlings chirruped away and continued to dispense their charity.

Never before did the Theatre Royal empty with such urgency.

There is no easy way to remove starlings from an opera house, but suffice to say that a day later, and before the second night of the opera festival, they were persuaded to vacate their ornate perch.

NOTES FOR THE FIFTH OF OCTOBER

Anne Devlin

When I was nine, my father Paddy Devlin put a pen in one of my hands and an electoral register in the other and showed me how to write election addresses onto polling cards. As a result, by the time I was seventeen, politics was my rock and roll.

I remember a photograph of myself – it's the first photo I have ever really liked. I look ... womanish. I am staying with Joan, she's a secretary in the party office. She works with my dad on elections and lives in a flat overlooking the Botanic Gardens. My mother and father have left me there, for the weekend, with a cooked chicken. She lent me one of her swimming costumes. Black with a black mesh midriff. Because, for the first time since I was a kid, I have a midriff that summer. In the photo I'm on her balcony in sunlight. Well actually, I climbed out of a window onto the porch above the front door and posed: hello, Brigitte Bardot.

I still think I look like the girl in the picture two weeks after my seventeenth birthday when I run for the bus. It's parked outside Queen's, in the forecourt in front of the Union. It's the single-decker Ulster Transport bus that will take us to Derry. The bus is full when I reach it, but my friends have kept me a seat. They are students and graduates mostly, and I am a schoolgirl. I shouldn't even be on the bus, but I joined the young socialists earlier in the summer and they can't get rid of me. Even when they set me tasks like sewing a new banner. I cannot thread a needle, so I buy white adhesive fabric from which I cut out letters and stick them onto the banner with a hot iron.

And because four of us have been to see *Yellow Submarine* in the cinema a few months before, we sing on the bus: we all live in a fascist regime.

When we arrive in Derry there are occupied police tenders parked in steep side streets. It's the first time I've been to Derry and I'm busy thinking, what are all those police vehicles doing on the slopes?

Until Roger, who looks like John Lennon in an Aran sweater, says, 'Oh, look, Blue Meanies!'

In Duke Street when we are stopped, James puts a megaphone to his mouth, and makes a speech. The problem with standing next to a megaphone is you can't hear anything but noise; you need to stand in front of it to hear. In front of me are four lines of people and James is talking into the backs of their heads. I must have got distracted, because suddenly, these lines of marchers have melted until there is no one, except in my frame of vison: a dark uniformed figure, peaked cap shading his eyes, his arm raised in front of his face, the truncheon an extension of the arm, his other hand cupping his elbow. He swings his left knee towards the raised arm in perfect balance, while facing me, from the middle of a line of men. He screws up his face and snarls, like the principal dancer whose balletic movement I am blocking: 'Get out of the road! If you don't want to get hurt!'

Like a coiled spring released, his left leg comes back, his right arm comes down and I run, back along the street to where I find James, standing on the edge of the pavement. He looks odd. Then I notice a trickle from his hairline to his jaw and onto his collar. A man moves swiftly towards us and guides us into a closed public house, where he gives me a pan of hot water and cloth and leaves, me feeling like Saint Veronica.

In the lobby of the City Hotel, a row of telephone booths with those concertina doors fully extended are occupied by cubs and veterans phoning their copy, in urgent, carefully paced sentences to national editors.

We believed that Britain was a fairer place to live than where we did. My family never looked to Dublin. All my mother's sisters went to England for work. My father's paper was *The Manchester Guardian*; my grandmother read *The Universe*. The Beatles were the Irish in England, and Liverpool was Pepperland. I stayed up all night when Harold Wilson was elected. I never understood why the English could keep changing their government and we had the same one for fifty years.

And when the *Six O'Clock News* came on from London on 5 October, we watched young ghosts of ourselves pass, on the other side of a glass wall. I gathered those fifty years into my face. And no one came back from Derry.

PHENOMENAL GRACE

Susan McKay

Pat Hume is looking at old photos from the Duke Street march. 'All men,' she says, 'Or nearly. That's how it was.' Her husband marched that day. She was at home, eight months pregnant and with the couple's three small children.

Pat's memory of the morning of what became Bloody Sunday in 1972 is, 'Oh my God, I think I'm pregnant again.'

There were women on Duke Street that October day in 1968, great women. But mostly, in those early days, the women of Derry were not marching but minding. Struggling nonetheless. No one could have gone out if they had not stayed at home. The chant might have been 'one man, one vote' but it was women who bore the brunt of rearing families in the gerrymandered slums.

John Hume used to say, 'I'm the parcel but Pat delivers me.' It's an oddly charming statement, but there's something enigmatic about it – maybe because Pat's role as the wife of that visionary leader is really quite complicated, as John was well aware. What everyone who knows them acknowledges is that Pat was every bit as involved in the transformation of Northern Ireland as her husband. He could not have done a thing without her.

She is an unsung hero who doesn't want to be sung. She does her best to dissuade me from writing about her. 'I'm boring as hell,' she says. 'Write about the women who were out there campaigning – write about Máirín Ó Dochairtaigh, Kittie O'Kane, Sheila McClean, Cathy Harkin.' Yes, yes, R.E.S.P.E.C.T. – but, to get back to Pat.

341

Mary Robinson said the great civil rights campaigner Inez McCormack taught her that sometimes you can be more effective if you don't feel the need to take the credit. Mary Beard says that if women are to be included in history we need to look at leadership as being about more than just the single charismatic figure. We need to think collaboratively, and about power as the ability to be effective, to make a difference to the world.

Early evidence of Pat's power of influence: John was training to be a priest when he met her.

She was known back then as Babs, Babs Hone. Pat ran the Hume household. She was also the breadwinner – a teacher. A surprisingly stern teacher, I'm told. Some were misled by her beauty and her ready smile into thinking she'd be a walkover. She had shimmering blue eyes and a swathe of wheat-coloured hair which she wore in a plait. She was twenty-one when she taught her first class; there were fifty-six teenagers in it. The Humes relied on another woman, too. This was Molly Doherty, known as Nana. She looked after the children. Reliable, practical, and full of laughter, Molly kept the family afloat for twenty-three years.

Pat says that when she got in from school, Molly would be 'out the door like a shooting star'. She doesn't blame her. 'Our house wasn't the easiest,' she says. It wasn't just the 'five mad feckers', as the Hume children were described to me by one of them, Mo. There were also what Pat calls the 'unpredictabilities'. The house 'never emptied' she says. A constant stream of people called on the phone or to the door seeking help with problems which included, according to Mo, 'housing, brew not coming through, son lifted by the British army, someone had the shit kicked out of them, passport required'.

It was Pat who spent her evenings dealing with all of this, who attended funerals, and knew everybody. After John became an MEP in 1979, she formally took over the running of his constituency office. John was often away – setting up credit unions, attending parliaments, meeting world leaders. He was Washington, Dublin, Brussels, London, Belfast. Pat was Derry, she was the Hume's Derryness. But John took no significant decisions, ever, without consulting his wife. His trust in her political judgement was complete.

There were always visitors. John was hospitable; Pat was the host. He could make Irish stew. Under supervision. Once John invited a bishop and his wife to lunch. Pat, who was about to give birth, served boiled eggs. 'Every so often,' she admits, 'I would erupt.'

They lived under siege. For decades, every day brought hate mail, threats and abusive phone calls. From unionists, from republicans. IRA supporters stoned the house, and petrol-bombed it. Pat did her best to shield the children. Mo recalls her mother swearing, just once, and with just one word, when she opened the door one night to find her car and the windows of the house in flames. When the Hume–Adams talks were revealed, John was being denounced by the British and Irish establishments while acts of mass murder were proliferating in the North. It was hell, Pat says. 'I don't know how we survived.'

John, in truth, did not survive well. His health is broken, he has dementia and now another brutal illness that is stripping him of his faculties. Pat has become the memory John has lost. For years, she has been his guide, by his side to mediate encounters with strangers and friends, always gracious, always knowing what to say. If John says the wrong thing, people let it pass now. Pat says Derry has become a city of kindness.

Pat has had cancer and other afflictions. But she says she's reached her four score years and she looks back with gratitude. She has great friends, children she's proud of, grandchildren to snuggle up with on the sofa, and, as of this summer, a first great-grandchild She walks the banks of the Foyle. She loves Lisa McGee's *Derry Girls* and can recite and discuss in detail entire episodes. Remember the cream horn on Pump Street?

She loves to quote Seamus Heaney, 'there is one among us who never swerved / from all his instincts told him was right action / who stood his ground in the indicative'. She's thinking about John. I'm thinking about Pat too. Her modesty is part of what her daughter Mo calls her 'phenomenal grace'.

TEENAGE KICKS

Kate Kerrigan

I was at my friend Diarmuid's sixtieth birthday bash in a pub in Sligo dancing to Sister Sledge. The last time I danced to 'We Are Family' was with my sons in the kitchen of our new house. The open plan has so much potential for mid-afternoon 'joy' dancing. When I say 'we', of course, I mean 'me'. My sons find the idea of their mother dancing heinous. 'You're too old to dance,' said the eight-year-old, 'you could *hurt* yourself.' The Teen laughed, briefly, before shaking his head in disbelief at the sheer indignity of having me as a mother.

So, when offered a legitimate opportunity to dance at a party, I tend to go a bit mad. I was doing my trademark 'scoop' move to the left when I nearly banged into my mother's favourite writer, a national treasure. He was wearing Yeats specs and a three-piece tweed suit. What's that old boy doing here? I thought. Then I remembered it wasn't 1978 after all —and I wasn't in the youth club disco surrounded by sixteen-year-old bikers. I was a middle-aged woman in a pair of comfortable ankle boots and a black 'going out' dress throwing ludicrous shapes in the back bar of a pub in Sligo. I went off the idea of myself entirely and, defeated, sloped to the Ladies.

I made a conscious decision to give up recreationally studying myself in mirrors after I turned fifty. Aside from the practical necessity of daily maintenance make-up, I try to avoid them, but pub bathrooms on a night out are a necessity and my reflection was less of a disappointment than it usually is, due to a combination of broken light bulbs and zealous make-up application. I headed back to the dance floor just in time for Blue Monday. Is it really the case that Eighties music is retro? It still sounds so current to me. As the drum beat started pounding out I remembered the last time I danced to this addictive tune was with my friend Johnny. He was part of this Sligo gang. I met a lot of them here through him. He died a few years ago – at fifty. I danced for a minute or two in his honour, remembering the fun we had dancing in Dublin nightclubs together, back in the day. Then I felt too sad to dance. Johnny should be here.

As I get older and lose more friends, I have found the fearful shock of death can give way to a sort of bleak resignation. I went over to the quiet corner where I'd been standing earlier and sought out my drink. Everyone was merry. Birthday boy Diarmuid was standing at the edge of the floor, next to the bar. Momentarily alone, he was surveying the room with a big, daft grin on his face. 'Sixty – hi,' I could hear him saying in his Northern accent. He was smiling from the inside out.

'Teenage Kicks' by the Undertones came on – the anthem of all arty eighties types – and I watched as my husband launched himself across the room. He was joined by other beer-fuelled comets all rushing towards the euphoric recall of youth, and within seconds the dance floor was heaving with middle-aged punks. I looked on as my old man and Diarmuid threw their pointed fingers at each other shouting the words of the chorus, and I thought, I don't care how old we are, we are still banging hot! The artist Alice Maher, cool as a cucumber, was sitting across the room watching the scene unfold as well, and we nodded at each other and laughed at the scene before joining them. This was our music, our time – these are still *our* boys – twenty or eighty – it makes no difference.

Sure, some of us are gone and nights like this remind us of them. We must never forget that we're the lucky ones. We are still here, still alive, still dancing – we *will* be the eighty-year-old punk generation. Teenage kicks are not just for teenagers, after all.

MISSING BRENDAN KENNELLY
Gudrun Boch-Mullan

The Frankfurt Book Fair is the oldest, and to this day the world's largest, trade fair for books. The five-day annual event in October has a history that goes back all the way to the fifteenth century when printing was developed. For the past two years Covid prohibited the usual proceedings, but this autumn sees publishers and writers, presenters and the media back at the multitude of events. Every year, since 1988, a country has been chosen as special guest of honour. This year, Spain is the chosen country, but a lot of attention will also be given to writers from Ukraine, writers like Serhiy Zhadan and Katja Petrowskaja.

In 1996 Ireland was the guest of honour, incidentally just a year after Seamus Heaney had been awarded the Nobel Prize for Literature. Naturally, he was one of the many writers invited to read in Frankfurt. When I now look at the programme of 1996 it strikes me that male writers outnumbered female writers by far – wouldn't it be different nowadays?

Representatives of the chosen nation get special attention from German media around the time of the book fair. When Ireland was guest of honour, all papers had articles on Irish writers and documentaries were shown on TV. As a journalist I was commissioned by the *Frankfurter Allgemeine Zeitung* to write a piece on Brendan Kennelly, which I was delighted to do, as it would give me a chance to meet the poet, whom I admired for his work and his wonderful engaging personality. I was staying in Sligo at the time; a meeting in Dublin was quickly arranged.

That afternoon with Brendan Kennelly in the garden of Trinity College was unforgettable. We sat on a bench, birds picking around our feet (lovingly greeted by the poet); sun shining, words flowing, topics ranging from the drag and dread of alcoholism, the sorrow of a broken marriage, the joys and rewards of teaching, to the healing potential of poetry. In his soft, melodious voice he talked about his admiration for women, his own shortcomings and failures, his belief in the young – if only you encourage them! And accompanied by his infectious laughter, he said that teaching and writing were his ways to connect, so that he wouldn't die a lunatic.

Never had I met a celebrated professor so unassuming and self-doubting. What was unusual, too, was that he asked me, his interviewer, about myself, where I came from, what had brought me to Ireland? I told him about my home town on the Rhine where my ailing mother lived, who would soon have to move to a place where she would be looked after. He asked her name and where exactly she lived and pronounced her first name, Luise, so cutely, the French way, 'Louise'.

And then this magic afternoon came to an end, and I had to rush to Connolly Station to get the last train to Sligo. And he ran with me across the Liffey and down Talbot Street, while right and left people constantly addressed him, 'Hello Brendan,' 'How's it going Brendan ...' And then a quick goodbye at the station, and we assured each other that it wouldn't be long till we'd meet again in Frankfurt.

This was not to be. I would make it to Frankfurt, but just for a day, as my mother's move to a nursing home coincided with the time of the book fair and I had to be with her. But a day I would manage, if only to see Brendan Kennelly again.

To my unspeakable disappointment I was told he wasn't there, and wouldn't come, because of urgent heart surgery in Dublin. I couldn't believe it. Had he not run with me all the way from Trinity to Connolly Station just a short while ago, and no trace of impediment of any kind?

I made my way sadly to my home town on the Rhine and found my mother very composed and reconciled to the fact of having to move. Somewhat puzzled, she told me that she had been sent very nice sweets from Ireland, did I know anything about it? No, I didn't. But when I saw the box of Butler's chocolates at her bedside, it dawned on me who had sent them, and it brought tears to my eyes.

HER SMILE

Cyril Kelly

To enter her world
The code is three rings, two loud knocks.
And because it will take some time,
I stand there listening for the Zimmer frame
Advancing from the kitchen,
That clip and ferrule clop
Masquerading past the mirror dimming in the hall,
Past Aussie grandchildren fading on the wall.
I cast a waiting eye on her tiny garden,
On her Deora Dé, God's fuchsia teardrops.
Eventually I hear the staccato rhythm rattling to a stop.
She is just inside the door,
Putting on the wistful smile
Of a girl stepping out in a lovely frock.
I hear gnarled knuckles struggle with the chain,
With five brass levers of the mortise lock.
For me this moment is ordained with impending grace.
And I am ready,
Ready with my meagre offering of a meal,
Ready to be blessed by her badge of courage;
When the door opens
Her smile will be like a blossom
Bravely spreading
Through the autumn weathers of her gentle face.

HAYBARN

Leo Cullen

That old haybarn I knew in my youth: the stars sailed across its galvanised roof. The moonlight leaked in through its open sides and spilled on the deck of hay and on the face of the man who lay there, a man I well remember. He used to tell me things: how the wind always got into that barn, made the irons rattle and creak and sometimes give off alarming knocks as though, about to fall asunder, it was only held fast at the last second by one staunch rivet.

He was a tramp who, each summer, sloped by our farmyard, and for a few shillings helped at haymaking. And then, disinclined to work much anymore, but knowing where he'd find the doss, he bunked in the haybarn.

I still sometimes fall into a sort of trance and think of him: I see his sheepdog lying beside him on the hay. It startles, its ears cock; it looks at him, then settles again. When darkness first sets in, he sees the Great Bear constellation in the northern sky. Night goes on; the stars wheel around in the vault. Great Bear holds its steady gaze. Great Bear is his night awake companion. A car passes along the road below the high haggard wall; it makes such a fuss throwing its lights up into the boughs of trees and along the grooved ceiling of the barn. Then across the hills it beams, and off into the high sky towards infinity. Cars at night he finds reassuring, but also disconcerting: other souls abroad in the world.

There's a sudden noise of a door slamming in the dwelling-house above; lowing, too, sometimes, from the cows in the byre; sounds of hooves stamping against the concrete floor. And out there in the grass, scraping presences.

He lays a mat of jute bags between his clothes and the hay's prickly thistles; he keeps the ends of his trousers outside his wellington boots and tied with baling twine so the trouser legs can't ride over the boots and the rats can't crawl inside. He knows a tramp that had a rat go down his boot and, imprisoned there, bit off a toe. He knows another tramp who one icy night when the hay bench was hard as metal, got a raging rush of blood for a woman of his past, to fall asleep with a memory on his lips, and awoke badly bitten by frost.

I'm a poor sleeper, he'd say. If a fellow has to sleep in a haybarn often as he, surely it isn't asking too much to be able to sleep. Night comes at you from all sides, he'd say. There are ghosts out around farm buildings after nightfall. Clattering sticks against the buckets in the wind. They are ghosts of the dead who once walked up and down the road, ghosts of those who once built the high walls and planted the cypress saplings, now gnarled trees enclosing the haggard. Ghosts of men, with whom he once laboured during hay-making times: Johnsy the ex-miner from the local coal mines, and Ted, the horse gambler, from East Limerick. There's those enjoy bunking outdoors. Those that have choice. If I had choice, I'd bunk in a castle.

He is no longer around, long gone. Spent his final days in a county home until in a deep dream at last, there came a night when ambulance lights shone in through his county home window, and his haybarn lifted anchor and sailed him across the galaxies.

A TALE OF TWO STORIES

Kevin Marinan

In the last few years I've lived in hotels, friends' houses and a homeless shelter here in Ireland. I have seen things in Ireland from a few perspectives, and met people from many walks of Irish life. Here are two examples, one good, one not so good. But in reverse order, so we end on a happy note. This first story is from 2015.

It was raining. Pouring. Most people were either snoring, or preparing to try. I was in a town in the west of the country but had nowhere dry to sleep for the night. I walked down a path from the main town until I saw a large house that was surrounded by a new and expensive-looking grey wall. The property had a couple of outbuildings that I thought were probably for cars or storage: garden equipment or similar.

The main gate wasn't locked, so I sleekly nudged my way through it and walked up the path to the furthest outbuilding from the house. Unfortunately, the door to the outbuilding was locked, so I put down my bag and sat under the shelter of the door overhang. I had been relaxing for a few minutes, as best I could after a long day travelling, mostly on foot, when the front door of the house opened and a man with a dog on a leash approached me.

Now I understand how this person had no idea if I was a friend or foe, all he knew was I was an intruder to his property. As he and his animal walked towards me, I said, 'Hello ... I'm sorry for being here, but I just had to get some shelter from the rain. I'm on my way to Mayo but I have nowhere to stay for the night. I'm sorry for disturbing you ... I'll leave.'

What, dear listener, would you have done if you were in this man's position?

351

Anyway, he told me to leave immediately or he would let the dog loose. So off I went. Into the cold, wet night.

I walked back to the main street, huddled in a doorway and wrote this poem:

> *I'm nobody, and I'm nothing.*
> *Tonight I am unseen.*
> *Tomorrow I'll be nowhere,*
> *And your conscience will be clean.*

I found my way to my late mother's birthplace in Mayo the following day. She died when I was a teenager but every few years I try to get back to Ballina where she grew up and spend some time in the places she used to know.

My second tale is more recent. Although not a religious man, I was rescued from the streets by the St Vincent de Paul in Wexford. They never asked if I was a believer or not, which was a relief for me. I was given a room and meals in their town centre men's shelter. Room 22.

The men were mostly rougher and tougher than me. Although brought up on a Manchester council estate, I was lucky to have had Irish parents who made sure I was educated and wise to the world – not just to the street. Our house was full of books and we were encouraged to read them.

The St Vincent de Paul looked after me, and within a few weeks found me a place of my own. A small flat to live in. To write and paint in. To laugh and cry in. I'm still here.

So I wrote this poem:

> *I didn't die yet,*
> *So you needn't cry yet.*
> *I'm so happy on my own.*
> *Let the spring fly*
> *Into summer's high.*
> *Let our winter be alone.*

A PRINCIPLE OF FREEDOM

Lourdes Mackey

Neapolitan opera fans hoping to hear Margaret Burke Sheridan sing on Monday, 25 October 1920 were disappointed. 'The performance is cancelled,' a notice pinned to the closed doors of the San Carlo Opera House declared. 'La Prima Donna cannot sing because her compatriot is dead.' Her compatriot, Terence MacSwiney, had earlier faded away after seventy-four days on hunger strike. 'The brains of the Republican Army in Ireland died in Brixton Prison … this morning,' headlined *The New York Times*. His status as Cork's Lord Mayor and an elected public representative ensured that his hunger strike had resounded across the international press, like a tragic drama: a drama that echoed his own best-known play, *The Revolutionist*, but acted on the world stage, before a universal audience.

Terence MacSwiney wrote prose, poetry and plays and, according to his friend Daniel Corkery, loved literature and art with a passion almost as great as his passion for a free Ireland. His library was filled with Shaw and Ibsen and Molière. He had copied his choice of Rossetti's sonnets into a pocket notebook, to be recited as he pushed his bicycle twenty, thirty, forty miles away from his beloved wife, to speak brave words in some little hamlet, then wake at dawn in a strange house to read his favourite poem – Shelley's 'I Arise From Dreams of Thee'.

His wife, Muriel Murphy, was daughter to one of Cork's wealthiest merchant princes, brewer of Murphy's stout. Her family, she said in her testimony to the Bureau of Military History, 'was unionist, imperialist, capitalist, conservative and Roman Catholic'. Courtship with an impoverished Irish rebel was the last thing the family wanted, so her mother refused her permission to marry. This meant that if Muriel wished to inherit, she couldn't marry until she was twenty-five.

On 9 June 1917, the day after her twenty-fifth birthday, she and Terence MacSwiney were married in the English town of Bromyard, where he was then interned. More than half of his life with Muriel would be spent behind bars. In 1918 he was in prison for two major events in his life – the birth of his daughter Máire and his election to the first Dáil.

By 1920, Terence MacSwiney and his comrade, Lord Mayor Tomás MacCurtain, were the face of the Republican movement in Cork. MacCurtain's callous murder by the RIC, in front of his pregnant wife and children on 20 March, was a portent of terrible things to come – the arrival of the Black and Tans five days later. MacSwiney's speech, upon his election to replace his friend as Lord Mayor, contained his most famous principle: 'It is not those who can inflict the most, but those who can endure the most who will conquer.'

Less than five months later he was arrested in the City Hall. He refused food even before his court martial, which took only fifteen minutes to find him guilty of possessing seditious documents, likely to cause 'disaffection to his Majesty'. One of those documents was his own inauguration speech. Sentenced to two years in Brixton Prison, he responded, 'I shall be free alive or dead within the month.'

Muriel remained at her husband's side throughout his hunger strike. At the time it was believed that a person could not survive for longer than a month without solid food. Days passed into weeks and, filled with foreboding, she asked Michael Collins to intervene. Collins ordered MacSwiney to end the strike as he would, as Collins told him, 'be ten times a greater asset to the movement alive than dead'. MacSwiney refused. 'I am confident that my death will do more to smash the British Empire than my release,' he stated.

'His spirit is as strong as ever,' Muriel told the *Daily Mail*, 'I support him in everything.'

George Lansbury, editor of the left-wing *Daily Herald* and future leader of the British Labour Party (and grandfather to the actress Angela Lansbury), informed throngs of protestors in Trafalgar Square that 'the Lord Mayor of Cork is currently being murdered in Brixton Prison by the British Government'.

Soon demonstrators from Brisbane to Boston and Buenos Aires to Barcelona joined in the protest. 'Yesterday he was unknown outside of

Ireland,' reported Madrid's *El Sol*; 'today the whole world is familiar with his name.' In New York, two thousand longshore men, including many African Americans, refused to unload British cargo in what became known as the Irish Patriotic Strike. Marcus Garvey, the famed Black nationalist leader, conveyed the support of the entire Black community to the MacSwiney family, while the Mayor of New York warned the British Government that 'Terence MacSwiney has won the admiration of all the peoples who believe in rule of the people by the people.'

Letters and telegrams piled high on George V's bureau, beseeching him to intervene. The King favoured clemency, but his Prime Minister Lloyd George was resolute, and so was Terence MacSwiney.

A surge of shame swept England as one hundred thousand Corkonians lined the streets of his native city, on the Eve of All Saints' Day, to bid him goodbye. His sacrifice motivated many future revolutionaries, including members of the then fledgling ANC. MacSwiney's biographer, Dave Hannigan, writes about a young Ho Chi Minh, who, working in a London hotel when the death was announced, burst into tears, saying 'a country with citizens like that will never surrender'.

Nehru took inspiration from MacSwiney, and it is known that Gandhi treasured his copy of MacSwiney's *Principles of Freedom*, a collection of essays published posthumously.

Terence MacSwiney lived the heroic role he had written for the protagonist, Hugh O'Neill, in his play *The Revolutionist*. Hugh's last words are prescient: 'What's the good of being alive if we give in?'

THE HELLFIRE CLUB, WILLIAM WORDSWORTH AND THE WRONG SORT OF TOURIST

Kevin Mc Dermott

The trees are in their autumn beauty, and the woodland paths are dry, or they were earlier in the week when I walked Killakee woods to the Hellfire Club. It is a popular walk at Halloween. The atmospheric ruin on the summit of Montpelier Hill was built in the eighteenth century as a hunting lodge for William Conolly, the speaker of the Irish House of Parliament. Legend has it that the lodge became a drinking club for wealthy young men whose gambling and licentious behaviour attracted the Devil himself into their company.

South Dublin County Council plan to develop a visitor centre at the Hellfire Club. The proposed development, on the eastern slopes of Montpelier Hill, will command views across Dublin and the Wicklow Mountains.

As I walked the woods I thought of the poet William Wordsworth. I suspect that if Wordsworth were alive and living in the greater Rathfarnham area, he would be writing letters to the national newspapers stating his opposition to the plans of the council.

Wordsworth was a great letter-writer. In 1841 he opposed the building of the Kendal and Windermere rail line. He believed that members of the working class from Carlisle or Manchester would lack the capacity to appreciate the beauty and the character of seclusion and retirement that the Lake District offered to discerning visitors. He feared an influx of Sunday day trippers. In one letter Wordsworth stated that, 'A vivid perception of romantic scenery is neither inherent in mankind, nor a necessary consequence of a comprehensive education.' For the poet, the appreciation of natural beauty was a matter of sensitivity and discrimination. Communion with nature was a spiritual experience and the Lake District was a sacred place.

Famously, Wordsworth was a great walker. Indeed, he and his friend, Samuel Taylor Coleridge, helped popularise walking tours. And while Wordsworth feared that tourism would ruin the Lake District, he himself undertook walking holidays in France, Switzerland, Germany, Belgium and Scotland, as well as visiting Rome and Paris. He also did a six-week tour of Ireland in 1829, sailing off Glengarriff and climbing Carrauntoohil. Wordsworth was particularly impressed by Kerry and the Giant's Causeway.

The kind of tourists Wordsworth approved of were a select group: people like himself for whom a ramble in the mountains on a Sunday was a form of spiritual exercise which put them in contact with the sublime, with a sense of something greater than themselves. These ramblers were stirred by natural beauty and by views of the horizon, that resonant meeting of earth and sky.

My parents were not those kinds of tourists. From the perspective of Mr William Wordsworth, they were the wrong kinds of tourists. Although I grew up in Crumlin, a few miles from the Hellfire Club, we never went there on our Sunday drives.

My dad was a working man. For the last decade of his working life, he cleaned the industrial ovens in Boland's Bakery, a dirty, unrewarding job. On Sundays, he loved to dress up in a suit and tie and wear his best polished shoes. He didn't dress to traipse the mountains. In fact, I doubt the idea would ever have occurred to him.

Each Sunday after dinner we went for a spin. Dún Laoghaire, Bray, Glendalough.

We drove to places that were accessible by car and where you could stroll when you arrived. To the best of my knowledge, there was nothing spiritual about these outings for my parents. My parents did their worshipping at Sunday Mass.

If and when South Dublin County Council's plans proceed, and a road is built, and a tea room and coffee shop developed at the Hellfire Club, I will drive there on Sunday afternoons in November, when the veil between the world of the living and the world of the dead is pulled apart. And in that place of ghosts, I will position myself at a table that commands a view of the car park. And I will watch for a black Morris Minor, OYI 976. And inwardly I will cheer when it arrives. And my dad will get out and brush the cigarette ash from his jacket. And he will brush each shoe on the calf of his trousers to give them a quick buff. And my mam will look splendid in her coat and matching dress, with her square leather handbag and her sensible shoes. And these two ghosts will stroll around the Hellfire Club on the tarmacadam path. And if the weather permits, they will stop and look over Dublin Bay and admire the view out to Howth and beyond, northwards, to Lambay. They will appreciate the pretty view. And if it is not too cold, Dad will buy ice cream from the Mr Whippy van parked up on site. Or they will go and have a cup of tea in the café.

And I hope that when they settle and look around, there will be a glimmer of recognition, from my ghostly parents, of the ageing man sitting in the corner, smiling over at them.

And in my heart, I will feel the great joy of seeing those two again, the wrong sorts of tourists, but the best of good people.

PANGUR BÁN AND AUDREY

Gordon Snell

When Maeve Binchy and I first talked about getting a cat, most of our friends were enthusiastic. One said, cats are no trouble. If you go away for a few days, you only need a neighbour to look in, feed them and ask, 'How was your day?' We went ahead and never regretted it. Our current resident is Audrey, a fluffy white cat with a black tail she sometimes stares at, wondering if it belongs to her.

As Audrey sat beside me on the desk one day, I was reminded of one of Maeve's favourite poems, the one about Pangur Bán, the pet cat of a monk who, many centuries ago, paused in a work of translation to write a verse in the margin of his text about Pangur. So I decided to make a verse tribute to Audrey. And here it is.

Pangur Bán and Audrey

Pen in hand, a monk sat, bored –
This translation had him floored.
There on the desk beside him sat
Silky and white, Pangur, his cat.
Ready to purr at every stroke,
Ready to share a monkish joke.
Ready to soothe a monk when vexed
By tedious tangles in his text.

'Pangur my dear,' the cleric said,
'I'll write of you and me instead.'
So in the margin, then and there,
He wrote about that happy pair:
How Pangur dreamed of mice to catch
And he of making meanings match.
Each closeted within his mind,
Monk and Cat contentment find.

Twelve centuries have passed since then
And here sit I, with cat and pen.
You sit there, Audrey, sleek and white,
Pondering perhaps, what I should write.
Would you exult, if I describe
The story of your feline tribe?
How once, Egyptian Pharaohs kneeled
To pray your secrets be revealed?
Back then, your ancestors, with pride,
Were, like their masters, mummified.

I know for sure you wouldn't revel
In tales that claim that you're the Devil

Some saints who thought you Satan's daughter
Kept drenching you with holy water.
You'd rather hear the Hindu creed
That you're the goddess Shasti's steed.
Or learn how once, when he was down,
You brought Dick Whittington to town.

Oh how I wish that you could read
And understand my rhyming screed –
I yearn that I could learn instead
What thoughts are floating through your head.
Perhaps, as some believers state,
Reincarnation is our fate.
Then we could both achieve our goals
By simply swapping over souls.
Then each one would the other be:
I would be you, and you'd be me.

But here's the snag – would memory's store
Recall what we were like before?
If not, then better 'tis by far
To stay exactly as we are.
I as a man, and you as cat
Knowing precisely what we're at.
Audrey hears not these musings deep
For now I see, she's fast asleep.

NOVEMBER

NOVEMBER DEAD LIST

Louise Kennedy

When I was a teenager in the 1980s, my grandmother came to live with us in the small midlands town we had moved to after we left the North. All her life she had lived in Belfast, only to find herself a hundred miles from home, a widow lodging in someone else's house. As my sisters and brother and I grew up and her health failed, she seemed to retreat from the everyday goings-on in our house. She took to sitting in one of our gold velour armchairs, the tube of her catheter bag slung over the sleeve of her dressing gown like the straps of a handbag, telling stories of her girlhood.

I read somewhere that there was no such thing as teenagers until after the Second World War. My grandmother, Hannah Maguire, grew up in Ardoyne during the Twenties. She went to work in a linen mill at fourteen, yet she and her friends had distinctly teenage preoccupations. They bobbed their hair, scrimped, saved and mended to dress in the flapper style, danced the Charleston and went to the pictures. These interests did not always sit well with Hannah's mother, a severe woman who had been left a widow in 1915 when her husband was killed at the Front. She thought Hannah vain and frothy and rarely missed an opportunity to say so.

Hannah's idol was the Italian actor Rudolph Valentino. He was given roles that exploited his dark hair and eyes, his smouldering good looks. He played an Arab sheikh, a tango dancer, a French aristocrat, a bullfighter. He dressed in extravagant costumes and gave audiences scene after scene of brooding glances and passionate clutches. Off-screen he was at the centre of an infamous sex scandal, which only added to his appeal.

But in 1926, Valentino died suddenly of peritonitis. My grandmother learned of his death at the pictures, from a Pathé news reel. The headline read:

VALENTINO DIES!
THOUSANDS THRONG STREETS!
FAIRBANKS, BARRYMORE CARRY COFFIN!

The film flickered and jumped and my grandmother could hardly believe what she was seeing. A hundred thousand people, mostly women, lined the streets of Manhattan for his funeral. Mounted police had been deployed to corral them away from the funeral home, and the women responded by dragging the officers from their horses. Windows were smashed and the rioting continued well into the night. My grandmother told me that the patrons of the Forum picture house in Ardoyne, themselves no strangers to civil disorder, were deeply impressed. Valentino's body was laid out on a plinth surrounded by lilies and palms, and covered with a heavy cloth embroidered with the letters IHS. 'He's a Catholic,' someone said, and Rudolph Valentino was one of their own. The millies clung to each other and cried, their cupid's bows pursed as tight as the looms they worked, their bobbed hair so full of setting lotion it barely moved. Valentino was dead. Hannah, having lost her father when she was a child, knew what that meant: that she would think of him every day, that nothing would ever be the same again.

Valentino's last film was a big-budget epic called *The Son of the Sheik*. It was set 'not east of Suez, but south of Algiers'. Valentino played both the sheik and his son, and my grandmother couldn't decide which of them she loved the most. Over the following months she saw the film dozens of times, until she knew it by heart. The line that made her cry every time was, *My young lion. Your people would gladly pay ten thousand francs to look at your handsome face again.*

One Saturday in November Hannah put on her coat, pulled her cloche hat over her ears and went out. She crossed the Crumlin Road to Holy Cross Church and went up the steps. There was a heavy box on a marble table in the hall with a sign pinned to it that said:

NOVEMBER DEAD LIST

She tried to remember the last time she had seen her father, but his face had long since faded from her memory. All she could see when she tried to conjure up his image was how he looked in the only photograph they had of him that was taken five weeks before the telegram came. She took a piece of paper from her pocket and opened it carefully. In her best script she had written:

John Maguire 1881–1915
Rudolph Valentino 1895–1926

She had almost put 'Rifleman' in front of her father's name but thought better of it; her beloved Valentino needed no introduction. She folded the paper, kissed it quickly and slipped it into the slot on the top of the box. She whispered goodbye to the two men she had loved and stood with her heart pounding in her chest. When the priest read the names from the altar the next day her mother would kill her.

NORTHERN SKY

Clare O'Dea

No doubt about it, my passport picture was displeasing to my twenty-year-old self. Taken when I was sixteen, the image preserved a moment in time when I had a DIY perm and owned dungarees – which, unhappily, I chose to wear the day the photograph was taken.

I was next in the queue in Pulkovo International Airport, St Petersburg. The grey-uniformed border guard had a severe, matronly air, not unlike the nuns of my schooldays. 'Dokumenty!' she said. I closed the page on the offending image and handed over my passport.

Dokumenty. The first word I heard spoken by a real Russian in Russia, after two years of studying the language. She did not care to smile, but I beamed. That St Petersburg airport could not have been more drab and dreary, but for me it was the gateway to my dream, a dream paid for in countless pints served, tables wiped and ashtrays cleaned.

The guard studied my six-month student visa and found it acceptable. Then, although the Soviet Union had ceased to exist five weeks earlier, she stamped the page with the letters CCCP, pronounced SSSR in Russian. I suppressed the urge to cheer.

We had been warned about the cold. I had picked up a man's overcoat from a second-hand shop in Temple Bar, and old-lady-style plastic ankle boots from Connolly's, the only thing I could find with a warm lining. I looked like a girl who had borrowed her dad's coat and granny's shoes, or, to some eyes, a strangely dressed boy. My short hair and old overcoat certainly confused the Russians, who often mistook me for a citizen of one of the Baltic States.

My stay in St Petersburg was full of drama and wonder, perhaps as much to do with my age as the monumental changes taking place in the country.

But even amid the strangeness, I developed a routine. To get to class in the morning, I took the metro to Admiralteyskaya and walked across the wide Neva river to University Embankment, picking up a fried cabbage pie from one of the elderly street vendors along the way.

One day in particular stands out in my memory. It was still winter, and the beauty and the cold seemed to go hand in hand in the city. The language faculty of St Petersburg State University, across the river from the famous Bronze Horseman statue of Peter the Great, was in a crumbling old building that had once housed an obscure ministry in a Tsarist administration. I was waiting in the entrance hall of the university building when, idly, I started reading the student noticeboard. One slip of paper advertised a Russian-English dictionary for sale. To my amazement, someone had scribbled a phrase in Irish on the neatly written ad – *Bás don Bhéarla!* Death to the English language!

Ireland was two thousand miles away. Who on earth? I looked around, half expecting someone to step out from behind the staircase and say 'Gotcha'. I found a pen and wrote a message back. *'Cé scriobh é seo?'*

The graffiti writer answered the next day. After a few messages back and forth, we had a time and place to meet. His name was Kirill and he brought along a friend and an archaic-looking tape recorder. Kirill was as pale as he was earnest. With his black coat and scraggly beard, he could easily have played a young Rasputin in a cheap TV series. The students explained they were dedicated to preserving endangered languages in the former Soviet Union and elsewhere, and had started learning a handful of languages from books. They wanted to hear a native speaker pronounce Irish words. That I was the daughter of a native speaker was good enough for them.

They led to way to an empty room on an upper floor. I had no misgivings. How could I not trust two shy boys who were passionate about endangered languages?

The tape recorder whirred on the table while I read out the short texts they had provided, my *blas* eliciting frowns and raised eyebrows from the students. They had no idea of the vagaries of Irish pronunciation. A simple phase like *an sean bhean bhocht* – the poor old woman – is full of revelations if you are not aware that an S is not always an S and an H has superpowers.

Kirill and his sidekick were delighted. Could this be the beginning of a beautiful friendship, I wondered. But when I was done, the linguists ushered me out with smiles and nods, eager for me to leave so they could listen back to the tape. All they had wanted from me was my voice.

In return, they gave me this memory, without which I might not be able to summon the feeling of being twenty years old in a foreign city with the future stretching as wide and bright as the northern sky.

A WORD WITH GAY

Patrick Griffin

It almost seems like I have lost a member of my family. And yet I met Gay Byrne only once in my life. On that memorable evening I went to a Kilkenny bookshop to have Gay sign a copy of his book *The Time of My Life*, which was co-authored by Deirdre Purcell.

On my arrival I was met with a seemingly endless chain of bodies which extended out of the bookshop onto the street and ended up somewhere out of sight around a corner.

It was as if all these strangers were friends. Conversation flowed and the topic was focused on one person only – Gay.

Bit by bit we inched our way towards the doorway of the bookshop. We were streamed parallel to another line of smiling customers who were coming out of the crowded shop, with books in their hands, in most cases open to the page on which Gay had put his signature.

When, after an hour or so, I finally got to the counter and bought my copy of his book, I was directed to a table where Gay sat.

I assumed that with the vast amount of books he had already signed, and facing an equally long group of eager fans, he would quickly scribble his signature and pass on to the next person. But no, that wasn't Gay's way of doing things. As always he was in control, while I was in awe, a quivering fan rendered almost speechless.

He took my book and carefully opened it to the page where he would sign his name.

As I stood face to face with this icon of broadcasting, I was thinking about a moment when even the master was taken by surprise: an occasion when Gay was completely fooled on air.

One Monday morning in 1977, Gay introduced a piece of music. Back then, Gay would give a signal to the sound booth to have the next LP or single placed on the turntable. Only, on this occasion, what came over the airwaves was not the performer and song he'd just announced.

At some recent party, Gay, who was an accomplished pianist, had been secretly recorded while he was playing old-style jazz piano. On the morning in question on his radio programme, someone in the control room – presumably his producer – substituted the song already announced with a recording of Gay's piano playing. Gay was completely taken by surprise. Being the consummate performer, he joked about it and accepted it graciously. Listening at home, I felt inspired to dash off a comic poem. I typed it as quickly as I possibly could on an old Remington and got it to the post office just before closing time.

The following morning, I was tuned in to the programme as usual when I heard Gay mention that a listener had written a piece about his piano playing and that he would read it out on the next day's programme.

A combination of delight and panic set in. Here was my one opportunity, I thought, at getting my moment of radio fame courtesy of this master of the airwaves.

That also meant I had one chance to keep the recording for posterity. It was a matter of having a blank tape at the ready, and a cassette recorder that I hoped wouldn't let me down at the last moment.

Wednesday morning arrived. 'Tico's Tune', the instantly recognisable signature tune of *The Gay Byrne Hour*, came blasting out of our old Pye radio and I waited and waited through chit-chat and music and ad breaks. And then I heard Gay start to talk about how someone had taken a good-humoured dig at him and his piano playing. This was it. 'It's a brave man who would take on the writing of poetry on such a subject,' he said. Then he read my poem out.

It was more than just a reading; it was a performance. Gay had brought my few words to life far better than I could have ever imagined. Family and friends congratulated me, but it was Gay who had performed the magic.

Over a decade later, in the Kilkenny bookshop Gay looked up at me. 'Young man, have you read my book?'

I was almost on the verge of saying to him, 'No, but you read my poem on the radio.'

Instead, shyly I managed to mutter, 'Not yet.'

He shook my hand, smiled and replied, 'Well, I suggest you do.'

I had nothing to add. Gay Byrne had spoken to me. I was thrilled.

And best of all, I still have that tape.

Thank you, Gay.

From the Gay Byrne Hour, Radio Éireann, 1977

... Moving on to something rather lighter in vein, we have, I promised you the other day that somebody was taking – not for the first time – the you-know-what out of me, a listener in Carlow, Patrick Griffin, who wrote a poem about my piano playing. And it's a brave man who will undertake the writing of poetry on such a subject, and it's called Gaybo's Piano Roll Blues, *and I intend to read it to you right now.*

Gaybo's Piano Roll Blues, by Patrick Griffin

'Sing a few bars,' everyone cried, 'we'd love to hear an oul' song!'
'Well now you're lucky,' Gaybo replied, 'for I've brought me piano along.
And to think that I nearly forgot it! Sure I wouldn't have brought it at all,
But tonight when I left for the party, it was standin' right there in the hall.
"Are ye goin' to the party without me? Do I have to get down on me knees?"
Asked the overstrung upright piano, as he spoke through his ivory keys.
Well me heart nearly broke as he stood there, and I thought, now what harm
    can I do?
If I bring him along to the party, and play an oul' medley or two.
So I pulled the piano behind me, and dragged it along up the street,
Though we got funny looks and strange glances from the people we happened
    to meet.
We finally got to the party, and everything was in full swing
And I knew it was worth all the effort when somebody asked me to sing.
"What a pity we don't have a piano," the drunk in the corner cried,
And I said, "It's funny you should ask me, 'cos I happen to have one outside."
So they wheeled in the upright piano, and I said now I'll play just for you.
Someone said, "play some songs by Tchaikovsky!" and the drunk asked for
    'Rhapsody in Blue'.
So I started to finger the keyboard, and everyone else sang along,
But two and a half minutes later, I came to the end of the song.
Then I closed the lid of the piano, but somebody shouted "Encore!"
And I had to be truthful and tell them that I just couldn't play any more.
"Is that all?" they cried when I finished, and I said, "That's the one song I play."
So they said, "carry on, play the same song again," and I looked at them all
    in dismay.
But they told me to go on and play it, "Sure we won't mind the same song
    at all,
For we can't tell what song you're playin', when we're lyin' blind drunk in
    the hall!"
So if you are asked to a party, you're sure to be asked for a song.
Here's some advice that I'll give you – bring your piano along!'

THE TENTERS, WHERE THE FUTURE IS A HUNDRED YEARS OLD

Henrietta McKervey

Imagine if the future were a hundred years old.

As spectator sports go, looking on while a man from Dublin City Council climbs a ladder and unscrews a street sign from the front of a house doesn't sound like it would be up to much. But it's unexpectedly moving to watch him carefully remove the hundred-year-old green-and-white enamel sign from the wall.

He goes to stow the sign (one of the few remaining original Cló Gaelach ones, complete with distinctive Gaelic Revival flourishes) in his van.

'Wait!' I say.

'It's okay,' he replies. 'Don't worry! It's only going to be restored. We'll bring it back after.'

'No, it's not that,' I say. 'Can I take a photo?'

He holds the sign up, his arms wide, the words 'Oscar Square' in Irish and English captured between his hands. An angler showing off his catch.

When he's gone, I take a second picture: the rectangle of grey, unpainted space now revealed on the white wall. This is the first time daylight has touched this small part of the façade in a hundred years.

A centenary is quite something for any estate. Where I live, in the Tenters – an area in Dublin 8 roughly the same size as St Stephen's Green park – this centenary marks something else too: Ireland's first ever tenant purchase scheme. The name comes from the area's previous incarnation as a crucial part of the weaving industry, when cloth was stretched by hand and strung out to dry on vast wooden frames. The word 'tenterhooks' has the same origin.

Imagine, at the height of the Civil War, Dublin was building social housing. Making homes, communities for working families. Creating opportunities for future generations. Just a few years earlier, Dublin had the worst housing in the British Isles, with half of all city dwellers living in tenements. Estimates from 1918 suggested 50,000 new houses were needed, yet only thirty-seven were built. Alderman Tom Kelly believed that good housing was a weapon in fighting tuberculosis, and he battled for funding for the Tenters. There was a selection process for new residents: a family had to be already living in the city (many came from tenements); the head of the household had to be working; and there had to be a minimum of three children.

Twenty-two acres, twenty-six roads. One of the shortest, Cow Parlour (its name doesn't suggest a former city dairy, but rather nods to its Huguenot ancestry) makes an appearance in Ulysses as Boulevard Bloom. An area was reserved for a school and a church, and public space included in the form of Oscar Square park – distinctive these days for its huge cherry blossom trees and Emergency-era underground bomb shelter. Paths run from each of four gates, meeting in the centre of the park at a circular plinth with a statue and two curved benches. The design must have appeared pleasingly formal and neat on paper once; today, the grass around the centre is dotted with dog-churned bald patches.

Four hundred houses, five rooms in each. Front gardens were for flowers, back gardens for growing produce. Plumbing for an indoor bathroom was included, and each home was fitted with a single electric light. Every week the rent man set up shop in the middle of the estate.

The concept of tenant purchase wasn't always understood. In the 1960s, a man went over to pay his rent one Wednesday, only to be told his forty years were up, the house was his. He had never realised it, but he had, week by week, brick by brick, bought the home his family lived in.

A woman who moved into her house with the very first tranche of twenty-five tenants sought out the rent man a week later. She was confused: where was the other family, the ones who were going to live upstairs? There is no other family, she was told; every room is yours. The house is yours.

Imagine: at a time when the present was so unsettled, care was given to the future. A new state, making a commitment to its own working people.

A month later, I watch the sign go back on the house, fresh and bright, and the grey rectangle disappears again. And I wonder, did a woman stand where I am and watch as it was installed a hundred years ago? And, just for a moment, did she hold her breath and let the present fall still?

KEVIN BARRY IN THE UMBRELLA STAND

Síofra O'Donovan

When you are the descendant of a hero, you live in their shadow. I tried to run from the overwhelming charisma of this boy-hero-great-uncle Kevin Barry, whose story was sung by Paul Robeson, Leonard Cohen and every traditional Irish band you can think of. Yet my grandmother, Kevin Barry's sister, would not allow the song to be sung in the house. It was maudlin, she said.

But Kevin wasn't maudlin. An oval portrait hung of him in my father's study – a copy of a painting by somebody in the H Company of the IRA. The face and shoulders of Kevin Barry had a slightly airbrushed look, set against a monochrome and patriotic green background. Kevin had a quiff of hair like Tintin and he was wearing a trench coat with the collar upturned. He beamed eagerly around my father's study, like a friendly family ghost. Beside this portrait was one of my grandfather, Jim O'Donovan, in a rectangular frame, painted by Leo Whelan. A true die-hard, my grandfather's convictions had him locked up long after the War of Independence. His face, in the portrait and in real life, was sterner and more chiselled. And when I was brought to see him in his nursing home, he never looked at me. I looked at him, in his wheelchair, at his hand with missing fingers – blown off when he was demonstrating a hand grenade he'd just invented. I found the stubs of his missing fingers fascinating. And for some reason, we called him 'Beep-beep', although I have no idea why. I heard more recently that he occasionally demanded bottles of whiskey from my father and other visitors. He needed an anaesthetic for the past and for the tragedy of his wife Monty, my grandmother, who lay prostrate on her bed down the corridor in the same nursing home, paralysed by several strokes. A woman of acerbic wit and sharp intelligence was living her final years in this terrible limbo.

My grandmother Monty was the first dead person I ever saw. I stole a glimpse of her in the open casket at her funeral in the nursing home chapel. I never forgot her still, waxy face and the smell of candles and incense hovering around her. My father quickly took me out to the cold corridor with my cousins and we were told to wait there until the funeral service was over. I heard the drone of praying, and the priest muttering gloomily from the altar.

She, Kevin Barry's second-youngest sister, was gone. My grandfather was gone too by 1979. They were all slipping away, leaving my father angry and intolerant of our inability to grasp who these people were. He wanted me to be the custodian of our family history, but I did not want to do it. He would sit in his green armchair and tell me stories of how Kevin Barry cycled over the Wicklow hills to drink in the hotels in Glendalough and Aughrim, and how my grandfather locked himself in a room at night in the family home in Shankill, speaking German to his secret friends in Nazi Germany. And how my great aunt Kitby, Kevin Barry's older sister, sailed to America with Countess Markievicz, on de Valera's orders, to fundraise for the Republic. But my father always came back to Kevin. Kevin spinning around on his bike in his Belvedere cap, drinking, dancing, pulling Belgian girls, out on the streets in ambushes, down alleyways carrying arms. And in the end, hanging on the gallows, just like in the song. I resisted, but the stories seeped into me, there was nothing I could do, because they were part of me.

Although I grew up with these gripping tales of espionage and family militarism, it was Kevin Barry who made the greatest impact on me. The rest of it was just too frightening and strange, such as the thought of my grandfather Jim drinking tea with Hitler – which he didn't, of course, this was a product of my over-fed imagination – or speaking to Hitler on his radio from the family home (which he didn't do either). I took refuge in our family hero, the boy who beamed at me from the oval portrait in my father's study. I wrote essays about Kevin Barry for history class, described the ambush on the Monk's Bakery in detail. I could see his face as he was driven with the British soldiers to Bridewell prison. Irate, but amused. He was hanged the day before my birthday and, although we lived decades apart, his death was a shadow that followed me everywhere.

ARMISTICE DAY IN DONEGAL

Seán Beattie

For generations, thousands of emigrants in the northwest set sail from Derry Quay on their way to the New World. Most were heading for America, never to return. But in 1917, the tide went into reverse. Europe was at war, and America came to the rescue.

Under the Draft Law enacted by President Woodrow Wilson, all males between twenty-one and thirty were enlisted. Most expected to see service on the battlefront on mainland Europe, but a small number were dispatched to bases scattered across this island at the edge of the continent. One of these was in the townland of Ture in Inishowen, County Donegal, hundreds of miles from the hostilities. Those stationed there had drawn the lucky straw. Instead of the grime and stench of the trenches, they enjoyed the bracing air and verdant pastures of Lough Foyle, ten miles north of Derry City.

The first to arrive in January 1918 was a small group of tradesmen, carpenters, engineers and supervisors who were tasked with constructing a base from scratch with imported American timber. By 4 July, all buildings had been constructed, just in time to celebrate Independence Day by flying the Stars and Stripes. The recruits were mostly in their late teens or early twenties, so commanders at the base organised a sports day, followed by a dance in the evening. Several musicians were among the recruits, and they hastily organised their own orchestra, which they christened the Troubadours. To get the gender balance right for the big social event of the evening, army cars were ordered to bring local girls from Derry City and the neighbouring towns of Moville,

Carndonagh and Buncrana. With a new generator imported from America, the banks of the Foyle glowed as darkness fell amid the music and dancing. It was by all accounts a fairyland of mirth, sound and happiness.

For the young ladies, it was a night to remember. No more country waltzes or 'Shoe the Donkey', a traditional mazurka, which was a light-hearted, two-hand dance played in every parish hall: instead, the melodies of Irving Berlin and popular Tin Pan Alley tunes would have floated across the Foyle that night. The customary tea and sandwiches were replaced by minerals and cookies, with no scarcity of American cigarettes. Not unexpectedly, romance blossomed, and there were at least two weddings that could be traced directly to the base, where couples met for the first time.

During the day, recently assembled sea planes took off from the base in the hunt for enemy U-boats. For the few months that the base was in operation, there were many U-boat sightings but only one that is thought to have been destroyed.

And finally, the news that all were waiting for arrived – the cessation of hostilities, and the signing of an Armistice at eleven o'clock on the eleventh day of the eleventh month in 1918. The Armistice Day Banquet and Dinner organised by the Welfare Committee at the air station was a special celebration, and the menu included many newly invented delicacies to mark the occasion, such as Roast Stuffed Liberty Chicken, and Peace Bread with cider and cigars as extras. Celebrations led by the Troubadours went on into the night. There was a slight touch of sadness, too that friendships, formed along the banks of the Foyle, were about to end.

Armistice Day brought a sigh of relief to many Irish families who had sons fighting in Europe. My own family in Inishowen had reason to celebrate: my uncle John Beattie, who had emigrated to America in 1905 and enlisted in the US army under the draft of 1917 had survived the war. There was an added bonus when he turned up at the family home to greet his widowed mother. And he caused a stir at local dances which he attended in full army uniform.

The Americans departed in style, travelling in batches of a hundred, and parading in the streets of Derry on their way home, cheered on by thousands lining the city thoroughfares. Unlike their colleagues on the Western Front, nearly all were going home; only two recruits who were sent to Donegal did not return, one being drowned in the Foyle and another falling victim to the Spanish flu.

Little did anyone guess that the Americans would be back in another couple of decades when Europe would again be a battlefield. The story of the U-boats would have a different ending, as the city quays became the base where they were berthed, before being sunk to the bottom of the ocean off the north Donegal coast.

And not much remains of the American base of a century ago – a red-brick pump house on one side of the Derry to Moville road, and a vast concrete apron on the other, all now wrapped in the silence of peace.

THE POPPY

Brian Patterson

It's sometime in the early 1950s. Still a young boy, I'm staying with my grandparents in Limerick. On this grey, rainy November day, my grandmother is taking me out with her onto the streets of Limerick. Everything smells of wet. This is the 'flag day' of the British Legion and we're going to spend it selling little paper poppies, to raise money for the Legion. Who or what the British Legion is doesn't mean very much to me. But something else – the thought of a cream cake in the Stella Café in the late afternoon, when my gran's feet have finally had enough.

Long after my grandmother had died, I began to realise that selling poppies for the British Legion on the streets of republican Limerick in the 1950s must have required a lot of courage. And I began to understand what motivated her to do that. Her family, the Reillys from the Liberties in Dublin, had for generations been suppliers of fodder for the horses of the British Army in Richmond Barracks. So it was natural that many young men in the family volunteered and enlisted to fight in the Great War. Their motivation, I think, was neither pro-British nor anti-Irish; it was simply a family tradition. During the war, her brother Tom served in the Royal Irish Rifles; another brother, John, was an army padre; her Uncle Ned lost a leg; Uncle Charles lost a foot; Uncle Bill was listed as missing and, somewhere in northern France, 'Known Only Unto God'. The Great War loomed large over her family.

Perhaps the saddest story was that of her uncle, Thomas Hewson Curtis, who enlisted in South Africa and served throughout the war on the Western Front. In October 1918, in the final days of the war, he returned to Dublin on a short leave. At the start of his journey back to the front in Belgium, the mailboat, the RMS *Leinster*, was torpedoed by a German submarine sixteen miles out of Kingstown, as Dún Laoghaire was then known. He drowned along with 350 others. His death, leaving a young widow and a small child in Pretoria, was pointless. The war by then was effectively over: it had only days to run.

Something like 210,000 Irishmen, north and south, served in the British Army during the Great War. Lutyens' Garden of Remembrance at Islandbridge commemorates the 50,000 – that's almost one in four – who lost their lives. In the south, the ones who survived came home to an Ireland that had been 'changed utterly'. Having fought for the Crown Forces, many were ostracised and treated as traitors – often by their own families. As Talleyrand said, 'treason is a matter of dates'. The fledgling Irish State turned its back on them, and many were destitute. The uncomfortable truth for us is that the British Legion did more to help these traumatised Irishmen than did the government of the Irish Free State.

Some years after that flag day in Limerick, and I'm now a rebellious teenager, spending Christmas in my other grandparents' house, just outside Cork. This family, originally from Yorkshire, settled in Ireland in the 1920s and also had deep connections to the Great War. My grandfather has served in the British army and survived the war, minus an eye. Christmas Day is choreographed around the Queen's speech – it's carefully arranged so that we'll all be squashed around the dining table, listening in silence to the speech on the wireless, with the smells of the cooking turkey wafting in from the kitchen. My grandfather, as always, wears his poppy at home. But not in public.

At the sound of the 'God Save the Queen', we'll all stand and then drink a toast to Her Majesty, before starting the noisy, festive Christmas meal. But on this particular year, on impulse I refuse to stand, saying sullenly, 'She's not my Queen.' My grandfather is shocked and annoyed. My grandmother gives me a stern lecture in the kitchen. In her Yorkshire accent she tells me, 'I' thy Grandad's house, thou do as Granddad sez! Thou stands to attention for 'Queen.' Over sixty years later, I still cringe inwardly when I think about my insolence.

And so, at 11 a.m. this Remembrance Sunday morning, you'll find me at Islandbridge, standing quietly at the War Stone, with my collar turned up against the cold. Amongst the russet, golden, autumnal trees, I'll be wearing the red poppy of the British Legion. And I shall wear it in respectful memory of those who fought in all wars and died for our liberty. But also in memory of my brave grandmother, her brothers and uncles – and to atone for my impudence to my long-dead grandfather.

THE SUNDAY OF BLOOD, NOVEMBER 1920

Chris Shouldice

On that Sunday in late November, one hundred years ago, the sight of a small spotter plane circling the Croke Park pitch at Jones Road caused concern to my father, Jack Shouldice, and the other members of the Volunteer Dependants' Fund Committee. They had organised a charity football match soon to take place there. They had received a visit that morning from officers of the IRA Dublin Brigade, sent by Michael Collins, warning them to expect a raid by the Crown Forces. This would be a reprisal for a series of actions taken early that morning in the Southside of Dublin City, in which fourteen British intelligence officers had been killed. My father, who was then Secretary of the GAA Leinster Council, was asked to liaise with the Fund Committee.

In a statement given to the Bureau of Military History in 1952, my father said,

'The match had been fixed some weeks in advance – the teams taking part had been selected from counties Tipperary and Dublin, and I was in charge of the arrangements. We were rather unfortunate in the date selected …'

After the warning from Michael Collins's people, he continued, 'I consulted with GAA officials present including Alderman Nowlan, Luke O'Toole, Andy Harty and Dan McCarthy. They considered that if we called it off, the GAA would appear to be identified with what happened the previous night in Mount Street. Raids anyhow were common, but we never anticipated such a bloody raid. Though anxious about the outcome, we decided to carry on. Stiles-men, ticket sellers and ground staff had been appointed and the gates opened about 1.30 or 2.00 p.m. ... the game was not in progress more than fifteen minutes when lorries of the raiders swooped down on the grounds and without any warning burst their way to the railings surrounding the playing pitch, opened fire on the people on the far side and on the players. Fortunately they were scattered and only one of them, young Hogan of Tipperary, was shot dead. The other players threw themselves flat and managed to crawl off, mingling with the crowd. Many were tumbling over the wall into the waste ground on the Ballybough side. It was among the spectators on this side that the greatest havoc occurred. Fifteen people of both sexes were killed, hundreds wounded or injured in the mad scramble that followed, trampled or torn with barbed wire on the walls.'

Dad went on to describe his own predicament that day, saying, 'I had my little office under the old stand but vacated it when the shooting started and mingled with the crowds, with armed forces all around. The searching went on for an hour or more, the people having to keep their hands up, with machine guns trained on them ... not more than four or five were detained, on suspicion. I was one of that number. A small diary was found in my possession, which appeared to a drunken officer searching me to be suspicious, and he ordered me to be detained in one of the dressing rooms, to be dealt with later, which did not look too healthy for me. Sometime later another officer came along, fortunately a decent and sober man, examined the diary, and said out loud that he didn't see anything suspicious here, and quietly to me, "There has been enough bloodshed here today and I advise you to get away as quickly as you can." I obeyed the order with alacrity – I was the second last to get away, and the last was a young lad, released after me.'

What pleased Dad most, however, was that during the following week, all but £5 of the total gate receipts of £165 was handed in by the ticket sellers, to the benefit of the Volunteer Dependants' Fund. What would surely have pleased him more, were he alive to see them in a revitalised Croke Park, were events such as the record crowd of 90,000 for the 1961 Down v Offaly All-Ireland football final; the Special Olympics of 2003; the fantastic Ireland v England rugby match in 2007 when the huge crowd respected the 'God Save the Queen' anthem; and Queen Elizabeth's visit in 2011 heralding a new spirit of Anglo-Irish reconciliation. What followed then were the Eucharistic

Congress of 2012, the visit of Pope Francis in 2018, and this year, the remarkable celebration of the Islamic Eid festival, the audience including Jewish and Christian dignitaries.

What a remarkable panoply of events the green sward of the old Jones Road ground has experienced since that dreadful day, when blood flowed, on Sunday 21 November 1920.

THE BICYCLE AND US

Lelia Doolan

Cappoquin Library is home to a bicycle called Rozinante, or Roz, ridden many years ago full tilt from Ireland to India. It was the first of a family of bicycles with no gears whatsoever. They carried an intrepid, passionate, humanitarian writer and prodigious spirit from nearby Lismore, Dervla Murphy, all around the world. It's her birthday today. Dear Dervla, here's a small card with much love.

A few weeks ago, in one of the endless tidyings of life, I came across a postcard that we had made for the celebration of revolutionary women in the West of Ireland during the commemorations for 1916. It's a black-and-white photograph of a group of young women in sensible tweeds and men's hats, standing by their bicycles. They look cheerful and resolute.

It got me to remembering how important and what an egalitarian machine that two-wheeled friend has been to poor people over the last couple of centuries. The bicycle despatches run by the women member of the Citizen Army and Cumann na mBan kept local intelligence flowing during times of secrecy and revolution here. Many were those swift, apparently harmless journeyings. My aunt Delia, small and freckled, carried the butter that she had made along with the messages she was asked to convey from Drumquin to Clarecastle. Think of those strong but weary legs. I remember reading that Máire Comerford – mighty, tiny Cumann na mBan heroine – cycled the sixty miles from her mother's school to attend Thomas Ashe's funeral in Dublin in September 1917. They left Wicklow at 5 a.m. and were in good time for the funeral Mass at noon.

Those young women, and young men, had their counterparts worldwide. In the Russia of 1917, if the 3rd Cycling Military Battalion had not switched

389

from the Imperial to the Bolshevik side, what a disaster might have become the people's revolution. True too, in Gandhi's India and Mao's China, as people there rose to protest or oppose. On a journey with An Óige to China years ago with my sister Mary, we often witnessed the furniture of an entire household being conveyed on the front and back of a modest bike by a very skinny cyclist. In India, I saw a family – father in the saddle with a knapsack child, two babes in a basket out front, one on a carrier, and another in a small handy-looking trailer with their mammy.

As a child, for self-propulsion, myself and my brother Matt had a tricycle and a small car which you sat into and pedalled on the ground to get along. We would shout to Mother: 'We're off for the two days,' and make sorties to the bottom of the garden. But at last, we graduated, after wobbles, to the noble iron steed. In Ireland, all my growing-up life, we were a cycling country.

My brothers cycled to matches, the uncles cycled to dances forty miles away, romantic souls of every sort cycled to meet their fellas halfway across the country who cycled the other half to meet them. Swathes of all sorts of citizens criss-crossed the island, and came back to work or to the farm in the early hours. Men wore their caps; women wore their headscarves. We whooshed down hills, shouting at the wind! We cycled to the sea for a swim, to school, to college in Earlsfort Terrace ... my dear pal Miriam Ann O'Connell rode a very small Low Nelly and I had a very High Nelly so we must have been quite a sight, bowling along the Green. Another aunt, Anne my godmother, was an inveterate bicyclist, often to funerals, miles and miles away – to the Spa, to Kilfenora, Liscannor, Ennistymon, Corofin, Anywhere. Prodigious journeys. There was a destination to all of it, a place or a person and an event to arrive at. Mother flew along with a basket on the front, holding the messages, and a child on the carrier. Fathers, too. Our father, Paddy, cycled home, uphill, to his dinner in the middle of the day from the Custom House in Dublin to a mile beyond Rathgar and cycled back after ...

There were cycle parks like forests in the middle of O'Connell Street, full to bursting and manned by low-sized fellows with green-ribboned caps, who for sixpence or so stuck half a raffle ticket in your handlebars and gave you the other half. And, generally, kept a sharp eye out for passing villains.

In those days, bicycles were of the sturdy, big black variety. Men's had a crossbar and women's had an upward bar of curved metal. People sat upright, like they do in Holland where cyclists own the country. In the violent seventies, I criss-crossed Belfast on a faithful *rothar*, carrying all sorts of video equipment and getting a fool's pass from the various barricades in so-called no-go areas.

During the early days of the lockdown, a good neighbour and myself were able to cycle off to a nearby inlet for swimming. Nowadays, I meet waves of helmeted figures, all slim and Lycra-clad, hurtling along, communing with the tarmac. I have no trust that they are really going to meet the beloved or to bring back a pound of butter from the shop. For them, the bicycle seems to be a means of high-speed dreaming. As Flann O'Brien says – they may have become half man, half bicycle.

With its revolutionary possibilities, zero emissions, and egalitarian credentials in a world of unequals, to honour you on today's birthday, dear Dervla, 'tis time we sent Greta Thunberg a bicycle!

FOR DERVLA

Raja Shehadeh

For Dervla Murphy

It was thanks to a young Irishman working at the Edinburgh International Book Festival that we were introduced. He told me that a famous Irish writer would be visiting Palestine and would like to meet me.

I have met many writers and journalists over the years who came to visit my country and see for themselves what was happening there. But, as I was to find out, you, Dervla, were different.

It was the autumn of 2008 when you called from the Balata Refugee camp in Nablus. You said: 'I will be coming to Ramallah. Can we meet?'

I was shocked to hear that you were living in Balata, one of the poorest and most turbulent of the refugee camps. I was sure you were the only non-Palestinian living there.

When you arrived at my office in Ramallah, I asked you, how was the taxi ride from Nablus?

'I never take taxis,' you told me. 'I always take the bus.'

Then you said: 'There's a demonstration in the central square. Shall we go and join them?'

I was ashamed to say that I rarely take part in demonstrations and gave the excuse that we could not, because we had to wait for my wife Penny to join us for lunch.

I took you to one of Ramallah's good restaurants but you would not even have a salad.

'I only want a beer. I haven't had one for the past two weeks in dry Balata.'

You then told me how you only have a big breakfast which lasts you the whole day.

'I needn't bother about food after that,' you said.

To someone like me who is so passionate about food, this came as a shock.

I was concerned about your safety in Balata, that people might take you for a Jewish settler or that you might fall while trekking through the rocky hills without marked paths. I convinced you to buy a walking stick and I drafted a letter in Arabic which you could show if stopped or harassed by Palestinians who were suspicious of you. As I learned later, you never used either.

All this revealed my ignorance about the sort of person you were.

Many travel writers place themselves in trying and dangerous situations in order to write about them. Your purpose was to understand, and make the world better understand, the plight of the Palestinians, and that was why you placed yourself in the most dangerous areas.

After you had consumed two large beers, I drove you to the bus stop and left you there, still worried about what might happen to you.

A week later you phoned. You had left Balata and were now in the most threatening of all cities in the West Bank, the old city of Hebron. There you lived among the resilient small population of a thousand Palestinians in the Old City who had managed to remain after the residents were pushed out – more than 7,000, leaving behind a ghost town. These Palestinians were the target of daily harassment by the 800 hard-line Jewish settlers now living there, protected by twice this number of Israeli soldiers.

Soon after you moved in you phoned:

'I cannot tell you how angry I am. I cannot remain quiet. I feel I need to do something.'

I got worried that you might react in a violent manner that would lead to your deportation from the country. I tried to calm you down.

All this was proof that I still did not know the kind of person I was dealing with.

You've had years of experience of the most brutal regimes around the globe that you visited in your travels. This was just another. You well knew how to control your anger, how not to lose your trust in the basic goodness of humanity and write with passion and intelligence, helping your readers understand the true situation in my country as few could describe it.

The next time you called you had made it to the Gaza Strip after you persistently tried for years to reach that large prison.

The outcome of your repeated visits to Palestine was two superb books. Talking to you over the course of your visits made me realise how I had suppressed my own anger. Reading your books helped me see how you used your anger to write lucidly about the injustice in Palestine.

We were to meet in Dublin in March at the International Literature Festival. You were kindly willing to come to Dublin from Lismore. I was so looking forward to seeing you again. But it was not to be. The pandemic prevented us from meeting.

Short of seeing you in person, I extend to you over the air, my dear, dear Dervla, warmest wishes on your ninetieth birthday.

ERSKINE CHILDERS: THE RIDDLE OF THE MAN

Peter Cunningham

No novelist gets close to Erskine Childers when it comes to living the life of the books. James Bond and George Smiley played out the fantasies of Ian Fleming and John le Carré, but Childers first invented the modern spy thriller, and then spent the rest of his turbulent life trying to outdo the adventures of his own creation.

Robert Erskine Childers was born in London in 1870 into a family with distinguished political connections. When he was six his father died of tuberculosis and his mother was removed to an isolation hospital from which she never emerged. Childers and his four siblings were sent to Ireland, to Glendalough House, County Wicklow, to their mother's family, the Bartons, wealthy Anglo-Irish Protestant landowners with Irish Nationalist leanings.

After school, he went to Trinity College, Cambridge, and then settled in London as a junior committee clerk in the House of Commons. Following a sciatic injury, his passion became sailing and with an eighteen-foot sloop he undertook expeditions into the Baltic. In early 1900, he served as an artillery driver in the Boer War. Invalided home, he began work on a novel that would be published in 1903 as *The Riddle of the Sands*.

Childers's book seized upon contemporary English suspicions of an imminent German invasion and turned them into a bestseller. The novel's hero, Carruthers, works in the Foreign Office and has all the well-bred, insouciant qualities found fifty years later in Commander James Bond. During a hot August, Carruthers accepts an invitation to join his friend

Davies in the Baltic. Carruthers slowly realises that he has been invited, not as a deckhand, at which he is hopeless, but because he speaks German, which Davies does not. He learns that the point of their mission is not duck shooting, as Carruthers was led to believe, but tailing the boat of a shadowy figure whom Davies suspects is an English traitor involved in setting up secret German naval bases in the shelter of the Friesian Sands.

Subtitled *A Record Of Secret Service*, the novel is remarkably modern: the technical sailing data give the book its backbone, a new realism that would become a mainstay of authors like John Buchan, Eric Ambler, Alistair MacLean and many others.

Most writers would have used this success to build a publishing career, but all of Childers's subsequent interest seems to have been in outdoing Carruthers. In January 1904 he married Molly Osgood, daughter of a wealthy doctor, whose wedding gift to the newlyweds was a 51-foot gaff-rigged yacht, which they named *Asgard*, after the mythical home of the Norse gods.

An idealist, well read and intelligent, Molly was a fierce opponent of imperialism; soon Childers became a champion of Home Rule for Ireland.

In May 1914, he met a figure straight out of spy fiction. Darrel Figgis, an Irish poet and novelist, had been tasked by Irish Nationalists, including Sir Roger Casement, with purchasing German arms for the Irish cause; Figgis chose the yacht-owning Childers to transport the contraband. They travelled to Hamburg together, posing as Mexican partisans, and in the offices of Magnus Brothers signed a contract, using false names, for the purchase of 1,500 Mauser rifles and more than 30,000 rounds of ammunition.

Two months later, Erskine and Molly sailed the *Asgard* from Cowes in the Isle of Wight to the mouth of the Scheldt in Zeelandic Flanders, where, in the company of a smaller yacht, they rendezvoused with a German tug. On Sunday 26 July, in high seas, Childers skippered the *Asgard* carrying 900 rifles into Howth, and became an instant hero for the Irish cause.

Soon after, with Britain now at war with Germany, he saw no irony in joining the Royal Navy. After the war, he was back in Ireland, where Arthur Griffith, the founder of Sinn Féin, believed him to be a British spy.

In October 1921, Childers, now a Sinn Féin TD, was at Éamon de Valera's direction appointed secretary-general to the Irish plenipotentiaries sent to London to negotiate what would become the Anglo-Irish Treaty. Despised by Griffith and barely tolerated by Michael Collins, Childers privately briefed Dev as to what he perceived to be the Irish surrender to British demands. Dev's refusal to accept the Treaty was at least partly primed by Childers, as were the leader's subsequent equivocations, which, despite the Treaty being accepted democratically by the Dáil, led to the Irish Civil War the following year.

Childers cut a somewhat forlorn figure among the military men and was mainly confined to a house in Macroom, where he wrote anti-Treaty propaganda. On 10 November 1922, summoned by Dev to Dublin, he stopped over in Glendalough House, his childhood home. The Free Staters were waiting. Childers was found in possession of an unlicensed semi-automatic pistol, given to him by Michael Collins. He was brought to Dublin, tried by National Army court martial and on 20 November was sentenced to death by firing squad.

His life had been lived out as the survival fantasy of a small boy whose parents had suddenly disappeared, a life of perpetual action in which he was the hero. He was taken out at dawn in Beggar's Bush Barracks on Friday 24 November 1922. Like Carruthers, to the end he remained the epitome of upper-class English composure. He shook the hand of each man lined up to kill him, and then, blindfolded against his wishes, his last nonchalant words to them were, 'Take a step or two forward, lads, it will be easier that way.'

BLOOD IN THE WATER

Bernadette Buda

The tanks rumbled down Üllői Avenue into Budapest. Dawn was breaking. November 6, 1956. Only thirteen days before, the small nation of Hungary had successfully revolted against Russian oppression. In Irish terms, this was Hungary's 1916. Now, the tanks, bearing the capital letters CCCP of the Soviet Union, were on a mission to smash this Hungarian revolution.

That same day, thousands of miles away, a plane carrying the members of the Hungarian men's national water polo team touched down at Darwin, Australia. Confused and anxious for news from home, they were nonetheless determined to do their best to represent their battle-torn home country in the 1956 Olympic Games in Melbourne.

Weeks before, when the revolution started, they'd been in the hills above the city of Budapest, guarded by Russian minders, with no access to a pool, radio or telephone. In the city below, fires burned, gunshots could be heard and the players didn't know if loved ones were dead or alive. They had trained hard for four years. Now the trip to Australia was in jeopardy. The uncertainty was excruciating, especially for the youngest player on the team.

Ervin Zádor, at twenty-one, was a rising star in the Hungarian team. From humble beginnings, thanks to an unbeatable spirit and an exceptional swimming talent, he had worked his way up in the game. His tenacity and endurance were lauded by his more experienced Olympian teammates.

As a six-year-old, Zádor once stood in the hall of the famous Olympic swimming pool on Margaret Island, in Budapest. He looked up in awe at the names of past Hungarian champions, etched into a marble wall, and decided that one day his name would be up there too.

So when word came that the Hungarian Revolution had succeeded, and the team could participate in the Games, Zádor was elated. They boarded a plane for Australia, exhilarated over the new independence of their country. However, their fitness level was an issue for concern. They hadn't trained in a pool for weeks.

Rumours reached them en route that tanks were pouring into Hungary to reimpose Soviet rule. Immediately upon landing in Australia, the one team member who could speak English grabbed a local newspaper to find out what was happening back home.

The news wasn't good. The revolution had been crushed. One dream was now shattered, but the dream of an Olympic gold medal still remained.

From the start of the Games, many spectators, aware of the suppressed revolution, cheered on the Hungarians. The boys delivered. The team adopted an innovative defensive strategy to compensate for the missed weeks of in-pool training. It worked. They remained undefeated up to 6 December 1956. On this day the most infamous water polo match in Olympic history was to take place – the Melbourne Bloodbath.

Water polo was never a game for the faint-hearted; aggressive physicality and clever tactics make the sport gripping to watch. Kicks and punches occur regularly, especially underwater. In Hungary, huge respect persists for water polo, one of its most popular and successful sports.

Exactly a month after the Russians crushed the Hungarian Revolution, the two teams that entered the pool that day were Hungary and the Soviet Union.

The stage was set for a historic contest. Eight thousand spectators crammed into a 6,000-seat stadium. The Russians were booed and whistled at on every touch of the ball. The crowd chanted 'Hajrá Magyarok!' (Go Hungary!). Apart from the atmosphere, the conditions for the two countries were fair and equal. The Hungarian players knew, by beating the Soviet Union, they would give a massive lift to all Hungarians.

Ervin Zádor later recalled the strategy had been to provoke the Russians.

'We play, they fight. Back home we were obliged to learn two hours of Russian every day. So, in their own language, we were able to tell them how much we disliked them. Soon they were fighting with us.'

The strategy worked. With two minutes to go in a ferocious game, the Hungarians were leading 4–0 when Zádor got punched by his Russian marker, Valentin Prokopov. The blow created a deep cut near Zádor's right eye which welled up with blood. Instructed to leave the pool, the injured player left a trail of bloody water behind him. Seeing this, many spectators rose from their seats, demanding the game be brought to an end and that the Hungarians be declared the winners. Others clambered furiously over barriers to have a go at the Russian players. The referee halted the match a minute early, and the police had to intervene and escort the Russian players to safety. The next day the image of Zádor's bloody face made the front pages around the world.

Because of his injury, Zádor could not participate in the final against Yugoslavia. The team won 2–1, and the Hungarian water polo team were awarded gold medals.

About one-third of the Hungarian Olympic delegates did not return to Hungary behind the Iron Curtain. The defectors included half of the water polo gold medalists.

Zádor made it to the United States, settling in Linden, California. He never played water polo again, but coached Mark Spitz, who went on to become one of the greatest Olympic swimmers of all time.

Zádor didn't see Hungary again for over forty years. He returned in the summer of 1999, ten years after the fall of the Iron Curtain.

In 2002, the surviving members of both teams had an emotional reunion in Budapest. The handshake that should have taken place in 1956 in Melbourne finally happened in Budapest. They agreed that the game symbolised something much greater than the sport. Players on both teams were victims of political circumstances.

It was on this visit to Hungary that the Olympians were brought back to their training pool on Margaret Island. Once again, Zádor found himself standing in the hall where he'd stood as a six-year-old, looking up at the names of Hungarian champions etched into the marble wall. There, among the names of his 1956 teammates, he saw the two words: Zádor, Ervin.

THEN AND NOW

John F. Deane

Of course they come back, the dead, because they are there, just beyond the reach of our material being, on the other side of that nothingness we are scared of; the dead have their own work to do, on earth and throughout the heavens. And they are there, too, because we keep haunting them. They are still alive in us, we need them, as we hunger for hope and meaning. The New God that our age holds to, is not the Most High and Almighty God, he is Burning-bush, and Whinny-hill, and Furze-bloom. He is no longer a gilt tabernacle bathed in ethereal light but he is there, too, alongside our dead, he is goldcrest flitting in the berberis, he is the small flock of sparrows bathing in the pool left along the potholes in our country roads. And that is why, remembering the days when the pink rose rambled, when blackberries plashed purple kisses on my lips, I can still find contentment this side of nothingness, because I, too, am ghosted by the presence of those I have loved, and lost.

Father, for instance, who came, for the first time, to the island and took up fishing from the high rocks beyond Purteen. After a long day's work suffered in an airless and paper-ridden office, he was happy to escape into the free and bewildering air, there at the rim of the world. He stood, late evenings, stirred by the wonder of the Atlantic, awed by the teeming life of the ocean. I, then still unthought of, am there, too, on the cliff ledge near him, waiting. They did not yet know each other, but there was Mother, native to the island, picnicking with her sister Patricia on the strand. I see them, sitting on a tartan-printed blanket laid out on the sand; there is a basket of sandwiches, a bottle of rose-red wine and some Waterford cut-glass tumblers. They are laughing together, youth and promise copious as the blue sky above them. I am there, too, as yet unthought of, watching from the breaking waves, and waiting.

And now all three of them are ghosts, they have become island, having touched all boundaries and frontiers, all shores, and gone beyond them. Their bodies have become clay, dust of original stardust, their spirits part of the eternal Spirit that is brooding over all islands, over the allclay of our being, over the everysoul of creation. Patricia died, aged twenty-four, from the dreaded consumption, and I was scarcely two months old but she, my gentle and beautiful godmother, haunts me still. I keep a shard of the most pure, the whitest quartz, filched from her grave, and it holds me to her, though we scarcely met at the difficult junction, into, out of, time. When I came upon her photograph – the date in mother's teacherly hand, underneath – I felt a sense of loss again, and of defeat: 1939, that century's monstrous war machines already turning, Patricia, aunt and godmother, barely nineteen, in studio pose, a flawless loveliness, the flaw lurking within. She was gazing out at us from the picture, assured, looking to some certain and future promise – my now, her then, coming together in this moment's Eucharist – aware perhaps, too early, that our human dreams are clouds; this earth, our cherished place, a moment's sunlight, a long dark.

And so I sought and seek the words that will undo time – she alive again, resplendent in memory, where a life long gone remains whole in its promise, and undefeated. She, and I: compacted of island stone, sea and sky; bones of the spirit and pores of the body, the ongoing flood of imperatives, the tempests of sorrow, the peaceable kingdom.

And after her, Father left for the worlds beyond our mortal being, and Mother, too. Though each of them, long gone into that world of light, leave strong and varying glimmers in the memory, and a haunting presence in their son of love and faithfulness. So I have stood, at the sea's edge, stunned again at the knowledge of my own ageing, Father, Mother, Patricia, decades gone into that ocean of all unknowing. And – since time itself is not real, since it is merely a figment of our imagining, so that then is now, now then, I call to them from this wind-blown strand, bracing myself against the power of evolution and cosmos, and call out to them, watching for them still, and the rain comes slanting down and vanishing into the heaving sea, and the myriads of raindrops, in their perfection and their beauty, meld with the waves of the ocean, and with its breakers.

DECEMBER

AT RUADHÁN'S WELL

Donal Ryan

The land was opened around Ruadhán's Well
So a ring fort appeared by the path
And a small lake below it
Centred by a stand of reeds.

We all marvelled at these brand new ancient things
And cast regretful eyes along the razed hedgerow,
The stumps of ash and oak.
But what about it?

There were plenty more trees,
And more regrettable
Were all the years spent not knowing
Of the ring fort or the lake.

The solitary farmer that had kept them secret
Was dead, and the distant cousin
That fell in for the land was more given
To openness, to views, to airy spaces.

He was at the service this year,
Standing midway between the priest and the spring head,
Straddling the border between the patterned commonage
And his inherited freehold.

After the singing and the blessing,
In that restless uncertain time
Between the end of prayer and the start of gossip,
He stepped forward from among the congregation.

Tall and broad-shouldered,
Oblivious to the rising swarm of speculation
He lifted a cup of the cool water to his lips
With a steady hand.

A finger of evening sun
Touched the gold of his wedding band,
Then pointed in every direction at once
As a dozen hearts sank.

Stepping back from the sacred shore
He drew his hand across his lips
And smiled as the next person passed.
God bless us, he said, that water is sweet.

His note was struck of spring and stone,
Of the earth beneath him, the vaulted sky above.
We heard ourselves echoed
In every syllable

As he accepted the hands of the Faithful,
The grudging blossom of their regard,
The gratitude of his new neighbours
For the felled trees.

ALTERNATIVE WINTER SOLSTICE

Christina Park

Newgrange was out, of course. Only a lucky few ever get to witness a winter solstice there, to sit in the perfect darkness of that ancient chamber waiting for dawn to find its way in. So, my friend Cathy and I decided on our own midwinter ritual: we'd walk to the top of Djouce Mountain in Wicklow to meet the sunrise.

It had seemed like a great idea from the comfortable distance of a fireside pint. But reality bites pretty hard in the grim pre-dawn of a winter morning, gazing out from the only car in the carpark. Wrenching ourselves out of bed had been bad enough. But now, where was the mountain?

The Djouce we knew from sunny weekend outings was a gentle hike leading up to a glorious panorama that took in Dublin city, the sea, even as far as the coast of Wales. But a thick bank of cloud had enveloped the car soon after we left the motorway and started climbing. We'd see nothing up there, maybe not even the path beneath our feet.

However, there was no turning back now. Clinging on to the prospect of a greasy fry down in Enniskerry afterwards, we forced ourselves out of our warm cocoon into the clammy air.

Conifers framed the path before us in monotone gloom: winter and the night had leached all colour from the earth, and all scent but the clean, thin note of pine.

The fog held what little light there was to itself, the way lying snow does. Out from the trees, it stuffed the space like fabric, so our voices were confined to a small pocket around us.

A stinging wind found us on the boardwalk that leads up the mountain, beading the mist on our jackets. Steps lead to a memorial rock dedicated to the hillwalking enthusiast JB Malone, originator of the Wicklow Way. Normally this affords a spectacular view of Lough Tay, its black prehistoric waters lying in a cup of granite. That morning, though, you would not have known there was a lake, or a wide valley all the way south to Lough Dan.

It was in conditions such as these, in 1946, that a plane carrying a group of French Girl Guides crashed into the mountain. Fresh from the trauma of the Second World War, they were on their way to a holiday camp with their Irish counterparts in Rathfarnham. Without the navigation tools we have today, the pilot was relying on visual clues as to location: there were none. All on board survived the crash, largely because the fuselage broke away from the plane on impact.

Yet the mountain doesn't seem to hold these recent memories. Once past the regimented rows of spruce on the lower slopes, there is little to suggest modernity. Even the weathered railway sleepers of the boardwalk, slick with wet, suggest something far older than themselves: that ancient network of wooden roads that crisscrossed our island's bogs in the Iron Age, trees laid down to take people safely from village to village through *talamh bog*, soft ground, avoiding tar-black pools and bog holes that might suck you down forever.

The shifting glow gave no angle of light to orient us: we had only this road to trust. In that surreal alertness of early waking, we might easily step back two thousand years, be walking this road back to a crannóg to be greeted by a dog's bark, the scent of wood smoke; or up to the cairn near the summit, whose ghost is still marked on Ordnance Survey maps. A reason, perhaps, for the original name *Dioghais*, meaning 'fortified height'.

Half-formed thoughts weaved, like our own breath, into the pearly air. Higher, and the cloud began to shred, opening pockets of distance. It hastened like a river current, a drift of imagination made manifest. Were we the mountain's dream, our bright jackets moving in and out of visibility as the veil thinned and thickened?

And then everything changed. First the blush hit the high cloud far away up the mountain. Then, even as we turned and pointed, the mist around us began to suffuse with pink. We stopped, wordless, as the glow intensified, bathing us from every angle in peach-gold. We were standing in sunrise.

Other gifts unfolded: hoar frost picking up the dawn colours, fantastical wind-sculpted ice in frozen bog holes. The cloud fell back, revealing a dark scattering away up the mountainside. Deer, heads lifted. Gone.

The last slope was short, but steep. We bent breathless against a snow squall then crouched in the lee of the boulders at the top – just in time to see the sun clear the clouds, searing bronze, in all her pagan glory.

Taking out our flask of hot port we toasted the solstice, tasting the approach of Christmas. Pitying those still sleeping.

JOHN McCORMACK AT CHRISTMAS

Tom McGurk

He was kept in his own special container, a leather-bound valise, at the back of the radiogram. He only came out on very special occasions, like the Waterford Crystal, the polished napkin holders and the Maid of Erin linen tablecloth.

My mother would unpack him with all the sensitivity of a brain surgeon at work. Each vinyl LP, wrapped in its own tissue paper, was slowly extracted, laid out on a clean tablecloth and rigorously dusted.

Next, the record was finger-tipped onto the turntable with a brand-new needle already in place in the playing arm. Finally, with elaborate care, it was slowly lowered onto the spinning vinyl.

A slow humming at first, a few little bumps and then, flowing out of this ancient electrical time-machine, the magnificent singing voice of John Francis McCormack.

Truly Christmas was here at last … the high priest himself had arrived.

Even today, years later, to hear that voice is to gently push open a door into Ireland's past. By now the original McCormack sound has metamorphosed through many technological generations, in the search for the original sound. It's been a one hundred-year journey from shellac cylinders to vinyl and finally computerisation to digital.

McCormack's record career and record sales were enormous. He recorded a vast array of songs, sold millions and became both the doyen of Irish America and globally the most famous Irishman of the age. Given the ravages too of decades of emigration that he lived through, McCormack, an emigrant himself, became an Irish global icon.

His voice now echoes down those long queues for Ellis Island and Botany Bay. No wonder then that listening to him on those childhood Christmas nights was often to sit in the valley of adult tears. Older now, we recognised of course that Christmas nights are all about those who are there and those who are no longer there.

Can we these days ever imagine what it must have been like for those generations of Irish mothers and fathers who waved their children onto ships, many with the real expectation that they might never see them again? Many never did. Children who in time shrank to mere letters and cards and packages of shamrock for St Patrick's Day. It is still difficult to hear McCormack's emigrant laments without sensing his huge listening audience of ghosts.

Around me as a child on those Christmas nights, jaws would tighten, eyes close and heads lean back into McCormack's long unfaltering lines, his breath control and that ringing high register. Here was a voice that sounded like the rarest of vintage port.

It was not a huge resonant operatic voice, one to smash glasses up on the high shelves, but rather an engaging, melodic register that charmed and enchanted. With its artistic super-structure it was Renaissance but its chassis was Irish.

After the party games and the singsongs had petered out, McCormack's audience would be summoned to gather around the gramophone for the final act in this, the Irish Christmas litany.

Papal Count John McCormack had wooed the world's opera houses but at this particular moment, in this dying of the year, he was ours alone.

Annually the melancholy procession would begin: 'The Last Rose', 'Kathleen Mavourneen', 'Molly Brannigan', 'The Harp That Once Through Tara's Halls', 'The Boys of Wexford', 'Mother Machree'. We were suddenly adrift in a Hibernoland of shamrocks, round towers, wolfhounds and that collie dog, forever frozen in time on the LP labels, listening to his master's voice.

The music and the emotion would build, pumping up the room. This was our bard telling our story, from dispossession to famine to emigration to liberation. Songs of love, songs of broken hearts and songs of defiance. Little post-colonial Ireland shaking a fist at the big bad world.

Within McCormack's own lifetime, almost a million Irish had emigrated and at his concerts around the world they would gather to hear him. On Christmas nights especially, in those thousands of emigrant homes across the globe, tears would flow; children would solemnly study tearful adult faces as their High Priest's plangent recital filled the drawing rooms of the Irish diaspora stuck in their moment.

It was McCormack's great luck that Tom Moore's extraordinary marriage of high Victoriana and Celtic melodic genius preceded him. Poor old Moore, he was savaged by Irish history but his songs have survived his detractors.

McCormack's friends included James Joyce. Yes, the same one. Joyce, a decent tenor himself, was curiously obsessed with McCormack. He won a Feis Ceoil medal singing and he and McCormack once sang together in the same Dublin Horse Show Concert in 1903.

A reviewer commented on the occasion that 'Mr. James A. Joyce, the possessor of a sweet tenor voice, sang charmingly "The Salley Gardens" but gave a pathetic rendering of "The Croppy Boy".' However, he concluded that 'Mr. J.F. M'Cormack was the hero of the evening.'

Famously, Joyce's wife, Nora, was reputed to have said at his Zurich funeral, 'Poor Jim, he had a lovely voice, he should have stuck to the singing instead of bothering with writing.' But Joyce in the end gave McCormack the ultimate accolade: the great tenor's persona wanders through *Ulysses* and in *Finnegans Wake*, Shem and Shaun, the rival twins, are most probably portraits of James Joyce and John McCormack.

In 1938, with his Pavarotti-like world fame, McCormack gave his final concert in the Royal Albert Hall to an audience of 11,000.

Were we to bury an Irish time-machine, to be dug up in a thousand years, to see what we were once like, what would we place in it? Probably a *Book of Kells* reproduction, surely a hurling stick, maybe some potatoes and of course, John McCormack LPs. I suspect that wherever, whenever there will be Irish, they will still be hearing the master's voice calling.

CHRISTMAS 1963: AN AUDIENCE WITH SÉAMUS ENNIS

Jim Galvin

My mother had left us, leaving my Kerry-born father and me unsure how to celebrate the Nativity. How to fill the void? Home was Finchley, the north London constituency of a then relatively unknown Tory MP, Margaret Thatcher. But then a gift horse arrived, an invitation to join Irish friends for Christmas dinner. It must have been the common bond between expatriates that prompted the kind gesture.

In the 1950s, for some obscure political reason, our host had been exiled from his post in the Irish Customs and Excise and was forced to move to London for work. His wife had been a dancer in Jimmy O'Dea's revues. We got to know the couple through her son, a folk singer.

Our host, an erudite man, had a comprehensive knowledge of Irish traditional music. He knew most of the major performers. During a less than entirely happy sojourn in the UK, Joe Heaney, the great sean nós singer, had briefly stayed with the couple; they said that he would sometimes sing himself to sleep at night.

Christmas morning dawned; the religious rites were observed. It was an Irish mile's walk to our hosts' abode. For my father, at 18 stone and built like a modern Munster rugby prop forward, it was a chore, because of his gammy leg: a tubercular knee infection had left him unable to bend his left leg.

Upon arriving, we entered the sitting room and unexpectedly encountered another guest. Tall, lean, with long thin hands, he was wearing a grey double-breasted suit and an immaculate white shirt and tie. We had just met Séamus Ennis.

He had been in the UK making a documentary programme. Like many gifted artists, he did not take great care of himself, and his current neglect had led to a medical crisis. He'd been hospitalised, and from there he'd contacted our hosts. As a special, seasonal concession, the hospital allowed him out for two days on the basis that he would abjure all alcohol. He gave his word, but then a promise made under duress is not binding.

After less than ten minutes Ennis had complete control over us, his audience. He had a soft, melodic, baritone voice. We hung on his every word.

After the meal we sat by the fire. A bottle of Jameson whiskey, twelve years old, appeared along with beer. I vividly recall how the whiskey was handled with almost sacramental care, Ennis gently cradling a bottle, nursing it like a newborn. I alone abjured the water of life.

There was some mention of Ennis's work for Radio Éireann and a little talk about his earlier pioneering research with the Irish Folklore Commission in the 1940s. However, the bulk of the now near monologue was about his time with the BBC in the 1950s, recording traditional music in England, Ireland, Scotland and Wales.

In my childhood, on Sundays, there were two particularly special programmes on BBC radio. The first was *As I Roved Out*, the programme Ennis collected for, and the second was *The Naturalist*, which was introduced by the plaintive cry of the curlew.

Ennis talked of his odyssey along the highways and byways searching for the vast, varied trove of traditional music and culture. At one point, when speaking about his travels in the Hebrides, he reached into an inside pocket as if to produce a fountain pen, but instead drew out a penny whistle and piped a melody to illustrate his point.

Then, as carousing friends were wont to say, 'it was later'. The fire had dimmed; the whiskey had been consumed. Ennis was weary. It was time for us to go, and Ennis to rest with our friends.

The trudge home was slow but we were inured to the cold. It had been a magical reality for a few hours. I had a slight buzz in my head the next morning. My father did not feel at his best.

I moved to Dublin in 1971. I never met Ennis again, although I saw him on television in that decade. However, I do remember at a later date watching his daughter Catherine Ennis, an acclaimed international musician, play 'Easter Snow' as a tribute to her father, and I recalled that cold Christmas day, transformed by Séamus Ennis. The apple did not fall far from the tree.

COURAGE IN THE ALLEYS: HUGH O'FLAHERTY

Joseph O'Connor

On Christmas Eve, in Rome, I went for a walk – through the shadowed, cobbled backstreets that lead from the old working-class quarter of Trastevere, by the banks of the Tiber, to the Vatican.

In the houses, families were gathering. Radios played Puccini. The darkness of the alleys seemed sanctified by hope. I was thinking of Hugh O'Flaherty.

I can't remember the first time I heard his story, but I've an idea it was in Listowel, County Kerry. Late one night, perhaps in John B. Keane's bar, someone told me about Hugh O'Flaherty's courage in Rome during the Second World War, how he and a small band of fellow activists saved thousands from the Nazis. Home in London, the more I researched him, the more amazed I was. Five years ago, when I was wondering what to write a novel about, Hugh came knocking on my windows.

His courage is gripping but it is also inspiring. It always had the makings of a tense psychological thriller, I thought, with a beautiful soundtrack ranging from Italian opera to Palestrina, and that's what I hoped to create when finally I sat down to write his story. But there are other colours and implications to that story too, including the ones that altered my own life.

Born in Cork, raised in Kerry, Hugh came of age around the mistrust of English soldiers that was one bequest of the Black and Tans. Yet his journey took him to a point where he lived stubbornly by his own moral compass, even when faced with the threat of Gestapo interrogation and execution.

He was that rarest of things – a person who wouldn't take orders from any side. Commanded by the Irish government, as well as the Vatican and the Germans, to cease his work, he continued his secret and perilous mission, saving 7,000 escaped British and American prisoners from death.

His small group of trusted activists came from very different backgrounds. Sir Francis Darcy Osborne, Britain's ambassador to the Holy See, was a public school-educated aristocrat, who had at one time been close to the late Queen Mother. He and Hugh became co-conspirators. Newark-on-Trent-born Lieutenant Colonel Sam Derry of the Royal Artillery was a tower of strength for the Escape Line, a stunningly brave soldier who had himself escaped Nazi camps several times, on one occasion by jumping from a moving train. There was John May, a Cockney, a servant at the British embassy, described by Derry as 'a brilliant scrounger'. It's touching that this group of such high-minded human rights defenders also needed one thief.

Also central to the Escape Line was Delia Kiernan, known to fans of Irish folk music as the great Delia Murphy. Married to Ireland's senior diplomat in Rome, Thomas Kiernan, the first director of Radio Éireann, Delia quietly flouted Dublin's insistence on non-involvement in the war, showing tremendous personal courage in assisting Hugh.

It was in February 2020, as Covid came to Ireland, that I sat down to write Hugh's story. What a blessing, when I remember the fear and unease of those months, the headlines, the sufferings, and the courage of carers. The world shrank to two kilometres, but I was going to Rome every day. I decided to call the book *My Father's House*, after a saying of Jesus, 'In my father's house are many rooms.' Hugh hid fugitives in attics and cellars, in outhouses and monasteries, in the many secret rooms of hidden Rome. Every morning, I made myself write a thousand words about him. He was of the things that helped to keep me sane. I walked around Rome with him, looked through his eyes, attempted to understand a man so many times more heroic than I could ever be.

I set the story on Christmas Eve, because the Romans love Christmas but also because the story of the first Christmas has its own vein of persecutions. There are angels but there is also Herod. I wrote hundreds of sentences and would almost hear Hugh telling me, 'No, that's not right,' or 'I didn't talk the way you have me talking, I was from *Kerry*, not Dún Laoghaire.' Sometimes Hugh made me laugh. Once or twice, he made me cry. Morning after morning, sentence after sentence, his story appeared on my pages. Looking at it now, a finished book, I sometimes wonder where it came from – through that frightened, panicky time, when even in isolation we relied so much on each other.

But I know, of course. It came from the Hugh O'Flaherty who lived in my head through the lockdown, my lamplighter through the book that is now his.

I thought of him, as I walked the backstreets of his beloved adoptive city on Christmas Eve. His stubborn, quiet defiance. His hidden passion for justice. His extraordinary modesty. His love. The stars of Christmas glittered in the cold Roman sky, over St Peter's and the Colosseum, over the steeples and palaces.

In the alleys through which he led so many thousands to freedom, I felt his brave and noble spirit move like a rumour.

A Roman, a scholar, a Kerryman. A hero.

CHRISTMAS CHEESE

Lisa McInerney

At the start of November, I was in Dublin airport, in a café that was selling mince pies at the till and playing Christmas songs on loop. All the classics – Elton John, Wizzard, Mariah. I am partial to a bit of cheese, whether the foodstuff or the metaphorical kind, but not at the start of November. What I deem appropriate in a Christmas countdown – you know, how much cheese, and when to consume it – is informed by the job that I had when I was sixteen. We were coming up on the millennium, the Celtic Tiger was still warming up to a roar, and after school and at weekends I worked in a small supermarket in Gort, south County Galway.

There was a seasonal rhythm to supermarket work in the late nineties, but it was gradual, and it was contained. In 2021, middle-aisle specials in Aldi or Lidl mark ski-pants season, home-gym season, barbecue season, and that which begins a week or two before Halloween and is referred to in my house as 'German Biscuit Season': Christmas, for which the harbingers are stollen and lebkuchen.

In the nineties, Christmas in the supermarket began with the arrival, in the franchise delivery, of ingredients needed for Christmas baking: jars of mincemeat and apricot jam, marzipan, royal icing, mixed peel, candied fruit, tubs of glacé cherries, almond essence. After that came the Christmas music.

Head office sent only one CD per month, so you can imagine how many times I'd hear each song in a week. For December, on the hour, every hour, we'd have what I then regarded as the more unfortunate Christmas songs: 'Mistletoe and Wine', or 'Keeping the Dream Alive' (which is a Christmas standard, despite its having nothing to do with Christmas), or David Essex's

'A Winter's Tale', in which he lamented his lover ditching him, leaving behind only footprints in the snow. I associated these songs with the peculiar delectables on the shelves and so, as the days rolled on, I came to love them – in secret, until now. It was a perfect, cheesy storm: the momentum of the Christmas countdown, the novelty of the foods, the over-identification with the schmaltzy lyrics. I was sixteen; there was probably some boy or another I was thinking too much about.

While David Essex crooned about whoever broke his heart I stocked the shelves, at last, with the real fripperies, but fewer than we would come to expect in the age of breathy M&S ads that extolled all that was hand-rolled, sumptuously enfolded or Courvoisier-drenched. Instead there were tins of Danish butter cookies and USA biscuits; boxes of Roses no one wanted to get the task of wrapping because they were infernally trapezoidal; Cuisine de France mince pies; selection boxes shaped like Christmas stockings; packages of herby stuffing; bottles of Sandeman port and Harveys Bristol Cream, and Blue Nun, of course, for the very urbane.

And the Christmas *RTÉ Guide*! When the bumper issues came in, suggesting that we spend at least a week slothfully watching old classics in our pyjamas, it was unequivocally Christmas. From then till Christmas Eve there would be full trolleys at the tills, harried but cheerful customers, and managers in new jumpers actually deigning to pack bags. It felt meaningful, properly affecting to a kid just figuring out the tempo of adult life. At other times of the year, space wasn't made on the shelves for items that were scrumptious just for the sake of it. Managers hid in offices. There weren't sinfully early showings of classics on the telly. Hearing 'A Winter's Tale' eight times a day would have been much harder to stomach if you hadn't been promised a week off and your weight in biscuits.

It's said that retail staff detest Christmas music, and I imagine the craiturs above in the café in Dublin airport, listening to 'Stay Another Day' in November, would qualify. But this never happened with me. I worked up an appetite for what was syrupy stacking shelves in a supermarket, and never got so full that I felt sick, for this is the advantage of keeping Christmas contained in December.

And after we closed on Christmas Eve, and the boss brought us to the pub for a hot port and a pat on the back, I would join my mam for Midnight

Mass, so full of toddies or sticky ballads that I was moved even by religion. Sixteen, hopped up on the glorious odysseys of the past couple of weeks, tears rolling down my face for what seemed to be no reason at all.

TINS

Paul Howard

There is no doubt in my mind that the Christmas songs of my childhood were the greatest Christmas songs ever recorded. The fifteen-year period between Wizzard's 'I Wish It Could Be Christmas Every Day' and Cliff Richard's 'Mistletoe and Wine' represented a golden age for Yuletide tunes – if not a cultural high point for civilisation.

Every year, I still marvel at the power of these songs to reconnect me with my childhood. For instance, Wham!'s 'Last Christmas' never fails to bring me back to a cold night in December 1984, when my friends and I spent several hours collecting grocery items for the St Laurence College Loughlinstown Christmas Bazaar.

We walked the length and breadth of Ballybrack that night, dragging my mother's red tartan shopping trolley behind us, knocking on doors, asking people to donate food items for the grocery stall.

At the end of the night, we went back to my house and laid out our bounty on the kitchen table. It was mostly tins. Heinz spaghetti spirals. Yellow pack tomato soup. Batchelors processed peas. Tesco's own-brand prunes in their own juice. Del Monte mixed fruit cocktail. And then something so revolting that I couldn't believe it was real at the time, just as I can scarcely believe it today – a full Irish breakfast in a tin.

The picture on the label suggested that, somehow, crammed inside this Tardis-like aluminium container, were four tablespoons of baked beans, one thick slice of bacon that resembled the sole of my foot when I stayed too long in a hot bath, half a grilled tomato, six button mushrooms and – swimming in the tomato sauce – a tiny, skinless sausage, looking pale and apologetic, like a limp penis.

The fire in the kitchen was roaring and it smelled of smoky coal – the good stuff. On the portable black-and-white television, there was a video for a Christmas song I'd never heard before. George Michael on a skiing holiday, mooning over an ex-girlfriend with pouty lips and big hair, when we all still believed that that was George's type.

As we sat at the table, looking over the dozens and dozens of tins we'd collected, I had an idea. How funny would it be if we swapped around all the labels? If we took the label off the pineapple rings and stuck it on the cock-a-leekie soup? If we took the label off the peach slices in their own juice and stuck it on the salmon chunks in brine? If we took the label off the Scotch broth and stuck it on the pear halves in syrup?

Very funny, we decided.

So we set to work. As carefully as our clumsy, adolescent fingers would allow, we removed the labels from each and every tin.

Halfway through this operation, my mother walked into the kitchen and asked what was going on. I told her matter-of-factly that we were swapping around the labels on all the tins we'd collected for the school bazaar. My mother had a very strong sense of right and wrong – but she also knew good comedy when she saw it.

She weighed up what I told her, and said, 'I'll go and get you the good glue.'

The 'good glue' was a tube of Evo-Stik that was once kept in the kitchen drawer but my parents had taken to hiding it ever since watching a *Today Tonight* special report about teenagers sniffing solvents at the Papal Cross.

Having retrieved the glue from its hiding place, my mother committed to the idea fully, offering helpful suggestions as to which label should go on which tin – sweet on savoury, savoury on sweet, and oh, how giddy we became thinking about the likely reaction when each tin was opened.

By the time we returned to school in January I'd forgotten all about it. Brother Fred – our First-Year religion teacher, who'd been in charge of the grocery stall at the bazaar, welcomed us back and said he hoped we'd had a nice Christmas.

'I hope you had a happier Christmas,' he continued, 'than the woman from Ennel Court, who decided to make spaghetti bolognese on New Year's Day and discovered that her tin of chopped tomatoes contained black cherries in syrup. I hope you had a happier Christmas than the family from Achill

Road, who were served peas on toast for their breakfast on St Stephen's Day. And I certainly hope you had a happier Christmas than the woman from Ashlawn Park, who, on Christmas Eve no less, emptied a tin of fruit cocktail into a trifle she was making – only to discover that it contained something so vile that I can barely bring myself to describe it to you. A full Irish breakfast … in a tin.'

I don't know if Brother Fred ever suspected that I was responsible for switching all those labels. What I do remember is the struggle he had trying to keep the smile from his face.

BRINGING IN THE CHRISTMAS
Kathleen MacMahon

There are women who go all misty-eyed at the mention of Christmas. I'm not one of them. I don't feel the need of it. I *like* the deep mid-winter. I like curling inwards on dark nights. I like a bit of quiet as the year slows towards its turn. Christmas, I could do without.

It's a festival of things nobody likes. There's nobody who really likes Brussels sprouts, no one can honestly say that wine is better drunk hot with orange slices and cloves, and I don't for a minute believe that anyone in all honesty loves turkey.

Here's the thing ... *I know I'm not alone.*

We're the alley cats of the season. A secret Christmas resistance, a tribe of festive naysayers. We seek each other out, making common cause by saying the unsayable – because, hey, what's not to like about Christmas?

... It's a celebration of happy families, a feast of warm houses and full larders and conviviality, a frenzy of gift buying and giving. But 'Remember,' as Jane Eyre so wisely said, 'the shadows are just as important as the light.'

If you're prone to melancholy, as I am, you can't help but see the shadows. The bright lights of Christmas pick out all the world's flaws, like dandruff at a disco. Grief, loneliness, want – all suddenly become visible to the naked eye.

Christmas is open-heart surgery for the soul ... the shopping streets are its operating theatre, with our most tender feelings – all that love, all that desire – exposed for everyone to see.

It doesn't help that we're addicted to the notion of perfection. The perfectly chosen gift, the perfectly shaped tree, the perfectly cooked Christmas dinner ... and all that expectation dangling over a gaping void of disappointment if it falls short.

It was way easier when standards were lower.

When I was growing up, Santa didn't bother to wrap presents. His supply chains were unreliable – he might leave a note explaining why he'd left you the Barbie bath instead of Barbie's horse, the Wham! album instead of The Who. Santa's presents often arrived without batteries… and you had to wait twenty-four hours for the newsagent to open before you could use your new Walkman.

Some things were lost in translation, like the year I asked for a baby doll and was horrified to find, when I stripped off the baby's clothes, that it was a *boy* baby. My mother whisked it off to the kitchen with a look of grim determination on her face and came back two minutes later, problem miraculously solved.

It's hardly surprising – from a feast to celebrate the birth of a baby to a virgin mother – that Christmas continues to demand miracles of women. In our grandmother's day, the practice of 'bringing in the Christmas' started early in the year. A few pennies were diverted from the housekeeping money to start a store of dried fruit and nuts for the pudding.

Now, bringing in the Christmas involves stocking up on selection boxes and tins of fancy biscuits and Christmas crackers and new pyjamas, and the worst of it is that you have nobody but yourself to blame. Because *you* made all these things a tradition and Christmas won't be the same if any of them are forgotten. Times change but the pressure on women remains.

'Who are you going to this year? Oh, is it *you* doing it? And how many are you having?' It's a miracle if there's no row over who's turn it is to host it and who goes to who, and who can't be left alone, and who has the potential to wreck it if they're invited, and who'll wreck it if they're not invited. Covid is the ghost of Christmas past, but there's that part of you that hankers after the quiet of it, because this year there's no getting out of it, and before you know it you're going to be standing at the kitchen sink on Christmas Eve trimming those Brussels sprouts that nobody's going to eat … but it's at this precise moment that you will catch a glimpse of your reflection in the window and see your life from the outside in – like a Christmas card, all warm, twinkling lights and happy Christmas faces, and that's when the person on the radio will play the one piece of Christmas music you actually like – a piece so beautiful even you will have tears in your eyes listening to it.

With a bit of luck this blessed wave of goodwill and gratitude might carry you through Christmas Day – it will certainly last while the kids open their Santa presents, and the smell of a freshly peeled mandarin orange pulled from the bottom of a Christmas stocking takes you back to your own childhood. You might even manage to stay on the Christmas surfboard through the table setting and the gravy making and the eating of the turkey, which even *you* have to admit is actually delicious, but by the time the plates have been cleared and the Brussels sprouts are wrapped in cling film and stored in the fridge, you will be well and truly over it. The wave breaks, leaving behind a kitchen full of washing up. There's no room in the green bin for all the wrapping paper. Only the plain biscuits are left in the tin, but don't despair, because the best bit is still to come, the bit when you crawl into bed on Christmas night and count the sleeps until *next Christmas*.

BULGARIAN WINTER WONDERLAND

Wendy Erskine

In the music video for 'Last Christmas' by Wham!, glowing, attractive and happy people with skis cavort in the snow before retreating to an Alpine lodge. Although there are some lingering, sad looks because George's partner is now with Andrew, the overall impression is of wonderful times. The snow is thick and white. And everyone wears beautiful coats.

In the Milk Tray advert of the seventies, a man, sleek in black, descends the slopes by ski, leaping periodically into an azure sky, all because his lady needs the chocolates.

When in 1984, a handwritten note was pinned on a noticeboard in a Country Antrim school asking, 'Are you interested in a ski trip?' these two key, snow-related references were no doubt in the minds of many of the students who thought, do you know what, yes, I *am* interested in a ski trip. And so, a group gathered to hear that the trip would happen the week before Christmas. It would cost £140. And it would be to Pamporovo in Bulgaria.

Practically no one had ever skied before. And most of us, in our parochial teenage way, weren't sure where Bulgaria was. But we couldn't sign up quick enough.

In order to prepare for the downhill experience, it was arranged that we would travel to a place some distance outside Belfast for dry skiing lessons. The dry ski centre approximated an arrangement of what seemed to be outsize bristle doormats on a 45-degree slope. But some people loved the dry skiing. They immediately had a knack for it. I found it difficult to get up the slope, never mind come down it. 'Don't worry love,' the instructor said. 'When you actually get on real snow, I can tell you are going to be a natural.'

This was something I doubted.

In the weeks leading up to the trip there was also the hiring of the salopettes. In the shop I stared forlornly at the reflection in the mirror, a two-piece ensemble of salopettes and ski jacket in baggy brown nylon. I imagined a Veda loaf hesitantly moving down a mountainside.

'Have you not got anything in black, or tighter?' I asked.

'Are you imagining yourself as the Milk Tray man?' the woman asked.

'Oh no way, not at all,' I said.

Although I *was* imagining myself as the Milk Tray man. 'Well', the woman said, 'brown's all we got'. But I did get some new clothes for the trip: a thin, fake leather jacket and thin, fake leather skirt. People said I would be freezing. I didn't care.

And so, the week before Christmas a plane took off from Aldergrove to Plovdiv in Bulgaria, thirty suitcases stuffed with the same brown padded nylon from the same shop. But when it touched down there was no whiteness. Just tarmac. Black tarmac.

'Where's the snow?' we demanded. The teachers weren't overly perturbed. 'Where we're heading to is sixty miles away', they said. 'It's up in the mountains. There'll be snow up there.'

The bus made its way towards Pamporovo. At one point, one of the teachers said, 'Kids, you do realise that we're behind the Iron Curtain.' We peered out, expecting to some corrugated iron structure. But all we saw was no snow.

At the hotel there had been a mix-up with the booking. Everyone would now have to share a single bed with another pupil. There was, it must be said, a little snow. A light skiff. Enough for a paltry snowball maybe, but not enough for skiing. The disappointment hung heavy. There was a disco that played Europop and also, perhaps surprisingly, Killing Joke; it became a regular night-time haunt for everyone. But we were up a mountain in a tiny little village with only a couple of hotels. Although there was no snow it was freezing. The fake leather jacket and skirt were a mistake. Days were spent lying on the single beds eating sweets and talking about what we would do at Christmas when we got back home, or trying on each other's clothes. We

429

were bored a lot of the time. In the evenings in the hotel there was a band that would play Beatles covers while we ate our dinner. Not too many people were sorry when the week was over and the brown salopettes were returned unused to the shop.

Two years later, in 1986, the record label 4AD released a recording of traditional folk songs performed by the Women's Chorus of Bulgarian State Radio. It sold 100,000 copies and I loved listening to it. And so, when I recalled this holiday, my memories of the coach journeys through the countryside and the mountains out the window of the hotel room were transmogrified a little since they were soundtracked by the amazing and strange close harmonies of those Bulgarian women. But in the mix, Wham! was still there.

A CHILD'S CHRISTMAS IN MARINO

Declan Kiberd

Nen wasn't really my granny; but I only found that out when I was twenty-four and she was well into her eighties.

My real granny died after giving birth to my mother in 1915. And that left my poor grandfather Tom Keegan shattered, with a young family to raise. They were tumultuous times, for he was a Gaelic Leaguer and a member, with his brothers, of the Irish Volunteers.

The following year his brother Eddie was shot through the lung in the Easter Rising and fired from his job in *The Irish Times*. It all became too much for Tom and he sent each child for care to a relation. My mother was sent to her grandmother's home, where a few years later she caught the Spanish flu, so-called.

'Don't tell me you're going to leave me now,' was all her stricken father could say. But nobody in the family died and suddenly everything got very much better. A wily parish priest told Tom he had found the perfect wife for him: an elegant lady with a lovely humorous temperament named Alice from Howth. Her father, who rejoiced in the name Napoleon McKenny, had owned the Royal Hotel there, but he was busy drinking himself and the family out of it.

Alice had been to a posh Loreto school, where they played cricket. She needed a good husband and Tom was surely the man. It all worked out perfectly. The children all came home and they soon came to love Alice as a mother. And she made each of them the food they liked and soon yet another girl was born to the happy couple.

431

There was only one complication. Tom had been one of the Howth gun runners. He sent his six daughters to Scoil Bhríde, the first Gaelscoil for girls, where they grew ever more independent under the inspiration of Louise Gavan Duffy. Eventually they formed the nucleus of Celtic, a very successful camogie team.

But their new mother was an unrepentant monarchist. Somehow, they all agreed to disagree and never was a cross word exchanged.

During my childhood years my granny Nen began to post me, all the two miles from Marino to Clontarf, a children's magazine called *Look and Learn*; this would allow her to test my knowledge of English kings and queens. I wasn't too interested, but of course I played along. And it was of great use when I went to Trinity.

One year when I visited her home, she brought me out to the coalhouse – no longer a gun depository – and with a wicked wink, she handed me a cricket bat, prompting my lifelong adoration of the game.

But her monarchist tendencies came to a climax every Christmas Day. All the family, now with the next generation of children, assembled for her wonderful meal. But before we could sit at the table, the great moment was always preceded by Nen shushing everyone to listen to an address to country and commonwealth by the then young English Queen, Elizabeth.

Nen used to get so stressed that the inexperienced monarch would fluff a line that she invariably sat down in her favourite chair and smoked her one cigarette of the year. Her hands would tremble as she listened and the cigarette ash would grow so long that eventually it fell into the one glass of sherry she drank every year. She would finally gulp the whole lot back and say with relief, 'She did that very well!' And then the sumptuous meal was served.

Perhaps the smoking was done out of a displaced anxiety about coordinating a meal for so many; but I never thought so. She really wanted a royal triumph. And I found it personally hilarious to see all those camogie champions kept at bay, silent and respectful, through this whole performance. Then when it had ended, one of my aunts would quietly switch the radio, and later the television, off.

In the week before each Christmas, Nen went on a royal progress through Marino, demanding what she called her 'Christmas box' from each shop proprietor, and she always got one. She brought me on one of these expeditions, confiding that she had only been once to the city centre, which was all of two miles away from Marino, and that was for a performance of the Abbey Theatre's first version of *The Plough and the Stars* in 1926.

Her family members, all the Keegans, hated it – Nen included – because they felt that O'Casey was mocking esteemed Northside neighbours like Fluther Good.

In 1976, I invited Nen to the fiftieth-anniversary production of the play. I thought her take would be interesting. Siobhán McKenna played brilliantly the loyalist Bessie Burgess. When she died near the climax of the play, shot by a random bullet, there was absolute silence in the Abbey auditorium as Bessie lay dead on the floor. But Nen suddenly broke the silence with her penetrating falsetto: 'She did that very well.'

I could sense the irritation all around us, and I could have sworn that the great actress half-opened an eye to see whether she could spot the culprit. I had intended taking Nen to meet the cast; after all, she had seen the original Abbey production, and would have been interesting on the comparison; but she had already had her say, so instead, as quickly as possible, I drove her back to the political sanctuary of Marino.

Nen has long ago left us; but her words echoed in my head when they recently buried the English Queen, by then exactly the same age that Nen was when she died. And, watching the well-ordered rituals, I thought of how she would have relished them. A few weeks later, when Ireland outplayed England in a game of cricket, I wondered what Nen would have said about that. Probably, 'They did that very well.'

PIANO MAN

John Toal

I've a thing about clean hands, and I can trace it right back to my first piano lessons aged six. Before you got to touch the pristine white keys of Mrs Frame's upright piano, you washed your hands in hot water and Imperial Leather soap, and then you dried them on a clean, starched towel. A whiff of that exotic, luxurious aroma still brings me right back there. My next piano teacher was a Sister Frances, a Good Shepherd nun who announced one day as we sat side by side at the piano that she thought I should take organ lessons. Her thinking was, and the phrase she used – because it has stuck in my mind ever since – was, 'Because every parish needs a priest that can play the organ.' So that's kind of jumping guns, counting chickens and putting carts before horses all in one.

The truth was, although I loved music, and although the piano was a huge part of my life, I never wanted to be a classical pianist. I'd had a traumatic experience at Newry Feis playing Handel's 'Arrival of the Queen of Sheba' where my right foot shook so much I kept holding the sustain pedal down and the whole thing ended up like the Queen of Sheba arriving in a pot of soup. But I did fancy the idea of being the piano man. The guy at the centre of the craic. The person who would check on a night out to see was there a piano, what sort of nick was it in, was it locked and would it be okay if, y'know, later on ...?

So I worked out chords for TV themes and chart classics of the time, from Howard Jones to 'Axel F', and I spent ages at our piano at home, tinkering around with chords, making my own funky arrangements of songs in Irish from a glorious little book called *Cas Amhrán* (my version of '*Na Cleagana*' was an undiscovered classic).

434

My father had a lovely singing voice, and came from that generation of, 'If you're going to sing a song, sing an Irish song.' So for him it was the 'Ould Claddagh Ring', 'The Cliffs of Dooneen' or 'The Granemore Hare' … and I have to say it's a perpetual sadness that for all the long evenings we sat in the living room looking at each other, and all the Saturday nights that he belted out songs in the kitchen while enthusiastically burning sausages to *Céilí House*, I never even thought to accompany him on the piano singing one of his songs.

I have played piano in the National Concert Hall before. We'd come down from Newry to Dublin for a big competition when I was about seventeen, and when no one was looking I sneaked out past the eight double basses, through the big heavy door, onto the stage, and found the grand piano unlocked. So I played 'The Wexford Carol' to a silent ovation from an empty hall. Thank you Dublin!

And then one day a son came along who also played the piano.

A few Christmases ago I realised that while I can do 'The Wexford Carol' and a bit of O'Carolan and 'The Boys from the County Armagh' in whatever key you want, 'Spanish Train' by Chris de Burgh, this guy, this guy can do 'Wuthering Heights', 'Bohemian Rhapsody', all the ABBA stuff, Elton John, you name it, all the trimmings, fistfuls of notes all in the right order, augmented and diminished chords, and if he doesn't know it, he'll work it out quicker than me.

And as a parent that's both exhilarating and sobering. Because the genes have worked and found a new generation. But they're stronger, they're sharper, and they're quicker. So over time I found myself at the family and friends' Christmas parties, not in the hot seat at the keyboard calling the next song, but sitting on my *cajón*, a sort of tea-chest box percussion thing beside the piano, tapping out a rhythm, and watching young goldenballs working his magic. Prouder than punch like, but waiting like a greyhound in a trap for somebody to call a tune that he didn't know, ready to jump in and remind people, 'I used to be good at this, you know …'

One day I came home from work and before I got to the front door I could hear Mícheál Ó Suilleabháin's beautiful, sweeping piano piece 'Woodbrook' – one of my favourites – coming from our living room. And I stopped and listened, wondering, is that a recording? and then I realised it was the son playing the piano.

It's hard to describe what that feels like. A child of yours has gone to the trouble of learning a piece that you love, that he loves, and that's momentous and significant and moving. But it's more than that. It's like when we used to talk about handing on the faith, that they grasp something that you showed them, like catching a first fish, so that in all that they do and in all the places they go in life, they hold on to something from you.

SILENT NIGHT: WALKING THROUGH THE SNOW

Eileen Battersby

The hard-packed snow crunching beneath his feet was comforting, a distraction from the burning sensation in his fingers. It was very cold and clear; a white moon shone as bright as day. The tall trees lining the valley seemed black, suddenly menacing. But Josef Mohr, dedicated assistant priest at St Nicholas Church in Oberndorf, near Salzburg, Austria, rarely complained about anything, and particularly not then, having recovered after yet another bout of illness. Although sickly and destined to die young, Mohr was pleased with his lot in life. From early childhood he had always found joy in music, had been a chorister, and was a violinist.

On the night before Christmas Eve in 1818, he had enjoyed watching a performance of the Nativity enacted by travelling players. It was to have been staged in the newly built church, but the organ was refusing to cooperate. A neighbour had instead hosted the event. Mohr smiled at the image of a baby born in a stable. His own mother had provided for him through her needlework; his father, a mercenary soldier and deserter, had abandoned her before she gave birth. Humble beginnings were something the kindly priest understood.

Musical talent had helped Mohr secure an education and in time, having been given a special dispensation – required because of his illegitimacy – he had entered the Catholic seminary in Salzburg. His proudest moment was being ordained at the early age of twenty-three.

Pleasant thoughts of the evening's entertainment and the atmospheric view of the snow-covered valley reminded him of some stanzas he had written two years earlier, during his first official posting as an assistant priest. It was there, in Mariapfarr, a place of pilgrimage, inside the twelfth-century church dedicated to the Virgin, that a beloved painting had profoundly moved him. This likeness of a mother and baby – 'Holy infant, so tender and mild' – is believed to have inspired his poem which was to become one of the most famous carols ever written: one which would eventually be sung in more than 300 languages, with 733 copyrighted recordings. American master singer-songwriter Paul Simon, when asked was there any song he wished he had written, immediately replied: 'Silent Night'.

Shortly after Mohr had completed his poem, he had become so ill that he returned to the less harsh climate of Salzburg, to Oberndorf, a village just north of the city, not far from the Bavarian border.

Now it was the night before Christmas Eve. Father Mohr began to hurry.

Aware he needed a carol for the approaching Midnight Mass, he decided to consult his friend, Franz Gruber, the local schoolmaster. Gruber, five years older and the son of linen-weavers, was the organist and choirmaster at St Nicholas. Mohr knocked at Gruber's door, recited his poem and outlined his request. Gruber listened, intrigued. In a matter of hours, despite the absence of a functioning church organ, a melody had emerged: a simple arrangement for guitar and voices.

During that Midnight Mass two hundred years ago, '*Stille Nacht*', or 'Silent Night', was heard for the first time. Mohr played the guitar, and the two friends sang, while the choir came in to repeat the last two lines of each of the three verses. Mohr was unworldly. He never objected to being sent from parish to parish; he donated his modest earnings to charity, and would die of heart disease a week before his fifty-sixth birthday. Franz Gruber was different: he married three times and was twice bereaved. Thriving until his death at seventy-six, he would compose various arrangements of 'Silent Night', including for organ – and for organ and orchestra – as well as scoring other carols and masses. His name as the composer is far more widely remembered than is that of Mohr as the lyricist.

Some weeks after that Christmas of 1818, an organ builder arrived at St Nicholas Church to repair the faulty instrument. Gruber tested the organ by playing 'Silent Night', so impressing the visiting craftsman that he asked to copy the music.

'Silent Night' began moving across northern Europe.

By 1834 the famous Strasser Sisters had performed 'Silent Night' for King Frederick of Prussia, who then decreed that his cathedral choir would sing it each Christmas Eve. Twenty years after it was first sung in an Austrian church, 'Silent Night' was sung in German, in New York, on Christmas Eve by another Austrian singing family, the Rainer Singers. Mohr had died three weeks earlier.

Ironically, considering the wealth of the British choral tradition, 'Silent Night' was not translated into English until 1863.

Created on an impromptu inspiration, 'Silent Night' has often united humankind at times of darkness as well as celebration. By December 1914, the fifth month of the First World War, a temporary truce was agreed when about 100,000 of the serving troops on both sides began singing Christmas carols. It was competitive, with the Germans initiating it by singing 'Silent Night'. Most British soldiers didn't recognise Josef Mohr's words, but they all knew Franz Gruber's tune. One of the many stories about that brief ceasefire tells of how one distinctive voice singing 'Silent Night' soared out across No Man's Land. It was claimed to be that of the Wagnerian tenor, Walther Kirchhoff, a star of the Berlin Opera, then serving as Crown Prince Wilhelm's aide-de-camp.

On that Christmas Eve into Christmas Day in 1914, with goodwill among men on both sides, as food parcels and cigarettes were shared, the meditative simplicity of 'Silent Night', devoid of the anthem-like bombast of many carols, caused opposing sides to see the enemy as merely other men.

Early into what would prove a far longer war than initially anticipated, that truce – the only one there would be – disturbed some leaders, yet delighted ordinary soldiers, many of whom would die once the fighting resumed.

Josef Mohr's gentle sentiment in 'Silent Night', then as now, suggests a better, more peaceful world is possible.

CHRISTMAS CONCERT

James Harpur

i.m. Eileen Battersby

It's strange how intimate it feels to be
Waiting in the wings with a stranger –
As we, the last performers, sharing smiles
And nods, pace up and down an area
Of six feet square, like caged panthers,
Our director's torch the only light by which
I, the next one on, rehearse my lines,
And you, the final reader, dart your eyes
At words on Joseph Mohr and 'Silent Night'.

Still we pace and gurn at one another
And whisper 'You'll be fine, don't worry'
With a shoulder pat, a squeeze of elbow.
Until suddenly my turn arrives –
As if I am a parachutist pushed
From dark to light – and look!, the orchestra –
The audience – like angels, glittery
With necklaces and rings and bracelets –
The herald announcing my name; a hush.

And maybe heaven will be similar to this?
'We shall all be changed in a moment
In the twinkling of an eye ...' into glory

And see the singers waiting to declare
That 'all is calm, and all is bright ...'
I say my words and brush you as you enter
To speak the final piece, your final piece ...
Before that fateful drive in two weeks' time
On the road that leads from Sheephouse.

Thank God our endings are concealed from us,
The future just an intuition at best –
And non-existent when we're in the present
Released from what we feared so much;
As now, at curtain call, we lead the others out
And in a chain of hands we bow together
And bask in grace, the shining host before us,
Letting the final music echo in our souls:
'Sleep in heavenly peace, sleep in heavenly peace.'

NIGHTWOOD LIGHT

Vincent Woods

Watch the span of the year. The weather sweeping in – deep and sudden
clouds that shroud the land, mountains vanished, hills vanished, lakes
and rivers one with sky, water finding water, rain pouring, drenching,
pelting, pissing, hurtling down, scattering woman, man, beast to shelter
and awe, thunder cracking off rock, lightning sizzling forking blue and
yellow, scorching trees, sparking old fears buried deep in flesh-memory,
rain, rain, rain soaking earth, sunburst after, greenness greener than ever,
birds tentative in the high trees, frogs spawning from old wells, energies
running deep in and out of the earth, frost whitening the frilled edge of
things, hedges and old roads, ruined stone … snow crowning the crooked
edges of high ground. Wind that would raise the devil out of seven hells,
swirling summer winds out of nowhere, wind in winter driving gouts
of chill blackness. Light and its fading, winter darkness darker than ever
remembered, saturated, pitch, star-scattered, vast, fading again to spring
out of long solstice silence, light, light, light lengthening out of nightwood,
into may and flower, white-scent, elder, rose
Spiders webbing
        grave swans nesting in monastery reeds
          ghost fish treading the riverandlakewaters

CONTRIBUTORS

Farah Abushwesha is a BAFTA-nominated film and television producer. Her screen credits include Netflix Original *Irreplaceable You*, *The Last Photograph* and *Woken*. Notable television credits include *Stags*, *No Return*, *The Singapore Grip* by Christopher Hampton and Agatha Christie's *The ABC Murders*. Author of two acclaimed filmmaking books, she is a recipient of the BFI Vision Award (2020).

John Banville is the author of many novels including *The Book of Evidence* and *The Sea*, and has been the recipient of the Man Booker Prize, the James Tait Black Memorial Prize, the *Guardian* Fiction Award, the Franz Kafka Prize and the Prince of Asturias Award. His most recent novel, *The Lock-Up*, is published by Faber.

Aoife Barry is the author of the bestselling *Social Capital* (HarperCollins Ireland). She has written several radio essays, which were broadcast on *Sunday Miscellany*. Her essays and fiction have been published by *Banshee*, *ThiWurd* and *Visual Verse*. She is an award-winning freelance journalist and broadcaster based in Dublin.

Bibi Baskin, writer, journalist, radio and television presenter, followed her interest in Ayurveda to India where she became a hotelier. The author of *The Happy Book*, she now lives in Co. Cork.

Eileen Battersby (1956–2018) was literary correspondent of *The Irish Times* for many years, and particularly championed fiction in translation. Four-time Arts Journalist of the Year, she also won the Critic of the Year award and published three books: *Second Readings*, *Ordinary Dogs* and a novel, *Teethmarks on My Tongue*, published by Dalkey Archive Press.

Seán Beattie resides in the Inishowen peninsula, Co. Donegal. He is editor of *Donegal Annual*, the journal of the Donegal Historical Society. His doctoral thesis on the Congested Districts Board was published as *Donegal in Transition* in 2013 by IAP/ Merrion Press. His interests include local history and sea swimming.

Blanaid Behan was born and raised in Dublin. Married with two sons, she now lives near Oxford. After a career in television, she spends much of her time swimming in interesting locations, some of it competitively.

Denise Blake, a regular *Miscellany* contributor, was born in Ohio, USA, and lives in Co. Donegal. Her poetry collections *Take a Deep Breath* and *How to Spin Without Getting Dizzy* were published by Summer Palace Press. Her third collection, *Invocation*, is published by Revival Press.

Gudrun Boch-Mullan grew up in Germany. She completed her studies at Marburg University in 1975 with a PhD in English literature. Married to an Irishman since 1984, she spent as much time in Ireland as possible while working in Germany as a lecturer and radio editor and presenter. She now lives in Donegal.

Zainab Boladale was born in Lagos, Nigeria and raised in Co. Clare. A DCU Journalism graduate, she made her television debut as a presenter on the RTÉ children's programme *news2day*. Since 2019 she has reported for *Nationwide*, bringing viewers personal stories of resilience, highlighting talented young Irish people, and showcasing events from around the country.

Mary Jane Boland is from Skibbereen, Co. Cork, and lives in London. In 2014 she was awarded a PhD from the University of Nottingham for her thesis on national identity in pre-Famine Ireland. She now works as an advisor to Lord Puttnam and is head of research at Atticus Education. Her father, Dr Michael Boland, was diagnosed with early-onset Alzheimer's Disease in 2007. He was fifty-nine, she was twenty-three.

Dermot Bolger's fourteen novels include *The Family on Paradise Pier*, *An Ark of Light* and *A Second Life*. His seventeen plays include an adaptation of *Ulysses* and *Last Orders at the Dockside*, both staged by the Abbey Theatre. His tenth poetry collection, *Other People's Lives*, appeared in 2022. He is a younger brother.

Muriel Bolger is an award-winning travel writer, author, amateur artist and music-lover. Her adventures in travel writing saw her live a five-star lifestyle in tandem with the daily challenges of being a mortgage-holder and raising three teenagers on her own. Later in life she turned to fiction and art; the music of Puccini has been a constant joy and solace.

Eva Bourke is a poet and translator. She has published seven collections of poetry, most recently *Seeing Yellow* (Dedalus) and several anthologies and collections in translation. With Borbála Farragó, she edited the anthology *Landing Places: Immigrant Poets in Ireland* (Dedalus) and with Vincent Woods, *Fermata: Writings Inspired by Music* (Artisan House). In 2020 she was awarded the Michael Hartnett Prize for Poetry. She is a member of Aosdána.

Mark Brennock is national director of communications with the HSE. He worked as a journalist for twenty-three years, mostly with *The Irish Times* as chief political correspondent, Northern editor, foreign affairs correspondent and deputy news editor. He also worked for fourteen years with the communications agency Murray Consultants.

Latvian-born **Katrina Bruna** moved to Ireland in 2020 to pursue a degree in law alongside her lifelong passion for creative writing. Katrina's short non-fiction stories explore themes of tradition, culture, belonging and identity, highlighting elements of the shared human experience we so often overlook in the rush of modern life.

Originally from Hungary, **Bernadette Buda**, a teacher of English, moved to Ireland in 2008 and became an Irish citizen in 2017. Writing non-fiction stories and practising yoga have been her passions. A regular contributor to *Sunday Miscellany* since 2017, she has participated in the programme's live events and in the *Miscellany50* anthology (New Island, 2019).

Niamh Campbell won the *Sunday Times* Audible Short Story Award in 2020 and the Rooney Prize for Irish Literature in 2021. Her second novel, *We Were Young*, is currently on paperback release with Weidenfeld & Nicolson.

Jennifer Carey is a recent History and Geography graduate from Trinity College Dublin. She wrote and edited in English and Irish for a number of university publications including the award-winning *University Times* newspaper where she was a member of the editorial board. She now works in broadcasting.

Tim Carey was born in Milwaukee, USA, but has lived for most of his life in Dublin. He has written a number of history books including *Mountjoy: The Story of a Prison*, *Croke Park: A History* and *Dublin Since 1922*. He is a regular contributor to *Sunday Miscellany*.

Marina Carr's plays include *Girl on an Altar*, *iGirl*, *Hecuba*, *By the Bog of Cats* and *Portia Coughlan*. Her work has been produced by, among others, the Abbey, the Gate, Druid, the Royal Court and the RSC, and translated into many languages. Awards include the Windham-Campbell Prize, the Susan Smith Blackburn Prize and the Macaulay Fellowship. She is a member of Aosdána.

Kate Carty was born in Nottingham to Irish parents. She graduated in law and qualified as a solicitor, becoming Chief Crown Prosecutor for Nottinghamshire. Kate took early retirement, moved to Westport and since completing her MA in Creative Writing at NUI Galway in 2018, has had pieces published locally and broadcast on *Sunday Miscellany*.

Senator **Tom Clonan** is an academic, writer, journalist and an independent security analyst. A former Army Officer (Captain), his PhD revealed shocking levels of sexual violence within Ireland's armed forces. An advocate for citizens with disabilities, he is a parent of four children and carer for his son Eoghan, who suffers from a rare neuro-muscular disease. He is the author of *Blood, Sweat and Tears* and *Whistleblower, Soldier, Spy*, both published by Liberties Press.

A.M. Cousins was born in Kilmore and now lives in Wexford town. Her poems have been published in various literary journals including *The Stinging Fly*, *The Irish Times* and *Poetry Ireland Review*. A regular *Miscellany* contributor, her first collection of poetry, *REDRESS*, was published by Revival Press (Limerick) in 2021.

446

Maurice Crowe was born in Westport, Co. Mayo. His father was from Clare, his mother from West Limerick. As his father worked in the bank, the family moved regularly, from Westport, to Galway, to Ennis, to Hospital, and to Dublin. He lives in Clare, beside the Shannon estuary.

Leo Cullen is the author of a short-story collection, *Clocking Ninety on the Road to Cloughjordan*, and a novel, *Let's Twist Again*, both published by Blackstaff Press. His work has appeared in the *Irish Press, Sunday Independent, The Irish Times* and many other publications, and been broadcast on RTÉ Radio 1, Lyric FM and BBC Radio 4.

Peter Cunningham's books have been translated into many languages. His most recent novel, *Freedom Is A Land I Cannot See*, immerses the reader in the lives of Dublin families as Ireland fights for her freedom in the early 1920s. His prizes include the prestigious Prix de l'Europe. He is a member of Aosdána.

Gerald Dawe, Belfast-born poet, has published ten collections, most recently *Another Time: Poems 1978–2023* (The Gallery Press). He has also published numerous non-fiction books including *Politic Words: Writing Women/Writing History* (Peter Lang). He lives in Co. Dublin.

John F. Deane is from Achill Island and has published several collections of poetry, most recently *Dear Pilgrims* (2018) and *Naming of the Bones* (Carcanet, 2021) and a memoir, *Song of the Goldfinch* (Veritas, 2023). He is the founder of Poetry Ireland and its journal *Poetry Ireland Review*. He is a member of Aosdána.

Roslyn Dee is an award-winning travel writer, broadcaster and columnist with the *Irish Independent*. Formerly Assistant Editor of the *Sunday Tribune* and Associate Editor with DMG Media, she is author, with her late husband, photographer Gerry Sandford, of *A Sense of Place: Irish Lives, Irish Landscapes*. From Derry, she now lives in Wicklow.

Anne Delaney lives on the Northside of Dublin with her husband, Con, and retired from the Department of Justice some years ago. She's enjoying her retirement very much, having time to 'play bridge, walk with the Irish Ramblers Club and read all the books I've missed'.

Anne Devlin, playwright, prose-writer and screenwriter, has written about the core year in the Civil Rights Movement, 1968, in many forms, including in her short story 'Naming the Names' and her stage play *After Easter*. Her play *Ourselves Alone* charted women's involvement in the republican movement. Her latest book is a collection of stories, *The Apparitions* (Arlen House, 2023).

From Cheekpoint, Co. Waterford, **Andrew Doherty** followed his family into the commercial fishing way of life. The author of *Before the Tide Went Out* (2017) and

Waterford Harbour Tides and Tales (2020), he has contributed to various publications and radio and television programmes. He leads walks and talks on land and river and blogs at tidesandtales.ie.

The late **J.M. (Joe) Dolan**, who died in 2023, was an IFTA-award-winning freelance sound recordist in film and television who worked for RTÉ, TG4, BBC, Channel Four, Granada TV, FR3 France, ZDF Germany and most European networks as well as ABC, NBC (US), CBC Canada, and Channel 7, Australia. Two projects particularly close to his heart were his short film, *A Father's Letter*, which he directed, and sound recording for *Out of the Marvellous*, Charlie McCarthy's film about Seamus Heaney. He was a regular contributor to *Sunday Miscellany*.

Lelia Doolan has been an actor, producer, director, teacher and writer in theatre, television, film and journalism. She founded the Galway Film Fleadh and Cinemobile service bringing cinema around Ireland, and led the building of an arthouse cinema in Galway. She is active in social and environmental issues.

Séamus Dooley is Irish Secretary of the National Union of Journalists. Educated at St Saran's Secondary School, Ferbane, he is a graduate of the College of Commerce, Rathmines. A former editor of the *Roscommon Champion*, he began his career with the *Tullamore Tribune* and also worked with the *Irish Independent*.

Mia Döring is from Dublin. She writes fiction, essays and poetry and is the author of the bestselling memoir *Any Girl*, a memoir of sexual exploitation and recovery (Hachette, 2022). Her writing has been published in *Ropes Literary Journal, Litro Magazine, The Irish Independent, The Huffington Post, Irish Country Magazine* and more.

Dominic Dromgoole was the Artistic Director of Shakespeare's Globe Theatre in London from 2006 to 2016. He is the author of *Astonish Me! First Nights That Changed The World, The Full Room, Will and Me,* which won the inaugural Sheridan Morley prize, and *Hamlet Globe to Globe*, which was a *New York Times* Book of the Year.

Bernard Dunleavy is a Senior Counsel. A former Chair of the Programme Board of the RHA, he is also a Director of Children's Books Ireland. He spends as much time as possible swimming in the sea and making marmalade.

Inspired by the recent wave of historians and geographers exploring human dependency on the natural world, **Ann Marie Durkan** is completing a PhD at DCU examining the place of animals in twentieth-century Dublin. She is fascinated with this trans-species approach, which uncovers how modern human societies are the result of the efforts of a multiplicity of species.

For two decades, **John Egan** was a broadcast journalist with RTÉ Radio and BBC News in London. In 2000 he left public-service journalism for an editorial role with Barclays

PLC. On his return to Ireland, he joined Shell and worked in his native Co. Mayo as Community & Communications Manager for the Corrib Gas Project.

Wendy Erskine's two prize-winning collections, *Sweet Home* and *Dance Move*, are published by The Stinging Fly Press/Picador. She edited *well I just kind of like it*, an anthology about art and the home for Paper Visual Art Books. She is a Fellow of the Royal Society of Literature and was a Seamus Heaney Fellow at Queen's University in 2022.

Brian Farrell has worked as a photojournalist since 1979. In 2003 he left his position as photo editor of the *Sunday Independent* and moved to Co. Sligo with his family. He writes regularly for *Sunday Miscellany* about his memories of growing up in Finglas and his many experiences while working with a national newspaper.

Alan Finnegan was born in Dublin in 1972, graduated from UCD in 1993, and spent the following decade in Italy and Spain. He returned home in 2004 to help manage his family pub in Dalkey, where he can still be found pulling pints and telling tall stories.

Nicole Flattery is the author of the short-story collection *Show Them A Good Time* and her debut novel, *Nothing Special*. She is the winner of the An Post Irish Book Award, the Kate O'Brien Prize, the London Magazine Prize for Debut Fiction and the *White Review* Short Story Prize. Her work has appeared in *The Stinging Fly*, *The Guardian*, *The White Review*, *The London Review of Books*, *The Irish Times* and *Winter Pages*.

Catherine Foley is a writer, broadcaster and journalist. Her most recent publication is *Amhrán Sráidbhaile/Village Song* (2023), published by Arlen House. Other books include *Sorcha sa Ghailearaí* (2003), *An Cailín Rua* (2004), *Samhradh an Chéasta* (2010), *Ag Marú Maicréal* (2019), *Cuisle an Chósta* (2019) and *Beyond the Breakwater: Memories of Home* (2018).

Quentin Fottrell is a managing editor, reporter and columnist for *MarketWatch* in New York. His writing has appeared in *The Wall Street Journal*, *The Irish Times*, *Town & Country* and *The Sunday Times*. His book *Love In A Damp Climate* explored relationships and social changes in early-noughties Ireland.

Born in London to Irish parents during World War II, **Jim Galvin** worked in the City upon graduating. His interest in Irish traditional music allowed him to meet many musicians. In 1971 he moved to Dublin with his Irish wife. He is retired, but a far-flung family ensures he travels widely.

Margaret Galvin grew up in Cahir, Co. Tipperary, but lives in Wexford. She has worked with the library service and as editor of *Ireland's Own*. She has published six collections of poetry, most recently *Our House, Delirious* from Revival Press, Limerick. Her poetry and prose are often broadcast on *Sunday Miscellany*.

Claire Garvey was born in Cork and is a graduate of UL and the University of Maynooth. She has been interested in writing since winning a commemorative plate for her 'holy poem' in a Year of the Child competition in 1979. She lives in Dublin with her husband, three children and two dogs.

Rory Gleeson is an author, playwright and screenwriter. His novel *Rockadoon Shore* was published by John Murray. He wrote the short film *Psychic* and the play *Blood in the Dirt*. His writing has featured in *Granta*, BBC Radio 4, *The Tangerine*, RTÉ Radio, *The Irish Times* and *The Dublin Review*.

Patrick Griffin from Kilkenny is a Francis MacManus Short Story Competition winner and contributor to RTÉ's *Sunday Miscellany*, *A Living Word* and *A Word in Edgeways*. His work has been anthologised and performed at the Frank O'Connor Short Story Festival and at Bewley's Café Theatre, Dublin.

Antonia Gunko Karelina was born in Donetsk, Ukraine. In her early twenties she spent a year and a half in Canada, then returned to Ukraine, got married and moved to Kyiv. She received a master's degree as a translator, and continues to work in this field. She is temporarily living in Ireland 'while the best warriors on this planet fight for freedom!'

Michael Hamell loves hurling, rambling and books. Now retired after forty years' involvement in agricultural and environmental issues mainly for the European Commission, he and his family live close to Croke Park as he waits with dented optimism for Dublin to win another all-Ireland hurling final.

Conall Hamill was born in Dublin and grew up in Clontarf. He taught for many years in St Andrew's College, where he co-founded the One-Act Drama Festival and was involved in creative writing and journalism. He has acted with Co-Motion Theatre Company and has been a regular contributor to *Sunday Miscellany* since 2016.

James Harpur has published eight books of poetry, including his latest, *The Examined Life* (2021), an odyssey through boarding school; and *The Oratory of Light* (2021), poems inspired by St Columba and Iona. His debut novel, *The Pathless Country* (2021), set in Galway, London and Limerick during the early twentieth century, won the J.G. Farrell award and was shortlisted for the John McGahern Book Prize. He lives in West Cork.

Donal Hayes is a writer and radio documentary maker living outside Kinsale. Published and broadcast 'in all the usual places', he is married with three kids and two dogs, and is happiest with a biro in hand, staring out the window.

Nuala Hayes is an actor, storyteller, independent broadcaster and author. A regular *Miscellany* contributor, she trained at the Abbey Theatre and has performed in plays by many of Ireland's major playwrights. She is interested in oral storytelling and has collected stories throughout Ireland. Her *Laois Folk Tales* was published in 2015 by the History Press.

Mr Justice **John Hedigan** is a retired Irish judge who has served on the Court of Appeal, High Court, and the European Court of Human Rights. Current chair of the Irish Banking Culture Board, he also served as chair of the National Archives Advisory Council from 2017 to 2022.

Neil Hegarty grew up in Derry. His novels include *The Jewel* and *Inch Levels*, which was shortlisted for the Kerry Group Novel of the Year award in 2017. He is co-editor, with Nora Hickey M'Sichili, of the essay collection *Impermanence*, which was adapted for radio by RTÉ.

Dr **Rachael Hegarty** is a Dubliner, a poet and an educator. Her poetry collections have won awards and critical acclaim. Her fourth book, *Wild Flowers on the Darndale Roundabout* launches on Earth Day 2024. Rachael's kids say she uses F words too much: Finglas, Feminism and Fecking poetry. However, they like when she's on *Sunday Miscellany*.

Rita Ann Higgins has published twelve books: ten books of poetry, a memoir in poetry and prose in 2010, *Hurting God*, and a book of essays and poems in 2019, *Our Killer City*, from Salmon Publishing. *Tongulish, Ireland Is Changing Mother* and *Throw in the Vowels: New & Selected Poems,* are all published by Bloodaxe.

Sharon Hogan is a cross-discipline artist: a writer, actor and visual artist (photography, drawing, painting, sculpture), she also holds an MA in Dance Performance from the University of Limerick. She has worked extensively as actor, writer and director, on stage, radio, television and film, throughout Ireland and the UK.

Conor Horgan is an acclaimed photographer, writer and award-winning film-maker. He has written five films including *One Hundred Mornings* (2011), which won the Writers' Guild of Ireland Award for Best Feature Film Script. He lives in Dublin with his cat, Amy.

Paul Howard is a satirist, novelist and TV writer, who is best known as the creator of fictional rugby jock Ross O'Carroll-Kelly, as well as his work on the BAFTA-award-winning TV show *Bad Sisters*. He lives in Co. Wicklow with his wife, Mary, and a basset hound named Humphrey.

John Hurley was born and raised above the family newsagents in Miltown Malbay where his daily interactions with local characters inspired his love of a good story. Now retired as a teacher of English in Crescent College Comprehensive, he has more time to write, support Miltown, Clare, Limerick and Munster, and share his love of storytelling with his two beloved grandchildren.

Frank Kavanagh was born in 68 Clanbrassil Street, in the old Liberties of Dublin; the house no longer exists. He is trying to grow old gracefully, but it's hard at seventy-four, when your bones start to creak and you forget to remember. He claims to be one of Patrick Kavanagh's 'standing army of 40,000 Irish poets'.

Joe Kearney hails from Callan, Co. Kilkenny. He is a novelist, multi-award-winning documentary maker and regular contributor to *Sunday Miscellany*. His most recent book is a short-story collection, *The Beekeeper and the River* (2022).

Born in Dublin, **Frank Keegan** graduated from DCU and worked in banking and IT, followed by a career change to become a commercial pilot and airline captain. He served in the Reserve Defence Forces, retiring with the rank of Commandant. An associate lecturer at Munster Technological University, he is married with four grown-up children.

From Listowel, Co. Kerry, **Cyril Kelly** taught in Dublin for many years and has been a regular contributor to various programmes on RTÉ Radio, notably *Sunday Miscellany*, where he is a familiar voice.

From Newry, Co. Down, the late **John Kelly** (1935–2022) was a leading figure in UCD for many years, with roles as university registrar and deputy president, senator, and professor of chemical engineering. A champion of causes such as women in engineering, student disability services and more, he published *Joyce the Student* (Gleoiteog Press) in 2021.

Louise Kennedy grew up in Holywood, Co. Down, and worked as a chef for nearly thirty years. Published by Bloomsbury, her short-story collection *The End of the World is a Cul de Sac* won the John McGahern Prize; her debut novel, *Trespasses*, won Novel of the Year at the An Post Book Awards. She lives in Sligo.

Angela Keogh is the author of a novel, *The Winter Dress*, and a number of stage plays, most recently *The Girls in the Boat*. She is studying traditional Irish music in Leitrim, and teaches creative writing at the Hedge School. She lives in Co. Carlow.

Kate Kerrigan is one of Ireland's most popular novelists, with over fifteen novels to her name, including her *New York Times* bestselling Ellis Island trilogy. London-born Irish, Kate is currently touring the UK and Ireland with her one-woman show *Am I Irish Yet?* She lives in Killala, Co. Mayo, with her husband and two sons.

Declan Kiberd teaches at Notre Dame, Dublin. He was for many years professor of Anglo-Irish literature at UCD and a member of the board of the Abbey Theatre. He has lectured in over thirty countries and has published over ten books. *Inventing Ireland* won the *Irish Times* literature award and *Irish Classics* the Truman Capote Award for Literary Criticism in English worldwide. A member of the RIA and the American Academy of Arts and Sciences, he publishes regularly in *The Irish Times*, the *TLS* and *The New York Times*.

Liam Lally is a retired primary school teacher. Originally from Belmullet in Co. Mayo, he has lived most of his life in Dublin.

Born into the Parish, Limerick city, **Mae Leonard** has lived in Co. Kildare for over fifty years. A folklorist and local historian, she is a long-time contributor to *Sunday Miscellany* and *A Word In Edgeways* and is regularly published in *The Irish Times, Ireland's Own* and the *Limerick Leader*. She is a listed writer in schools and libraries.

Brian Leyden is the author of the bestselling memoir *The Home Place*, the novel *Summer of '63* and *Sweet Old World: New and Selected Stories*. His one-act stage play, *Remember Me*, premiered in the Hawk's Well Theatre, Sligo, in May 2023. His new novel is *Love These Days*.

Jackie Lynam is from Dublin. Her poems have been published in various anthologies and journals, and her non-fiction pieces broadcast on *Sunday Miscellany* and published in the *Irish Independent. Traces*, a collection of poetry and essays, will be published in autumn 2023.

Born in Dublin in 1941, **Charles Lysaght** is a lawyer and biographer. He wrote the definitive biography of Brendan Bracken, the Tipperary-born son of a Fenian who served as minister of information in the wartime government of his friend and hero Winston Churchill.

John MacKenna is the author of twenty-three books, the most recent of which is *Absent Friend*, a memoir of his friendship with Leonard Cohen. He has also written for the stage. He teaches creative writing at Maynooth University and at the Hedge School. He lives in Co. Carlow.

Lourdes Mackey's work has featured in *The Irish Times, The Irish Examiner, Cork Words 2, Crannóg Magazine, Flashback Fiction* and in the UEA's *Suffragette Stories*. Her fiction has been placed or listed in various national and international story awards. With a keen interest in history, she contributes regularly to *Sunday Miscellany* on diverse topics. She lives in Cork.

Kathleen MacMahon is a novelist, short-story writer and journalist. Her novels have been listed for the Kerry Group Irish Novel of the Year, the Irish Book Awards and the Women's Prize for Fiction. Her short stories have been published in *The Stinging Fly, The Irish Times* and *The Lonely Crowd*. Her work has been translated into over twenty languages.

Manchán Magan is a writer and documentary maker who presents *The Almanac of Ireland* on RTÉ Radio 1. He writes occasionally for *The Irish Times*, and has presented dozens of documentaries on issues of world culture for TG4, RTÉ and Travel Channel. His books *Thirty-Two Words for Field, Tree Dogs* and *Listen to the Land Speak* are acclaimed bestsellers.

Born and raised in Manchester, England, **Kevin Marinan** moved to Ireland in 1997. His mother was a native of Mayo and his father was a Clare man. Writing has been both his hobby and his profession for more than twenty years. He has three adult daughters, one grandson and one ex-wife.

Niall McArdle's work has appeared in *The Irish Times, Banshee, Spontaneity, The Lonely Crowd, RTÉ Guide* and *Phoenix Irish Short Stories*, and has been broadcast on RTÉ Radio. He has been shortlisted for the Hennessy Literary Awards, the RTÉ Short Story Competition in honour of Francis MacManus, the Benedict Kiely Short Story Competition, and the Cúirt New Writing Prize.

The late **Larry McCluskey**, a regular *Miscellany* contributor, was a seasoned drama festival adjudicator. Artistic director for many years of Drumlin Players, he toured his one-man show, *Awhile With Seamus Heaney*, to Edinburgh and beyond in 2016, to widespread acclaim. Former CEO of Monaghan VEC and Chairman of Cootehill GAA, he wrote the popular 'Off the Fence' column for the *Anglo-Celt* newspaper.

Barry McCrea is the Keough Family Professor at the University of Notre Dame where he teaches literature on its campuses in Indiana, Dublin, and Rome. He is the author of two scholarly books on European literature, and of a novel, *The First Verse*. He is currently finishing his second novel.

Kevin Mc Dermott is a Dublin-based writer. He is the author of six novels for young adults. His writing for radio includes plays, feature-length documentaries, essays and short stories. His poems and stories have been published in journals in Ireland, the UK and the US, and broadcast on RTÉ.

Dr **Rosaleen McDonagh**, BA, M Phil and PhD, is an activist for the Traveller community. She is a writer, a playwright, a Human Rights Commissioner and the first member of Aosdána from the Traveller community.

From Co. Wicklow, **John McDonald** studied Environment Design at TU Dublin, before gaining an MA in Design: Professional Practice and an Advanced Diploma in Teaching and Education. He has a keen interest in history and especially the overlap between culture, society and the built environment. He lectures on the Interior Architecture programmes at MTU in Cork.

A distinguished broadcaster, writer and journalist, **Tom McGurk** worked in Ireland and the UK with, among others, RTÉ, Granada TV, Thames TV, BBC and Channel 4. His film scripts include *Dear Sarah* and *The Need to Know*. A long-serving *Sunday Business Post* columnist, his investigative journalistic achievements include the publication of new evidence on Bloody Sunday, a principal factor in launching the Saville Inquiry.

Chris McHallem, a regular *Miscellany* contributor, trained as an actor at London's Central School of Speech and Drama and as a writer at IADT in Dún Laoghaire. Recent work includes touring with Conor McPherson's *The Girl From the North Country*, and a radio adaptation of his own one-man stage show, *Strutting and Fretting*, for RTÉ Radio 1's Drama on One.

From Derry, **Susan McKay** is Ireland's Press Ombudsperson, and the author of books including, in 2021, *Northern Protestants: On Shifting Ground*. Her award-winning journalism has appeared in *The New York Times*, *The New Yorker*, the *London Review of Books*, *The Guardian* and *The Irish Times*, and she was Northern editor of the *Sunday Tribune*. She was a founder of the Belfast Rape Crisis Centre.

Playwright, novelist and actor **Jim McKeon** (1942–2023) of Bishopstown, Cork, was the author of over twenty books, including an acclaimed biography of Frank O'Connor. An avid sportsman, he played League of Ireland football for Cork Celtic for five years, and won a basketball all-Ireland medal with Cork.

Henrietta McKervey has published four acclaimed novels. She features in the collection *Impermanence* (broadcast on RTÉ) and the anthology *A Little Unsteadily Into Light* (New Island). She won a Hennessy First Fiction Award and the UCD Maeve Binchy Travel Award. She contributes to the *Irish Independent, The Irish Times* and RTÉ Radio 1.

Lisa McInerney has written three novels: *The Glorious Heresies*, *The Blood Miracles* and *The Rules of Revelation*. Her prizes include the Women's Prize for Fiction, the Desmond Elliott Prize and the RSL Encore Award. She is published in eleven languages. In 2022 she was appointed editor of *The Stinging Fly*.

Geraldine Mitchell is a Dublin-born poet and writer who has been living on the Mayo coast for over twenty years. A Patrick Kavanagh Poetry Award-winner, her poetry is widely published and anthologised and she has four collections to her name, the most recent of which is *Mute/Unmute*.

Judith Mok was born in the Netherlands and has been resident in Ireland since 2002. As well as many books in Dutch, she has published novels, stories and poetry in English, including *Gods Of Babel* (Salmon, 2010). Her most recent publication is a fictional memoir, *The State Of Dark* (Lilliput, 2022).

Clare Monnelly is an actor/writer whose debut play, *Charlie's a Clepto*, was nominated for three *Irish Times* Theatre Awards. She has worked on stage with the Abbey, the Gate and Druid and on screen in Sky One's *Moone Boy* and RTÉ's *Nowhere Fast*. She says that writing gives her 'a stronger sense of purpose'.

Tom Mooney is the author of *All the Bishops' Men* (Collins Press) and is a former editor of the Echo group of newspapers. He is curator of the annual Wex-Art visual arts festival and creative director of Jazz at Johnstown. He has programmed events for Poetry Ireland, Creative Ireland and Culture Night.

Sarah Moore Fitzgerald is a professor at the University of Limerick with specialisms in psychology, pedagogy and creativity. She has published seven novels for children. Her work has been adapted for the stage and translated into twenty languages. In 2022 she won *London Magazine*'s annual award for short fiction.

Daniel Mulhall is a former Irish diplomat who has served as ambassador to Malaysia, Germany, the UK and the USA. Since his retirement, he has been Global Distinguished Professor of Irish Studies at Glucksman Ireland House, NYU, Parnell Fellow at Magdalene College, Cambridge and a Fellow at the Institute of Politics, Harvard University. His latest book is *Pilgrim Soul: W.B. Yeats and the Ireland of His Time* (New Island, 2023).

Kathleen Murphy, a regular *Miscellany* contributor, is a proud Irish Traveller and a devoted married mum of a young daughter. She recently qualified as a primary school teacher, and has a PGCE from Sunderland, an MSc in Human Rights from UCD and a BCL from Maynooth University.

In a journalistic career of almost fifty years, the late **Paddy Murray**, who died in 2022, worked for many newspapers including the *Evening Herald, Irish Daily Star* and *Sunday World*. He edited the *Sunday Tribune* from 2003 until 2005 and was an *Irish Times* columnist in recent years. He published *And Finally: A Journalist's Life in 250 Stories* (Liffey Press) in 2021. Married to Connie, he described their daughter Charlotte as his greatest achievement.

Grace Neville graduated from UCC and Lille and Caen universities. She is professor emeritus of French and former VP at UCC. She is a member of numerous committees on higher-education transformation at the French Ministry for Higher Education, French National Research Agency and French universities including the Sorbonne. She holds the Légion d'honneur.

Kerry Neville is the author of two collections of stories, *Necessary Lies* and *Remember to Forget Me*. In 2018 she was a Fulbright Fellow at University of Limerick, where she was Visiting Faculty in the MA in Creative Writing Program. She is an associate professor and co-ordinator of the MFA and Undergraduate Creative Writing Program at Georgia College and State University.

Mark O'Connell was born in Dublin in 1964. Although he often dreams of living in Kerry, he never really left Dublin. He lives in the capital with his wife and four children. A former political correspondent with *The Sunday Business Post*, he has, since 2000, been a full-time practising barrister.

Novelist, screenwriter, playwright and broadcaster **Joseph O'Connor** is the author of many novels including *Star of the Sea, Shadowplay* and most recently, *My Father's House* (Harvill Secker). Among his awards are the Prix Zepter for European Novel of the Year and the Irish Pen Award for Outstanding Achievement in Literature. His work has been translated into forty languages.

Michael O'Connor taught for many years at St Nicholas Montessori College, specialising in adult education, Montessori theory and literature. He has had poems published in *The Irish Times*, *The Stony Thursday Book*, several *WOW!* anthologies and *Literature Today*. He lives in Ballybrack, Co. Dublin.

Author of two non-fiction books about Switzerland and Ireland, **Clare O'Dea** published her first novel, *Voting Day*, with Fairlight Books in 2022. Formerly an *Irish Times* journalist, Clare moved to Switzerland from Ireland in 2003. She lives with her family on the invisible border where the French-speaking and Swiss-German cultures meet.

John O'Donnell's work has been published and broadcast widely. Awards include the Irish National Poetry Prize and Hennessy Awards for Poetry and Fiction. He has published five poetry collections. His short-story collection *Almost The Same Blue* (Doire Press) was nominated as one of the *Sunday Independent*'s 2020 Books of the Year.

Mary O'Donnell work includes poetry, four novels, three short-story collections, essays and journalism. Her 2020 collection *Massacre of the Birds* (Salmon) is translated and published in Brazilian Portuguese with Arte y Lettras. Other work is available in Hungarian and in Spanish. She is a member of Aosdána.

Síofra O'Donovan teaches writing workshops in schools, mental-health and prison facilities using the dynamic and archetypal 'Hero's Journey'. The recipient of many writers' residencies and arts awards, her books include *Malinski* (Lilliput Press, 2000), *Pema and the Yak* (Pilgrims Books, 2006), *Yours 'Til Hell Freezes* (Currach Books, 2020) and *Lost in Shambhala* (Amazon, 2023).

Mary Kate O Flanagan is an award-winning writer, journalist and storyteller. A story editor and script midwife for film and television, she was a Grand Slam Champion Storyteller at The Moth in Los Angeles and a Champion Storyteller at The Dublin Story Slam. Her theatre piece, *Making A Show of Myself*, will tour Ireland in 2023 and 2024.

Lani O'Hanlon is a movement therapist and writer living beside the sea in West Waterford. Her writing is published widely and regularly broadcast on *Sunday Miscellany*. She won the Poetry Ireland Trócaire Award in 2022, and her collection *Landscape of the Body* is published by Dedalus Press (2023).

Emer O'Kelly is a commentator and critic who has worked in newspapers, radio and television. She was a newscaster with RTÉ for eighteen years, a foreign correspondent, and is currently drama critic for the *Sunday Independent*. A frequent contributor to *Sunday Miscellany*, she lives in Dublin.

Olivia O'Leary is a journalist and broadcaster. She has presented current-affairs programmes for RTÉ, BBC and ITV. In recent years she presented RTÉ Radio 1's *The Poetry Programme*. The O'Brien Press has published two collections of her radio columns for RTÉ's *Drivetime* programme, *Politicians and Other Animals* and *Party Animals*.

Michael O'Loughlin was born in Dublin in 1958. He has published many volumes of poetry, including *Poems 1980–2015* (New Island, 2017), and most recently *Liberty Hall* (New Island, 2021). He has been Writer Fellow at Trinity College Dublin and UNESCO Writer in Residence in Prague. He is a member of Aosdána.

Mary O'Malley has published nine collections of poetry, of which the latest is *Gaudent Angeli*. A member of Aosdána, she has recently received a doctorate from the University of Galway, her alma mater, and has held residencies in Tarragona, the US and Paris. *The Shark Nursery* is due from Carcanet in 2024.

Dr **Fionn Ó Marcaigh** is a zoologist from Dublin. He wrote 'Eternity Along The Strand' for *Sunday Miscellany* on a Saturday morning in March 2020, after the last Irish Wetland Bird Survey of the season. He has continued to participate in scientific research and was awarded a PhD by Trinity College Dublin in 2023.

Joe Ó Muircheartaigh is a Dublin-born journalist and author who has long since reconnected with his country roots by living and working in counties Clare and Kerry. He divides his time between the West Kerry Gaeltacht community of Baile na nGall and Ennis, and works with *Kerry's Eye* newspaper.

Daisy Onubogu is a writer currently readying her debut novel for publication. Prior to that she enjoyed a varied career across law, tech start-ups, venture capital and ESG advocacy. She likes to travel and is a fan of books, pies, medium sarcasm, social justice and facilitating connections to make things happen.

Helen O'Rahilly is a former television executive at the BBC and RTÉ. She commissioned award-winning programmes for both broadcasters over her long career. Having lived in London for thirty years, she returned to Dublin in 2019 to live a quieter life.

Fran O'Rourke is emeritus professor of philosophy at University College Dublin. His latest book, *Joyce, Aristotle, and Aquinas*, was published in 2022. With guitarist John Feeley he has performed Irish traditional songs from the works of James Joyce in many parts of the world, from Shanghai to San Diego.

Christina Park is a writer and editor based in Wexford. Her feature and travel articles have appeared in *The Irish Times*, *Irish Independent* and *Business Post*, and her poetry in journals including *Poetry Ireland Review* and *The Stinging Fly*.

Brian Patterson is a former CEO and chair – and now a leadership coach and mentor. He's also part of a writing group, which grew out of a UCD Lifelong Learning course on memoir writing, the members of which encouraged him to submit his script 'The Poppy' for *Sunday Miscellany*.

Colin Regan got his love of words from his mother Mae and his secondary-school English teacher, Arthur Lemon. He got his love for a bit of devilment from his father, Oliver, along with his Roman nose. He and his wife, Maggie, have two children, Eliza Rose and Oscar Gordon Regan.

An NCAD graduate, **Alannah Robins** has exhibited in the RHA, Dublin and galleries in London, Istanbul, Helsinki and Sweden. Her pan-European participatory project, 'Carrying the Songs', involved over four hundred storytellers and (so far) twenty-five artists. She is founder-director of Interface, a studio and residency programme in Connemara with a focus on intersections between science and art.

Donal Ryan is a novelist and short-story writer from Nenagh, Co. Tipperary. His work has won numerous awards, been adapted for stage and screen, and translated into over twenty languages. He teaches Creative Writing at the University of Limerick.

Barbara Scully is a well-known writer, columnist and broadcaster from Dublin. She is regularly published in the national press and magazines and is a familiar voice on radio. Her first book, *Wise Up: Power, Wisdom, and the Older Woman* was published in 2022 and has been widely well received.

Oliver Sears is a London-born, Dublin-based gallery owner. He is the son of a Holocaust survivor and founder of Holocaust Awareness Ireland. 'The Objects of Love', an exhibition of his family story, showed at Dublin Castle and the 92NY in New York.

Pauline Shanahan is an actor, writer and, more recently, a comedian. With comedy she has gigged all around Ireland and the UK. She has also played at Electric Picnic, the Vodafone Comedy Festival and the Edinburgh Fringe Festival with her show *What's Cooler than a Hipster? A Spinster!*

Raja Shehadeh is Palestine's leading writer. He is also a lawyer and the founder of the pioneering Palestinian human rights organization Al-Haq. He is the author of several acclaimed books including the Orwell Prize-winning *Palestinian Walks*. His latest book is *We Could Have Been Friends, My Father and I*. He lives in Ramallah, Palestine.

Ian Sherry worked for many years for Northern Ireland's Ordnance Survey. Author of *Listening to the Curlew* (Lagan Press), he writes on farming and other subjects for *Small Farmer's Journal, American Surveyor, Mules and More* and many other publications. Now living in Rostrevor, Co. Down, he farms a few acres outside the town.

Paula Shields is a writer and arts journalist currently on the arts show *Arena* on RTÉ Radio 1. Other highlights include making the IFTA award-winning TV documentary *Fairytale of New York* and judging the 2017 and 2018 *Irish Times* Theatre Awards.

A chartered engineer with a Masters in Engineering Science, the late **Chris Shouldice** (1931–2023) worked as a rural electrification area engineer with the ESB, later with GE in the US, CIE and Teagasc. He was Chair of the Solar Energy Society of Ireland and Council member of the RDS (science & technology). With a keen interest in history drawn from his father Jack, an officer in the Easter Rising, he contributed regularly to RTÉ Radio.

Frank Shouldice is a writer, journalist and film-maker. He directed the multi-award-winning documentary *The Man Who Wanted To Fly* and also produced/directed numerous RTÉ Investigates reports including *Running For Our Lives*, *Belturbet, the Bomb that Time Forgot* and *Milking It*. In 2015 he published an historical memoir, *Grandpa, The Sniper*, and subsequently toured *Six Days*, his spoken-word stage show, around the country.

Gordon Snell is the author of many books for children. He has also written song lyrics and librettos, novels, plays and books of humorous verse, and has worked in both television and radio as a writer and interviewer. Husband of the late Maeve Binchy, he lives in Dalkey with their cat, Audrey.

Gerard Stembridge was born in Limerick and educated at DBS Sexton Street and UCD. He has written and directed for television, film and theatre. His radio work includes *Scrap Saturday* (RTÉ), *Daisy, The Cow Who Talked* and *Hiding Out* (BBC Radio 4). He has published five novels.

From Newry, **John Toal** is an award-winning broadcaster for BBC Radio Ulster and BBC Radio 3. He's about the same age as *Sunday Miscellany*, grew up listening to it and has been writing for the programme for a number of years. He lives in Co. Down.

Colm Tóibín is the author of ten novels, including *The Master* and *Brooklyn*, and two collections of stories. His first book of poetry, *Vinegar Hill*, was published in 2022. His work has been translated into more than thirty languages. He is Laureate for Irish Fiction.

Peter Trant, writer, actor and retired teacher, was born in Derry and raised in Carrigans, Co. Donegal and in Clones, Co. Monaghan. After many years living in London he now lives in Monaghan.

A regular voice on *Sunday Miscellany*, **Olive Travers** is a retired clinical psychologist from Donegal. A selection of her essays, drawing on her own personal experiences and observations, *Nets of Wonder*, illustrated by Barry Britton and with an accompanying podcast featuring music by Eamon Travers, is published by Beehive Books.

Fred Tuite is a careers consultant in Kilkenny city. From Skerries in Co. Dublin, he attended UCD and qualified as a teacher of English and French. Later he qualified as a guidance counsellor and worked for many years in Co. Laois. He has contributed to *Student Yearbook* and *Essential Guidance* and edits *Guideline*, the journal of the Institute of Guidance Counsellors.

William Wall is the author of seven novels (most recently *Empty Bed Blues*, New Island, 2023), six collections of poetry and three of short fiction. His work has won multiple prizes and awards and been translated into many languages. He holds a PhD in Creative Writing from UCC and translates from Italian.

Grace Wells is an award-winning eco-poet and environmental writer. Nature, spirit-of-place and environmental concern are the large themes of her writing. She has published three books of poetry with Dedalus Press, most recently in 2022, *The Church of the Love of the World*. She lives in Ennistymon, Co. Clare.

From Clonmel, **Joe Whelan** has worked in construction ever since leaving school at fifteen. In 2015 he inherited his uncle's sheep farm in the Comeragh mountains. After attending writing workshops in Carrick-on-Suir and Clonmel, he has had his work – poems, plays and stories – published, featured at various festivals and broadcast on *Sunday Miscellany*.

Jonathan White was born in Dublin, grew up in New York and for forty-five years has plied his trade as an actor on stages, screens and wireless sets the length and breadth of Ireland and beyond. He's now following in the footsteps of his father, Seán J. White, who was a *Sunday Miscellany* regular in the 1970s.

Vincent Woods is a writer and broadcaster. His plays include *At the Black Pig's Dyke*. With Eva Bourke he co-edited *Fermata: Writings Inspired by Music*. He wrote the libretto for Gavin Bryars' composition 'Wittgenstein Fragments', premiered by Louth Contemporary Music Society. He lives in Dublin and is a member of Aosdána.

ACKNOWLEDGEMENTS

I'm very grateful to Elaine Conlan, *Sunday Miscellany* broadcast co-ordinator, who has made an enormous contribution to the preparation of this anthology; to Jane Byrne, Ben Moore and Aisling Grennan; to Patricia Harrington of RTÉ Legal; to Tracey Diamond of RTÉ Communications; to all in RTÉ's Sound Department; and to Carolyn Dempsey, for all her great work on the programme in previous years.

Clíodhna Ní Anluain, who produced *Miscellany* for ten years and edited many superb anthologies, offered invaluable advice.

Thanks to Ann-Marie Power, head of RTÉ Arts and Culture, and Peter Woods, head of RTÉ Radio 1, for their kind support.

Thanks also to copy-editor Susan McKeever, and to Mariel Deegan, Aoife K. Walsh and Djinn von Noorden of New Island Books for their skilful stewarding of this book to publication.

Thanks to my parents, ever-generous first listeners, and to my husband, Conall, for his endless wise counsel and insight.

Final thanks to all *Miscellany*'s excellent contributors, who make the programme what it is, week in, week out.